THE

HISTORY AND ANTIQUITIES

OF

Bicester,

A MARKET TOWN IN OXFORDSHIRE:

TO WHICH IS ADDED

AN INQUIRY

INTO THE ~~HISTORY~~ OF

Alchester,

A CITY OF THE *DOBUNI*,

THE SITE OF WHICH NOW FORMS A PART OF THE COMMON
FIELD OF WENDLEBURY IN THE COUNTY OF OXFORD.

BY JOHN DUNKIN.

WITH AN APPENDIX, AND THE WHOLE OF KENNETT'S GLOSSARY.

1816.

ADVERTISEMENT.

The chief part of the materials from which the following work is compiled was collected, from a wish to ascertain what reliance could be placed on the traditionary history of Bicester and Alchester. Necessarily engaged in other pursuits, which allowed but a very limited opportunity of indulging the desire of research, several years elapsed in collecting documents for and reducing the history into its present state. And as the utmost extent of the author's expectations was to afford a moment's entertainment to those friends who might peruse the manuscript, he was surprised to find not only a general willingness to further the object of his inquiries, but an anxiety that the work when completed might appear in print. To gratify this disposition, proposals were issued to publish it by subscription, and the numbers that immediately offered themselves as subscribers proved the interest they took in its fate. That the book might be accessible to all, it has been chiefly attempted to condense as much matter as possible in the smallest compass.

With this view it was originally intended that the body of the work should contain only the titles of the charters, grants, and other documents relative to the priory, markets, fairs, &c. which are printed in Kennett's Parochial Antiquities, deposited in the public archives, or remain in the possession of private individuals; and that a separate Appendix should be published, in which copies of the whole should be inserted, together with translations of those which are written in Latin, &c. This plan was relinquished at the request of several of the subscribers, who suggested that to the general mass of readers an English translation of the chief papers, together with an abridgement of the others found in Kennett, with copies of those necessary to form a continuation of that author's work, would be sufficient, while an opportunity would be thereby afforded of re-printing the whole of the Glossary. In thus complying with the wishes of the subscribers, surely the public will not think there needs any apology.—Of the manner in which the performance is executed every reader will judge for himself; and since excuses will avail nothing, perhaps it is best to be silent.—The author trusts, however, that he may say without presumption, that considerable exertion has been used in collecting the most authentic documents relative to the places of which he treats—that no pains have been spared in endeavouring to obtain the most correct information of their present state, and that in all cases he has strictly adhered to truth and impartiality.

Availing himself of this opportunity, the author gratefully acknowledges himself under particular obligations to the following gentlemen, who readily assisted him in the prosecution of his work, and kindly furnished him with original documents, translations, or communications.

John Coker, Esq.
John Caley, Esq. F. A. S. Keeper of the Records in the Court of Augmentation.
John Satchell, Esq. Kettering.
Alfred John Kempe, Esq. Blackheath.
Mr. William Upcott, Librarian of the London Institution.
The Feoffees of Estates for Charitable Purposes in Bicester.
Rev. John Markland, Bicester.
Rev. Richard Fletcher, ditto.
Mr. John Kirby, ditto.
Mr. Henry Chandler, ditto.
Mr. Thomas Harris, ditto.
Mr. William Rolls, ditto.
Mr. Richard Smith, ditto. &c.

viii   ADVERTISEMENT.

He has also to acknowledge the readiness shown by Sir G. P. Turner, Bart. to furnish him with the unpublished documents remaining in his possession relative to the Priory, while he has to lament the affliction that deprived him of the benefit which would have resulted from the fulfilment of his intentions.

Bromley, Kent, January 1, 1816.

ERRATA.

Page.
22. Line 8, *for* There are 15 hides and an half land of 22 carucates, *read* There are 15 hides and an half. Land of 22 carucates.
28. Line 7, *for* From Doomsday Book it is evident, *read* From Doomsday Book it is clear.
36. Line 5, *for* hence villains were found, &c. *read* and villains were found, &c.
37. Line 6, *for* and hence poor *laws* were found necessary, *read* and in consequence poor *laws*, &c.
40. Line 12, *The quotation should close at* feathers, *instead of* drawing-room.
52. Note, *for* It is not known whether the three deaneries, &c. *read* It is not known when the three, &c.
56. Note, *for* The money paid for the running of swine in a forest, *read* The running of swine in a forest.
58. Line 11, *for* G. Basset and Egiline his wife gave all their lands, &c. *read* G. Basset and Egiline his wife gave to the priory all their lands, &c.
58. Line 4, *for* gave for the health, *read* gave to the prior and convent for the health.
63. Line 18, *for* Bishop of Lincoln, Bath, &c. *read* Bishops of Lincoln, Bath, &c.
93. Line 12 of Note, *omit the word* couchant.
134. Line 21, *for* his treatment from the French, *read* his treatment from that people.
238. Line 16, *for* last years, *read* decline.
336. Note, *for* Hietto, sheep of two years old. Vide Glossary. *read* Hietto only.
330. Line 3, *for* 1535, 27 Henry VIII. *read* 1534, 26 Henry VIII.

THE

HISTORY AND ANTIQUITIES

OF

BICESTER.

CHAPTER I.

Situation and Name.

BICESTER, a considerable market town in the hundred of Ploughley in Oxfordshire, is situated near the north eastern boundary of the county, at the distance of thirteen miles from the city of Oxford. It is a town of very remote antiquity, and is commonly supposed to have been indebted for its origin to the Saxons; but the precise date at which that event occurred, and the circumstances attending it, are totally unknown. The etymology of its name is almost equally undetermined; though several antiquarian writers of reputed erudition, in their endeavours to trace it, have offered some plausible conjectures on the subject.

Skinner in his *Etymologicon Linguæ Anglicanæ*, states that Bicester was originally called by the Saxons Burenceaster, or Bernacester, from Buren or Bern, signifying grain, and Ceastre a town or station; but Dr. Plot, in his Natural History of Oxfordshire, contends that it obtained that appellation from the forest of Bernwood, on the edge of which it then stood, and that it was subsequently denominated Burgcester from St. Eadburgh, to whom the priory and parish

SITUATION AND NAME.

church were dedicated: in later times, by corruption, Burcester, and since Bisseter. These conjectures however, Kennet regards as unworthy of attention, and asserts that the town never was seated nearer than three miles to the forest above mentioned [1].

An anonymous writer, in a MS. History of Alchester, since printed at the end of Kennet's Antiquities, derives the name of Bicester from the apostle Birinus, whom he supposes to have advised the Saxons to erect a fort here, which they in consequence called, after him, *Birini castrum* [2].—This idea is treated as improbable by Hearne, but Kennet allows it to have some weight, and seems to have hesitated whether to prefer it or the two following opinions. First, that Bicester might be derived from the Saxon Beorn, a word equivalent to *castrum primarium*, the principal fortress, which he conceives may have been given to the place on account of the advantage it afforded to the West Saxons, as a military post against the Britons and Mercians; or secondly, as hinted by Harrison, in his Description of England [3], that it might come from Bure, the name of the stream or rivulet which runs through the town [4]. With this latter opinion Hearne perfectly coincides, observing that it was named from its situation on the river *Bruern* or *Bourn*, and that the true writing is *Bruerncester* or *Bourncester* [5]. With all due deference to the assertion of this eminent antiquary, however, the editor of the Beauties of Oxfordshire, observes that "it does not seem likely so trifling a stream as the Bure could impart a name to a set-

---

[1] Plot's Oxfordshire, (Oxford, 1705) p. 356.
[2] History of Alchester, apud Kennet, p. 687.
[3] Holinshed's Chronicle, vol. i.
[4] Kennet's Parochial Antiquities, p. 27. The variation in the name of this town may be some argument to derive it from Birinus; for as he has run the changes of St. Birine, St. Beryn, St. Burine, &c. so has this place followed the change of initial syllables, Birine-ceastre, Beryncester, and Burincester.
[5] Oxoniana, vol. iii. p. 80.

tlement of consequence; and it is certain that Berncestre was, in the age of Birinus, a frontier garrison, and was possibly built about his time, and by his advice, from the ruins of Alchester[1]."

Amidst so general an uncertainty, it would appear presumptuous in me to attempt settling this matter; for, if earlier writers could determine nothing with precision, much less is it now to be expected: besides, probability is not of much weight, since inquirers often find, in their researches after the origin of names, that the most unlikely is the true one. Nor is the traveller more surprised at the insignificant spring at the foot of the Abyssinian mountain, from which the fertile and overflowing *Nilus* takes its rise, than the readers of history are at the trifling circumstances which have given appellations to persons and places renowned in the historic page.

CHAPTER II.

Description of the West Saxons.

As it is generally allowed that Bicester and the surrounding villages owed their origin to the West Saxons, and formed part of their kingdom, a brief account of that people, and of the means by which they obtained possession of the country, may be interesting to the present inhabitants, some of whom are very probably their descendants.

The warriors usually comprehended under the name of Saxons consisted of three tribes or nations, Saxons, Jutes, and Angles. Of these the Angles were by far the most numerous, and accounted themselves the most honourable; insomuch that they affected to despise the Saxon name, and, when addressed as

---

[1] Beauties of Oxfordshire, by Brewer, London, 1818, p. 534.

such, would answer with disdain "We are not Saxons, but Angles." They originally inhabited that part of the continent which forms the duchy of Sleswick, and were among the foremost to engage in the expedition against Britain, to which it is thought the whole nation passed over under different leaders. By their valour they obtained possessions in every part of the country; but in the counties of Oxford, Buckingham, &c. they are described as forming the bulk of the inhabitants. Their persons were elegant, tall, strong, and robust; their hair, and complexions, generally fair; their eyes commonly blue, stern, and piercing; and they are characterized as more capable of enduring the austerities of winter and the pangs of hunger, than the anguish of thirst and the heat of the summer sun. Their moral character, even as it is represented by some of their own writers, would appear to have been destitute of every virtue except that of valour: but charity is inclined to doubt the faithfulness of the representation, and throw in some brighter tints; especially as other authors enumerate the additional virtues of chastity, hospitality, and kindness towards each other. The following may be considered as a narrative of the West Saxon military achievements, in this part of the country, and forming a history of the principal events connected with Bicester previous to the conquest.

CHAPTER III.

General and Military History preceding the Norman Conquest.

In the year 495, about thirty-six years after the landing of Hengist, the first Saxon invader of Britain, a fresh body of these warriors arrived under Cerdic and his son Kenric, and on the very day of their debarkation were engaged by the Britons. For that people, perceiving that the Saxons had determined upon the ruin and subjection of their country, were resolved to resist the intruders to the utmost of their power. Uniting themselves under the renowned Ambrosius and Arthur, they fought various battles with such success, that forty years of incessant warfare elapsed, before the Saxons, though assisted by numerous reinforcements, could effect the establishment of the kingdom of the West Saxons, which included the site of Bicester and its neighbourhood.

The Britons inhabiting these parts so powerfully resisted the remains of the Saxon army which escaped the destructive conflict of Mount Badon, that they were totally unequal to further conquest during the life of Cerdic. A new generation of warriors arose, and victory repaired to the standard of his valiant son, Kenric: but the Britons, no way dispirited with the loss of Hampshire, concentrated their forces at *Beranbyrig*, now Banbury, (A. D. 556) and sought, by a desperate effort, to regain their lost honour. Their troops were drawn up in three lines; each consisting of three distinct bodies, and the cavalry, the archers, and the pikemen were distributed according to the principles of the Roman tactics. The Saxons charged in one weighty column, boldly encountered with their short swords the long lances of the Britons, and maintained the conflict till the evening, when victory was yet doubtful: still, however, the fact of the fortresses remaining in the hands of the Britons proves that the contest terminated in their favour.

New multitudes of German warriors continuing to increase the armies of the Saxons, and to pour into the country at opposite points, distracted the attention of the Britons; nor could the courage of despair, evinced in the fatal battle of

Bedford, preserve the British fortresses of Eglesburg or Aylesbury, Bensington, and Eynsham, from falling into the hands of the enemy. Thus dispossessed of their strong holds, and overwhelmed by numbers, the Britons beheld the whole of their country parcelled out into districts, over which the principal chieftains assumed the sovereignty. On this occasion the midland counties were made to constitute the kingdom of Mercia.

Though Oxfordshire has been usually considered as annexed to that monarchy, a great part of it was really subject to the West Saxons; and though the Britons were driven to the westward, they remained for some time powerful and independent; the West Saxon garrisons of Cirencester and Eynsham were frequently harassed by their incursions, and in the last days of their freedom they displayed a valour and resolution worthy of a better fate. Numbers however ultimately prevailed: the parties of the Britons were successively cut off; and when Penda ascended the Mercian throne, he directed the whole strength of his kingdom to effect their destruction: those few who escaped the sword were consigned to abject slavery.

Hitherto the resistance of the Britons had engaged the common attention of the various tribes of Saxons, and produced a friendly co-operation; but when that people were entirely suppressed, the different monarchs fiercely commenced their inroads upon each other's territory. Among the foremost in showing his ambition was the West Saxon prince, who continually assailed his Mercian neighbours. These finding it difficult to defend their borders, collected their forces, and fought a desperate battle against the West Saxons at Cirencester. Both parties having tried their strength, and neither obtained the victory, it was considered prudent to form a league between the kingdoms. In this season of peace the West Saxon monarch was visited by the missionary Birinus[1], who had been dispatched to attempt the conversion of the kingdom by Pope Honorius.

The opportune arrival of Oswald, king of Northumberland, at the court of Kynigels, in the year 623, to unite himself in marriage with the daughter of that prince, contributed greatly to the success of Birinus. By their united persuasion, Kynigels was not only induced to embrace the Christian faith, but also to found an episcopal see at Dorchester, of which Birinus became the first bishop[2].

---

[1] Though it required no common spirit of missionary zeal to venture among these barbarians, little is known of the former part of the life of Birinus, or what induced him to attempt the conversion of the West Saxons. He is introduced to our notice as an ecclesiastic applying to Pope Honorius for a deputation; and the account goes on to state, that he was accepted, encouraged, and afterwards sent to Genoa, to receive ordination from Asterius, at which place it was expected he might have an opportunity of learning the Saxon language from the Franks who frequented it for the purposes of trade.

Malmsbury and other ancient writers say that from thence he travelled through France to a sea port on the Channel, where having performed the sacred mysteries, he embarked in a Saxon vessel for the shores of Britain. That when at a considerable distance out at sea, he recollected he had left behind a corporeal containing the blessed sacrament; and considering it vain to solicit the return of the pagan sailors who steered the ship, and impossible to leave the treasure behind him, supported by a strong faith, he stept out of the ship upon the waters, which instantly became firm under his feet, and walked to land, where, having secured the vessel, he returned on board in the same manner, the ship remaining stationary from the moment he left it. The ship's crew were of the nation to which he was sent, and being struck with the miracle, lent a docile ear to his instructions, became the first fruits of his mission, and gave an earnest of his future success.

Milner says, "This prodigy is so well attested by most of our judicious historians, that those who have had the greatest interest to do so, have not dared openly to deny it:" but it ought to be recollected that this author is disposed to believe that many miracles took place during the conversion of our Saxon ancestors. Hist. of Winchester, vol. i. p. 89, 90.

[2] It is said that Birinus was stung to death with snakes; and that none of that species could ever after live within the sound of the great bell of Dorchester abbey church. Mag. Brit. vol. iv. p. 476.

A. D. 643. Cenwalch having succeeded to the West Saxon kingdom, shortly afterwards divorced his queen, who was sister to Penda, the warlike and cruel king of Mercia. That monarch, indignant at what he conceived an unpardonable insult, immediately invaded Wessex, and defeating Cenwalch, forced him to seek refuge at the court of the king of the East Angles, with whom he resided three years, and was baptized. At his restoration, he voluntarily gave to Cuthred, his brother's son, to hold as a principality under him, all that part of his kingdom which lay on the north side of the Thames, computed at 3000 hides by the Saxon Chronicle; at the same number of villages by Huntingdon; and at a third share of his whole dominions by Malmsbury. The donation, it is not improbable, was made at Ashendon, in the forest of Bernwood[3].

A. D. 680. Ethelred, king of Mercia, having reduced all the country on this side of the Thames, and annexed it to the Mercian kingdom, Theodore, archbishop of Canterbury, anxious to gratify the ruling power, new modelled the bishops' see at Hatfield, and appointed Eta, a monk of the monastery of Hilda, at Whitby, to the bishopric of Dorchester, which, from the time of Birinus, had belonged to the West Saxons, but was henceforth united to Mercia.

Oxfordshire remained annexed to Mercia till Cuthred, king of the West Saxons, no longer able to bear the insolence and extortion of the Mercian kings, gave battle to Ethelbald, at Burford, A. D. 752, when that monarch was defeated. By this victory Cuthred recovered the principal part of the county, and it remained attached to the West Saxons till Offa the Mercian, determined to regain it, marched an army across the frontiers, (A. D. 775), about Souldern or Fritwell, (where ran a branch of the Roman Way, since called the *Portway*,

---

[3] Bernwood was disforested in the reign of James I.: it extended from Borstal to Weston Underwood.

or, by some, *Wattle-bank*), to Bensington, which place he besieged. Kenwulf coming to its relief, sustained a signal overthrow, and was forced to fly beyond the Thames; while Offa destroyed the fortress, and took possession of the county, which his successors retained till Beornwolf was defeated by Egbert, at the memorable battle of Ellendune, (perhaps Ellingham in Hampshire), when the county of Oxford was united to the West Saxon kingdom. Shortly after this, Ludecan usurped the regal power in Mercia, but was slain by the East Angles, 825. The Mercians then set up Wiglaf to rescue them from the West Saxon yoke; but Wiglaf was conquered by Egbert, who permitted him notwithstanding to hold Mercia as a tributary kingdom.

The reign of Wiglaf's successor Berthwulph, a like tributary prince, was disturbed by the Danes, who overthrew his army and forced him to seek refuge in a foreign country, where he died, A. D. 852. The Danes, after taking much spoil, and committing great devastation, marched southward, which afforded Burrhed, the succeeding monarch, an opportunity of strengthening his power by an alliance with King Ethelwolf, which seems to have had the effect of securing his dominions, as it does not appear that the Mercians were again visited by these ruthless invaders until 867, when, having succeeded in despoiling York and Nottingham, they penetrated into this kingdom, but were compelled to retreat by the exertions of Burrhed and his ally Ethelred, aided by the brother of the latter, afterwards the illustrious Alfred.

In 870 the Danes again issued from York, and entered Mercia, marking their rout with blood and ruin. The East Angles, finding their former submissions would not preserve them from the miseries of war, flew to arms, but being totally defeated, the enemy seized upon Reading, and ravaged the surrounding country. To deliver his kingdom from these dreadful enemies, Ethelred collected all his forces, and fought several battles with them. One of these took place at Ashendon, near Bernwood, (A. D. 871): but the courage of Alfred, after a severe conflict which continued without intermission the whole of the day, could only effect a temporary victory; for, within fourteen days, the Danes having concentrated their forces at Basing in Hampshire, whither Ethelred had pursued them, again offered battle, and were in turn victorious. The Saxons retreated towards Bernwood, the scene of their former success; " perhaps," says Kennet, " hoping for assistance or security from the Roman fort of Alchester." The Danes immediately followed, and having divided their army into two parts, fell upon the English, who were encamped on the west side of Gravenhill, where Ethelred and Alfred had cast up strong entrenchments, part of which still remain in Merton woods. The Danish troops, at the first onset, were broken; but having rallied again, they beat the Saxons, and remained masters of the field. According to their usual custom, they interred the slain in the wood on the adjoining hill, which henceforward obtained the name of Gnepen-hul, the hill of graves, or sepulchres of the dead. Dr. Plot considers this fact to be established by the circumstance of some Danish armour and immense numbers of bones having been discovered near that spot. As additional evidence on the same point, Kennet states that a Danish spur was found on opening the ground for the foundation of a garden wall for Sir William Glynn, at Ambrosden.

Victory having thus declared in favour of the Danes, they immediately marched and burned Reading; but Burdred having consented, by the payment of the infamous Dane-gelt, to become tributary, they afterwards withdrew beyond the Humber. When however they had destroyed every thing in that country they again returned into Mercia; and Burdred perceiving they were bound by no treaties, once more had recourse to arms. Being defeated, he abandoned his country in despair, and fled to Rome, were he soon afterwards died. The Danes then committed the government of Mercia to Ceolwulf, on condition of his assisting them in their depredations, and surrendering the kingdom on demand. Affairs however did not remain long in this state: the Danes bestowed a part of Mercia on Healfdune; and Ceolwulf, sensible of the danger and difficulty of his situation, delivered up the remainder to the celebrated King Alfred.

It is said that while the Danes continued at Northampton, the Saxons constructed a wall and ditch to prevent their incursions into these parts. If so, it is not improbable that the wall was raised on the bank of the original ditch, or on a branch of that made by Offa, (and thence called *Avesditch*), which marked the western boundary of the Mercian kingdom. A rampart is also represented as having at that time been erected on a spot at Mixbury, afterwards called Beamont, and another at Ardley: without doubt there were others at intermediate distances, but their sites remain undetermined.

The genius and success of Alfred procured a general respite from Danish violence; and in 886, his policy induced him to reduce Mercia from the rank of a tributary kingdom to that of a province, the government of which he committed to Ethelred, his son-in-law. Great numbers of the Danes were, however, scattered throughout Mercia; and, after the death of Alfred, they resumed their ravages in straggling bodies. These were taken into the pay of Edward and Ethelwald, who struggled for the sceptre, and harassed the country with their conflicts (A. D. 904). The surrender of Oxford, and the subsequent death of Ethelwald, leaving Edward undisputed sovereign, he directed his attention to the subjection of the Danes, and accomplished his design, by the assistance of his sister Ethelfleda, widow of Ethelred, governor of Mercia. This heroic princess (who inherited more of the spirit of the great Alfred than any of his other children) despising the humble cares and amusements of her own sex, commanded armies, built cities, and performed exploits which would have done honour to the greatest princes. Having governed Mercia eight years after the death of her husband, she died in the year 920, and Edward took the government into his own hands.

In those distracted times, between 911 and 914, the Danes made this county a scene of devastation, and entirely destroyed the old town of Berincester, and the villages of Fulwell, Woolaston, Shelswell, Bainton, and Saxonton, some of which have never been rebuilt.

The exertions of Edward and Athelstan seem to have secured peace to these parts until the time of Edwy, when the ecclesiastics Odo and Dunstan excited the people to revolt, and persuaded them to call his brother Edgar to the government.

Fortunately the administration of Edgar was popular, and and his reign peacable; but that of his successor was marked by Danish invasion and outrage. To gain the friendship of the barbarians, and, if possible, thereby to prevent their depredations, a marriage was proposed between Ethelred and the daughter of one of their princes; but the people smarting under their violence, secretly resolved (probably countenanced by Ethelred) on a general massacre, which in Oxfordshire was carried into effect with every circumstance of cruelty, on St. Brice's festival, Nov. 13, 1002, the churches themselves affording no protection. This treachery was severely revenged by the Danes, who, with an immense army, invaded, ravaged, and imposed a heavy tribute on the country.

For many years, without any intermission, Oxford paid tribute to the Danes, during which time it was subject to every calamity, and was in part destroyed by fire; but the sufferings of the county reached their height, when Sweyn, A. D. 1013, marching from Gainsborough, issued orders for his soldiers to plunder the churches and ravish the women, in every part of the country on this side Wallingford. This brutal order was as brutally executed; but the subsequent death of Sweyn, and the elevation of Canute, brought peace to the exhausted Saxons.

The policy of that prince was to allay the animosities between his Danish and Saxon subjects, and to attempt effecting a cordial union between them: nor was he unsuccessful. Notwithstanding the number of Danes that were settled in Mercia, the country henceforth enjoyed peace. At what time the inhabitants of Bicester, and the surrounding villages which had been destroyed, commenced the re-erection of their habitations, record does not inform us, nor can it be discovered why those of *Berncester* preferred the other side of the brook to the site on which the town had previously stood: conjecture is useless; since we hear nothing more of the place till it is found constituting a part of the vast possessions of Wigod [2] *de Wallingford*, in the reign of Edward the Confessor [3].

CHAPTER IV.

Roads.

THE bad state of the Oxfordshire roads [1] was long proverbial, and there were few more deservedly stigmatized than those in

---

[2] Perhaps " de Wallingford" has been added to his name in later ages, to distinguish this thane or nobleman by his residence, which was at Wallingford, as it is generally admitted that surnames were introduced by the Normans.

[3] Kennet, Antiq. p. 23—50.

[1] In ancient times the roads were repaired either by sums levied upon parishes, or by the services of individuals; and in the days of popery it was considered as an highly meritorious act of piety to devote money to this purpose; hence the

the neighbourhood of Bicester. At certain seasons the latter were absolutely impassible, and at all times attended with danger to the traveller. Much improvement, however, has of late years been effected by the introduction of turnpikes. The road leading from Bicester to Aylesbury was the first on which the experiment was tried. For this purpose, an act of parliament was obtained, 10th Geo. III. A. D. 1770, enabling trustees to borrow sums of money, for repairing and widening the road; permitting them to erect gates, and receive moderate tolls for the liquidation of such sums, for the term of twenty-one years from the time of the passing of the act[a]. By the successive acts of 1791 and 1813, the trustees have been enabled to direct their attention to further improvements; and the communication between Bicester and Aylesbury may be considered as convenient as local circumstances will admit. The tolls are of 4d. for every beast of draught, 2d. for every horse not drawing, 1s. 3d. per score for oxen, &c. and 10d. for calves, sheep, &c. besides double tolls on Sundays. The exemptions are limited to carriages, &c. employed in the public service; to carriages, &c. employed in purposes of husbandry, not going beyond the limits of each respective parish, and to those used for the purpose of going or returning from public worship.

In 1793 an act was obtained for " amending, widening, and repairing the road from Clay-hill, in the turnpike-road between Neat-Enstone and Chipping-Norton, in the county of Oxford, over the Heyford-bridge to the Water-lane, in the

---

frequency of donations towards mending the highways, many of which still continue to be received. See Hist. of Bromley, p. 21.

[a] The act, as usual, does not dispense with any law, custom, or usage which requires statute work, or sums of money to be paid in lieu of repairs of the road; but directs the continuation of the same, or a yearly composition, to be paid to the surveyor of the roads of the parish in which such highway is situated. Act, p. 20, 22.

town of Bicester, and from Bicester to the turnpike-road in Weston-on-the-green." The term and powers of the act were further enlarged and extended in 1813, and " the road branching out of the turnpike-road at Bicester windmill, to the turnpike-road leading from Blechington to Onslow-bridge, in the county of Oxon," included in those directed to be repaired.

In the same session (viz. 1793, 31st Geo. III.) was another act passed for " repairing and widening the road from the market-place in Bicester to the Buckingham turnpike-road, in Aynho, in the county of Northampton." By the extension of its term and powers, A. D. 1813, "the road branching out of the turnpike-road at Bicester Town's-end, and joining the Buckingham turnpike-road, in the parish of Finmere, co. Oxon, was incorporated with the above ;" since which the repair has commenced.

The tolls and all exemptions on these roads are similar to those on the Aylesbury road already described; and the time allotted for the operation of each of these acts is limited to twenty-one years [3].

There are several other roads leading to the neighbouring villages of Launton, Bucknell, &c. which remain in their original state; but as they are not often used for purposes of traffic, their condition is not so much a matter of public consideration.

---

[3] See the different Acts.

CHAPTER V.

General Description of the Town.

Bicester is situated in a flat country, surrounded by rich arable and pasture land. The air is extremely healthy, and the water pure. The neighbourhood, which is well adapted for the chase, has long been the annual resort of gentlemen addicted to that diversion.

The parish, including both the townships, Market-end and King's-end, may be estimated to contain about 2600 acres, of which the greater part is in good cultivation. Graven-hill and Merton are the only woods to which it is contiguous.

The town consists chiefly of one irregular street extending about a mile and a half in length, with two others branching from it called Crockwell and Water-lane.

That part of the principal street named *New-buildings* is in all probability the most recent part of the town, as they are not mentioned in any of the ancient writings quoted by Kennet; and the circumstance of an hermitage standing on the site of the house now occupied by Mr. William Horwood, may be adduced as proof that there were no other buildings adjoining in the reign of Edward III. except the chapel of St. John the Baptist; both of which were probably surrounded by a plot of ground, then called " the Hermitage Close," which extended into Crockwell.

Within the recollection of many of the present inhabitants, the site of the turnpike was known by the name of *Butts-corner*; from which it may fairly be presumed, that this spot was anciently without the boundaries of the town; the name intimating that butts, or ends of lands, (in the field) extended to that spot[1]. Perhaps it may be proper to add, that the

---

[1] This opinion seems warranted by Kennet's Glossary; though some may con-

garden belonging to the turnpike was formerly the common pound.

Crockwell probably derived its name from an ancient triangular well of excellent water, at present covered by the corner house, at the bottom of that street, but which was formerly open and exposed. When it was deemed advisable to build over the spring, part of its waters were conveyed into a well on the waste, and part to a small reservoir, called the Horse Spring, then under the wall, but now in the close of John Coker, Esq. The well has been since removed, and that which is now found near the spot, was made at the expense of the above gentleman, about the year 1794. A few years ago, Mr. Thomas Harris, a wool-comber, formed the adjoining premises into a bath, but as the speculation was not successful they have since been converted into a dwelling-house. The name of Crockwell appears as early as A.D. 1211, when a Walter de Crockwell is mentioned in the priory annals, whose name, it is very probable, was derived from this place. In 1245, a messuage in Crockwell is described as given by William Longspee to the canons. Crockwell was inhabited by some indigent people, who received alms of the priory, in 1277; and for some years has been the abode of the poorer class only [a].

---

jecture that it derived its name from having been the spot on which the butts for the practising of archery were formely placed.

[a] Until within the last eighteen or twenty years, houses in Crockwell were let to the poor at a moderate rent, (from 15s. to 2l. per annum, according to their different state of repair, and the extent of garden attached); but about that period two individuals (one of whom is since dead) commenced a kind of speculation in these cottages, to the full extent of their property; and by dividing and subdividing the old houses, were not satisfied by rendering them small and inconvenient, but enhanced the rent beyond all proportion; so that at present there are cottages, without a foot of ground attached, and at most consisting of two or three rooms, which are actually let for 7l. per annum.—Disgraceful indeed to the avaricious and unfeeling owner!

Traces still remain of a back road through the brook into King's-end, which served for the use of teams when the drivers wished to avoid the town. After the turnpike-road was made, this way was rendered impassable, and the ground added to Mr. Coker's close, on the condition of his allowing a footpath through the adjoining Dovehouse close: part of these closes were formerly called Crockwell Moor.

Sheep Street, in old writings, is called St. John's-street, most likely from its leading to the chapel of St. John the Baptist: and it appears to have borne that name from a very early period down to the sixteenth century. The present name is derived from the sheep-market, which is kept in it. This street, together with the market-place, is inhabited by the principal tradesmen of the town, whose dwellings are in general very respectable. The *Market-hill* is a small square, having on one side the *King's Arms Inn*, which is the first in Bicester. The *Shambles* are a long range of open buildings, erected for the express accommodation of the butchers, but which are now little used; that class of the town's-people preferring shops attached to their own dwellings. Formerly this place was much resorted to, and was crowded by a row of butchers' stalls on each side, besides the shambles. The *Town-hall* is an adjoining building, bearing the date of 1686, but erected in 1622[3]. Its eastern end is surmounted by a turret, with a bell and clock; the former of which is used to collect the officers and townsmen when they meet here on parochial business. The ground floor is let to some of the inhabitants, and partly used as a dwelling-house. In this hall the charity school was held about fifty years ago, but it has since been transferred to a smaller room built over the *Cage* and *Engine-house*.

---

[3] The date of the erection of the "Towne Eaule" may be found on the back of one of the old writings in the Wallingford chest.

Opposite these stood the *pillory* and *whipping-post*, which was removed some years since, and the irons belonging to it affixed to a post in the Shambles. The *stocks* still remain in front of the cage.

One branch of the brook crosses the street just below the end of the *Water-lane*; under an arched bridge guarded by a parapet on one side, where the channel is considerably enlarged for the accommodation of the inhabitants of the town, in washing and watering horses. On the embankment is a single row of houses which constitute the principal buildings of the Water-lane. The *Meeting-house*, on the opposite side of the road, stands upon the site of some buildings which were destroyed by the dreadful fire of 1724, which extended its ravages as far as the back of the King's Arms. Adjoining the turnpike was a very ancient *mill*, mentioned in Doomsday Book, the *dam* of which, a fine body of water, was greatly admired by strangers. The mill-house has been improved, and is now a handsome structure, but has lost much of its picturesque appearance, from the water having been lately arched over, and the space covered with green-sward.

At a short distance from *Blind-lane* stands the *Pest-house*, erected for the reception of persons afflicted with the small pox. The *Work-house* is a substantial building belonging to the feoffees of estates for charitable purposes, but let to the parish, and capable of accommodating forty poor individuals. Nearer to the Market-hill is the handsome residence of Mr. Davis.

The *Causeway* extends from the town brook to the church-yard, and was originally a raised bank (as the name implies) for crossing the brook: the whole of the hollow way has been of late years filled up, and the brook arched over; but, in rainy seasons, the bank is frequently overflowed, and the houses inundated. A small lane leads to *Place-yard*, so called from its being the site of the Priory.

DESCRIPTION OF THE TOWN.

The *Church-yard*, which is considerably elevated above the highway, is used as a thorough-fare from one township to the other. The church is the place of worship common to both townships.

King's-end, according to Kennett, is built on the site of the old town of Berincestre or Bicester, which was destroyed by the Danes about the year 913. A few houses afterwards erected on the spot obtained the name of the *Village of Bigenhul*, which, however, gave way to that of King's-end, the township having been known by the latter appellation so early as 1399. Till of late years there was a large green, with several houses upon it; these have been pulled down, and the green added to the pleasure grounds of John Coker, Esq. the lord of the manor, whose seat is the chief ornament of the town. For the accommodation of those poor who were deprived of habitations by taking down the houses on the green, some buildings have been erected upon the land adjoining King's-end turnpike.

There is no manufacture of great importance now carried on at Bicester; though formerly the making of sack-cloth, and of common leather slippers, together with the combing of Jersey wool, formed the employment of a large proportion of the inhabitants. Some of the poor have been of late years employed in the lace trade; but even this seems declining, and time alone can discover whether the new business introduced, viz. the plaiting of straw, will rise to any consequence. Many ancient writers have spoken in praise of the excellence of Bicester malt liquor, a reputation which at present it most justly retains. The town derives great benefit from its market and fairs, which are well attended by dealers in cattle.

CHAPTER V.

State of the Inhabitants, Tenures, &c.

THE earliest authentic records represent Bicester as forming a part of the *Honour of Wallingford;* but as there is no particular account of the village anterior to Doomsday Book, and that volume is universally considered as valuable a piece of antiquity as any age or nation could ever boast, a short account of it may not be uninteresting.— The idea of this undertaking was most likely suggested by the survey instituted by the celebrated King Alfred; and reflects honour on the memory of William. Executed at a time (A. D. 1082) when the Conqueror's authority was fully established, and the land divided among his chieftains, it conveys a minute account of every part of the kingdom. To attain as near to correctness as possible, the commissioners were empowered to examine upon oath the *lords of each manor,* the *presbyters* of each church, the *reeves* of every hundred, and six *villains* of every village, relative to the quantity of meadow, pasture, wood, and arable land in their district, the names of the proprietors, the nature of their tenures, the number of tenants, cottagers, and slaves, of all denominations, who lived upon the different estates, and their probable value. The work was executed with fidelity, and every particular entered regularly in the register. Oxfordshire was the fourteenth county surveyed (A, D. 1084), and the following is a correct extract of the part relating to the village of Bicester.

Idē. Ro. (De Oilgi) tenᵭ Bernecestre p. ɪɪ. Maner. Ibi sᵗ. xv. hidæ ʔ diᵐ. Tra. xxɪɪ. car̃. De hac tra. ɪɪɉ. hidæ sᵗ in dñio. ʔ ibi. vɪ. car̃. ʔ v. serui. ʔ xxvɪɪɪ. uiłłi cū. xɪɪɪɪ. borᵭ hñt xvɪ. car̃. Ibi ɪɪ. molini de xl. soliᵭ. ʔ xɪɪ. āc p̃ti. Silua. ɪ.q̃ɀ lḡ. ʔ una laᵗ   Valuit. xv. liɓ. M. xvɪ.

Translation.—" Robert (De Oilgi) holds Berncester for 2 manors¹. There are 15 hides and an half land of 22 carucates² of which 3 hides are in demesne, wherein are 6 carucates, and 5 servants and 28 villains, with 14 borderers, and they have 16 carucates. There are 2 mills³ of 40 shillings rents, and 12 acres of meadow. A wood of one quarrentine in breadth and one in length. In the days of King Edward it was worth 15*l*. now 16*l*.³

The total change of measures and manners renders it difficult to understand the precise meaning of the terms used in the survey, and adopted by writers in the following ages. Investigation has proved that no definite number of acres can be obtained from these loose measures, varying according to the custom of the counties. A *hide* of land, for instance, according to Gervaise of Tilbury, is 100 acres; the Malmsbury MS. computes it at ninety-six: but, in the reign of Henry III, a hide at Chesterton is reckoned at no more than sixty-four acres, and valued at forty shillings⁴. The *carucate* is equally ambiguous, and only signifies as much arable land as could be tilled by one plough: according to a computation

---

[1] Now the manors of Bicester and Wretchwic.
[2] One standing at the bottom of the Water-lane, the other at the north end of Mr. Coker's close.
[3] Kennett, p. 65.
[4] Hyde from the Saxon byb a house or habitation. Kennett's Glossary.

made in the twenty-second year of Edward III. it contained 112 acres, though some charters reckon it at 100, and others as low as forty acres. Kennett reckons the *quarrentine* at forty perches, or a furlong [5].

The various descriptions of inhabitants are better ascertained. The *servi* or peasants were those usually denominated *pure villains* or *villains in gross*. These were without any determinate tenure of lands; and, at the arbitrary pleasure of their lords, appointed to such servile works, and for such wages as they chose to give them. They were absolute slaves in person, issue, and stock; and might be removed and sold at pleasure. The *villani*, or *villains regardant*, were of a superior degree, and held some cottages and lands, for which they were burthened at appointed seasons with some stated servile work or offices, such as mowing, reaping, plowing, sowing, &c. and were conveyed from one proprietor to another, as appurtenances of the manor to which they belonged [6]. The *bordarii*, or borderers, were less servile in condition than the villains: they had a *bord* or cottage, with a small parcel of land, allowed them, on condition

---

[5] Glossary, art. *Carucate, Quarrentine,* &c.

[6] Kennett's Glossary contains the following instances of their persons being conveyed with their lands so held in villainage. "William de Longspee confirmed to the Priory of Burcester land in Wrechwike---cum villanis et eorum sequelis et catallis (p. 216). So Hamo de Gattone conveyed his lands in Wrechwike, cum omnibus villanis et eorum tenementis et sequelis (p. 272);---villanos, cum villanagiis omnibus, catallis, et tota sequela ipsorum; (p. 288);---una cum villanis, coterellis, eorum catallis, servitiis, sectis, et sequelis. p. 310). In the charter of Gilbert Basset and Egiline his wife to the priory of Bicester,---Terram nostram de Votesdun et de Westcote, cum omnibus pertinentiis suis, scilicet dominium nostrum cum villanagio (p. 151). He adds, this tenure is now extinct, yet the footsteps of it still remain in those customary services which are now reserved from some tenants to the lord; as particularly from the tenants of Mr. John Coker, lord of the manor of Burcester, Kingsend." None of the tenants, however, of the present Mr. Coker perform any service, and the nature of the above is now unknown.

applicable to the village of Bicester, but is generally descriptive of the state of the whole kingdom.

It does not appear that the introduction of the Norman government materially affected the inhabitants of Bicester. Their lord was the friend of the conqueror, and maintained his influence with him till the day of his death: nor is it clear that his son-in-law introduced any change. In the disputes between King Stephen and the Empress Maud, Brien Fitz-count, the superior lord, with his feudatory vassal Gilbert Basset, adhered to the empress during every turn of fortune; and on the accession of her son Henry II., they were rewarded by the following very important charter of privileges, 2d Henry II.

Translation.—"HENRY, by the grace of God King of England and Duke of Normandy, &c. to the bishops, earls, barons, justices, and all my ministers and faithful servants, French and English, of all England and Normandy, health. I command you that all the men and merchants of the Honour of Wallingford, that they may enjoy firm peace throughout England and Normandy, wherever they may be. And ye shall know me to have given and granted to them in perpetuity all laws and customs, well and honourable, as better and more honourably they enjoyed them in the time of King Edward, of my great-grandfather King William, and the time of my grandfather King Henry. I grant to them also, wherever they may go with their merchandise, purchases, or articles for sale, throughout all my land of England and Normandy, Aquitain and Anjou, *by water and by land, by wood and by strand*; they shall be free from tollage, pontage, passage, picage, pannage, and stallage; in shires and hundreds, and divisions of shires and hundreds; from aid of the sheriff[11], and

---

[11] Bailiffs of sheriffs had a customary fine to pay them; from these the men of the Honour of Wallingford were, by this privilege, exempt.

service of geld and Danegeld [12], from hidage [13], and *bloodwite* [14] and *bredewite* [15], from murders, and various services appertaining to murders [16], and from works of castles, of walls, of ditches, of bridges, of footways, and from all customs and secular exactions, and servile works [17]; they shall not be molested by any law to be made above ten pounds. I prohibit and command, that nothing above this be made, lest any thing above this vex or disturb. Witness, Theobald Archbishop of Canterbury and others.

"Dated at Oxford, the first day of June, A. D. 1156."

This charter was confirmed, and enlarged with many additional privileges, by Henry III.

The above charter clearly defines the usages and customs of the nation before and after the conquest; and confirms the testimony of historians, that almost every crime might be compromised by paying a certain sum of money, which the injured party and his friends were obliged to accept of as a compensation. But it is equally true, that in these and subsequent ages, violence frequently prevailed, and the exe-

---

[12] Geld, a tax. Dane-geld, a tax imposed by the Danes, which was continued on extraordinary occasions, for many years after the Conquest.

[13] Hidage, a tribute raised on every hide of land.

[14] A customary fine paid as a composition for the shedding or drawing of blood.

[15] A fine arising from any default in the assize of bread.

[16] By the laws of Edward the Confessor, if any person was murdered, the murderer was to be apprehended by the fribourg where the body was found, and delivered up to justice. If he could not be immediately taken, a respite of one month and a day was allowed to the said inhabitants; and if he was not then produced, a fine was imposed of forty-six marks, of which sum Henry I. appointed forty marks to be paid to the king, and six to the nearest relations of the party murdered. The inhabitants of Wallingford were exempt from this fine.

[17] Either personal labour, or a contribution in money. Kennett's Glossary.

cution of the laws was interrupted; so that men were obliged to seek their safety in unlawful combinations, examples of which are mentioned by Hume. This subject, however, appertaining more properly to general than to local history, those who wish information respecting it are referred to that author, or Dr. Henry.

From Doomsday Book it is evident the *whole* of the manors of Bicester and Wretchwic belonged to Robert De Oilgi. When these were afterwards granted to Gilbert Basset, senior, it does not appear that any part of them was alienated; and that they descended to his heirs in the same undivided state, for several generations, is evident from an inquisition taken of the Honour of Wallingford, A. D. 1212, reciting Richard De Camvil as holding seven knight's fees, which Kennett makes Bicester, Wretchwic, and Stratton, the original grant. But if these knight's fees contained the whole parishes, it is difficult to reconcile two grants the same year to Bicester Priory, one of which is expressly said to be by James le Bret, *lord of Biggenhull*, and the other by the prioress and nuns of Merkyate, who had a mansion and estate in Bicester; unless we suppose the latter manors were granted by the Basset family, who still remained superior lords of the fee, and that they were held by some unspecified tenure [18]. The other names which shortly after occur, as possessing land, &c. are Robert Clerk (A.D. 1214), Robert Fitz-Michael (A.D. 1217), and Thomas Brito (A. D. 1222); and these are noticed for their donations to the priory. But the virgate of land is expressly stated as given to Robert Clerk [19] for *his homage and service*, a circumstance which goes very far to warrant the conclusion that the other persons held their lands in the same way.

A. D. 1245. A sum being laid on every knight's fee, for

---

[18] Kennett, p. 176 & 177.   [19] Ib. p. 180.

marrying the king's eldest daughter, the prior of Bicester Priory paid three marks [20].

No better statement can be given of the situation of the villains not only in Bicester but throughout the kingdom, as it regarded their services, than the following extract from an account of the "Tenants, Rents, and Services," within the manor of Bicester, in eight parchment folios, taken in 1325, 18-19th Edward II., now in the possession of John Coker, Esq. lord of the manor, and quoted at large in Kennett's *Paroch. Ant.*

Translation.—" Robert son of Nicholas Germayn holds one messuage and half a yard land in villainage, at the will of the lady; and is bound to perform one ploughing in winter, and one weeding, and one *wedbedrip* [21], at the will of the lady, and shall have one meal, and is bound to perform one mowing for half a day; and a whole yard land of the same tenure shall have gratuitously at *vespers* [22], which are called *evenyngs*, as much of what is mown as a mower can lift up with his scythe, and carry home with the same; and half a yard land of the same tenure shall have in the evening gratis, with a companion, as much of what is mown as a mower can lift up with his scythe and carry home; and the mower shall have his breakfast from the lady prioress: and the said Robert, and all other copyhold tenants of the lady, are bound to turn the grass which has been gratuitously mowed in the meadow called Gilberdesham,

---

[20] Kennett, p. 235. [21] One customary day's work. Gloss. art. *Bedrip.*
[22] Time of even-song, at which it was presumed he would be present. Kennett observes that the daily claim of a faggot by the wood-cutter is derived from these customs; and adds, with true clerical anxiety for the welfare of his flock, that it is no better than theft, and ought to be punished accordingly. Glossary.

without receiving a dinner, and there to toss up the hay, and make it into cocks; and he is bound to carry four cartloads of hay to the yard of the prioress, and he shall have one breakfast from the lady prioress : and a yard land of the same kind shall perform three days work in autumn, to wit, one day's work without a dinner, with three men, and one day's work without a dinner, with one man; and if he be a binder, he shall have at the said day's work one sheaf of wheat for seed of the last wheat that was bound: and he is bound also to perform one day's work at the will of the lady, with his whole family except his wife, and shall dine with the lady; and as often as the binder has his dinner, he shall not have the sheaf; and he is bound to carry four cart-loads of wheat in autumn, to the manor of the lady, and he shall have one breakfast; and he is bound to be assessed at the feast of St. Michael, at the will of the lady prioress; nor is he allowed to sell a male horse nor an ox of his own feeding, nor to put his son to learning, nor to give his daughter in marriage [23], without the permission and will of the prioress : but if the lady prioress be present, the said Robert shall fetch and carry eatables and drinkables to the prioress during the time that she shall tarry in the county, at her will; and he shall also pay rent per annum, at the four usual times, 2s. 6d. and suit of court."

Under the article *Libere Tenentes ad Terminam Vitæ Cottag.* are the following entries :

"Matilda le Tallier holds by the court roll one messuage, with its curtilege, to the end of her life, and shall pay at the four usual feasts 4s. per annum, and suit of court.

"Isabella Maunde, &c. 2s. John Monkes and Matilda his wife, by written indenture, &c. 3s. John Abbot holds

---

[23] What would the present generation of farmers say to these restrictions?

till the end of his life, by the court roll, one acre and one rod of land, laying in the fields of Bicester, in five parcels, at 18*d*. per annum.

"Alice, who was the wife of Richard le Grey, cotterel and native to the lady, holds one messuage, two acres of land, and half an acre of meadow; and is bound to perform one day's weeding, and one day's customary work, and one day's haymaking, and to find one man to make hay with the aforesaid Robert, the son of Nicholas, and to make three customary days' work in autumn, without food, and shall pay 12*d*. rent per annum."

From the above extracts it plainly appears that many of the natives, cottars, and villains, were bound to perform their various services without food, or, at least, with only one meal from their lords. The land which they held by these services was their only wages: but, at the close of harvest, they usually had an extra meal or dinner, called the *harvest-home*[24]. On this day all the families of the customary tenants were bound to give their services, except their wives and shepherds, the former being supposed to be unable to leave the house, and the latter their flocks. This day of rejoicing was usually celebrated with singing and feasting; and from this the present custom of keeping harvest-home had its origin. Nothing, however, shows their state of bondage more conspicuously than the prohibitory clauses relative to the marrying of their daughters and the education of their sons, both grounded on the fears of the lord lest the children should be unable to perform the stipulated services.

From the same folios above mentioned it is evident that the lords of the manor provided a public bake-house, to which

---

[24] Anno 1293. Homines de Heydington ad curiam domini singulis annis inter festum Michaelis et Sti Martini venient cum toto ac pleno dyteno sicut hactenus consueverunt. Kennett, p. 320.

every tenant was expected to take his victuals to be dressed, where a regular toll was paid: it is entered as follows:—
"John the baker, and Christiana his wife, hold to the end of their lives, as aforesaid, four houses, with their curtilages, and one oven, with customary suit to it, and pay 2s. per annum, and suit of court." With the same benevolence they provided a mill for grinding corn, and here also a regular toll was taken [25].

It would appear pretty evident that mechanical professions were accounted more honourable than the practice of husbandry, since the laws prohibited any man from putting his son to any employment except *agriculture*, unless he possessed 20s. per annum in land [26]. The very cursory notice made in the folios of the persons attached to mechanical professions, leaves us ignorant of their state in Bicester; though we may safely conclude they were few in number, very ignorant, and, perhaps, inferior in condition to Robert Germyn: indeed, it is not improbable the mechanics or tradesmen, described in the different rolls, were nothing more than natives of the lordship, occasionally exercising such professions on the estates.

It has been already stated that every baron held a court, in which petty offences against members of the same fee were

---

[25] The mill spoken of must not be confounded with the present King's-end wind-mill, which was erected by the father of Sir Thomas Grantham, under a lease from the great-grandfather of the present Mr. Coker, who has in his possession the original lease.

[26] Dr. Henry reckons an estate worth 20s. per annum equivalent to 10l. at present; and adds, "if any person applied to husbandry work till he was twelve years of age, he was not permitted to abandon it, and follow any other line of life." He considers this law made on purpose to increase the number of labourers, at this time on the decline through the wars between the rival houses of York and Lancaster. Henry, vol. x, p. 53 & 54. See also p. 171, where the statutes 7th Henry IV. chap. 17, are quoted.

tried, and to which it was expected that every villain would bring his cause. It is true, they might remove them into the king's court: but even there, the villain could obtain no redress against the impositions of his own lord; for the indictment was immediately quashed, on the lord's appearing in court, and proving the prosecutor to be his slave: the law immediately presuming that, *as such*, he was incapable of possessing property, the lord's power extending over himself and all he had, except to the maiming, or taking away his life, or ravishing his relations; yet against all others could the villains maintain an action, none beside having any right to call them slaves [25].

In the *court-baron* the accounts of the year were usually settled, the services of each individual registered, and the fines paid. On the first Saturday in August, 1343, one of these was held for Bicester, when the accounts were given as follows:

"William Rede, for himself 2d. with two oxen.

"Agnes Serich, for herself 3d. and for one *ancilla* (maid servant) with four several beasts.

"John Cope, for himself 3d. with one turkey (*Africano*).

"Isabella Brown, for herself 2d. and for one *ancilla*.

"Robert Frerehews, for himself 2d. and suit and service to the lord with four beasts.

"William Symms, for himself 1d. to drawing corn for the lord.

"Richard Duke 3d. for himself and his servants drawing corn for the lord [26]."

---

[25] Archæologia, vol. ii. p. 312.

[26] The court-baron is closed by the inquest of the jury, as follows; "Inquisitio capta, &c. super sacramentum juratorum qui dicunt, super sacramentum suum, quod Juliana Hardy, quæ tenuit de domino unum messuagium et unam virgatam terræ in bondagio, diem clausit extremum, et accidit domino nova heriota 2 boves pret. 16s. post cujus mortem venit Walterus Hardy,

In a court-baron held at Wretchwic, the first Saturday in August, 1382, after the accounts were given for homage, pannage, and other profit to the lord, a by-law was made to reinforce all former orders for the regulation of *hunting*, under the penalty of 2s. fine for every offence; and " whereas the tenants' bees had been disturbed by the huntsmen, no further molestation should be given, under the penalty of forfeiting 4d. for such trespass."

Anciently there was also a court held by the lords of the HONOUR OF WALLINGFORD; but, on the attainder of John de la Pole, Earl of Lincoln, for rebellion against Henry VII., his manor of Ewelm escheating to the crown, it was by Henry VIII. constituted an honour, by the annexation of several manors, among which was Wallingford [27]. It is therefore probable that the lords of Ewelm assumed all the privileges connected with the demesnes thus annexed; and that they deputed their steward, bailiff, and others, to hold the courts of the Honour of Wallingford. At Bicester (a part of that honour) it was customary to hold this court on Easter Monday; and those inhabitants who neglected to attend it were usually fined one penny, or summoned to Ewelm. This court has been discontinued for many years, and tradition

---

et dat domino de fine 66s. 8d. pro licentia ingrediendi et tenendi prædicta messuagia et terram in bondagio, secundum consuetudinem manerii, reddendo et faciendo opera similia sicut prædicta Juliana solebat facere, et fecit domino fidelitatem, et cepit pleg. de fine, &c. Item dicunt, &c. quod Hugo King et alii de Wrechwyke vendiderunt arbores in gardinis suis, sine licentia domini, &c. de cætero non vendant sub pœna 12d., &c. Item dicunt &c. quod Richardus Syrech, Robertus Hardy, et Johannes Prynce, Hugo Page, et Johannes Page, extraxerunt bona sua extra domum domini, &c.

"Memorand. quod die Dominica in festo St. Andreæ Apos. 17 Ed. III, omnis status de Wrechwyke elegerunt Hugonem Kyng ad officium præpositi, et juramentum suscepit." Kennett, p. 456.

The *præpositus* (bailiff) appears evidently to have been elected by the men of Wrechwic, to do all the offices of equity between the lord and his tenants. Gloss.

[27] Magna Britannia, vol. iv.

ascribes that circumstance to a Mr. Howlet (circa 1769), who discovered it to be illegal.

A. D. 1425. Notwithstanding the scarcity of *inns* and *public houses* throughout the kingdom, it is evident some of these existed at this time in Bicester; for, in the bursar's accounts, 3d Henry VI., we find the names of "Joan Spinan, Alice Bedale, and other innkeepers," who sold to the convent " 132 flaggons of beer for 4*s*. 10*d*[28]."

After the commencement of the fifteenth century, a happy change took place in the condition of the lower orders of the people. The wars between the houses of York and Lancaster had greatly thinned the population, and the proprietors of estates found that the slaves, who laboured for them, and not for themselves, were often very stubborn, untractable, and indolent; so that, by degrees, they discovered that their work could be performed better and cheaper by hired servants. The manumission of the slaves had, in many instances, been effected by the necessity of arming them, and the feudal laws admitted no slave to bear arms. The clergy, too, often imposed the liberation of the slaves as a species of penance for certain failings. Time also convinced the landholder that his estates would be better cultivated, if the villain had an immediate interest in the produce; and that the raiser of the same would be better able to dispose of it than the lord or his steward. Hence arose the practice of receiving rents instead of services and produce. The granting of leases, which afterwards followed, completely emancipated the villain[29]; so that, by the reign of Elizabeth, a celebrated writer observes,

---

[28] Kennett's Glossary, p. 574. At this period public inns were very rare; travellers were usually entertained at religious houses for three days together, if occasion served: and indeed many spent their lives in travelling from one convent to another:—in this case their well-meant hospitality became a nursery for idleness.

[29] Henry's Hist. Brit. vol. x. p. 54.

no persons existed to whom the former laws relatively applied [30].

. The clergy and monks, under the stale pretence of preserving the church revenues, were the last to practise what they recommended to others: hence, villains were found on ecclesiastical and monastic estates, long after they had disappeared from every other. On some they existed at the Dissolution, and passed to the lay grantees of the property to which they were annexed; and I have no doubt that this was the case with those on the estate belonging to the prioress of Merkyate, in Bicester. Hence, though they had long before obtained their freedom in other respects, Kennett mentions the tenants of Mr. John Coker, then lord of the manor, as continuing, in 1695, to perform certain stated services.

. In ancient times, when every person on an estate was considered as a part of the family of the lord, and dependent on him for protection and support, it was his interest to allow his vassals the greatest privileges compatible with their situation. Hence, there were few or none of them who had not some small portion of land attached to their cottages, which they cultivated either after they had performed their customary day's work, or in the days that intervened. Most of them had cattle of some kind, and were permitted to turn them out to feed on the waste lands belonging to the lordship, or on the common fields after the removal of the produce. But, after their manumission, they lost all claims to these privileges. Their wages were thenceforth considered as their only means of support; though, as they in most instances con-

---

[30] Hume's Hist. Eng. vol. ii. p. 215. Henry VIII. granted a manumission (1514) to two of his slaves, and their families; for which he assigns this reason: "God at first created all men equally free by nature, but that many had been reduced to slavery by the laws of men. We believe it therefore to be a pious act, and meritorious in the sight of God, to set certain of our slaves at liberty from their bondage." Rymer, vol. xii. p. 470. Smith's Republic, p. 160.

tinued to reside on the manor, the freedom of commonage was winked at till the practice of inclosing began to prevail. And great as have been the advantages derived from the reformation of religion, it was attended with many immediate evils. It increased the number of poor, while it diminished the means of providing for their maintenance; and hence *poor laws* were found necessary. The retrenchment of numerous holidays indeed afforded opportunities for additional exertion; but it is clear that civil liberty upon the whole tended rather to depress than raise their pecuniary circumstances. The majority no longer kept a cow or a pig upon the common, or even poultry in their yard; their labour was barely sufficient for their support, and wages did not keep pace with the rise of provisions. Inclosures thinned the number of the farmers also; and though some were elevated, others were thrust into the lowest walks of life, so that their children were blended in its meanest ranks. The classes of peasant and farmer, which formerly approached each other, became widely separated,---distress and poverty took up its abode in the cottage, while luxury and pride retired to the farm-house.

These observations have anticipated those which would have arisen from the conveyance of the manor of Bicester Market-end with its royalties and appurtenances, by the Earl of Derby, (A. D. 1596) to T. Wykins and T. Clements, for the term of 10,000 years to come, the particulars of which will be hereafter given. Previous to that event, the greatest part of the township belonged to the lord of the manor; but, after the execution of that deed, the estate was divided, and sold in separate lots; so that, though the above-mentioned gentlemen and others afterwards obtained a release, together with a conveyance of the reversion in fee at the expiration of the 10,000 years, many of the different estates continue at present to be held on the original lease, and the tenure is from that circumstance usually denominated *Derby-hold*.

30th Geo. II. The act of parliament, in 1757, for the inclosure of Bicester-field, states that Sir Edward Turner is seized of great part of the land, and of the patronage to the church; John Princep, the vicar, as having right to the small tithes; the chancellor, masters, and scholars of Oxford, as trustees for the professor of physic; the trustees of the poor in the parish of Bicester; the tithing-man for the time being; John Pardoe, Esq. John Cook, Jasper Robins, William Roberts, William Blake, Ann Wilson, Sarah Box, William Humphrey, William Tanner, John Walker, Edward Lock, Mary Horn, Robert Maynard, John Major, Thomas Allen, Daniel Horwood, James Nixon, Thomas Slater, and divers others, *land-owners*, having *all* right of common, at stated times, and by a determined stint.

The act also describes William Shillingford, Richard Kirby, John Barker, John Hicks, William Rolls, Dorothy Harris, Thomas Eyles, Jacob Thomas, Matthew Clarke, John Ring, and others, as having right to commonage, in virtue of being owners of certain cottages or tenements [11].

To all and each of these a certain proportionate quantity of land was directed to be assigned, as near to their dwelling as possible; or else a sum of money was to be paid, equivalent to the advantages relinquished. These lands were thereafter exempted from all common pasture, estovers, &c.

Land was also assigned to Sir Edward Turner as rector impropriate, in lieu of all tithes and dues of corn, grass, hay, wood, &c. anciently claimed in the common field, the inclosed lands being directed to be discharged of the same.

A parcel of ground was allotted to the vicar, as a composition for small tithes, which he was henceforward to relinquish: and, in consequence, the proprietors of the several lands, ancient messuages, and tenements, who were subject to the payment of rectorial and vicarial tithes, were bound to

---

※ These last mentioned enjoyed a " cottage common, viz. for great cattle only," and this right did not extend over the meadows of Town Langford and Swallow. Act of Parl. p. 6.

fence and maintain the quickset hedges for nine years from the time of inclosure; these lands, cottages, or tenements, hereby becoming discharged of all tithes or moduses. But these allotments were neither to prevent the vicar from having tithe in ancient inclosed lands, messuages, cottages, gardens, mills, woods, under-woods, furze grounds, or parcels of land, whereof the owners had no right of common in the inclosed field; nor to lessen the title to oblations, mortuaries, or Easter offerings, or surplice fees, arising out of the town of Bicester: nor to defeat or lessen the title or right of Sir Edward Turner to the tithe of the ancient inclosed lands, as rector impropriate.

Special clauses are introduced, that nothing may prevent "or lessen the right of every person or persons whomsoever, having title or interest, with workmen, labourers, horses, teams, carts, or carriages, to come, go, be, pass, and repass, in, over, and upon all or any part of the meadow or pasture, called the *Mortar-pits,* at all times, for digging and taking away mortar;" "or on a certain piece of land, called the *Stone-pit-piece,* for digging and taking away stone at all times, in as full and ample manner as before the passing of the act."

The act closes by providing that the lords of any and every manor within the limits of the field are to enjoy the same privileges, of courts, rents, and services, as appertained to them before; and that nothing shall be construed to the damage of the king and his heirs [12].

Thus terminated the right of commonage enjoyed by the inhabitants of the Market-end. The inclosed lands were certainly improved in value, but many of the poorer inhabitants were ultimately considerable losers, since the sum received in compensation was gradually dissipated, and the privilege gone for ever. The expenses of inclosures could not be defrayed by others, and these also were obliged to sell; so that the

---

[12] Act of Parliament, p. 19.

evil fell upon those least able to bear it. It is not meant to insinuate that any imposition was practised; but in all great changes, the poorer orders of society are certain of being sufferers, their circumstances not allowing them to benefit by the proffered advantage.

Having thus stated the gradual changes in the relative situation of certain classes of society, it only remains to be observed, that it is of late years the farmers have attained a high rank in life. A writer pertinently remarks, " in the year 1750 farmers' daughters carried butter and eggs to market, in *green josephs*, fastened round with a leathern girdle; now they wear riding-habits and plumes of feathers [33]: but if such was their state in 1784; we may notice the steps they have advanced since that time. Their perverted education (consisting usually of music, dancing, and drawing,) has swelled them into the courtly *misses* : the dairy is now abandoned; they have their suppers, balls, and parties : and we may shortly expect to see the convenient farm-house turned into a modern *villa :* instead of the careful house-wife, attending her business, and the wants of her family, find that the *lady of the mansion* must be spoken with in her drawing-room."

Anno 33d Geo. III. The bill which afterwards passed into an act for the inclosure of King's-end field, stated, that the arable, meadow, lay, pasture, and waste lands contained by computation about 1200 acres [34]: that John Coker, Esq. lord of the manor, was seized of a considerable part of the above lands, together with part of the tithe of corn, hay, and grain, growing and renewing yearly within the same field : that Sir Gregory P. Turner, Bart. as rector impropriate of Bicester, was seized of certain glebe lands; and entitled to the remainder of the above great tithes : that Joseph Eyre, in right of the vicarage of the said parish-church, was seized of some

---

[33] Gent. man's Magazine, 1784.
[34] According to Young's Agricultural Report, p. 91, the field contained 1400 acres in cultivation, and 100 of common.

glebe lands, and entitled to all the small tithes growing and arising within the township of Bicester King's-end; and that Dame Elizabeth Dashwood, widow of the late Sir James Dashwood, Bart. was seized of the remainder of the said open and commonable arable, meadow, lay, and pasture land. That these lands of the several proprietors, lying intermixed and subject to the right of commonage, were inconvenient, and incapable of improvement, in their present state.; they therefore prayed the authority of parliament to effect an inclosure of the said lands, which was accordingly granted.

By the act three gentlemen who are described as quality men were appointed to survey, divide, and allot the said field among the above proprietors, according to the extent and quality of their respective estates; and they were provided with ample powers for the sale or exchange of any portion of the common that might be necessary to carry the act into effect, and connect the several parts of each estate. These commissioners were directed, in the first place, to mark out such public and private roads, ditches, fences, drains, gates, stiles, &c. as might seem requisite; so as that each public carriage road should be at least forty feet in breadth between the fences; the same to be made at the sole expense of the person through whose land it might be, within two years from the passing of the act. They were further directed to allot sufficient parcels of the inclosed land for stone or gravel-pits, so that there might be no deficiency of materials at any time for making and repairing the public roads in the township.

Land was also appropriated to the lord of the manor from the commonable land, in compensation for right of soil, tithe [35],

---

[35] It may be curious to trace the history of the great tithes in King's-end field, a memorandum is therefore submitted. An unknown benefactor bestowed them on Kirtlington parish church: that church and the tithe were given to a Cistertian Abbey, at Aulney in Normandy. The abbot of that place alienated the church of Kirtlington and its appurtenances, for the rent of 40s. per annum, to the prior and convent of Bicester. At the Dissolution they passed into the hands of the king, who granted them to Roger Moore,

&c. to which he was before entitled. To the rector and vicar, such other parts of the field as should compensate for their several yearly tithes, as well from the field, as from such tenements, gardens, inclosures, &c. as are within the township. In those cases where the owners or proprietors of cottages were found not entitled to lands or common right in the field, yearly rents were to be assigned, which were directed to be paid to the vicar, up to the day of his death, or removal. A special proviso, however, was introduced, to preserve the vicar's right and title to mortuaries, Easter offerings, and surplice fees, as they became due within the township.

The act further proceeds by directing the glebe land to be inclosed at the expense of John Coker and Dame E. Dashwood; securing the title of deeds or settlements on any of the estates; settling the titles of claimants to trees, fences, &c.; allowing the vicar to borrow money to carry the inclosure into effect; and closes by securing the rights of the lord of the manor.

The advantage accruing both to the farmer and landholder from inclosures is confessedly very great, though it is impossible to state the amount of the advance of land, either in Bicester or King's-end-field, without access to a rent-roll. If any reliance may be placed on the agricultural report of Mr. Arthur Young, it would seem that rents were trebled at Bicester, and that at the time of his writing, land was generally let from 20s. to 25s. per acre [36].

Esq. from whom they passed by marriage to the Blounts, and were finally sold by them to the ancestors of Mr. Coker.

[36] The same writer says that Mr. Coker is against leases, and never gives them; as they tell the farmer when he may begin systematically to exhaust the farm. In this rich country no great expenses are wanted in improvement, and if draining is necessary, Mr. Coker is at half the expense.—However, since the publication of that work, Mr. C. has granted short leases.

ABSTRACT
OF
RETURNS FOR THE EXPENSE AND MAINTENANCE OF THE POOR.

	King's-end.			Market-end.		
	£.	s.	d.	£.	s.	d.
Money raised by poors' rate and other rates, ending Easter 1803, within the year.	112	17	5	1281	13	10¼
Average assessments in the year 1783, 1784, and 1785.	39	1	8	567	1	8
Ditto 1776.	36	3	7	296	8	10
At what rate in the pound, 1803		1	6		6	6
Money expended out of work-houses, 1803.	106	0	10	953	6	4¼
In ditto 1803.				238	10	2
Money expended in suits of law, removal of paupers, and expenses of overseers and other officers.	1	12	9	47	6	9
Total of expenditure of the poor, 1803.	107	13	7	1239	3	4
Ditto ditto in 1776.	35	10	3	286	2	2
Do. average 1783, 1784, and 1785..	34	3	6	534	13	8
Expenditure for other purposes, church-rate, county-rate, militia, highways, &c..	5	3	10	22	12	10¼
Total expenditure 1803	112	17	5	1261	16	2
Money earned by the poor out of the work-house, 1803..				3	17	6
In work-house..				31	4	3

	King's-end.	Market-end.
Number of persons permanently relieved out of work-house..	15	67
In the work-house, permanently relieved..		27
Children relieved under 5 years of age..	3	21
From 5 to 14 out of the house..	10	30
No. of persons occasionally out of the house..	4	77
No. of persons included in the preceding columns above 60 years of age, or disabled from labour.	5	29
No. relieved not being parishioners.	3	180
Benefit societies holding their meetings in this place.		2
No. of members		119

POPULATION.

The following Table shows the number of houses and inhabitants in Bicester in the years 1801 and 1811, as stated in the parliamentary returns of these two periods.

	Houses.				Occupations.			Persons.		
	Inhabited.	Uninhabited.	No. of Families.	Building.	Agricult.	Trade and manufc.	Not included in these class.	Males	Females	Total Persons.
1801.										
Bicester King's-end.	44	1	48		pers. 112	pers. 80	pers. 4	103	93	196
Market-end.	364	5	461		811	826	113	837	913	1750
	408	6	449		923	906	117	940	1006	1946
1811.										
Bicester King's-end.	47		60		famil. 33	famil. 22	famil. 5	112	113	225
Market-end.	337	4	438	3	193	215	84	886	1035	1921
	414	4	498	3	172	237	89	998	1148	2146

CHAPTER VI.

Origin of Parish Churches.

THE first missionaries who laboured among the Anglo-Saxons commenced their work in the courts of the different monarchs, and were generally rewarded by the conversion of the royal family, and the principal courtiers. Personal attentions, and munificent grants, naturally followed, and stimulated their exertions among the inferior inhabitants. But, in general, the missionaries of the different kingdoms took up their residence in the capitals, and formed themselves into communities for the purpose of advancing each other in religious knowledge, and instructing the youth who were to succeed them in their sacred calling. From these societies, which afterwards assumed the pompous titles of chapters and cathedrals, the bishop regularly dispatched the different members, to dispense the offices of religion among the distant converts. And such was their estimation among the people, that no sooner did they appear in the streets, or on the high-ways, than the multitude swarmed around them, showing them every possible mark of respect, and receiving their words as those of an oracle. To facilitate the exercise of devotion, *auxiliary churches* were erected, and a few of these scattered through extensive districts offered the only means of worship. The public inconvenience of attending them was severely felt; but, as Christianity gained ground among the people, and was embraced by the lords of vast domains, the latter endeavoured to procure churches on their own estates. In their application to the bishops for this purpose, they pleaded their unwillingness that their tenants and slaves should neglect public worship, and their inability to permit their absence for the time their journeys to distant churches demanded. Their petition was granted, on their settling a sufficient endowment for the maintenance of a priest. This endowment usually consisted of a certain portion of land, of slaves to till the glebe, and of oblations made by the tenants. The churches were in general founded by the owners of the lordship, who, in consequence, became the patrons, obtained the right of presentation, and were allowed a seat within the rails of the chancel. When this was not the case, the priest built them out of the oblations of the neighbourhood, and the lay patrons endowed the living, the extent of whose lands formed the boundaries of the parish. As population increased, and these large domains were divided, the same objections applied to the parish church as were formerly advanced against the auxiliary. The same precautions for the perpetual maintenance of a pastor were taken, and another place of worship erected: but it differed from the former in many respects. The lands of both were granted *in pure and perpetual alms*, i.e. with all the advantages of a free and independent tenure, without burden or reserved rent; but the former was considered the MOTHER CHURCH, and at stated festivals the whole of the parishioners were required to attend divine service therein [1]. Even when Cuthbert, tenth archbishop from Austin, obtained the privilege of *burying-grounds* (A.D. 758) being attached to churches, the privilege did not extend to these *chapels of ease*, and for many centuries the dead were constantly brought for interment to the mother church. A part of the church also was allotted for the use of those who attended the chapels, and was usually distinguished by the name of the hamlet. They were also required to contribute a certain sum towards defraying the repairs of the church; and there is no doubt these usages were continued in many places until the Reformation [2].

In the time of Augustine, the tithes of all parishes were divided into four parts, of which one part was applied to the support of the bishop, a second to the clergy, a third to the

---

[1] Collier's Ecclesiastical History, vol. i. p. 229-230; Lond. 1708.

[2] Kennett, p. 585-596. A convincing proof that the inhabitants of Stratton-Audley anciently brought their dead to the burying-ground of Bicester will be found in the annals of the priory, A.D. 1425, in which the parishioners were fined for the illegal burial of two corpses in their chapel.

poor, and a fourth to the repair of the church. These were originally collected by the *itinerant priests,* or those at the head of the rural deanery, and were paid to the bishop to form a common fund for himself and the clergy who lived with him, or were sent abroad. When the cathedrals were endowed, however, the bishops gave up their claim to the fourth part; and in the time of Alfred, the whole tithes were finally appropriated to the priests, the poor, and for the repair of the churches. In those manors where no churches were built, the lords were permitted to receive the tithes as trustees, and, when they were erected on the estates in after ages, reserved the two parts (viz. for the poor and repairs of the church) to themselves. The clergy, however, regarded these privileges with envy; and, by their persuasion, they were settled on some religious house, or resigned to the parish priest, yet still charged with these uses, and not as absolute property. The innovation of ages has totally changed the application; but hence came the practice, and depends the custom, of the rector or impropriator maintaining the chancel [3].

We have a very full and ample proof of this in a deed quoted by Kennett, Par. Ant. p. 59, which contains a donation of the above-mentioned two parts of the tithe of the parishes of Burchester and Wretchwic, with those of Blechingdon, Weston, Bucknell, Ardulfley, Northbrook, &c. by Robert D'Oilgi, A. D. 1083, to the church of St. George, which he had lately built in the castle of Oxford, and endowed for a fraternity of secular priests. On the building of Osney Abbey, the whole of the endowment was transferred thither, and the monks continued to receive the tithes of Bicester and the adjoining hamlets, till they were assigned to Bicester Priory, in consideration of an annual payment of 60s. A. D. 1299.

---

[3] Kennett, p. 79-80.

CHAPTER VII.

First Parish Church in Bicester.

BEDE having asserted that "many churches were built and endowed by Birinus," among the West Saxons, after Christianity was planted in that kingdom, Kennett justly concludes that it is highly probable one of these was founded at Bicester, both on account of its distance from the cathedral of Dorchester, and the security it was likely to derive from the fortress. This opinion will receive additional strength from the circumstance of the situation of the present edifice, if it be granted that the old town of Berncestre stood in King's-end, and partly in the close of Mr. Coker[1], and that the parish burying-ground has never been changed. It is also probable that it was one of the auxiliary churches, from its having been the head of the rural deanery, and a mother church, from remote antiquity, and that the original structure was afterwards converted into the parish church, on a sufficient endowment being appointed for a priest by the lord of the manor. That the glebe lands were his gift appears certain from his retaining the two parts of the tithes till they were bestowed on St. George's Church in the castle of Oxford, A. D. 1083. Though we have no precise data for ascertaining the form or materials of the original church of Bicester[2], recent discoveries have placed it beyond doubt that the present edifice has been constructed out of the remains of some

---

[1] Many of the foundations of the old town remain in Mr. Coker's close.
[2] Many of the first churches in Britain were constructed of wattles; and even after the Conquest, some historians make mention of wooden churches,

former church, built of stone, and decorated with carved ornaments. In common with others, we may presume that the windows were glazed with horn, and the dim light transmitted through its narrow windows shed an awful gloom through the place, rendering candles necessary at noon-day. Ancient canons ordained that the image of the saint to whom the edifice was dedicated should be fixed in the church, or a portrait of him painted on the wall, or on a tablet, and hung over the altar, inscribed with the name and the time of the foundation[3]. The patron saint we may fairly presume to have been St. James, from the most ancient fair having been kept on that day.[4]. The additional ornaments of the altar were the crucifix, Mary, and John. The whole body of the church was left open for the people indiscriminately to stand or kneel at their devotions, the lay-patron alone having a place allotted to him within the rails of the chancel. Whether any persons of note were buried within its walls we have no means of ascertaining; but the presumption is against that belief, as these would prefer the church of the adjoining monastery.

Kennett represents the church as having originally stood at the north end of Sheep-street, and states that the present edifice was built about the latter end of the fourteenth or the fifteenth century, when the older structure was demolished. This opinion he founds on an old writing, which recites that, in 1406, John Gybbes of Watlington released all right and claim in a certain tenement of Bicester, nigh the church-yard, opposite the priory gate, &c. This (says he) proves the removal before this time, unless we sup-

---

[3] Kennett, p. 609, quot. Spelman, tom. I. p. 318.

[4] "At Burcester the wake is observed on the Sunday following the festival of St. James, and a fair is there kept on the said festival, and on the two days immediately before and after; which is a good argument, though other authorities be wanting, that the old parish church of Bicester was dedicated to St. James, as the new church might be to St. Edburg, patron of the convent." Ken. p. 612.

pose the *cœmeterium parochiale* was distinct from the old church, on which the new one was afterwards built.

In what way the sums necessary for building this fabric were raised, or who were the chief contributors to the undertaking, are points alike unknown. According to tradition, the tower was originally intended to have been erected near the present chancel (and the massive thickness of the walls seems to countenance the statement); but that the design was relinquished by the generous offer of the vicar to build a tower at the west end, at his own expense, which he afterwards carried into effect; and the present structure attests his taste and liberality[s].

It is not improbable that this parish anciently included many of the surrounding villages, which afterwards became separate parishes, and acquired authority over their own hamlets. Stratton-Audley for a number of ages was attached to and dependent upon Bicester, as its mother church, and the vicar's chaplain performed the offices of devotion in that chapel. No burials were permitted, but the dead were uniformly brought to Bicester; and when, in 1425, the chaplain presumed to inter there one of the inhabitants, the prior and convent sued and recovered damages of the village. Nor do I read of its ever being able to assume independence till after the Reformation.

The high antiquity of a chaplain, as attached to the parish priest of Bicester, may be gathered from an ancient deed confirming the hermitage and chapel of St. Cross, at Muswell, to the church of Missenden, A. D. 1106, bearing date 7th Henry I., and signed "William the elder priest of Bicester, with William his chaplain."

---

[s] If there is any foundation for the tradition, it is not unlikely the building of the fabric was considerably advanced, either before the proposal was made, or the original design relinquished, which, from the appearance of the semicircular arches, was cruciform.

The presentation belonged to the lords of the manor till the foundation of the monastery by Gilbert Basset, when the church was conveyed by charter to the prior and canons, who henceforth became its patrons and annexed it to the priory. As little more can be collected than the bare names of the vicars, it is intended to mention their appointment, under the various priors who succeeded to the government of the monastery.

CHAPTER VIII.

Deanery of Bicester.

IT is not known at what time rural deaneries were first instituted, but they were probably copied from secular divisions. The office of the dean was to receive complaints, inquire into grievances, to stay personal suits on offer of compensation, and to inflict the lesser censures of the church. They had at first the decision of all testamentary and matrimonial causes, and were assisted by a chapter formed of the neighbouring clergy; but their office was at last usurped by the archdeacon, and became nominal as early as the reign of Edward I., though the title is still preserved [1].

The antiquity of the Deanery of Bicester extends beyond any authorities extant, and probably is nearly coeval with the introduction of Christianity into these parts. It originally consisted of ten churches: but in after ages the two deaneries of Kirtlington and Islip being added, together with the

---

[1] Kennett, p. 632—655.

THE AUGUSTINE ORDER.

church of Ambrosden [a], in the deanery of Cuddesdon, the number was augmented; and, according to Willis, it now contains the following churches, viz. Ambrosden, Audley, Blechingdon, Burchester, Bucknell, Chalton, Chesterton, Kirtlington, Finmore, Frinkford, Fritwell, Goddington, Hampton-poyle, Hampton-gay, Hardwick, Heyford-*old-pontem*, Heyford-warren, Hethe, Islip, Launton, Lillingston-Lovel, Merton, Marston, Middleton, Mixbury, Newton-Purcel, Oddington, Stratton-Audley, Somerton, Stoke-lyne, Tusmore, Wendlebury, and Weston.

The seal of the Deanery of Bicester was found among the ruins of Alchester, and is described as containing the impress of a pelican standing on a font or pedestal, opening her breast with her bill, and feeding a brood of young-ones with her blood. The form of it was oblong-oval; and round the margin, near the extremity, was the inscription "*S. Decani Berencestre* [b]."

CHAPTER IX.

The Augustine Order.

THE Augustine Order derived their origin from the saint whose name they afterwards assumed; and though their founder drew up no rules for the particular government of a community, but simply made the Scriptures his guide, his followers

---

[a] Kennett remarks, that "at the time of the taxation under King Edward I., the church of Ambrosden still continued under the deanery of Cuddesdon, but at the election of a new see at Oxford, or near that time, was transferred to the deanery of Bicester." p. 632. It is not known whether the three deaneries of Kirtlington, Islip, and Bicester, were united.

[b] Kennett, p. 632.

THE AUGUSTINE ORDER.   53

contrived to extract the following regulations from his works, which they bound every brother and novitiate to observe [1].

I. That no man call any thing his own, but have all things in common—that to all be distributed according to their wants—that those who were poor abroad, do not go haughty, nor those who were wealthy despise the poor—that none have any property, or take care for food or raiment, but give all he has to the poor—that none be admitted without trial—and if any depart the monastery, to carry nothing away with him.

II. After prescribing the service of the church, the Canons are enjoined to work from the morning to the ninth hour, and read from the sixth hour to the ninth—when they must go abroad, it must be by two-and-two, and not to have any idle discourse.

III. They are enjoined the love of God, and of their neighbour—to be all of one mind—to be present at prayer at the appointed hour—to subdue the flesh by fasting—to listen to what is read at dinner, nor to grudge what is allowed to others who are sickly, or of a weak constitution—not to be affected in apparel—not to do any thing which may give offence—not to gaze on women—not to conceal any thing that is given them—to take care of the sick—if they should revile one another, to beg pardon— the person offended to forgive.—They are enjoined obedience to superiors—the superior not to be presumptuous [2].

Their dress consisted of a *black mantle* for an outer covering, which reached down to their feet, was open, and much like a cloak with a hood to cover the head, but had no sleeves;

---

[1] They bore the common name of "monk" till the eleventh century; but having become extremely lax in their rules, a council at Rome, after condemning simony and keeping of concubines, ordained the clerks should lodge and live together, and put into a common stock what they received from the church. Stevens's Dugdale, vol. ii. p. 64, 65.

[2] Stevens's Dugdale, vol. ii. p. 126.

they wore beneath this an *amice,* originally made of skins or serge, which covered the shoulders, and hung down to the middle of the back. Under these they wore an *albe,* made much like a surplice, reaching below their knees, but the sleeves were narrow; when it only reached the knees, it was called a *rochet.*

They covered their heads at first with *scull-caps,* worn on the hood of the mantle; afterwards their caps were made wider at the top than the bottom, but still round and flat. About 500 years ago they were made square, all of wool, having as it were four horns, which appeared but little outwardly.

Such were the rules and dress of the black canons[3] of the Order of St. Augustine. Their rules embraced the three vows of poverty, chastity, and obedience, with occasional voluntary penance, in common with the other Orders. And however, at this enlightened period, men of different persuasions may feel inclined to deride their fastings, flagellations, and other acts of mortification, they may be abundantly defended by the tenets and practice of the church for many ages preceding the establishment of this order. Their dress is liable to no more exceptions than the present dress of the clergy, or the uniform costume of alms-houses or charity-schools. Their rules are generally drawn from the Scriptures: and though, in a few cases, they may appear rather strained or misapplied, surely none but the fastidious will conceive themselves justified in condemning them.

---

[3] The "black canons" were so denominated, from the black habit worn over their surplices. They came into England with Athelwulph, confessor to Henry I., and in a few years multiplied prodigiously. Stevens's Dugdale, vol. ii. p. 69.

CHAPTER X.

Priory of St. Edburg.

THE Priory of Bicester was founded by Gilbert Basset, grandson of the first of that name, A. D. 1182, in the 28th and 29th of Henry II. for a prior and eleven canons of the Order of St. Augustine, (in imitation of the number of Christ and his eleven disciples,) and dedicated to St. Edburg. His lady Egiline de Courteney surviving him, and by her munificence contributing towards the endowment, was reckoned a co-founder. It is not known whether he erected a new building, or converted his own mansion into a monastery for their reception[1]. On their introduction he gave them the following charter of endowment[2].

Translation.—" To all the faithful of our holy mother the Church present and to come, Gilbert Basset sends greeting. Be it known unto all of you, that I have given and granted to John, Prior of Berncestre, and to the Canons serving God there, for the welfare of the body and soul of my Lord King Henry, and for the welfare of my own body and soul, and of the bodies and souls of Egilina my wife and of my children, and for the souls of my predecessors and successors, the Church of Berncestre with all its appurtenances. And in addition

---

[1] "Some say that Bassets house was where the late Priorie stood." Leland's Itin. p. 3. vol. vii. It is, however, thought by several in the present day, that the foundations which still remain in the Horse-close in an area, apparently once surrounded by a moat, together with their proximity to the monastery, warrant the conjecture of that spot having been the site of his mansion, and that it was encompassed by a considerable park.

[2] Kennett, p. 135.

thereto, all the land which is between the croft of Gilbert the miller and the messuage which was Adam's, and the messuage itself, as far as my park road, together with five acres which the aforesaid Adam held. And the messuage which was Osmand Favel's, together with the croft. And the messuage of William the waggoner, and the messuage of Alward, together with the croft in which the two aforesaid messuages were. And also every tenth load of my wood, that, as it comes from the wood, it may be drawn into the Canons' yard as into my own. And a certain meadow which is called Hamma, extending from the croft of Seric de Wretchwic by the mill-dam as far as where the new brook runs into the old one, and the mill-dam itself, to erect a mill where there was one formerly; or if it can be more advantageously erected in any other place near the mill-dam, let it be done. Also pasturage in the pasture ground within my domain for three teams of drawing oxen, together with my drawing oxen. Also for four hundred sheep. The pasturage belonging to the church, as well in my domain as in the common pasture, and freedom from pasnage [3]. Also that their tenants holding of them shall be free and quit from all service, so far as respects me. Also the church of Ardinton with its appurtenances; the church of Comton with its appurtenaces; the church of Missenden with its appurtenances; for a perpetual gift, free and quit from all secular service and exaction in the meadows and pastures, in the marshes, in the mills, in the ways and paths, and in all places, as well and as freely as property was ever held by any person whatsoever. And I Gilbert Basset will warrant the aforesaid churches and the aforesaid possessions to the Canons aforesaid free from all secular service. And the aforesaid Canons must not give or exchange the aforesaid churches or possessions for any

---

[3] The money paid for the running of swine in a forest.

PRIORY OF ST. EDBURG. 57

other church or for any other possessions, nor to farm let. Witnesses;—Rob. de Whitefield, then vicar. Thos. de Dureval. Egilina my wife &c. Alicia Basset. Henry de Curtenai. Rob. de Almari. Hugh Durevall. Thomas Basset. Fulc. Basset. James de Gerardmulin. Walerona de Chrichlade. Rob. le Waleis. Bartholomew Chaplain. Rob. son of Ralph. William de Covele. William son of Richard. Warin Butler. Hasculf de Bixa. Thomas Briton. Adam Clerk. Richard Clerk de Calverton. And many others."

The first charter of foundation is in a long slip of parchment, with a seal appending of green wax bearing the rude effigies of a man on horseback and this inscription + Sigillum Gilberti Basset.

Soon after the grant of this charter, Gilbert Basset gave to the said Prior and Canons a second, reciting the chapel of Stratton[4] as an appurtenance to Bicester, with lands in the parish of Stratton: And in the same year, a third and larger, containing an additional gift of 40 acres of his demesne, 20 acres in one of the common fields, and 20 in the other. Both of these are signed by the same witnesses, and bear a seal of the same impression.

Kennett supposes the saint to whom this priory was dedicated, was the holy virgin of Aylesbury, who, together with her sister Eaditha, having taken the veil, were reputed saints. Their father Frewald gave them the town of Aylesbury[5].

List of Priors, Benefactors to the Priory: Vicars, &c.

John first Prior. Vicar unknown.

The Prior and Convent having cast a longing eye on the tithes of Stratton, given to the Abbey of Eynsham by the grandfather of their founder, sought a quarrel about one vir-

---

[4] Now Stratton-audley.   [5] Kennett, p. 134—138.

gate of land which had been lately given to them. By the interposition of Gilbert Basset the dispute was ultimately settled by the arbitration of Philip Prior of St. Frideswides and Richard of Aylesbury,—that in consideration of the proximity of Bicester convent, the tithes of Stratton should be assigned to it for a pension of twelve shillings per annum: which agreement was immediately confirmed by the founder. But instead of charging this sum on the temporalities of the priory, it was immediately thrown on the appropriated tithes of the church [6].

1193. Gilbert Basset and Egiline his wife gave all their lands of Wotesdune and Westcote their demesne, in pure and perpetual alms for the health of their own souls and Thomas their son; and in 1201 [7], G. Basset, after providing that his body should be buried in the Priory, increased its revenues by the gift of some land with two mills, which he had lately bought of Baldwin de Munz in the parish of Kirtlington, paying yearly to the monks of Aulney in Normandy eleven shillings and to the heirs of Ingram two shillings for all services. It is however doubtful if he was ever buried here [8].

1209. Richard de Camvill and Eustace his wife, daughter of the above founder, and now patrons of the Priory, gave for the health of their own souls and Thomas their son, all the tithe of hay in their domain in the villages of Bicester, Stratton, and Wrechwic, in pure and perpetual alms.

Near this time the Vicarage of Bicester was ordained by Hugh Wells Bp. of Lincoln [9] as follows.

---

[6] Kennett, p. 144.   [7] Ib. 151.   [8] Ib. 162.

[9] Previous to the ordination of vicarages, parish churches appropriated to houses of religion, were supplied by secular priests who were stipendiary curates; but when by the ordination of vicarages the stipend was exchanged for a standing portion of tithe, glebe and manse, such endowment bettered

The Ordination of the Vicarage of Berencestre.

Translation.—"The Vicarage of the Church of Berencestre, which belongs to the Prior and Convent of the same place, by authority of Council has been ordained after the following manner. The Vicar shall have for his stipend and for those of his Chaplain and Clerk forty shillings annually to be allotted in certain portions. And he and his Chaplain and Clerk shall have from the Priory sufficient food for himself, his Chaplain, and his Clerk, and he shall have from the Priory hay and provender for one horse : and their offerings ; to wit one penny for a burial, (*corpore præsenti*) and one penny for marriages, and one penny for purifications, and on Christmas Day three pence, on Easter Day two pence, and he shall have at each of the other two principal feasts one penny. Also Offerings in Confessions, and by Legacy, as far as six pence; and the Vicar and the Canons shall divide the overplus equally between them. He shall also have a sufficient dwelling-house out of the Priory. But the Canons shall bear all the lawful and accustomed burdens of the Church besides the parish burden. And the Vicarage is worth.... ....but the whole church twenty marks [10]."

1210. Egiline de Courteney wife of G. Basset having obtained the moiety of the manor of Wrechwic, formerly given as the portion of Eustace to Thos. de Verdun, consigned the half of the manor which Gilbert Basset had reserved to himself, with the whole of the wood of Gravenhull, in free tenure, to the Priory [11].

Robert second Prior. His appointment uncertain.

1211. Richard Camvill and Eustace Basset his wife, for the sake of their own souls and of their ancestors and suc-

---

his title, and made him a perpetual vicar instead of an arbitrary curate. Ken. p. 605.   [10] Kennett, 559.   [11] Ib. p. 174.

cessors, gave to Robert Prior of Berencester, and the Canons of that church, one messuage in the late tenure of Walter de Crockwell, with all its appurtenances, in pure and perpetual alms [12].

1212. James le Bret, lord of Biggenhull, within the parish of Berncestre, gave (with consent of Amable his wife) to the Priory four acres of meadow land in *Gore,* near the Ham (*i. e.* house or piece of land) of Gilbert, by charter [13].

Hervey third Prior. His appointment uncertain.

The same year the Prioress and Nuns of Merkyate in Bedfordshire granted to Hervey Prior of Burncestre two ridges of land in *Hodesham,* in exchange for one acre nearer their land in *Nyhenaker,* and half an acre of meadow near the meadow called Gilbertsham [14].

1214. Richard de Camvill and Eustace confirmed the donation of half the manor of Wrechwic given by Egiline de Courtney; and as a further benefaction, gave to Robert Clerk for his homage and service one virgate of land in the village of Bernecestre [15], to hold for the yearly rent of one pound of cummin; on condition the said Robert, or his heirs, should find one lamp before the altar of St. Nicholas in the greater church of St. Mary and St. Edburgh in Bernecestre; to burn every night entirely, and every day during divine service, and at canonical hours, for the health of the souls of him, his wife Eustace, Gilbert Basset, Egiline, and Richard Camvill their son.

By another charter they confirmed the gift of the manor of Wrechwic, and wood of Gravenhull, with the additional gift of a certain pasture called *Coubrugge* [16].

---

[12] Kennett, 175.   [13] Ib. 176.   [14] Ib. 180.
[15] This virgate of land was one part of Candle-meadow.
[16] Kennett, p. 180.

PRIORY OF ST. EDBURG.

Richard fourth Prior. His appointment uncertain [17].

1216. James le Bret, lord of Bigenhull, gave with the consent of Amable his wife, to Richard Prior of Berncester and the Canons of the same, a meadow called *Kinsitheam*, for the soul of his father Walter Bret, and for the souls of his ancestors and successors [18].

1217. Robert Fitz Michael, in consideration of one mark of silver and the yearly rent of one pound of cummin at Easter, granted to the church of St. Edburgh two acres of land in Buricroft, lying between the land of Nicholas son of Harold and the land of John Goddard. Soon after the same person gave two acres in *Fort furlong and Crockwell furlong*, by the service of one penny yearly [19].

1218. James le Bret gave to the Priory five acres of his land in *Crockwell furlong*, with a marsh called *Crockwell moor*, and four seilons or ridges of land to make there a *bercherie* or sheep-cote [20].

1219. Isabel, daughter of Hugh Gargate of Caversfield, in her pure widowhood gave to the church of St. Maries and St. Edburgh in Burncester, part of a croft which lay near to the court of the Canons (the other part having been already given by Muriel her sister) on condition the said Canons should receive her and her mother into their prayers for ever; and when they should depart this life, their names should be inscribed in the Martyrology of the Convent. Sybil de Caversfield confirmed one virgate of land in the

---

[17] On the authority of Kennett, I have given this prior's name as *Richard*, and considered him the fourth in office from John the first prior, though only the initial *R*. is given in the deed quoted—p. 183. Willis mentions Reginald as fourth prior; but as his name does not occur at length till his resignation in 1269, I have considered it too long a period for one person to hold the government, especially as they were commonly middle-aged before they received the appointment. See Willis's Abbeys, p. 172.

[18] Kennett, 186.   [19] Ib. 185.   [20] Ib. 187.

village of Stratton, which Isabel her daughter had given for the maintenance of one Canon for ever [21].

1222. Thomas Brito gave to the church of St. Edburgh for the souls of Gilbert Basset and Egiline de Courtnai ten acres of land in the field of *Magendune,* seven acres of which lay between the land of William Petre and William Wind, three in *Endepethe,* and three in *Lillesei* [22].

1225. The Prior presented a vicar to the vicarage, name unknown [23].

1227. Walter son of Richard de Kirtlington released and quitted claim to the Canons all his right and title to a new mill on the other side of Cherwell, with a parcel of willows, free passage over the river, and a parcel of land near the mill twenty-four feet towards the north, and seventeen feet in breadth towards the west side of the mill [24].

1228. In consequence of a dispute between Alan Basset baron of Wycomb concerning the advowson of Compton, Wilts, it was determined by the Bishop of Lincoln, Bath and Wells, that the Bishop of Sarum should have the presentation, but that two parts of the tithe of corn in the said parish and one croft near the house of the incumbent should remain a perpetual endowment to Bicester priory [25].

1229. Alice Basset, widow of William Mallet baron of Curi-Mallet, Somerset, gave some lands in Dedington to her nephew Gilbert Basset, who soon after gave them to the Priory [26].

1230. Walter Ingeram gave to the church and priory a plot of ground reaching in length from *Hoosford* to the mill o Kirtlington, with full liberty to plant or fell trees, sell or convert it to any other use [27].

---

[20] Kennett, 189.   [21] Ib. 194.   [22] Ib. 198.   [23] Ib. 201.   [24] Ib. 205.
[25] Ib. 207.   [27] Ib. 208.

PRIORY OF ST. EDBURG,

1231. The Prior presented a vicar to the church of Newton [28].

1233. Alan Basset baron of Wycomb left by will two hundred marks to the University of Oxford, for the maintenance of two chaplains, and made the Prior and Convent of Bicester his excecutors, who purchased three carucates of land in Arncote, with a wood in the said village, out of the rents of which they obliged themselves to pay eight marks yearly in two equal payments, for the support of two chaplains or scholars residing in the University of Oxford, who should pray for the souls of him and his wife; and on every special festival add a *placebo* and *dirige*. This land still bears (or very lately bore) the name of Prior's-hill.

The schools of Burchester [29] (Scholæ Burcestrienses) lay in School Street, on the north side of St. Mary's church.

1234. William Longspe, patron of the Priory, confirmed the former grants with pasturage for fifty-two yearlings at Erdington [30].

1236. The Prior presented to the church of Little Missenden [31].

1239. Robert [32] fifth Prior died; and the Convent, having obtained leave of their patron W. Longspe, elected Henry one of their canons.

1240. The Prior presented to the church of Little Missenden, Bucks [33].

---

[28] Kennett, 209.

[29] Kennett supposes the Scholæ Burcestrienses originated in this donation, and that the convent being thus obliged to maintain two scholars hired a tenement of the Abbey of Osney called Hastyng, and employed it for the instruction and residence of scholars.—This plan was adopted by the different orders in succeeding ages.—p. 213.

[30] Kennett, p. 216. [31] Ib. 220.

[32] Rob. Grosthead Archid. Oxon. Henricus Canonicus de Burnecestr. petita et obtenta licentia eligendi a Com. Sar. a conventu ejusdem domus vacantis per mortem Roberti Prioris in Priorem electus est. Dods. MS. vol. 107. p. 78. [33] Ken. 224.

1244. Phillippa, daughter of Thomas Basset, in her pure widowhood gave to the church of St. Mary and St. Edburg all her right in seven shillings yearly rent out of a tenement in Stodley, to be paid to the canons, on condition the said canons, for the health of her soul, and her ancestors' and children's souls, should find one lamp always burning before the altar of St. John the Baptist in the conventual church of Bicester.—Here she was afterwards buried [34].

Ralph de Chesterton gave the service of one knight's fee in Betterton, payable at the death of every Prior of Pothele [35].

1245. The Convent paid three marks towards the marriage of the king's son, a grant being made of twenty shillings on every knight's fee.

William Longspe gave to the Priory a pasture land called *Heesecroft,* lying on the east side of the highway leading to Wrechwic, as far as the bridge, with the whole meadow adjoining, to inclose and convert at pleasure; and also his whole right and title in a mill held by Robert Puff, saving to himself and his heirs the free grinding of corn for himself and family; and also a messuage in Crockwell, for which the said Canons used to pay fifteen pence; in consideration of their remitting sixty shillings rent per ann. which they had in the mill of Wivesley [36].

1249. Philip Basset, son of Alan Basset baron of Wycomb,

---

[34] This lady was the second wife of Henry Earl of Warwick, who died 13 Henry III. She afterwards married Richard Siward, from whom she was divorced.—Kennett, p. 233.

[35] It seems Thomas de Mazcey had given the manor of Westbatterton to the Priory of *Poghele* by the service of one knight's fee to the capital lord, to be paid at the death of every Prior, which manor was then in possession of Sir Ralph de Chesterton. By an indenture made between the parties it was agreed Sir Ralph should confirm the gift, and the Priors successively perform the service. This service constituted the donation to Bicester Priory.—Kenn. p. 233. [36] Kennett, p. 235.

gave to the church and convent sixteen acres of arable land, and one acre of meadow in the fields of this village, with four messuages in the said village, excepting a reserved rent to the lord of the demesne [37].

1254. The Pope grants to King Henry the tenth of all spirituals for three years. Bicester Priory was then valued at fifteen pounds, and the vicarage at thirty marks by the Bishop of Norwich.—Hervey Prior.

1261. John sub-prior of Bicester chosen Prior of Chetwood [38].—The religious were now become so unpopular as to occasion some of the inhabitants, in their grants, to prohibit their children giving their possessions to monasteries [39].

1268. On the death of Reginald seventh Prior, William de Quainton one of the canons was chosen to that office by leave of Henry Lacy Earl of Lincoln and Salisbury, their patron [40].

Isabel de Fortibus Countess of Albemarle granted a charter of confirmation to the Priory of five quarters of bread-corn to make hosts or consecrated bread for the service of the altar, out of the manor of Heyford-warrin originally given by her great grandmother Maud de Chesny in the tenth of Richard 1.[41] This grant was afterwards relinquished by the convent for a composition of six shillings and eight pence when the manor was granted to New College Oxon.

1271. Philip Basset gave by charter lands in Clifton, Heentone, and Dadingtone, with lands, tenements, and their appurtenances in Grimsbury in the parish of Bannebury, Northamptonshire [42].

1272. The remainder of Wrechwic came into the possession of the convent by gift of Ela, widow of James Lord

---

[37] Kennett, 241.   [38] Ib. 257.

[39] Ib. 264. Habenda et tenenda dictam acram terræ de me et hæredibus meis sibi et hæredibus suis vel suis assignatis vel cuicunque dictam acram terræ dare vendere legare vel assignare voluerit in quocunque statu sit exceptis viris religiosis——

[40] Kennett, 269.   [41] Ib. 270.   [42] Ib. 274.

Audley, and daughter of William Longspe [43]. She again two years afterwards renounced all claim to the two carucates in Wrechwic.

1275. John Pufgh granted to the canons his right in an acre of arable land lying in *Brodelond* in Bicester field; the canons releasing to him and Muriel his wife twelve pence yearly out of ten shillings annual rent due to the convent [44].

The convent purchased all the right and claim of Richard de Cülne and Christiana his wife in the water-mill in Kirtlington [45].

It appears by a parchment register that in 1277 the expenses of the religious were less than the receipts by twenty-five pounds six shillings and five pence.

Richard de la Vache granted and confirmed to Walter, prior, all the lands, meadows, &c. he held in the village of Wrechwic, by gift of Hamo de Gattone, the convent paying five marks and a half yearly, or, in default of payment, himself or heirs being allowed to distrain the goods or chattels on any part of the convent land in that manor [46].

1281. Walter, Prior, having caused Thomas de Meriton, one of his canons, to make an *In hoc* [47], in Arncot common fallow field, near the court or mansion house of the prior, on the east side in Nether Arncote, the abbot of Oseney complained he was much damaged thereby; and after much opposition it was agreed, nothing of the kind should hereafter be done without consent of the abbot [48].

1285. Henry Lacy confirmed the charter of Gilbert Basset and that of William Longspe [49].

---

[43] Kennett, 277.   [44] Ib. 284.

[45] "This was the chiefage or lord's rent, which the convent bought off for twenty shillings." Ib. p. 285.

[46] Ib. 238.

[47] An *In hoc* seems to have been an inclosure in some part of a common field which lies fallow, because it was agreed that the abbot of Oseney out of his mere liberality should allow the prior the crop of that croft for this turn.

[48] Kennett, p. 297.   [49] Ib. 306.

PRIORY OF ST. EDBURG.

1291. A general taxation of all ecclesiastical possessions in England, toward defraying an expedition to the Holy Land, granted to pope Nicholas IV, the whole was under the direction of John bishop of Winton, and Oliver bishop of Lincoln [50], when those connected with the church and priory were valued according to the following list.

Taxatio Ecclesiastica P. Nicholai.

	£.	s.	d.
Prior de Burncester' h't in Cestreton in t'ris et redd'	1	16	0
Wedlingbur' in redd' et p'ts	1	17	4
Wrechwik in t'ris redd' mol' p'ts pannag' et cur'	2	2	8
Feryngford in t'ris et pratis	0	1	0
h't man'ium de Grimesbur' in Decanat' de Bannebur' et com' Northt'	6	0	0
Ernecote in t'ris et redd'	3	14	8½
Stepel Aston in redd'	0	13	4
Blexh'm in t'ris redd' p'tis pastur'molend' et fruct' aial'	13	19	0
Westcote in t'ris et redd'	2	11	11
Cave'sfield in terr' redd' p'tis cur'	5	18	4
h't in ibidem in fruct' greg' et aial'	0	2	0
Decanat' Marleberg'			
Porcio prioris Burncester Eccl'ia de Compton £5 6s 8d decima.	0	10	8
Marleberg Prior'de Burncest' taxatio 10d. decima.	0	0	1
Ecc'lia de Burncestr' deduct' porc'	12	0	0
Porcio Abb'is de Alneto in ead'	1	6	8
It'm porcio Abb'is Oseney in ead'	2	0	0
It'm porc' Abb'is de Eynesham in ead'	0	12	0

---

[50] The collectors appointed in the diocese of Lincoln were the abbot of Oseney and prior of St. Catharine's at Lincoln. These deputed Ralph rector of Wooten, and Richard rector of Gilling, for the archdeaconries of Oxford, Bedford, and Bucks. Ib. 312.

1299. A dispute settled between the priory of Bicester and the convent of Asherugge respecting a common pasture near to Wrechwike, by an agreement that the prior and convent might enclose three acres of common pasture in Blackthorne, excepting meadow to be mowed, in any place where the tenants of the Priory and convent used to common [51].

1300. William de Thornberg ninth Prior quitting November 13th. Roger de Cottesford constituted prior.

The canons of Oseney agree to remit the tithes of Burncester, &c. to the Priory for sixty shillings per annum.

The convent of Bicester demise their prebendary church of Sutton with the chapel of Bockingham and their respective manors to the abbey of Aulney in Normandy, for two years at two hundred pounds rent [52].

1304. The tithe of Biggenhull and Nonnes Place was appropriated to the church of St. Maries Kirtlington, which church was appropriated to the Cistertian abbey of Aulney in Normandy. This year the abbot of Aulney demised the said church and its appurtenances to the prior and convent for the rent of forty shillings per annum.

1310. By an inquisition of the possessions of Henry Lacy Earl of Lincoln, the jurors found that he held the manor of Burncester by the law or courtesy of England of the inheritance of Margaret his wife, &c., and that there were in the said manor one hundred and sixty acres of land. That the prior held of the earl the site of the priory with four carucates of land, twenty acres of meadow, one water mill with other appurtenances, value forty pounds per annum; the church of the said town, value thirty marks, with the manor of Wrechwicke worth twenty pounds per annum, in pure and perpetual alms; and that Alice daughter of the aforesaid Henry and Margaret was the nearest heir of the age of twenty-six years and upward [53].

---

[51] Kennett, 336.   [52] Ib. 342.   [53] Ib. 360.

1317. The king at Walsingham confirmed the several donations made to the priory by special charter.

1320. Walter *de Burncester* [54] clerk, designing to give to prior and convent one messuage with ten acres of land in Grimsbury and Warkworth, petitioned for the dispensation of the statute of mortmain lately passed (A.D. 1276. Edw. I.) which, on the report of commissioners that it was not prejudicial to the king, was granted. This statute prevented many future donations [55].

1322. Richard Serich granted and confirmed to the prior and convent one messuage and nine acres of arable land in the town and fields of Bicester, held of John Puff, to have and to hold of the convent from the lords of the fee by usual service [56].

1329. A dispute which arose between Oseney abbey and Byrseter priory relative to the portion of tithes in Ardington Berks. decided in favour of Byrseter priory, under the hands and seals of the oldest inhabitants [57].

1331. Roger de Cottesford dying is succeeded by Robert de Curtlington eleventh prior. Admitted 6 calend. of December [58].

1342. Sir Richard de la Vache released and quitted claim to the prior and convent all his right and claim to the several lands and tenements which the said prior held in the manor of Wrechwyke, and to all suits and services which could arise from thence [59].

1348. Roger Warde became prior 3d cal. of June, on the death of Robert de Curtlington.

Nicholas Brode admitted vicar 16 cal. December [60].

---

[54] It was common for the religious to assume a surname from the place of their nativity or former residence.
[55] Kennett, 381. [56] Ib. 389. [57] Ib. 412. This document is very curious.
[58] Willis's Abbeys, vol. ii. p. 172. [59] Kennett, p. 453. [60] Ib. p. 559.

PRIORY OF ST. EDBURG.

1349. Nicholas de Shobington appointed thirteenth Prior, 10 calend July [61].

Thomas Cok curate of Middleton, William de Stratton curate of Launton, and Richard de Caversfield curate, jointly gave to the conventual church of St. Edburg in Burncestre all the lands, tenements, rents, services &c. which they had of the gift and feoffment of Thomas de Stapenhull in the villages of Burncestre and Middelington, to hold for ever of the capital lords of the fee [62].

John Osmond of Chippenham admitted vicar at Peterborough 15 calend. June [63].

1354. Peter le Grote fourteenth Prior resigning, Robert Blaket succeeded on the 5 of the ides of December, which dignity he retained until his death 1383 [64].

1356. The prior and canons admitted John de Aldwinkle vicar (John Osmond having tendered his resignation) on the nones of August; and Aldwinkle after retaining it fifteen years exchanged it with William Belhamy 20 November 1371, for the vicarage of Weregrove, Sarum [65].

1383. Robert Islip sixteenth prior confirmed April 1st [66].

1397. John Paulyn vicar, Richard Green curate.

October 14, Richard Parentyn appointed prior [67].

1401. Wm. Campion admitted vicar [68].

Circa, The parish church rebuilt in its present situation [69].

1411. Richard le Estrange lord of Bicester, and patron of the priory, granted to Richard Parentyn and his successors a pasture called Cowbrige mede, between the water course nigh the meadow of Biggenhull, and the priors' land called Cowbrige furlong, in full recompense for the free pasturage of three team of oxen, which liberty had been lost for a long time. This however is given and acknowledged as a full equivalent [70].

---

[61] Willis, vol. ii. p. 172. [62] Kennett, 471. [63] Ib. p. 559.
[64] Willis, vol. ii. p. 172. [65] Kennett, p. 558. [66] Willis, vol. ii. p. 172.
[67] Willis, ib. [68] Willis, ib. [69] Kennett, p. 558. [70] Ib. 546.

1413. Ralph Philip presented by the prior and convent, upon exchange with William Campion 10 March [71].

1425. 3 Henry VI. The chaplain of Stratton Audley at the instigation of the inhabitants presumed to bury two corpses in the said chapel when they ought to have been carried to the mother church of Bicester. Upon this violation of parochial rights, the prior and canons of Bicester the patrons and appropriators of the church made their complaint, and preferred a suit against the inhabitants of Stratton, and the prior in person went to London to prosecute and solicit in the cause, which was finally referred to the bishop of Worcester, who came to Bicester to try the same; which after due hearing and examining was determined in favour of the prior, and the inhabitants punished for their illegal offence [72].

By the *bursars'* account delivered 1425, it appears to have been customary for them to settle their accounts the day after Michaelmas [73].

1434. William Campion resigned the vicarage into the hands of the prior and convent, who appointed John Odam: admitted at Lydington Oct. 18. 1434.

1439. Richard Parentyn dying, John Wantyng succeeded to that office as eighteenth Prior [74].

1440. Richard Parentyn the late prior having held for life from the lord of the manor one parcel of ground called the *mulle piece* or mill piece, extending in length one acre called the *mulle acre*, lying near the highway under the wall of the priory close, called the horse close or *le horscrofts*, on one part; and the mete or boundary reaching toward the

---

[71] Kennett, 558.   [72] Ib. 577, 578.

[73] These accounts are given at length in the Appendix, and will be found to contain some very curious items.

[74] Willis's Abbeys, vol. ii. p. 172.

meadow nigh the *brech* on the other part, and abutting on the south upon Lamp-dytch near the aforesaid meadow, and on the north on the highway near the croft of John Russel, the same land was now granted by Sir Richard Le Strange to the priory by the service of one red rose on the feast of St. John the Baptist [75].

1453. John Wantyng resigning is succeeded by Edmund Wycomb, and the following maintenance appointed him:

Translation.—John Wantyng prior of Burcestre not having from any other quarter the substance of this world, from whence he is able to support himself, according to his proper state, rank and age, hath resigned the said priory. The bishop hath preferred to the same priory Edmund Wycomb, and assigns to the said John for his maintenance, a place called the *trymles* situated within the priory aforesaid, with its garden; also the said John shall have for the term of his life, for the clothing and stipend of his servant, five marks; also he shall have four cart-load of firewood from the wood or coppice of the said prior, and as much bread and beer, fish and flesh and other eatables and drinkables as two canons of the said priory have been accustomed to receive.: he shall have also every month two pounds of wax candles for his chamber; and shall have also every week twelve flaggons of beer and thirty-three conventual loaves for himself and servants [76].

In the third year of Henry VI. anno 1454. The prior and convent of Burcestre, entered into the following compact with John Odam, and granted this instrument for the perpetual endowment of the vicarage.

Translation.—Edmund, prior of the priory of St. Edburg Burcestre, and the convent of the same place, proprietors of the parish church of Burcestre aforesaid, and of the chapel of the blessed virgins Mary and Edburg of Stratton-audley, de-

---

[75] Kennett, p. 628.   [76] Willis's Abbeys, vol. ii. p. 332.

pendant on the same &c. John Odam priest, perpetual vicar of the parish church aforesaid &c. We the prior and the convent the proprietors aforenamed will and grant by these presents for us and our successors, that the said master John Odam perpetual vicar aforesaid and his successors in future time shall have and shall enjoy by right and title with the vicarage aforesaid, the manse of his vicarage with the gardens and customary places adjacent, and the tithes of vegetables and of hemp and flax growing in the gardens of the said parish, also all the tithes, oblations, mortuaries, altar offerings, commodities, profits, and emoluments whatsoever, arising at present or in future from the villages or fields of Burcestre, Wrechwic, or Biggenhull, and from other lands and places tithable or about to be tithed, within the boundaries or limits of the said parish church of St. Edburg, wheresoever situated, arising or in future to arise, and of all places appertaining to, or belonging, or in future to appertain to the same parish church, freely, fully and wholly, without impediment from us or our successors, excepting and reserving to us the prior and convent and to our successors all sorts of tithes of garbage and of hay arising from tithable places in the same parish, excepting also and reserving all sorts of tithes of all enclosures not gardens at present or in future in the said parish, in our hands without any fraud existing. But if any of these inclosures shall be in the hands of tenants, or occupied by their (kine) animals, then we will and grant that the aforesaid vicar and his successors shall have and enjoy the tithes of lambs, wool, cheese, butter, and the personal tithes, in every case reserving the great tithes in all those places to ourselves and successors, reserving also to ourselves and successors all sorts of tithes, oblations, and profits whatever arising in the village of Stratton-audley. And also we will and grant that the said vicar shall have annually two waggon load of good hay furnished and afforded by the prior and convent, to be carried to the manse of the said vicar at a proper time as heretofore accustomed, and 4 waggon load of fire-wood, out of the wood of the prior called the Priors wood near Arncote, to be cut down and carried at the cost of the said vicar, upon the reasonable arrangement of the prior and his deputies, after a proper requisition made by the vicar or his attorney. We the proprietors aforesaid also will and consent to the expense of maintaining a chaplain in the said chapel of Stratton, according to the tenor of the above composition, to celebrate and administer all holy rites to the parishioners there, by the consent, will, and assent of me John the vicar aforesaid, and also by the consent, will, authority and assent of the reverend father in Christ lord John by the grace of God bishop and diocesan of this place, to us and to our successors does appertain and belong; and not only the duty aforesaid, but also all other duties whatsoever incumbent on the said chapel or aforenamed church of Bicester, and to the vicar of the said church, in what manner soever belonging, the duty of repairing the vicar's manse or of furnishing meat and drink to the said vicar being alone excepted. In witness and affiance of which wholly and singularly we the Prior and Convent, the proprietors aforesaid, on the one part, to these indentures containing our agreement, and remaining in the keeping of the said vicar, have set our common seal. And I the vicar aforesaid on the other part, for the greater testimony and affiance of the premises, have procured the official seal of the reverend lord archdeacon of Oxford to be affixed. Given in the chapter house of the priory of Burcestre aforesaid, the twentieth day of January, (A. D. 1454,) thirty-third year of the reign of King Henry VI.[77]

1479. John Adams dies, and the Prior and Convent appoint Richard Brails vicar, who was admitted at Peterborough

---

[77] Kennett, p. 669, 670.

PRIORY OF ST. EDBURG. 75

July 29th same year. After holding it nearly two years and a half he resigned, and Thomas de Kirkby admitted at the Old Temple, London, 1481 [78].

1483. Richard Hindlest twentieth Prior enters into an agreement with the Abbot and Convent of Eynsham to pay yearly the sum of twenty shillings out of the mill at Old Clifton, near Dadyngton. The state of the premises no longer admitting the payment of forty shillings, the original sum is therefore remitted [79].

November 20th the same year the Prior died, and John Tooker the sub-prior was raised to that dignity [80].

1485. Thomas Banbury elected twenty-second Prior [81].

1486. The manor and church of Heyford being conveyed to New College, Oxon, the Prior and Convent released the rent of corn formerly given them by Maud de Chesney to make hosts, for the annual payment of six shillings and eight pence in money.

1498. William Stavely lord of Bignal gave by will twenty-six shillings and eightpence;—proved November the 1st same year [82].

1499. Richard Petyrton 17 July succeeds as twenty-third Prior, on the resignation of Thomas Banbury—is afterwards promoted to the abbacy of Nuttley, Bucks [83].

1503. William Dadyngton confirmed Prior in Dec.

1510. John Coventry elected twenty-fourth Prior October 11 [84].

1528. Robert Bruce twenty-sixth Prior died [85].

---

[78] Kennet, 621.
[79] Madox's Formulare Anglicanum, p. 107.
[80] Additions to Willis's Abbeys, vol. ii. p. 23.
[81] Willis, vol. ii. p. 173.
[82] He also "bequeathed his body to be buried in the chancel of the parish church of Bicester."—Kennett, p. 680.
[83] [84] Willis, vol. ii. p. 173,
[85] Cole's MS. vol. 27. p. 80, Brit. Mus.

1528. William Browne twenty-seventh and last Prior elected April 6th [86].

1529. Peter Gryffith appointed vicar on the resignation of Florentius [87].

1534. William Browne, Prior, and eight Monks, subscribed to the supremacy of Henry VIII. The following year were visited in general with other monasteries. It is probable the visitors here were Lee and Leighton, as their visitation included the diocese of Lincoln [88].

1536. The report of the visitors having disclosed monstrous vices and enormities which existed among the monastics in different parts of the kingdom, an act of parliament

---

[86] Cole's MS. vol. 27. p. 80.   [87] Kennett, p. 621.

[88] This step appears to have been taken with a direct design to produce charges against the monks, and thereby effect their ruin; they having lately fallen under the King's displeasure. The instructions of the visitors are very particular, and it seems almost impossible for the religious to avoid committing themselves in their answers to some of the eighty-six inquiries which the commissioners were directed to press. Among these were the questions whether divine service was kept up night and day at the right hours—how many were present and absent—the number of religious, whether according to the foundation—their former and present revenues—their mortmains and donations, and whether the founder was authorised to make them? They also were to examine their local statutes, inquire into the election of their head, see the rule of the house, number the professed, and examine the novices—to inquire whether the monastics observed their rule, but chiefly the three vows. Whether any had money without the master's knowledge—if there were any back-doors to the monastery by which women entered, or if boys lay with them.—Whether the rules of abstinence, fasting, silence, and hair shirts were observed—the habit worn, and every transaction of life in conformity to the order,—whether the superior and brethren acted towards each other as prescribed,—the edifice in good order,—the estates properly managed,—and church presentations rightly made?—and lastly, one brother was called to state another's views in entering that place, or managing its concerns: thereby exciting them to inform against each other. No wonder monstrous stories were propagated, doubtless many of them false: but they produced the desired end, the shocking enormities they were charged with excited the hatred of the people, and finally accomplished their suppression.—*Burnet's Hist. of the Reformation*, vol. i. p. 185.

PRIORY OF ST. EDBURG. 77

was passed for the suppression of all the monasteries whose revenues did not exceed two hundred pounds per annum. The preceding valuation having included the priory of Bicester in this number, it was accordingly surrendered by Prior Browne and his Convent, each of whom had pensions assigned them out of its revenues, though the amount of that paid to the Prior (viz. twenty-four pounds per annum) is alone preserved. 1537. Probably the last act of the prior and convent as an independent community was a grant of the right of presentation of the vicarage of Bicester to John Longland bishop of Lincoln, at which time that prelate collated John Phillips.

It is much to be regretted that the records of the Augmentation-office do not contain the original surrender of the monastery. The following, however, is the list of its revenues as delivered into that court, 29 Henry VIII.[b]

Oxon. Monast'rium de Burcester.

		£. s. d.
Burcester —	Firm' et Reddùs cu' Redd' Cust' Tenen'	13 10 4
	Firma terr' d'nicar' —	25 10 4
Wretchwyke —	Redd' et Firm' —	22 7 5
Stratton Audeley	Firm' terr' —	16 0 0
Ardyngton et Letcum-basset —	Firm' Rectorie' et Terr'	18 0 0
Kempton, Dodington Clifton et molehd' aquat' in Clyftonne	Exit' — —	32 0 2¼
Grymesburye juxta Banburye —	Firm' Manerij' — —	8 6 8
Nelthropp juxta Bannebuwye	Firm' Mes' — —	1 13 4

---

[b] The most grateful acknowledgements are due to John Caley, Esq. F.A.S. keeper of the records at the Augmentation-office, for his obliging communications, and for his ready assistance in procuring original documents.

Oxon. Monast' de Burcester.

			£.	s.	d.
Kirtlyngton et Tackleye	Redd' et Firm' cum Redd' tam lib' quam cust' ten'		11	17	8
Arncote in Hundreed de Bolingdon	Redd' Mess' et Terr'	–	4	11	10
Stepulaston	Redd' Mess' et Terr'	–	0	13	4
Middylton	Redd' Mess' et Terr'	–	2	0	0
Wendleburie	Firm' Cottag' et Terr'	–	0	10	0
Chesterton	Firm' terr'	–	0	5	0
Fryngforde	Redd' terr'	–	0	2	0
Hoyforde Warren	Penc'	–	1	6	8
Caversfelde	Firm' Manrij	–	2	13	4
Samforde	Firm' Mes' et terr'	–	0	5	0
Buckenhul	Firm terr'	–	0	5	0
Beamonde juxta Missenden	Firm' Man'ij	–	13	6	8
Westcote	Redd' Terr'	–	4	10	0
Blackenbull	Firm' Claus'	–	1	0	0
Compton Bassett	Penc' R͞cor	–	4	0	0
	Vendic Bosc Perquis' Cur'		null'		

Thus after existing for a period of three hundred and fifty-four years as the principal mansion in the town, did this monastery dwindle into insignificance and ruin, so that the most diligent inquiry can only rescue a few of the names of its principal buildings from oblivion, whose site neither tradition nor investigation can ascertain.

It is evident from the foregoing annals that the church of this monastery contained *three altars,* one of which occupied the east end, and was distinguished by the name of the high altar, and the others dedicated to St. John the Baptist and St. Nicholas. To the former of these, without doubt, the clause in the second charter of the founder applies, which di-

PRIORY OF ST. EDBURG.

rects that "one virgate of land in Stratton should be applied to finding a light for the church," and which according to ancient custom was placed on the altar during the celebration of divine service. This opinion seems also confirmed by the grant of Candlemeadow by Richard Camvill for the express purpose of maintaining lamps (or candles) for the altar of St. Nicholas, which were to burn every night entirely, "and every day during divine service, for the health of the souls of Richard Camvill and Eustace his wife, Gilbert Basset, and Richard Camvill their son."

The piety of Phillippa Basset, Countess of Warwick, provided a light for the altar of St. John the Baptist; and the circumstance of her being buried within the church would lead to the conclusion that she was afterwards buried near that altar [90]; indeed it is not improbable that both of the latter were founded as chanteries, and perhaps by the above benefactors, that after their decease masses might be perpetually sung for the repose of their souls.

Altars of this description were generally decorated with the image of the saint to whom they were dedicated. The private masses were seldom attended with any pomp, and almost without any attendant except the priest's boy, or some of the relations of the dead. On the anniversary a *missa ad requiem* was sung in the morning, and a *dirge* in the afternoon. This service was called the founder's *year's mind*; and if there were lesser commemorations, they were described as a *month's* or *week's mind* [91].

In common with other conventual churches, the religious had each a stall, similar to those now found in cathedrals,

---

[90] Kennett, p. 232.—The idea is suggested from her having granted seven shillings rent in Stodeley for maintaining a light to be set on this altar.

[91] A dole was frequently given on the anniversary. Peck's Desid. Curiosa, vol. ii. lib. vi. p. 38. Lond. 1732.

which they occupied during divine worship, and there is little doubt but that after death their bodies were buried in this church. This edifice also seems to have contained the ashes of several noble persons besides the Countess of Warwick.

The foundress, Egiline de Courteney, some of the Damories lords of Bucknel and Goddington, and one of the last lords Le Strange, are particularly enumerated as buried within the walls; but whether any tombs or monuments perpetuated their memory is unknown [92]. Even all traces of the pile itself have perished, and no document remains which can furnish a conjecture concerning it. On the Dissolution, the fabric was immediately destroyed, and most likely the bells, lead, and other materials sold, so that when Leland visited the place a short time after the surrender, there was not a vestige of its grandeur remaining. If, however, under the discouraging circumstances of the failure of traditional evidence, and the destruction of every fragment of the edifice, it be allowable to hazard a conjecture of its site, I should be inclined to place it within the smaller inclosure, on the northern side of the garden;—the space included within those lofty walls lying due east and west, and appearing proportionate to the extent of a church adapted to the use of this monastery [93].

---

[92] Gilbert Basset as some thinke was buried beyond the sea.

Æglean Courteney was buried in the Priorie of Burcester.

There were divers of the D'amories auncieat gentlemen buried in the Priory of Burcester.

There was also one of the last lords " le Strange " buried.—Leland Itin. vol. vii. p. 413.

One of these, Sir Richard D'amory, lord of Buckenhall (now Bucknell) was an eminent warrior in the reign of Edward III., and summoned to parliament from the twentieth of Edward II. to the year in which he died, A. D. 1330.

Ken. p. 413.

[93] I am aware there are those who consider the church to have been situated without the boundary walls, in Place yard. The matter might be decided by digging, as it is probable some vestiges of mortality would appear in the latter place, if the conjecture is well founded.

PRIORY OF ST. EDBURG. 81

Great part of the priory seems to have been left standing for many years, but nothing can be said of its original form. It is evident there were several spacious rooms; the *hall* or refectory, where all the canons dined; the *bursary*[94], where all accounts were settled; the *locutory*[95] or parlour, where the religious retired for conversation after dinner; the *chapter-house*[96], where all writings were drawn and sealed; and the *dortor* or dormitory, where all the fathers slept. Of all these we have only a faint idea of the dortor, which we gather from the bursar's accounts in 1425, and which represents that building as a long room covered with tiles, and each end surmounted with a weathercock[97]. How long these buildings remained in their original state after the Dissolution, is uncertain: the monastery afterwards became the residence of the Blounts[98], and was probably then of considerable extent; but the only part remaining, is a house now occupied by a Mr. Wilson who rents the gardens, and is forty-one feet in length, and sixteen feet and a half in breadth, one end of which forms a part of the boundary wall belonging to the monastery. From the situation of the building it is not unlikely

---

[94] "Computaverunt fratres Radulphus de Meriton et Stephanus de Oxon. de Bursaria domus Berncestre coram auditoribus." Kenn. p. 288.

[95] "Et Willielmo Hykkedon Latamo conducto per quatuor dies ad faciendum limen hostii Locutorii versus Aulam Prioris xyj den." Ib. p. 574.

[96] At Osney Abbey the dortor was an oblong room, divided by several partitions, between each of which was a bed open at the feet, and a candle which should serve for each of them till their time to arise at their nightly devotions. When the candles were lighted, the keys of this place were carried to the prefect or vicar, who opened it in the morning at the appointed time, when each monk had their summons to rise, and had an hour given them for private duty to prepare themselves for other services.—Peshall's Oxford, p. 304.

[97] The mention of eighteen corbelstones, explained by Kennett to mean niches for statues (Gloss.), conveys an idea of this building being extremely handsome. See Appendix.

[98] History of Alchester.

G

that it was the lodge, or the house appropriated to the lodging and entertainment of travellers: it has undergone many alterations; but from the form of the windows, and the exterior appearance of the structure, it seems to have been erected much earlier than the parish church.

Some years ago, another building stood within the wall on the right of the entrance, and was then used as an out-house. The windows were of similar workmanship with those which remain—the building has been since destroyed—the stone coping of the boundary is also removed, and the only remaining evidence of its former importance is the Gothic arch by which the house and garden are entered. A letter from Mr. J. Smith, the master of Bicester charity-school, (who with his father was employed many years in these gardens by the late Mr. Stratton,) states that they "found many earthen floors in the upper garden, under the southern wall adjoining *Clapyate*," which were probably the floors of the cells belonging to the monks. Near the centre of the same garden a circular well was also discovered, which he describes "about a yard in diameter, and walled with freestone." He adds: "My father and Master Hudson repeatedly tried to empty it; but after they had reached the depth of seven feet the water flowed in so fast that they were compelled to desist [100]. Close to the present building, my father also discovered a very neat coffin about two feet long; the bones were so small that he could not ascertain what they were, and there was no inscription visible. In the garden called the orchard, we found a neat little place

---

[100] This well was about the centre of the inclosed area, and, if the buildings and cells ran parallel with the boundary wall, was at nearly an equal distance from every part of the quadrangle. Hence it is reasonable to suppose that it was the chief water used by the monks. The freestone walls are now taken away, and in June 1814 it appeared an unsightly hollow full of muddy water.

walled with brick, and paved with six-inch square tiles ornamented with plain circles, and flowers of various kinds; the floor was about two feet below the surface of the ground."—The present occupier informed me that some time ago he found an immense arched vault, which on opening was half full of water; this he attributed to the falling in of the old drains, and on that account finding it useless, he removed the crown of the arch and filled it up. The adjoining premises are full of large foundations, once forming offices, &c. connected with the priory. There is a report that a large arch was standing close to the present farm-house, some years past; and that the farm-house itself occupies the site of the ancient lodge; and this report is confirmed by a deed quoted by Kennett, which states that the priory gate adjoined the church-yard.

The large pond in *Place yard* was doubtless originally designed for supplying the monastery with fish, as well as the moats in the Horse-close. Near the entrance of the garden is a smaller water, perhaps once a stew, where fish were preserved for immediate use, as the multiplicity of fast-days in the Romish calendar demanded a perpetual supply. There is a ridiculous story of a coach and six horses being lost in this water, though it is silent as to the owner, and the time when the accident happened; but there is nothing whatever which can countenance the report. On the site of the present rickyard, there was once a fine bowling-green, and a public-house known by the same name, much frequented by the principal inhabitants of Bicester: Time has laid his destructive hand on both, and their existence is almost forgotten.

In the days of superstition the canons of St. Edburg much encouraged the people to frequent St. Edburg's well, whose waters were considered a sovereign remedy in many diseases. Early as the days of Edward I. the spring had attained its reputation; and the road leading from the priory towards it was called *Seynt Edburg hes grene way*, and Via Sanctæ

Edburge. It was afterwards called *Edburg balk*, and thence corrupted into *Tadbury balk*; but even the latter name is now almost obsolete. "After the Reformation, the lame and blind ceasing to resort to this well with their vows and offerings, the saints having lost their honour and the wells their virtue, the current of the spring became stopped up, and all remembrance of it was fast hastening into oblivion," when, fortunately for St. Edburg, "the summer of 1666 proving remarkably dry, induced Mr. John Coker, then lord of the manor of King's-end, in which field it was situated, to open and cleanse the head of the spring; when such a sudden and great supply of water gushed forth, that had the old adorers lived, they would have esteemed it a miracle." From this circumstance the spring obtained the name of *New-found spring*, which it still retains. The narrow passage between the houses in King's-end, as well as the road now used as a foot-path to Middleton, was originally made for the sole purpose of visiting this well; for we are informed by Kennett that "the green balk extends half a mile in length, leading to no other place but the head of the spring [101]." This well is situated a short distance north of a barn &c. erected on the inclosure of the field, now in the occupation of Mr. Reynolds, and may be noticed as the head of the adjoining rivulet. A few years ago it was generally admired, as a clear and beautiful spring: but when I saw it last (in 1815) it was nearly choked up with weeds, and the surrounding ground a perfect marsh. Still I cannot close this article without indulging the hope that its ancient celebrity will secure the future notice of the inhabitants of Bicester, so as to prevent the spring from being neglected and consigned to oblivion.

In the thirtieth of Henry VIII. the priory, with great part

---

[101] In the time of Kennett the herbage of this balk belonged to the tithingman of King's-end. p. 138.

of its possessions, is said by Tanner to have been granted to Charles Brandon Duke of Suffolk, and brother-in-law to the King [102]: but it appears shortly after to have been again in the hands of the King; for in the thirty-second year of his reign (A. D. 1540) letters patent were granted to Roger Moore, Esq. conveying the site, lands, and tenements of the dissolved priory, to himself and his wife, and their heirs [103]. The grant included the patronage of the church, and the rights which were appertaining thereto, insomuch that we find him in the following year (1541) delegating the right of presentation *pro hac vice* to Bennet Wilkins and Thomas Shore of Bicester [104]. The monastery and estates passed to his descendants, who finally sold them; and after several purchases became the property of the Turners, in whose family it still remains.

The particulars of the possessions at Letcomb Basset belonging to the priory of Bicester are thus entered in the books which formerly belonged to the office of the Court of Augmentation, in order to be sold to Mistrys Russel, and the entry gives us a fair specimen of the way in which church lands were valued and disposed of at that time.

---

[102] Notitia Monastica: Burcester, Oxfordshire.

[103] "De Literis Regis patentibus Rogero More et uxore de terris et tenementis pertinentibus ad nuper Prioratum de Burchester alias Byssetur, in Comitatu Oxoniæ, sibi hæredibus masculis concessis." Michælis Recordæ, 32 Hen. VIII. Rotulo 44. Jones's Index to Public Records.

[104] To prevent the poorer classes of society from becoming sufferers by the dissolution of religious houses, and the consequent failure of that entertainment they were accustomed to receive at the table of the convent, it was ordered that hospitality should be kept up by the farmers of the land belonging to the late monasteries, under the penalty of paying every month six pounds thirteen shillings and four pence: yet the penalty not being often required, hospitality was neglected, so that the forfeitures being great, were abolished at the request of Parliament, 21 James I. Hist. of Henry VIII. by Lord Herbert.

P'cell possession' nup' Monast'ij de Burchestir in predico' Com. Oxon.[105]

Com. Bark.
Letcomb Basset. | val in | Item sum reddit. tent. terr. in letcom basset. p^d p. ann. soluend. ad fest. ibid } iiij^{li}

Memorandum the p'misses is entyre of themselfes and parcell off no honor Manor ne Lordshippe ne any of the ancyent Revennews off the Crowne nor of the Duchesse of Lancastre or Cornewall, and are not nyghe any the Kynge and Queene their maiesties howses reserved for their hynes acce'se.

It'm there are no parke lead ne mynes thereupon to th'auditor his knowledge.

It'm it is to be consydered what woodes or underwoodes be upon the same for that yt is unknowen to th'audytor.

Ex tertio die Maij 1557. per me Johani Thomson, audit.

vj^{to} die Maij 1557. Rated for Mystrys Russell. { The clere yerely value of the p'misses iiij^{li} whiche rated at xxvij yeres p'chase amounteth to } cviij^{li}

The mony to be payd in hand before the 22 of May 1557.

The parsonages of Bensington, Drayton, Stodham, Sherborne Clifton, and Overe[106], valued at fifty-two pounds per annum, are enumerated by Willis as part of the possession of Bicester priory, and stated to have been given by patent with the rectory and advowson of Stratton-Audley, towards the en-

---

[105] Harleian MS. No. 606. In the catalogue of the Harleian Library, the volume from whence the above article is extracted is conjectured to have formerly belonged to the office of the Court of Augmentation, as it is inscribed "Liber primus de lez Rates anno tercio et quarto Philipi et Marie regis et regine."

[106] Willis's Cathedrals, vol. ii. p. 422—426. But I strongly suspect it is by mistake that they are stated as part of the possessions of Bicester Priory, and that they originally belonged to Dorchester Abbey. See patent 34 Hen. VIII. 1542.

dowment of the first chapter of the see of Oxford, A. D. 1542. —They are also said to have been regranted on its removal to St. Frideswides, 1546, and still to continue annexed.

The manor of Grimsbury, valued at thirteen pounds six shillings and eight pence, with the estates of Kirtlington and Tackley, valued at twelve pounds one shilling, were granted in the thirty-sixth of Henry VIII. to Thomas Blencowe, Esq. of Marston, who appears to have been one of the tenants of the priory of Sheene [107]. The other parts of the possessions passed into unknown hands.

List of the Patrons and Vicars of the Church, subsequent to the reformation.

Vicars, &c.	By whom appointed.
John Wilkins, presented September 21, 1541.	Roger Moor Esq. granted the right of presentation to Bennet Wilkins and Thomas Shore of Bicester, *pro hac vice.*
Thomas Aspler, instituted March 8, 1558.	Agnes Wentworth widow.
Richard Aldridge, June 25, 1564. He resigned the living into the hands of John Kennal, guardian of the spiritualities Christ Church Oxon. August 16, 1565.	Dame Ann Chamberlain, widow of Sir Roger Ormeston.
George Osbath, instituted December 4, 1565.	Dame A. Chamberlain.
Robert Cauham.	
John Bird, B. A. presented February 15, 1604.	Sir Michael Blount, Kt. patron.

---

[107] I have corrected the amount of the valuation of these estates, as given in the Harleian MS. No. 6822, from the records in the Augmentation Office.

1606. The benefits arising from the composition entered into between the Prior and Convent, as proprietors and patrons of the church, and John Odam vicar, (A.D. 1454,) had been enjoyed by all his successors until very lately, when Sir Michael Blount, and Sir Richard his brother, in consequence of being seised of the priory, obtained possession of the instrument of endowment and other ancient writings relative to the vicarage, and determined to despoil it of part of its revenues. Accordingly they compelled their tenants to refuse paying the vicar John Bird any more tithes of wood, hay, &c. and they themselves would no longer discharge the vicarage of first-fruits, allow rent to be paid for the inclosed lands, or admit the claim of small tithes on their own estates. In this dilemma, deprived of the revenues of his church, and for want of the instrument of endowment unable to sue at common law, the vicar was compelled to have recourse to a suit in Chancery, whence he obtained a decree, ordering the payment of all arrears owing up to the time of the application, and directing that, for the future, twenty pounds per annum should be paid to the vicar for the inclosed lands, in equal payments at Michaelmas and Lady-day; the vicarage to be discharged from the payment of first-fruits, tenths, proxies, and synods; the vicar to have the tithe in the common field, and small tithes paid according to the composition—to be entitled to a close called the Dove-house-close, and to the profits of doves breeding in the dove-house—to a little *pightle* or pig-walk adjoining the said close—and finally to have two loads of hay brought home to his house, and four loads of wood yearly out of the wood called the Prior's wood at Arncote, to be cut down at the vicar's charge and request by the assignment of the proprietor. This decree was given May 4, 1608 [108].

---

[108] Papers given to the Rev. J. Smith by Mr. Cook of Magdalen College, Oxon, which may very properly be henceforth denominated *parish papers*;— my acknowledgements are due to Mr. Wright, for a sight of them in 1812.

Mr. Bird enjoyed this vicarage forty-nine years, and died September 19, 1653 [109]. Kennett places Mr. William Hall as his successor; but I am inclined to conclude that a Mr. Basnet or Barnet obtained the cure, which he held till the year 1666, when he was ejected as a non-conformist by the Bartholomew act; his name does not occur in Kennett's list, but he is particularly mentioned in Palmer's Non-conformist's Memorial, vol. ii. p. 309. His successors were,

William Hall.
Samuel Blackwell, inducted
    August 16, 1670.
Thos. Shewring, Aug. 1. 1691. Sir William Glynn, Patron.
Thomas Taylor [110],
Thomas Forbes,
Thomas Airson, 1708 [111].

1727. It appears that before, or about this time some disputes had arisen between the vicar and patron, respecting the endowments of the vicarage, part of which seem

---

[109] In the chancel of Wendlebury church is a stone inscribed " Here lies the Body of that reverend laborer in Christs harvest, pastor at Bisseter Ann. 49, and at Wendlebury Ann. 39, deceased September 19, 1653, John Birde, anno ætatis 77."

Anagram. Birde, Bride.
    " This Birdes the bride the lambe the bridegroom
    This graves the brides retireing room
    Old clothes must off new ones be on
    Against a joyful resurrection
    Thrice happy Birde thrice happy bride
    Thus to be wedded next Christ's side
    John Birde a bride mounting aloft doth fly
    To the sacred hills of blest eternity;
    Which place of rest now terminates his flight
    Crowning his faith with his redeemer's sight."

Monumental Inscriptions, taken May 25, 1660. No. 4170, Harleian MS.
[110] Kennett, p. 621.   [111] Churchwardens' books.

to have been claimed by the latter, and Sir Stephen Glynne indicating some desire to dispose of his estates in Bicester, the vicar by letter warned him against alienating any part which belonged to the church, and formally claimed the dove-house and closes adjoining. This letter, however, does not appear to have been sufficiently attended to, for the following year Mr. Airson considered it necessary to consult Serjeant Weldon on the case,—and it seems to have been ultimately laid before Sir Matthew Skinner, who in an opinion dated April 19, 1729, recapitulating the substance of the decree of 1608, says: "The dues settled by that decree can be recovered by a writ served on the several tenants [111]." The result was a relinquishment of the claims set up by the patron.

Mr. Airson died March 24, 1752, aged 71.

J. Princep appointed vicar 1752.
S. Cooke, 1769.—Wood, curate. } Sir Edward Turner, Bart.

Joseph Eyre, 1779 [112].—Turner.
John Smith. John Markland. } Sir G. P. Turner, Bart.

Vicarage.

The vicarage, which adjoins the church-yard, is a substantial edifice built partly in the Gothic style, and appears of considerable antiquity. From the view of it given in the plate of the church in Kennett's Antiquities, it is not impossible that it may be of nearly equal date with that structure, though of late years it has been somewhat modernized. An extensive garden is attached; but the circumstance of its abounding in bones, apparently human, has led many to conjecture that it anciently formed a part of the adjoining burying-ground, though there is neither tradition nor document which countenances the opinion.

---

[111] Parish papers. [112] Gentleman's Magazine.

This mansion has been the residence of the vicar or officiating clergyman for many ages; and is now occupied by Mr. Markland.

CHAPTER XI.

Parish Church.

HAVING already stated that the present parish church appears to have been erected about the latter end of the reign of Henry IV. or the beginning of Henry V.[1] our attention is now confined to a description of the edifice.—The church is neat, large, and commodious, consisting of a nave and side-aisles, chancel, and school-house, with a lofty tower and pinnacles[2]. The length is one hundred and twenty-five feet, and the breadth including the side aisles sixty-seven. The walls adjoining the chancel are much stronger than any other part, and open into the aisles with plain semicircular arches, a circumstance which seems to countenance the tradition that they were originally intended as the basement of the tower, though the plan was afterwards relinquished. The north aisle windows retain their original form, but most of the others have undergone considerable alterations, and there is little doubt those on the south were similar to those on the north side. A visitor in May 1660 observed that they contained specimens of painted glass, two of which were decorated with armorial

---

[1] At the time of Kennett's writing there was a tradition that the townships of King's-end and Bury-end were united into one parish at the building of the new church, previous to which the inhabitants of Biggenhull attended at their lord's chapel.—Kennett, p. 510.

[2] The edifice is built of stone apparently taken from Bicester stone-pits.

bearings, and on a third the following imperfect black-letter inscription, the deficiency of which another hand has partly endeavoured to supply in italics in the MS.

> Orā pro aīa *Jo̅hi̅s̅ Wilkyns* et pro bono ſtatu......
> ......*Alicieq; Matris ejus* .. *Wilkyns patris*....
> ......hanc feneſtram fieri........................
> ......quorum animabus propitietur *Deus Amen* [3]...

It is not improbable that most of the windows were decorated in a similar manner;—a relative, when nearly ninety years of age, assured me the chancel window was often admired for the painting it contained, in her youth [4]. Since those times, all have vanished, and nothing but plain glass occupies their place, divested of mullions and tracery. The period of these innovations cannot be ascertained, for in the churchwardens' books (the genuine annals of a parish) the sums alone, without the nature of the repair or alteration, are specified, and the vouchers are either negligently mislaid or purposely

---

[3] Harleian MS. No. 4170.—The same MS. notices the following particulars.
—— " In the north Ile against the wainscot these depicted.
  Ar. on a chevron between 3 lozenges 3 bulls heads.
    Paly of 6, a bend.
      Gu. 2 bars or, impaling s. 3 falcons levant ar.
      Gu. 2 bars or, impaling a. a lion ramp. s. quartering Barry of 6, g. and o.
      A. on a bend b. 3 bucks' faces quartering............
    quartering *Man*. 3d as 2d, 4th as 1st. Stanley.
" On a south window here these arms.
    Barry of 6 erm. and g. impaling A........
    Barry of 6, in chief a crescent: impaling 3 wolves heads couchant.
    B———————a bordure s. bezanty.
    Barry of 6 erm. and g. in chief a crescent: impaling a. 3 de lis b.
" In a north window.
    Erm. a fesse compony a. and b."

[4] Mrs. Hannah Chandler of Kensington: she died 15th December 1813; aged 88.

destroyed. Were the progressive alterations minutely remarked, we could forget the expenses of a churchwarden's dinner, while we read with pleasure the ancient state of the parish.

The appearance of the interior of the church before the Reformation may indeed be tolerably guessed at by the description of others handed down to us. A rood-loft or narrow gallery stretched across the body of the church at the entrance of the chancel, on which a rood or crucifix was placed, accompanied by a statue of the Virgin Mary and the beloved disciple St. John: the altar stood where the communion-table now stands, lighted with tapers, and decorated with similar figures, or a crucifix at least. At a low desk in the mid-aisle the litany or prayers for the dead were said [5]: the pulpit and font probably occupied their present places, and the remainder of the floor was covered with long open seats [6] many of which still remain, then indiscriminately used by the parishioners. In the changes of religion which took place between the days of Henry VIII. and Elizabeth, the altar was destroyed,—a communion-table placed in the body of the church,—was again restored, with all its appendages, and then once more displaced by the present table. At the latter eventful period the king's arms also finally triumphed over the cross, and the Ten Commandments occupied the station they now retain. Could we see the churchwardens' bills of those days, we could ascertain the number of copes, vestments, and sacred utensils necessary for the celebration of the ancient worship, all of which were provided by the parish.—Since that time, the laziness or pride of individuals gave rise to the reprehensible

---

[5] Peck's Desiderata Curiosa, p. 38.

[6] Before the Reformation, benefactions were often bequeathed for seating a church with benches or stools.—Wharton's History of Kiddington, p. 4.

plan of converting the open seats into *family pews*[7], and an increase of this practice, or of the population, soon produced a want of accommodation. This led some of the inhabitants and others to enter into a subscription for the erection of a gallery at the west end of the church[8] (A.D. 1693); and to secure the seats to the subscribers, their descendants, and others who might afterwards take places in it, a faculty was obtained May 20, 1700, from the vicar-general of the diocese, authorising them to "choose yearly *two supervisors*, who should place proper persons therein, and keep the said gallery with a lock and key[9]. The two wings of this gallery are expressly exempted from this inhibition, being declared private property. The length is stated at sixteen feet, but the depth is not specified;—the front seats appear to have been chiefly appropriated to the singers, from the period of its erection, and it is evident from various charges in the churchwardens' books of 1744 and others, that the parish provided a bassoon[10] for their use, until they obtained the organ. This instrument was

---

[7] Weever, who lived in the reign of Elizabeth and James I. speaking of epitaphs on the pavement of churches in and about London, says, "Many monuments are covered with seates or pewes made high and easie for parishioners to sit or *sleep* in, a fashion of no long continuance, and worthy of reformation."—Funeral Monuments, p. 701. London 1631.

[8] Gallery-wardens' books.—The principal contributors are Sir William Glynn; Ralph Holt, Esq.; William Busby, Esq.; Mr. Shewring, vicar, &c.

[9] In 1728, the door of the gallery seems to have been forced, probably by an individual whom the wardens refused admission into the gallery, as appears by the following entries.

	£.	s.	d.
For horse-hire and other expences, by going to the Justice with Goody Bull.	0	7	6
For a new key and mending the lock of the door.. ..	0	1	8

The present gallery-wardens, Mr. H. Chandler and Mr. W. Lines, were chosen September 7, 1809.

[10] Paid for mending the bassoon 16s. 3d.—Churchwardens' books for 1744.

PARISH CHURCH.

purchased of Sir Gregory Turner for fifty pounds, on the demolition of Ambrosden-house, and the sum principally raised by subscription, though the same books contain an entry in 1772 of " Paid Isaac Clarke, Osmond, and T. Stratton, on balance due for the organ, eight pounds three shillings." It was at first placed much nearer the front of the gallery, but shortly removed to its present position, on the representation of many of the inhabitants. For some time Mr. Osmond gratuitously performed the office of organist; on his leaving the town, no inhabitant being found capable of discharging that duty with credit, the bassoon was again introduced, till the appointment of Mr. Bayzand, since whose death the office has been filled by Mr. William Shears and Mr. T. Hicks.—The organ is generally admired for its fine tone.

This gallery-staircase also leads to two other galleries of later erection, built over the north aisle, and belonging to different inhabitants. A few years ago, *another* was constructed across the east end of the south aisle, for the family of Mr. Davis. In 1810, the still further increased practice of family pews having almost deprived the poor of the open seats, and many respectable families wanting accommodation, a new gallery was thrown over the entrance into the chancel. At that time it was placed beyond doubt, that the church was partly erected out of the materials of some more ancient edifice, carved stones being found in the centre of the walls, which were supposed to have ornamented the old church. This fabric was considerably injured by a dreadful storm which happened on August 3, 1765, the particulars of which are thus entered on the cover of the parish register by the officiating clergyman at that time :—" The lightening struck the ball from the weathercock, shattered the pinnacle, and destroyed the roof of the tower;' tore down the arch of the bell-window; damaged the stock and frame of the great bell, broke the chimes, took every pane of glass out of the window and partition, and threw them down into the church; it then tore up the pavement under the gallery, and ascending broke most of the lower windows throughout the edifice." The extent of the repair occasioned by this storm is only specified in the church-wardens' books by the round sums paid to the different tradesmen; a method of keeping those books much to be condemned and regretted by every curious inhabitant throughout succeeding generations.

The pulpit, reading-desk, &c. stand nearly in the centre of the church; the former rests against one of the pillars on the south side of the mid-aisle. In time of service they are covered with purple velvet purchased at the expense of the parish, A. D. 1810[n]. The font, near the north entrance of the church, is ascended by steps, appears very ancient, and probably stood in the old church; it is sufficiently large to admit of the immersion of the infant, as enjoined by the rubric, though now entirely laid aside.—Under the gallery hang a number of leathern buckets in case of accidents by fire, a ladder, &c. Soon after the formation of a Sunday-school, seats were erected near this place for the accommodation of the children. At the west end of the north aisle is a desk affixed to the wall, on which rests the ponderous volume of *Fox's Martyrology*; this desk was formerly placed in the chancel, and the book chained to it: the covers are now torn off, though they still remain chained together. There is no doubt that the book was placed in the church in the reign of Queen Elizabeth, and has remained there ever since.

In 1660 the following were the chief monumental inscriptions in this church, which were then entered in a volume marked Nº 4170 in the Harleian Library.

---

[n] It is likely that the former cushion, pulpit-cloth, &c. were the identical offering of Sir William Glynn, as I have seen no document which intimates that any articles of that kind have been purchased by the parish since that period.

"In the chancel against the north wall, a great gray marble raised monument, on a plate of brass affixed to the wall, this;

Orate pro aibus Willi Staveley armigi quondam dni de bygnell et Alicie uxris ej's filie et unice heredis dni Job'is Fraunces militis et dne Isabelle uxoris ej's filie et heredis dni Henrici Plesyngton militis, qui quidem Willies obit decimo die Octobris A.D.MCCCClxxxviii. predica vero Alicia obit 20 die Octobris A° dni MDc. quorum aiabus &c.

Against the south wall here a plate of brass, thereon this;

Here lyeth buried the xx day of September Anno Dñi 1551, ROGER MOORE Esq. a second son of More de la More in the County of Oxford, and Agnes his wife, daughter and heir of John Husye Esquire, the second son of Thomas Husye of Shapwicke, in the County of Dorset, who had ishwe by the said Roger Moore, Thomas, Mary, and Elizabeth; the which Thomas was one of the Gentlemen Pensioners unto Queen Elizabeth, and in her Majestyes service in Ireland, was slaine the 10th of Marce 1574, leaving no ishwe of his body, and Mary his eldest sister married Michael Blount of Mapledurham in the County of Oxford, Esq. and had ishwe Richard, Thomas, Charles, Katheryne and Mary, and Elizabeth his second sister married Gabriel Fowler of Tyselworth in the County of Bedford and had issue Rychard, Mary, Agnes, Elizabeth, and James.

Over all, these arms;

A fesse dauncetty paly of 6, s. and g. between three mullets s. quartering a chevron between three annulets g. a crescent. Impaling barry of six erm. and g. in chief a crescent. Over it two crests. The first, a demy lion ramp. a. charged with a fesse dauncetty; the second, a talbot pass. chained and collared, charged on the shoulder with a crescent.

Blount, O. 4 bars nebulée s. quartering, first, a tower, second, two wolves pass. within a bordure, in chief between these two coats a crescent; third, vairé; fourth, a pale; fifth, a

H

greyhound ramp.; sixth, a chevron between three pheons; seventh, as the first. Impaling *Moore*. Quartering, first, a fesse between three annulets; second, barry of 6 erm. and g. in chief a crescent; fourth as first. The crest, a wolf passant upon a crowne.

Fowler, Vert, on a chev. between three lyons pass. gard. three crosslets; quartering, first, three bars g. in chief a lyon pass. g.; second, a. three wolves heads erased, g. a bordure v. of castles o.; third .... a chief per pale.... and erm. in the first an owle. Impaling *More*, quartering the annulets and *Husye*. The crest an owle gorged with a crowne.

The two following are on brass plates in the wall which parts the Mid Aisle from the chancel in large Roman characters.

Here lyethe the body of JOHN COKER who departed this life the 14 of Feb. 1606. Here alsoe lyeth ye body of JOANE COKER wife of the said John Coker, who departed this life the 16 of May An^o 1618.

Here also lyeth the body of ANNE COKER wife of Cadwallader Coker eldest soñe to the saide John Coker and Joane his wife who departed this life the 20 day of Aug. 1625 [12].

Here also lie ye bodies of CADWALLADER COKER abovenamed and CATHERINE his second wife. He Dec. 15 Oct. 1653, Æt. 82. She 8 May 1635. Æt. 36 They had issue, John, Cadwallader, Frances, William, Catherine, Joane, and Elizabeth.

On an adjoining plate on the wall,

Here lyeth the body of JOHN LEWES, born in Lyñ in the county of Carnarvon, Gent. who for the love he bare to the said John

---

[12] The MS. Copy taken in 1660 gives an inscription as follows, which it describes as being on the floor. "Here lieth the body of CADWALLADER COKER who living succeeded his father abovementioned in his manor of Nun's Place, and after death in this grave, Obit Oct. 15, A. D. 1653."

Query, Has this inscription been removed, or is it covered by the pews?

Coker desired by his will to be buried neere him. He dyed in Oxford on the 21 day of September, 1612.

Near it is the following in black letter.

Heare lyeth buried the Bodye of Willm Hort at Hart Gent. who deceased the 5th of July 1584. And alfo with him lyethe buryed Ann his Wiffe, who was daughter unto Mr. Ashton of Croftone in the County of Lancafter Efquire and deceafed the 6 of Auguft followinge 1584 and had iffue 5 fonnes and 4 daughters.

Against a pillar not far off, a table of black marble, whereon this in golden letters;

ANNE CLEMENTS, the wife of Mr. Richard Clements, by whome he had 4 sons, George, Richard, Thomas, Benjamin, and 6 daughters, Elizabeth, Anne, Grace, Anne, Judith, Grace, she departed this life the 28th of May A. D. 1652, of her age 39.

> Reader, as in a glasse, thou perfectly may see
> How all things here below uncertaine bee
> She was her husband's, children's, parent's sole delight,
> By death's impartial stroke is taken from them quite.

In the south isle on a brasse on the ground this,

Here lyeth buried the body of RAFE HUNT, who was borne in Lankeyshire, in the Parish of Chilve, he was a long dweller in the town of Bissiter, and a good benefactor to the poore. He had two wyves, Ellen and Katherine, and had issue by Katherine one only daughter named Anne. He deceased the last day of November 1602.

Towards the bottom of the south Ile against the wall a brasse, thereon this,

Here lyeth buried the bodye of HOMFRYE HONT and ELIZABETH his wife. The which had Issue, fyve sonnes and three daughters, and was borne in Cliff Howse in Lankeshire and deceased the xxiiij day of Maye in the yeare of our Lord God 1601."

Such appear to have been the chief inscriptions in the

year 1660, the following monuments are among the most prominent which have been since added.

In the chancel is an elegant monument of white marble, secured with iron rails, to the memory of Sir Edward Turner Bart. and his Lady, at the top of which is a medallion containing the profiles of the deceased. The inscription as follows.

Under this Chancel in a Family Vault are deposited the remains of Sir EDWARD TURNER Bart. and Dame CASSANDRA his wife, late of Ambroseden Park in this County. He died October 31st 1766. She, October 18, 1770, aged each 48 years. He was Representative in three Parliaments; one for this county. He exerted himself as an active and vigilant Magistrate; adopted early in life the noblest political principles, and persevered in them to the end. He was learned without vanity, religious without ostentation; and excell'd in the great characters of Husband, Father, and Friend.

His sorrowful Widow (eldest daughter of William Leigh Esqr. of Adlestrop in the County of Gloucester) was beautiful in person, and engaging in her manner, won the esteem of all who knew her. A shining example of conjugal Affection, and every christian virtue. To her children an indulgent Mother, to Servants a kind Mistress, to the Poor, living and dying, a compassionate Benefactress, as a memorial to posterity of some, only, of the many virtues of this excellent pair their five surviving Children,

Sir Gregory Turner Bart. William Turner Esq. John Turner Esq. Elizabeth Wife of Thomas Twisleton Esqr. of Broughton Castle in this County, and Cassandra wife of Martin Bladen Hawke Esqr. eldest son of the Right Honourable Sir Edward Hawke, K. B : have erected this monument.

On a marble tablet over the chancel door;

H. S. E.

casta pia SARAH KENNETT, Filia unica et dilecta Roberti

Carver et Mariæ Conjugis, Uxor charissima Whiti Kennett S.T.B. Vicarii de Ambroseden[13].

   Nata   28 Maii 1675
   Nupta   6 Junii 1693
   Defuncta 2 Martii $169\frac{1}{4}$

Cujus mortem nimis immaturam lugent Maritus et Parentes mœstissimi M.DC.XCIV.

On the floor in the chancel.

Here lyeth y^e body of Mrs. SARAH KENNETT, who dyed the 2 of March 1693. Aged 18 years and $\frac{1}{4}$.

Opposite on a mural marble monument in the chancel,

H. S. E.

ROBERTUS CARVER,

Vir morum probitate dilectus et desideratus. Uxorem duxit Mariam filiam natu max. Willelmi Burley et Mariæ Conjugis,

---

[13] As the decease of this excellent young person is still annually commemorated in Bicester by a sermon and donation of forty loaves, on the 2nd of March, the following letter, written by Mr. Kennett to his friend Mr. Blackwall, conveying the intelligence of that sad event, may be deemed interesting.

" Oh! Mr. Blackwall, how can I write to you when I am so full of confusion and distraction, for the inestimable loss of my poor dear wife, whom my correcting father in heaven was pleased to take to himself this last night between twelve and one. You can scarce imagine the sorrow and lamentation of her father and mother and her desolate husband. We have scarce patience to talk of any thing relating to her funeral, only we all agree in this request that you would do the last office for the good creature, and preach her sermon either at Burcester or Amersden, as we shall think good when we come to be able to think. We think Monday must be the appointed day, which we know will be very inconvenient for you; but pray, good Mr. Blackwall, dispense with any inconvenience to grant a request that is so passionately made to you, and come hither time enough to doe that mournful service. If any extraordinary matter should detain you (but let nothing less than extraordinary doe it) dispatch this messenger with expedition; nay, whether you come or not let him tarry no longer than while you send some answer. Oh! this affliction was a sad surprise to me. I had but one day to spend in prayers and tears

Ex qua unicam suscepit Filiam Saram, quæ nupta Whito Kennett Clerico immaturâ morte præerepta est et juxta deposita: Obiit ille die 1º Aprilis, anno Salutis MDCXCVIII. Ætatis LIII.

In eodem pariter sepulchro super ossa Mariti jacet MARIA Uxor ejus. Obijt 19 Dec. A. D. 1722, Ætatis LXX.

On the chancel wall is a-marble tablet to the memory of 5 children of Samuel Blackwall, S.T.B. formerly vicar of this church.

Within the rail of the communion table on the ground,

M. S.

THOMÆ AIRSON hujusce Ecclesiæ per triginta sex annos Vicarii. Obiit Martii 24to 1752, Anno. Ætat. 71mo.

Also HANNAH, the wife of Thomas Airson, Vicar, who died June 13, 1751. Aged 69 years.

---

with her; when she spent many of her decaying spirits in rejoicing there had never been the least difference between us, in thanking me for all my love, in protesting her own true affection, and in a sensible way of expressing her resignation to God Almighty, and saying she had no other reason to be unwilling to die but only that she must part with a dear mother and dear father, and the dearest husband in the world. Oh, Mr. Blackwall, for my own sake I wish you may not these many years suffer the loss of an excellent wife; and for the sake of my sorrowful father and mother wish you may never suffer the loss of an only child.

"Your afflicted friend,

"March 2, 169¾. "WHITE KENNETT.

"My mother orders me to add that she shall never be satisfied if you are in life and health unless you come and preach her child's funeral sermon.

"To Mr. Blackwall."

The original letter is preserved among a collection of letters of Dr. Kennett to Mr. S. Blackwall, Lansdowne MSS. 1068, Vol. 2, Brit. Mus.

Notwithstanding this pressing request, it appears from a following letter that Mr. Blackwall could not comply with it. Mr. Coker was therefore prevailed upon to undertake the service, but while preparing his notes for the sermon, was suddenly seized with an "indisposition in the head," so that it was at last performed at Ambrosden by Mr. Northgrove.

Here lye four children of Thomas Airson, Vicar of this church, and Hannah his wife, viz. Mary, John, Hannah, and Thomas, who died young.

THOMAS FORBES hujus Ecclesiæ Vicarius ob. 1mo 4to die Octob. Anno. 1715. Anno Ætat. 44.

In the chancel on the floor, is a small marble stone,

Hic Jacet GULIELMUS Filius Stephani Glynne de Merton Armigeri, qui obiit 29 Decem. Anno Dom.

The date is obliterated[14].

On the ground going out of the chancel into the church three inscriptions to the memory of Thomas, Cadwallader, and Sara Coker, infant sons and daughters of Thomas and Sara Coker; and a fourth inscribed " Hearst Coker, Ob. 5 Novemb. 1719."

On the north-side of the mid aisle is a white marble monument, with a Latin inscription to the memory of Catherine Coker, daughter of John Coker, Gent. and Catherine his wife; and near it a similar tablet in remembrance of John Coker, Gent., and Catherine his wife.

On the north side of the middle aisle is a very elegant marble monument, ornamented with an erect figure bearing a sithe in his hand over a bust, from which are suspended two small medallions, with the inscription of Carolus II. Dei gratia.—Beneath is the following,

Spe Resurgendi;

Juxta depositi sunt cineres THOMÆ GRANTHAM Equitis Au-

---

[14] On the north side of the chancel, near an hatchment and helmet, are some irons fastened in the wall; these are said to have supported several funeral banners, streamers, &c. in honour of some of the Glynns, formerly patrons of the church. Query.—For what member of that family were they placed there?

rati, natus in hac Parochia de Bissister, Obijt Sunburiæ in Comitatu Midd^x Anno Ætatis suæ LXXX. Salutisque humanæ MDCCXVIII [b].

Grantham Andrews de Sunbury Nepos ex filia unicus et Hæres summa pietate et gratitudine erga Parentem et benefactorem munificentissimum hoc Monumentum posuit.

On the same side on a handsome variegated marble Tablet.

Near to this place lie the Remains of CADWALLADER COKER Citizen of London, who died on the eleventh day of January, in the year of our Lord one thousand seven hundred and eighty, and in the seventieth of his Age.

By a long and uniform course of assiduity, prudence, and integrity, he acquired with an unblemished reputation the means of exercising his natural disposition to benevolence, and at the same time discharged his duty to his Country, by promoting and extending her Commerce. His surviving Widow and six Children caused this stone to be erected in grateful testimony of the merits of an affectionate Husband and beneficent Parent.

On a black stone,

To the Memory of RALPH CLEMENTS, who departed this Life the 30th of Octob. A° Doñi 1683, in the 74 yeare of his Age.

On the south side of the middle Aisle,

In the first year of the Reign of our Sovereign Lord King James the 2nd 1685. The Honoured Sir Wm. Glynne of Ambrosden in the County of Oxford, Bart. Patron of this Church, gave for the use of such who are of the Communion of the Church of England, two large Flaggons of massy silver, One silver Salver, One silver Chalice and Cover, a large Carpet of purple velvet with gold and silk fringe for the Communion table, A purple velvet Cushion

---

[15] It is said that the metal coffin containing the body of Sir Thomas was stolen by some workmen several years ago, and the bones thrown into one corner of the vault.

—with gold and silk tassels, A purple velvet Cloth with gold and silk fringe for the ornament of the Pulpit.

Facing the middle Aisle (towards the Chancel) a marble monument inscribed;

To the memory of Mr. ROBERT JEMMETT of this Parish (a true Son of the Church of England) who died the 29 Day Octr. 1736, Aged 63 years.

And also ELIZABETH his disconsolate Wife who departed this life the 2nd Day of Octo^r. 1746, Aged 80 years. Who to the sacred Memory of her loving Husband erected this Monument.

He was sole giver of the Branch in this Church.

In the middle Aisle on the ground;

Under this stone lie the remains of ROBERT COKER, Esq. who departed this life the 16 Day of April in the year of our Lord 1789, Aged 79.

The Honorable Charlotte Coker, 1794.

On the south side are monuments to the memory of John Walker who died January 28, 1783, aged 80, and Ann his wife who died January 28, 1772, aged 58. John Walker who died September 2, 1810, aged 70; and Hannah his wife who died January 2, 1790, aged 38. At the west end a monument for Elizabeth, wife of Richard Walls who died November 3, 1737, aged 36. Their two daughters Anne and Elizabeth; and the above Richard Walls who died October 22, 1753, Aged 45.

Few of the remaining monuments containing more than the birth and decease of the person to whose memory they are erected, the limited nature of this work will not allow of the inscription being given at length; it is hoped, therefore, that the following abbreviation of their contents will be excused.

On the south side a monument to the memory of John King, who died May 4, 1760, aged 76. Edward Lock, his nephew, who died August 26, 1772. Edward Lock, *father*, January 13, 1762, aged 80. Sarah, wife of the latter, died February 2, 1748, aged 54. Elizabeth, their daughter, died October 12, 1733, aged 7 years. Sarah, their daughter, wife of Thomas Harris of Oxford, died May 27, 1765, aged 45. And John, son of T. and S. Harris, who died September 6, 1760, in the 12th year of his age.

Opposite, in the south Aisle, is an inscription to the memory of Sarah, wife of Joseph Kendall, who died July 11, 1803, aged 23. Nearly opposite to Walker's is a tablet which states that Elizabeth, daughter of John and Elizabeth Hicks, died June 19, 1741, aged 12 years. John, son of the above, died June 12, 1758, aged 35. John Hicks, sen. died November 21, 1760, aged 66. And Elizabeth, his wife, who died December 23, 1768, aged 74.

In the north aisle a monument to the memory of Thomas Russel, late of St. James's, Westminster, who died January 4, 1718, aged 48. His wife, Elizabeth Walworth, who died March 13, 1734, aged 64; and a memorandum of two sons and five daughters, who died infants. A monument in memory of Gabriel Burrowes, who died March 14, 1676, aged 42. William, the son of John and Ann Finch, died May 16, 1701. John Finch, citizen of London and grocer in this town, born at Warfield, Berks., died February 11, 1707, aged 58; and Ann, his wife, who died July 30, 1720, aged 81. On the same side a mural monument, which states that Mary, wife of John Burrowes, jun., died September 16, 1724, aged 29 years; and a memorandum of the birth and death of their three infants, Mary, Sarah, and Benjamin. A similar monument near the former, to the memory of Mary, the wife of John Burrowes, who died July 1, 1706, aged 39. John Burrowes, who was baptized March 29, 1666, and buried March 13, 1732, and four of their children. Inscriptions for Robert Evans, who died May 18, 1688, aged 56 years. Elizabeth, wife of John Woodfield, who died March 13, 1742, aged 61

THE TOWER.   107

years. John Woodfield, who died May 10, 1758, aged 82. John Blake who died May 24, 1777, aged 61. Ann his wife who died February 20, 1789, aged 59; and two of their sons. William Eagles of Aylesbury, who departed this life March 28, 1810, aged 62. And William his son who died December 31, 1808, aged 38.

The Tower contains a good ring of bells [16], clock [17] and chimes, the latter playing every four hours. It is divided into three stories; the first floor is the belfry, the third appropriated to the chimes, and the uppermost to the bells. Every evening at eight o'clock a bell is rung, which practice has been continued through every age since the Conquest, and may be properly denominated the *Curfew* [18]. From the top of the tower is a good prospect of the surrounding country. Its height is seventy-five feet, and the square of the base twenty.

THE SCHOOL.

This building adjoins the north side of the chancel, and is continued from the north aisle of the church, into which there is an entrance. It appears of later erection than the other

---

[16] The tower contains six bells and a *sanctus* or saints bell, the latter takes its name from being rung out when the priest came to these words, Sancte, Sancte, Sancte Deus Sabaoth, that all persons absent might fall down on their knees in reverence of the holy office going on in the church.—Warton's Kiddington, p. 8. Note.

John Coker Esq. has lately offered to be at half the expense of purchasing two additional bells to the tower, but the object has not been accomplished for want of equal liberality in others.

[17] The clock does not appear in the plate of the church in Kennett's Antiquities.

[18] I have adopted the popular opinion respecting the curfew-bell, in representing it as introduced by William, as a badge of servitude; but according to some the assertion is not well-founded, for there is evidence of the custom prevailing in most of the countries of Europe, and intended as a precaution against fires, which were then very fatal, most of the houses being built of wood.—See Henry, p. 335. vol. 6.

THE SCHOOL.

parts of the fabric; though at what time is unknown: but most probably soon after the Reformation. The inside is fitted up with desks and other conveniencies. Over it is a room formerly used as a library, and containing a number of books, some of which are valuable; the catalogue remains in the hands of Mr. Markland. The School is generally thought to have been endowed, though every writing relative thereto is said to be entirely lost. In the Magna Britannia it is called a Free school, "supposed to be founded by Simon Wisdome, an *alderman* [19] of this town; but," the writer adds, "we have no other grounds for our supposition than that he is found to have given constitutions and orders for the government of it in the thirteenth year of the reign of Queen Elizabeth [20]."

The school seems to have been placed under the immediate direction of the vicar, though at what time it ceased to be a *free school* is uncertain. The name of Kennett appearing in the list of benefactors in the catalogue of books given for the use of the scholars seems to intimate that it had not ceased to be such at the time when that gentleman assisted Mr. Blackwall both in the duties of the school, and the church; and even the bare reflection of our present ignorance of this institution is sufficient to produce the greatest regret, that any thing should have ever arisen to prevent the industrious, learned, and pious author of the Parochial Antiquities from continuing that excellent work down to his own time.

THE CHURCH-YARD.

The space allotted for a burying-ground is well adapted for an extensive parish and its dependencies, though some have supposed it to have once extended over a part of the vicarage garden. The ground is much higher than the ad-

---

[19] Perhaps "inhabitant." [20] Vol. iv, p. 399. ed. 1727.

joining streets, but whether arising from interments, or natural elevation, is uncertain. From its proximity to the old town of Berencester, and no vestiges of sepulture having been found in any other part of the parish, I am inclined to believe this spot is the original burying-ground, and not unlikely the site of the former church, notwithstanding the assertion of Kennett to the contrary.—A path is admitted under the north wall, and used by the parishioners as a thoroughfare; this is shaded by elms, and may be considered as the chief *promenade.* One of the principal objects in the church-yard is the stone pedestal on which the sun-dial is placed, inscribed with the churchwardens' names and the year of erection. The ascent is by several steps, which anciently were the steps to the cross; in the days of popery considered a necessary appendage to the church-yard.—There are several tombs, some of recent erection, but none above mediocrity; that at the end of the chancel, surrounded by iron rails, and erected to the memory of ——— Bowden, a butcher in London, was broken by lightning in the dreadful storm of August 3, 1765, and, until a few months ago, remained unrepaired. On the south side of the church-yard is the grave of Edward Bowden, who was murdered by his journeyman George Strap, and for which, as the stone informs us, he was tried, found guilty at Oxford, hanged, and his body given to the surgeons to be anatomized.

110 THE CHURCH-YARD.

The following is an abbreviated alphabetical list of names on the Tombs and Gravestones in the Church Yard.

TOMBSTONES.

NAMES	DIED	AGE	NAMES	DIED	AGE
Wm. Allen	13 Aug. 1797	55y^{rs}	Edward King	18 Aug. 1784	44y^{rs}
Thos. Eagles	24 Apr. 1787	70	Richard Kirby	14 Feb. 1772	55
Sarah his wife	25 Mar. 1749	25	Mary his wife	20 Dec. 1784	67
Eliz. ditto	27 Nov. 1798	82	William Robins	29 Aug. 1776	26
John Green	10 May 1723	78	Sarah his wife	16 Oct. 1772	25
Geo. Howlett	11 Mar. 1757	62	Ann Woodford	22 Dec 1759	83

GRAVESTONES.

NAMES	DIED	AGE	NAMES	DIED	AGE
Samuel Baker,	10 Mar. 1810	60y^{rs}	Fran. Jennings	13 Mar. 1801	56y^{rs}
Ann his wife	7 Aug. 1787	35	John Jones	7 June 1807	55
William Ball	18 Dec. 1785	76	Richard Jessop	24 July 1805	88
John Barker	21 Feb. 1776	60	Richard Kendal	12 Aug. 1813	73
John Bathe	23 Apr. 1791	44	John Kent	24 Feb. 1800	33
Hannah Bishop	21 Nov. 1792	81	Thos. Kingstone	24 July 1781	59
T. M. Blowfield	5 June 1814	55	Lawrence Lord	Mar. 1785	88
John Boffin	24 June 1811	41	John Pavier	3 Dec. 1782	72
Edw. Bowden	*Murdered* (by Strap) 21 Nov. 1774	55	Sarah Phillips	26 Mar. 1809	60
Rd. Buckle	12 Dec. 1786	43	William Potter	22 Oct. 1809	56
Ann his wife	13 May 1788	40	Susanna his wife	20 May 1803	59
Jon. Burnard	1 Nov. 1813	73	Thos. Reading	20 Aug. 1803	68
Eliz. his wife	2 Apr. 1797	62	Rd. Reading	1 Dec. 1812	42
William Busby	16 Mar. 1792	49	Henry Rolls	19 Jan. 1777	57
Robt. Carter	25 July 1787	55	John Sanders	25 Jan. 1802	34
John Castle	3 Nov. 1789	36	W. Shillingford	12 Sep. 1761	62
Eliz. his wife	12 Oct. 1786	42	Robt. Shirley	6 May 1808	77
Matthew Clarke	15 Dec. 1779	75	John Sirett	18 Oct. 1812	54
John Cleaver	2 Feb. 1794	76	John Stevens	14 Mar. 1803	37
Edward Crook	30 July 1801	39	Wm. Tanner	8 May 1799	46
Amy his wife	23 Aug. 1803	41	Thos. Timms*	14 Aug. 1754	49
Richard Cox	15 Dec. 1723	73	Johanna his wife	5 May 1785	84
George Foster	24 Aug. 1802	66	Wm. Whichelle	20 Sep. 1772	60
Eliz. Harris	10 May 1799	46	Paul his son	20 Sep. 1772	22
Jos. Humphrey,	11 Aug. 1781	85	Wm. Woodcock	27 June 1795	65
			Mary Wright	31 Mar. 1812	40

* Maternal grandfather to the writer. The stone is placed beneath the chancel windows.

CHAPTER XII.

Charity School.—Sunday School.—Hermitage, Chapel of St. John, &c.

It is most probable this institution took its rise on the decline of the Free-school before mentioned; the endowments or funds of which being diverted into other channels, or misapplied by those in trust, awakened in the minds of the inhabitants, and the surrounding gentry, the deepest concern for the education of the rising generation. Rightly judging that the diffusion of knowledge tends ultimately to the benefit of society, especially when extended to the lower classes, the following agreement was drawn up and circulated in the town and neighbourhood.—" Whereas profaneness and debauchery are greatly owing to a gross ignorance of the Christian religion, and for want of an early and pious education of youth, especially among the poorer sort; And whereas many poor people are desirous of having their children taught, but are not able to afford them a Christian and useful education; We, whose names are under written, do hereby agree to pay yearly, at four equal payments, the several sums of money over-against our names respectively subscribed, for the setting up a Charity-school in the parish of Burcester in the county of Oxon, for teaching to read, and instructing in the knowledge and practice of the Christian religion as professed and taught in the church of England, thirty boys out of the aforesaid and neighbouring parishes, viz.—Ammersden, Bucknell, Launton, Chesterton, and Wendlebury; and the better to encourage the same, we do further agree not to withdraw our subscription-money without giving a year's notice thereof; for which good purposes we do readily and willingly subscribe the following sums to commence from Michaelmas 1721.

Anonymous, 5*l.* 0*s.* 0*d.* John Ld. Bp. of Oxon. 2*l.* 0*s.* 0*d.*
Lord Abingdon, 5*l.* 0*s.* 0*d.* Rev. Mr. Airson, &c. &c.[1]

These subscriptions laid the foundation of the school, which was opened and continued in the Free School House, adjoining the church, for several years. It has been since successively removed to the Town-hall, and Guard-room, in which latter place it still continues. The school is at present supported by the subscriptions of the inhabitants of Bicester, and the collections made at an annual sermon preached for that purpose, in the parish church: but the objects of admission are now entirely restricted to the children of poor parishioners.

In the year 1725 a gentleman in the neighbourhood who subscribed largely to the school, declared unless the children were employed in some sort of work, to accustom them to labour, he would withdraw his subscription:

Upon this the trustees determined that the children should be employed in spinning Jersey; a woollen garter-weaver in the town agreed to supply them with work, and a person was engaged to teach them to spin. In June of the same year, the utensils were purchased, and about the middle of the month they made a beginning.

It was proposed that they should work during the school-hours only, six boys to work one day in the week, and the following day six others, &c.—At this time, all the rage was for employing the poor, and converting the parish-houses into work-houses, and it seems Bicester was not backward in trying the experiment [2].

How long this plan was pursued, we have no means of ascertaining; but, as the oldest inhabitants have no recollection

---

[1] The original agreement signed by the different subscribers, is still preserved among the parish papers, and is written on a long slip of parchment.

[2] Account of several work-houses for employing and maintaining the poor. p. 158. London 1732.

of any such thing, we may presume it was not continued for any length of time.

I have been informed that some of the neighbouring gentry have lately offered to add their subscriptions, if the number of scholars may be increased, by the introduction of children from the neighbouring parishes. This has been hitherto declined.

The boys are partly clothed and educated; are provided annually with a cap, blue coat, and leather breeches new. Their general appearance reflects great honour on the liberality of the parish; and as they sit in a conspicuous part of the church, the attention of the worshipper is naturally called to further acts of beneficence.

This school has lately received a considerable benefaction from W. Walker, esq. of Stamford Hill; who,—knowing it to have been the intention of his father, (the late John Walker Esq. of Hackney,) to settle a part of the interest of one thousand pounds 3 per cent. consols upon this institution, but which by some means was neglected,—did with a truly filial and pious liberality carry the design into execution; and by indenture appropriated the sum of sixteen pounds annually (deducting expenses), arising from the above interest, towards the support of the school: and as a further benefaction directed, that in case either or both of the church or meeting-house sunday-schools should be discontinued, the annual sum of seven pounds given to each, should revert to this charity.

The same indenture directs, that the trustees for the donation shall have the management of the school; appoint and remove the master, and examine and regulate its concerns. The children received, are directed to be those belonging to, or residing in the town: they are not to be admitted under seven, nor continued beyond fourteen years of age; to be instructed in the principles of the church of England, and in reading, writing, and casting accounts.

Mr. Walker, sen. was for many years a liberal subscriber

to the three schools in this parish; and it is hoped that the noble example he has set will excite in the minds of the opulent a spirit of emulation in similar acts of beneficence.

THE SUNDAY-SCHOOL.

As long as Sunday-schools are found productive of benefit to the lower classes of inhabitants in Bicester, the name of *Mr. James Jones* ought to be remembered with respect and gratitude. To that worthy man, the father of a numerous family solely dependent on his exertions, must the origin of these establishments in this place be ascribed. Deeply lamenting the ignorance and profaneness of the poor, and judging that much good might be effected by individual exertion, he resolved to offer instruction to as many as would attend on the sabbath, and on a stated evening in the week [3]. The novelty of the thing produced a great number of applicants, who were readily admitted; and the change which suddenly appeared in the streets was astonishing. But as Mr. Jones's plan embraced instruction in reading, writing, and arithmetic, he soon found that his circumstances were unequal to the unavoidable expenses incurred. In this dilemma he solicited the patronage of the parish. The good already accomplished had convinced every unprejudiced person of the necessity of providing for the continuation of a Sunday-school; though the policy of attempting to instruct the children in any thing more than reading, and in the principles of the Christian faith, was justly doubted. Even the advocates of Mr. Jones's plan were compelled to acknowlege that the charity-school already established, offered every advantage to all whose children could

---

[3] Sunday schools originated with Mr. Robert Raikes, a printer at Gloucester, on the representation of the disorderly conduct of the children in the streets on a Sunday, by a woman of that place in 1790. He at first defrayed the whole expense. The plan was carried into Yorkshire, and gradually extended over the kingdom.—*Gent. Mag.* 1804, p. 410.

avail themselves of daily tuition; and the advantages of Sunday lessons in writing and arithmetic were at best problematical. While these points were under discussion, the dissenters offered their patronage to Mr. Jones: their proposals being accepted, the school was immediately transferred to that society, and the children taken to the meeting-house. A. D. 1794.

This circumstance having decided the fate of the first school, no time was lost in endeavouring to establish another, not liable to the objections that had been made to the one that was first proposed. To further this object, the reverend Joseph Eyre, then vicar, preached a sermon, in which he urged every motive for the attainment of the design; he asked "Shall our brethren the dissenters be forward in so good a work, while we remain supine?" The appeal was felt, and a subscription was immediately raised for that purpose. The number of scholars of both sexes was limited to one hundred, over whom two masters and two mistresses were appointed: seats were erected for them in the church; and the ancient free-school appointed for their use, where they still continue to resort for the purpose of tuition.

The school has lately received a donation of seven pounds per annum from the late Mr. Walker.

THE HERMITAGE, CHAPEL OF ST. JOHN BAPTIST, AND INTENDED HOSPITAL.

1355. In the reign of King Edward III. a few yards beyond the present turnpike-gate in *New Buildings*, on the site of the house and garden occupied by Mr. William Horwood, (gardener) stood the solitary abode of *Nicholas Jurdan*, an hermit, and the warden of a chapel dedicated to St. John Baptist, which probably was not far distant, or perhaps adjoining the Hermitage.—This person on May 25th 1355, obtained of the king the following licence to erect and found a

THE HERMITAGE.

Hospital in Bicester, to endow it with the yearly rent of one hundred shillings, for the relief of the said poor, and to maintain one chaplain for ever.

"Rex omnibus ad quos, &c. Sciatis quod de gratia nostra speciali concessimus et licentiam dedimus pro nobis et hæredibus nostris quantum in nobis est *Nicholao Jurdan de Burcester*, heremitæ, custodi capellæ beati *Johannis Baptistæ de Burcester*, quod ipse quoddam Hospitale pro hospitatione pauperum et infirmorum in honorem Dei et gloriosæ Virginis Mariæ matris ejus, et beati Johannis Baptistæ apud Burcester, de novo fundare et centum solidatas terræ et redditus cum pertinentiis per annum juxta verum valorem eorum, exceptis terris tenementis et redditibus quæ de nobis tenentur in capite, acquirere possit. Habenda et tenenda eidem custodi et successoribus suis in subventionem sustentationis eorundem et cujusdam Capellani divina in Capella prædicta pro salubri statu nostro et Philippæ Reginæ Angliæ consortis ac Edwardi Principis Walliæ filii nostri carissimi dum vixerimus, et pro animabus nostris cum ab hac luce subtracti fuerimus, et animabus omnium fidelium defunctorum singulis diebus celebraturi in perpetuum, statuto de terris et tenementis ad manum mortuam non ponendis ideo non obstante, &c. Teste Rege apud Westminstre, 15 die Maii [4].

The silence of Kennett throughout the Parochial Antiquities, respecting this hospital, has led Tanner and succeeding writers to conclude that the design was never carried into execution [5]; perhaps in consequence of the death of the hermit. Indeed, the most minute inquiries afford no traces of such an establishment. The chapel of St. John Baptist is supposed by some to have been valued together with the priory, and demo-

---

[4] Kennett, p. 478.
[5] Tanner's Notitia Monastica. Burcester, Oxfordshire.

lished soon after [6]. And I am inclined to conclude that Kennett has been misled by tradition, or some relics of this chapel, to suppose the parish church stood in this neighbourhood, when in fact, no other sacred edifice was ever founded near the spot.

Besides, all ancient writings uniformly call the Sheep Street, *St. John's Street*, evidently from the chapel dedicated to that saint, either standing in or adjoining to it: whereas, if the old church had stood there, it mòst likely would have given its name to the street, especially as the chapel must have been of comparatively modern erection.—The idea of the church once standing here, may have arisen from the parish having used the chapel for public worship, while the church was rebuilding.

It is impossible to say of what nature the hermitage buildings were. The name and nature of the abode betoken solitude, we may therefore safely conclude, there were no houses about that spot. Indeed, this opinion is placed beyond doubt, by the following memorandum in a terrier of the lands belonging to the Prior and Canons of Bicester, taken in the first year of the reign of Henry IV. A. D. 1399. " Memorand.—Quod precedens terra dominica Dom. Lestraunge vocata *Wowelond*, jacet a fine villæ erga hermitag. et inter *Harry-furlong*, et buttat totaliter *into Stratton weye*." In the ancient writings of Mr. Horwood also, the entrance of the hermitage is said to be from the *Broadyates*, a proof that the site of New Buildings was known by those names in former times. And the circumstance of the deeds of some of the oldest houses in that street, acknowledging their being built about two hundred years ago, seems to warrant the conclusion, that the street was not formed before that period.

---

[6] Magna Britannia, vol. iv. p. 474.

CHAPTER XIII.

Dissenters in Bicester.—Meeting House.—Quakers.

It is uncertain at what time the opinions of the Puritans [1] were first known among the inhabitants of Bicester; though it is probable that the number who embraced them increased under the ministry of Mr. Basnet, a clergyman who held the cure of the parish during the great rebellion. To that class his subsequent ejection, at the passing of the Bartholomew Act, was doubtless matter of regret, but it does not appear to have occasioned any *secession* from the established church. This event seems to have been brought about after the passing of the toleration-act, by the preaching of the ejected ministers Mr. John Troughton and Mr. Henry Cornish; the former of whom had for several years kept an academy in the town, and occasionally preached in private. Having thus obtained a number of hearers, a barn was fitted up (*circa* 1692) in a yard opposite Coney-lane, and a congregation raised, over which Mr. Cornish was appointed minister: an office which he retained until his death [2].

As these divines are conspicuous in the annals of the neigh-

---

[1] The puritans objected to the whole hierarchy, which they declared was not of divine appointment, disallowed of the mode of cathedral worship, disapproved of set forms of prayer, sponsors in baptism, and bowing at the name of Jesus. They objected to the ring in marriage, and observation of saints' days, &c. See Neale's History of the Puritans, or Toulmin's Abridgement, v. i. ch. 5.

[2] The distress which followed the Bartholomew Act induced several of the ejected ministers to endeavour to establish schools for the instruction of youth in different towns and villages; others fled to their friends, and remained dependent on their generosity. But at the passing of the Toleration Act, most of them issued from their retreats and resumed their functions. The churches remaining closed against them, they erected meeting-houses in different places, their hearers they formed into societies which they denominated churches, and thus the first separate congregations originated.

bouring celebrated university, and their memory still cherished among the dissenters, a short account of their lives may not be uninteresting.

John Troughton was the son of Nathaniel Troughton, a clothier of Coventry, and educated under Samuel Frankland, in the free-school. In 1655 he was entered of St. John's College, Oxon; became afterwards fellow and bachelor of arts, and was expelled the college for non-conformity in 1662. When persecution rendered it necessary to preach in prohibited assemblies, he indulged no rancour against his opponents, and sought not to make his hearers become partisans, but true members of the church of Christ. He inculcated love and charity towards all, however they might differ in theological points, and himself maintained an amicable correspondence with many of the conforming clergy, by whom he was highly respected, on account of his great learning and moderation. On the issuing of the Declaration of Toleration, March 15, 1671, Mr. Troughton joined Dr. Langley and other non-conformists, in establishing a lecture in Oxford. Their meetings were held in Thame Street, without the north gate, and among the scholars who often came to scoff, Mr. Troughton was deservedly admired. Wood says, " the truth is, though the man was blind, occasioned by the small pox, ever since he was four years old, yet he was a good school divine and metaphysician, and had obtained much commendation by the university for his disputes. He was the author of several valuable works.

" This learned and religious person died in a house of one of the brethren in All Saints parish Oxon, January 20, 1681, aged 44 years. His body was carried to Bicester, and buried in the parish church; at which time Abraham James, a blind man, master of the free-school at Woodstock (sometime of Magdalen Col. Oxon) preached his funeral sermon[3]."

---

[3] Wood's Athenæ Oxonienses, p. 686. London 1721.

Henry Cornish was the son of William Cornish of Ditchèt, in Somersetshire: he was entered scholar of New Inn, and assisted the butler to enter battles in the buttery book. Wood stigmatizes his education as puritanical, and says that these principles increased under Dr. Rogers, principal of the Inn. While he remained in this seminary it is supposed that he took the degree of A. M., and became a popular preacher. In the convulsions which followed, he conscientiously joined the parliament party and left Oxford; on their success was appointed canon of Christ Church and B. D., and had the offer of D. D., which he refused. In 1646 he was appointed one of the visitors of the university; and with Langley, Corbet, Cheynel, and others, regularly preached at St. Mary's. After the Restoration he was displaced by the king's commissioners, though he still continued to preach as a non-conformist in these parts till silenced by the five mile act. He then retired to Stanton-Harcourt, and was patronized by the pious Sir Philip Harcourt. Here he remained preaching occasionally in private until the declaration of toleration issued by William III. when he joined Mr. Troughton, Dr. Langley, and Mr. Gilbert in preaching at Oxford. Ten years after the death of Mr. Troughton (A. D. 1690) he settled at Bicester, and assumed the pastoral care of a congregation of dissenters, probably formed by the labours of the ejected ministers. A barn situated in a yard opposite *Coney-lane* was appropriated to public worship, which we may safely infer from the different workmanship observable in the wainscot of the pews in the present meeting-house, was fitted up with seats for the accommodation of the people [4]. Here this gentleman, whose piety and talents were formerly considered equal to the important task of preaching before one of the first universities in the world, and who constantly attracted crowded audiences, when more

---

[4] It is not unlikely that the old seats were brought from the barn, and used in constructing the pews in the present meeting-house,

than eighty years of age preached to the inhabitants of Bicester[5]. To the honour of the dissenters Mr. John Oyliffe, the rector of Dutton, Bucks, asserts "they were as intelligent, good tempered, judicious, and loving people as a minister need desire. The good old gentleman was as tender of them as a father, and they carried it to him with the respect and tenderness of children; and vital religion exceedingly flourished among them." He died December 18, 1698, and was buried in Bicester chancel[6].

From the registers of the dissenters, which remain in the hands of Mr. William Rolls, it was evident that their first ministers considered themselves authorized to marry the members of their own community. The very first entry running in the following words: "January 24, 169$\frac{4}{5}$, Joseph Daniel and Jeane Abbot were then married in the chapel, certificates being received that the banns were lawfully published at Stonny Stratford and Bisseter congregation—by me, Henry Cornish."

It is followed by the entries of the baptism of different children; the first of which appears,

"February 18, 169$\frac{4}{5}$, Thomas, the son of Thomas Wilson, was then baptized by me, Henry Cornish."

The last entry of this divine is dated May 17, 1698; but throughout the whole of the register no other marriage is noticed.

It appears plainly from this book that Mr. John Troughton, son of the former, occasionally assisted Mr. Cornish in his pastoral labours, and on his death succeeded to his charge. During his ministry the barn was abandoned, and the present

---

[5] Wood says "In his old age he preaches in a barn for profit-sake to silly women and other obstinate people." Oyliffe says "As to profit-sake he was above it, having an estate of his own." I have endeavoured to steer a middle course in delineating his character.

[6] Wood's Fasti Oxonienses, p. 91.

meeting-house erected. After sustaining the important office forty years, he departed this life December 3, 1739, aged 73. As little more than the bare mention of the names of his successors occurs in any of the books, the list is subjoined.

Mr. J. Troughton was succeeded by Mr. Parke, Mr. Stuck, Mr. Fenner, Mr. Davis, Mr. Pickersgill, Mr. Hickman, Mr. Whitford, Mr. O'Bennett, Mr. Howell, Mr. Miller, Mr. John Dennant (in whose ministry a Sunday-school was established), and Mr. Richard Fletcher. This gentleman was ordained over the congregation May 29, 1799, and still retains the pastoral care.

THE MEETING-HOUSE.

At the erection of the meeting-house the dissenters in this town were numerous and opulent; and this structure is a lasting monument of their zeal and liberality. The building is 43 feet in length and 33 in width within the walls. The light is admitted by four lofty windows, with semicircular heads in the front, and two smaller on the back. Over the entrance is a pediment, in the centre of which an open volume rests on a label, inscribed with the year of its erection. In the book are the following words engraved " *Verbum Dei manet in æternum.*"

The interior is commodiously fitted up. Originally every part was in strict uniformity; but the erection of a gallery and some alterations have destroyed this effect; yet there are few who would not still view it with pleasure. The pulpit and sounding board were often deservedly admired for their elegant simplicity; but the latter has been removed some years, as it was supposed to occasion too great reverberation. Opposite the pulpit lies the body of the Reverend John Troughton, in whose ministry the building was raised. A flat stone covers his grave, inscribed " Here are deposited the remains of the Reverend John Troughton, many years a laborious and faithful minister to a congregation of Protestant Dissenters in this parish, and having served this generation by the will of God, fell asleep December 3, 1739, Ætat. 73. Also of Sarah his wife, who departed this troublesome world for a happy immortality, January 20, 1736. Ætat. 63."

There are several other inscriptions on the pavement, and two monuments affixed to the walls. One to the memory of the Sayers, grand children of Mr. Troughton, the ejected minister; and the other for Mr. W. Rolls, many years a deacon.

Adjoining the meeting-house is a vestry, of much later erection, which has recently been enlarged, and is chiefly used for the various services in the week.

The edifice is surrounded by a burying ground, and ornamented with trees. The entrance is in the Water-lane, with a terrace in front, formed at the expense of the late Miss Miller, who gave the cushion and pulpit-bible.

This spot was purchased after the dreadful fire of 1724, and was previously occupied by a range of buildings extending to the King's-arms-yard [7].

The ancient congregation was presbyterian, and Mr. Miller (I believe) was the last preacher of that class. The present is *independent*. The meeting-house is in the hands of trustees [8].

Their Sunday-school was established in 1794, and Mr. James Jones, the projector of these institutions in this parish, remained master till the illness which terminated in his death.

The benefaction of Mr. Walker appropriates 7*l.* annually to the support of this school, arising from the interest of 1000*l.* 3 per cent. consols, liable to the deduction of incidental expenses.

---

[7] See a paper now in the hands of Mr. Thomas Harris, a gentleman to whom I am extremely indebted for several important communications.

[8] The deed of trust is in the hands of Mr. James Gurden, sen., one of the deacons and a trustee, to whose kindness I am indebted for a sight of it.

THE QUAKERS.

The Society of Friends were formerly pretty numerous in this town; and had a meeting-house in a yard nearly opposite the *White Lion* public-house in Sheep-street. The meeting-house was fitted up with seats for the accommodation of the congregation; and from a large portable desk the speakers addressed the people. On the decline of the society the building was applied to other purposes, and finally converted into dwelling-houses. There are few of that persuasion now in Bicester, and whenever any of the speakers visit the town for the purpose of public worship, they usually obtain the temporary possession of the town hall.

CHAPTER XIV.

Fairs and Market.—Tradesmen's Tokens.

It is generally acknowledged that fairs and markets owe their origin to the concourse of people who usually assembled to commemorate the dedication of the churches. Hence anciently they were held in church-yards, and on the Sabbath day[1], till they were prohibited in the reign of Henry III. from being kept on that day or in those places. The oldest fair in Bicester is that usually held in Kingsend, by a charter granted in the first year of King Richard II. to Sir John de Worthe, then lord of the manor of Bigenhull, and now in the possession of Mr. Coker, though this is considered by Kennett

---

[1] A. D. 1204. Eustachius, abbot of Flay in Normandy, was one of the first ecclesiastics who preached against Sunday markets; and pretended to have received a letter from heaven, written by the hand of God, in which he threatened to rain sticks and stones, and boiling water on all who frequented them!!!—Henry's Hist. of Britain, vol. v. p. 434, apud Hoveden An, p. 457.

as no more than a confirmation of an ancient fair, deriving its origin from the dedication of the old church, which he presumes was consecrated to St. James, as the present structure is to St. Edburgh. The charter also contains a grant of a weekly Monday market, which has long been discontinued, and is as follows:

Translation.] "The king to the arch-bishops, bishops, abbots, priors, dukes, counts, barons, justices, sheriffs, mayors, ministers, and all bailiffs, and all other our faithful subjects. Know ye that we, of our special grace, have granted, and by this charter have confirmed for us and our heirs, to our beloved and faithful subject John de Worthe, Knt., that he and his heirs shall for ever have at their manor of Bigenhull, at Burcestre, one market every week, on the Monday; and one fair every year to continue for *three days,* to wit, on the vigil, on the day, and on the morrow of St. James the Apostle. Nevertheless that market and fair shall not be to the hurt of the neighbouring markets and fairs. Wherefore we will and strictly command that the said John and his heirs for ever shall have one market every week, on the Monday; and one fair every year for three days, as aforesaid. Witnesses the honourable Fathers S. Archbishop of Canterbury, Primate of all England; W. London; A. Worcester, Chancellor; and Thomas Exeter, Treasurer, our bishops; John King of Castile and Lyons, Duke of Lancaster, Mortimer, March, and others.

"Given under our hand at Westminster 20 day of Oct.

"By writ of privy seal."

This fair and market seems to have decayed afterwards, so that when the manor came into the joint possession of Humphrey Duke of Buckingham and John Felmersham, the former obtained a renewal of the charter granted to Sir John de Worthe. This grant is little more than a copy of the above, and bears date the 20th day of July, 17 Henry VI. 1438.

FAIRS AND MARKET.

The market was shortly after discontinued by reason of a new charter granted to Robert Brooke for one to be held in Bicester Bury-end. The fair however continues to this day, is annually proclaimed with music on the vigil of St. James, and is kept in the street of Kingsend [2]; many of the respectable inhabitants erect booths or affix a bough over their doors, and are thereby privileged to sell ale and beer during the fair. Formerly much leather was brought for sale; and as anciently these marts supplied the surrounding country with their commodities till the annual period of their return, the custom has obtained and continued of discharging curriers', shoemakers', and other bills at this time. From these circumstances, combined with the favourable season of the year at which it is held, this fair may be still considered one of the best in this country [3].

The statutes or fairs held on the three successive Fridays in October after old St. Michael in each year do not seem grounded on any charter; but on the necessity of an appointed time for masters and servants meeting together for the mutual accommodation of hiring and being hired. The origin of the custom may be traced from the decline of slavery; and the

---

[2] By the statute of 17 Edward IV. 1477, it was provided that "whereas divers fairs be holden and kept in this realm, some by prescription, and allowed before justices in eyre, and some by the grant of our lord the king that now is, and some by grants of his predecessors:—To every one of the same fairs there is of right pertaining a court of pye-powders to minister in the same due justice that every of the persons coming may have due justice, &c." Then follow clauses to regulate the same, and to provide remedies for every offence.—See Archæologia, vol. i. p. 190.

[3] Formerly the fair at Bicester was in so much repute, and attended by such multitudes, that it was judged necessary for the preservation of the peace in the night, to appoint watches both in Bicester and the surrounding villages. At the summer or St. James's fair three or four of the inhabitants used to take the office in rotation. The practice was discontinued by the falling off of the fair about twelve years ago.

statutes being held on three successive market days, seems to prove they had no other foundation than mutual convenience, because on those days the farmers were expected to be present on business. Such also was the opinion of Dr. Plot, who says " In the north of Oxfordshire it has always been the custom at set times of the year for young people to meet and hire themselves as servants, which meeting at Banbury they call the *mop*; at Bloxam the statutes, where they all sort themselves and carry their badges according as they are qualified; the carter with whipcord, the shepherds with wool, but the maidens, as far as I could learn, stood promiscuously [4]." These fairs are of course held in the market-place in Bicester.

Letters Patent granted to Robert Brooke for holding a new Market in Bicester Bury-end, 19 Henry VI. 1440.

Translation.] "The King to all, &c. health. Know ye that we out of consideration of the good services which our dear servant Robert Brooke renders, and shall render to us, of our special grace we grant to him, the picage, stallage, boothage, and tollage, together with the assize of bread and beer of our new market below the town of Burcester, in the county of Oxon, with all profits and emoluments which to us duly belong, or shall in any mode whatever by reason of the said market belong, in respect of picage, stallage, boothage, or tollage, for which truly we are informed nothing has been answered to us in these days, to be had and held by the said Robert or his deputy during his proper life, from thence enjoying such fees, profits, and commodities, as to the same in any manner shall belong, rendering from thence to us the annuity of six shillings and eightpence, to be paid to our receiver of Cornwall for the time being, or his deputy. The same being for all sorts

---

[4] Plot's Oxfordshire, p. 203.

of burthens and demands; any other statute, act, or ordination enacted or made to the contrary notwithstanding. In witness &c. Given by the king at Westminster the first day of June.

"By writ of privy seal and of the date aforesaid,
"By authority of parliament."

From the granting of the above charter that part of the town which had been heretofore known by the name of *Bury-end*[5] was called *Market-end*; and the market thus established seems to have speedily become one of the chief marts in the county. This eminence it retained till the year 1704, when the small-pox raged so dreadfully in the town that the market was entirely deserted; insomuch that the market-place was covered with grass, and bore the appearance of a meadow. It was long before the neighbouring villagers ventured again with their commodities, and trade being once diverted into other channels, the market never recovered its former importance. However, it is still much frequented by dealers in cattle, especially in the spring and autumn: but the practice of selling corn by sample has tended to lessen the appearance of business [6].

In 1769 Mr. Howlet having obtained the offices of high constable of the hundred of Ploughley and steward of the bailiwick of Bicester market-end, appointed three new fairs to be held in the market-place. The first on the Friday in

---

[5] On this circumstance Kennett grounds much of his argument in favour of the parish church being anciently situated in Sheep-street.

[6] I have heard many of the aged inhabitants say that they have formerly seen the whole market-hill covered with sacks of corn, &c.; the avenues leading to it crowded by the farmers' wives with their baskets of butter, eggs, and poultry; the parts around abounding with stalls of goods of every description; and the streets filled with cattle. They have generally closed this account by exclaiming, "Ah! those were rare days!"

Easter week, the second on the first Friday in June, and the other on the Friday following Christmas-day. Of these, the fair in Easter week is chiefly noted for the number of cattle usually brought for sale. The others are but little attended.

TRADESMEN THAT ISSUED TOKENS IN THE SEVENTEENTH CENTURY.

The coin of the kings since the Conquest was chiefly of gold and silver, though a bad policy sometimes debased it by alloy. The necessity of a smaller change compelled dealers and tradesmen to invent some token, as a medium for currency between themselves and their customers. Hence arose a diversity of these tokens, only current in their own neighbourhood. Under pretence of remedying this evil, but *really with a view of enriching a favourite,* a patent was granted (July 11, 1626) to the Dutchess Dowager of Richmond and Sir Francis Crane, Knt., to coin farthing tokens. They soon made many thousand pounds worth; and as a proof of the shameful imposition practised on the public, it is sufficient to state that out of an ounce of copper, which cost one penny, they made twentypence. Their patent was shortly after annulled, and all the tokens were left on the subjects' hands, who sold them to the braziers at tenpence or a shilling the pound.

Next came the *public farthing-token offices* in London. These gave one shilling in twenty to those who came to buy, and the country was soon inundated with them—gold and silver vanished—but when they returned to the patentees they disowned all that had not a double ring upon them, of which very few were found. Hereby the lower tradesmen were all ruined, who got their living by selling fish, vegetables, &c.

Then they put a brass or other mark in them, but still they were asserted to be counterfeited. At last the great quantity of royal tokens, and the refusal of the patentees to exchange them, put an entire stop to their currency. The necessity of change made tradesmen resume the issuing of tokens; and from their commencement in 1642 till they were cried down by proclamation in 1672 their numbers increased every year. The earliest town-pieces are those of Bristol and Oxford, 1652, but after 1666 they multiplied prodigiously[16].

The tradesmen who issued tokens in Bicester were, Gabriel Burrowes, John Borrows, Thomas Burges, Thomas Clements, William Hudson, William Stevens, and John Warry, of which the following is a description.

Burrowes, Gabriel, in (arms)—*Reverse*, Bisseter, Ironmonger, G.B.

Borrows, John, Iron- I.B.— *Reverse*, -monger in Bister, I.B.

Burges, Thomas—*Reverse*, of Biseter, 1665, T^{B}M.

Clements, Thomas, (arms)—*Reverse*, of Bissiter, Draper, T.C.

Hudson, William, of Bister—*Reverse*, in Oxfordshire, 1669, his halfpenny, W^{H}S.

Stevens, William, of Bister, 1669—*Reverse*, in Oxfordshire, his halfpenny, W^{S}E.

Warry, John, of Bister, three pipers, 1668—*Reverse*, in Oxfordshire, his halfpenny, I^{W}M. a heart[17].

CHAPTER XVI.

Manor of Nun's Place or King's-end and Village of Bigenhull.

At a very early period the nuns of the priory of Merkyate (now Market-street), in the county of Bedford, obtained the grant of a mansion and estate in Bicester, which were after-

---

[16] Snelling on Coins, p. 17. 1763.
[17] MS. Catalogue of Town-pieces and Tokens in the 17th Century. Quarto.

wards known by the appellation of the MANER OF NONNES PLACE, though at present neither the name of the donor nor the time of the donation is known. The earliest mention of this estate is found in an indenture made in the reign of King John (A. D. 1212) between the prioress and nuns of Merkyate, and Hervey, prior of Burncestre, for the exchange of two ridges of the nuns' land in *Hodesham* for one acre nearer to their land in *Nyhenaker*, and half an acre of meadow nigh to the meadow called *Gilbertsham*. A full statement of the lands constituting this estate may be found in the folios of lands, rents, and services taken in 1325; and by some considered as affording the best detail of the services of villainage extant: the original document is in the hands of Mr. Coker, the present lord of the manor. The services of one of their tenants, Robert, son of Nicholas Germayn, are stated at large in the list of tenures, &c., and a close translation of the whole court-roll is given in the Appendix. In the reign of Edward IV. the land was assessed among the temporalities of the prioress and nuns of Merkyate, and computed at the yearly value of fifty-six shillings and ten-pence, of which the tenths were rated at five shillings and eight-pence. A few years previous to the dissolution of the smaller monasteries (22 Henry VIII. A. D. 1530) a lease of it was granted by the prioress and nuns to John Gryffyth, a servant of the cardinal's (Wolsey), for twenty-one years, probably with a view to preserve the estate amid the impending storm which the religious saw ready to burst upon them [1]. Soon after the Dissolution, the rever-

---

[1] The lease is given at length in the Appendix.

At the valuation of the estates belonging to the priory of Merkyate, the account of this estate was entered as follows:

Dom' sive Monast' in s'ta Trini^{te} de Bosco juxt' Markeyate D'na Joh'a Zouch Priorissa ib'm.

                                                                                                            £. s. d.

Com. Oxon. Burcestre. Valet per Annu' in Firm' Man'is ib'm D'ni

Joh'i Gryffeth per Indentur' ostens'...................... vij xiij iiij

Records in the Augmentation Office.

sion in fee of this manor was granted by King Henry VIII. to John Denton, Esq. of Blackthorn, in the parish of Ambrosden, and in the year 1582 it was sold by him to Mr. John Coker [1].

The family of the COKERS derive their origin from Coker, a town in Somersetshire; but in the reign of Henry IV. John Coker, a member of that family, having married an heiress of the name of Veale, became possessed of a very considerable estate at Mapouder, in Dorsetshire, where he settled. John Coker, a descendant and younger son, who was born at Mapouder in the reign of Henry VIII. married a wife at Pollicot in Oxfordshire, and resided there a short time; but afterwards purchasing the manor of Nun's Place, he adopted the mansion for the residence of himself and his posterity, which, together with the estate, still remains in their possession.

The manor-house seems to have had its name changed to *Burchester Hall* during the time it was the residence of his son Cadwallader Coker [3], and to have been rebuilt by Mr. John Coker, his grandson, in 1682 [4].

To the last-mentioned gentleman the curious must acknowledge themselves under considerable obligations. From his papers Kennett derived some of the most valuable information in his Parochial Antiquities, and by his industry the

---

[1] Ex orig. penes Johan. Coker, armig. The reversion of this manor, together with the estate of Strippwike, at Ambrosden, were granted to Denton for fifty-seven pounds twelve shillings!

Jones's Index to the Public Records contains the following entry, "De Justiniano Champney et uxore occasionatis ad ostendendum quo titulo tenent Manerium de Burcester vocatum Nonnes Place in Com. Oxoniæ." Paschæ Recorda 17 Elizabeth. Rot. 64. This seems to intimate that this family held the manor, and it might be they resided in the mansion; perhaps they held it on lease from Denton.

[3] " De Cadwallader Coker occasionato ad ostendendum quo titulo tenet manerium de Burcester Hall in Com. Oxon." Michael. Recorda, 11 Jac. I. Rot. 295.

[4] See a plate of the mansion in Kennett's Par. Ant.

THE RESIDENCE OF JOHN COKER ESQ.

neglected well of St. Edburg was restored, after the lapse of more than a century, during which its virtues had been almost consigned to oblivion.—He and his descendants lie buried in Bicester church, in a vault beneath the family pew.—The last possessor, the Reverend Thomas Coker, is said to have entailed the manor and estates on the male branches of his family.

The present proprietor, John Coker, Esq., succeeded to the estate on the death of his uncle: by him the family mansion has been partly rebuilt, though many of the additional apartments remain unfinished. The front presents a handsome appearance, and by the inclosure of the green he has obtained a considerable pleasure-ground around it. To the exertions of this gentleman great praise is due for putting an end to the inhuman practice of bull-baiting, which formerly was a prevalent amusement in Bicester. The writer when a boy saw with pleasure his determined and laudable conduct in rescuing a poor animal destined to become the victim of this cruel sport from a savage mob, and never since that time has the practice been attempted to be revived. The insults he received on the occasion were shameful, but he had the reward of approving conscience and the benedictions of the humane. In every plan for bettering the condition of the poor or improving the town, Mr. Coker has been most ready to come forward with liberality, and it is much to be regretted that Bicester is not his constant residence.

Mr. Coker married in 1792 the Honourable Charlotte Marsham, the youngest daughter of the Right Honourable Robert Lord Romney, of the Moat, near Maidstone, Kent. His lady died in January 1794, leaving an only child, a daughter.

In the year 1798, when these kingdoms were threatened with invasion by the atrocious ruler of France, a general spirit of loyalty and patriotism manifested itself throughout all ranks and descriptions of the people. The university of Oxford was not backward in the laudable and spirited exertions displayed on this occasion. A regiment consisting of five hundred matriculated members of the university was raised, clothed, and armed at their own expense. Of this regiment Mr. Coker was unanimously appointed the colonel. In the subsequent year when the colonel applied to His Royal Highness the Commander in Chief to have his regiment reviewed by some general, His Royal Highness was graciously pleased to say that he would review it himself. Accordingly, on the 18th of June, in the year 1799, the regiment was reviewed by His Royal Highness in Port-meadow, when the most excellent and highly disciplined steadiness and military skill displayed by the corps drew from the commander in chief the strongest expressions of commendation and praise.

Upon the death of Sir Christopher Willoughby in 1809, Mr. Coker was unanimously appointed the chairman of the quarter sessions of the county of Oxford.

1814. At a numerous and respectable meeting of the nobility, gentry, clergy, and freeholders of the county of Oxon, convened by the high sheriff to consider of the propriety of addressing the Prince Regent on the occasion of his visit to the county in company with the Emperor of Russia and King of Prussia, Mr. Coker, after an eloquent and impressive speech, moved an address, which was received with unbounded applause and carried unanimously [5]. On the following Wednesday it was presented to His Royal Highness at Christ Church by the Earls of Abingdon and Harcourt, the Bishop of Oxford, J. Fane, Esq., and numbers of the most respectable gentlemen of the county.

VILLAGE OF BIGENHULL.

The village of BIGENHULL seems to have formerly stood south

---

[5] Times of June 22, 1814.

of Berencestre[6], and on the site of King's-end. Probably it only consisted of a few scattered houses, as all accounts represent it as having been very small. Without doubt some of the inhabitants attended at the lord's chapel, but it is most likely that the greater part of them took their places in the parish church. There was a tradition in the time of Kennett that it was a separate and distinct parish from Bicester Bury-end, on which point he remarks, " To support the tradition of two parishes, I find no better authority than the ruins of a chappel near Bignell-Farm and of a church in Burcester Market-end, near the Hermitage, at the north end of Sheep-street, long since also demolished. I rather believe that Bigenhull was only a distinct manor, like Wretchwic, within the precincts of Burcester, having a chapel subordinate to the mother church, and granted as a privilege to the lord of the manor."

The name of King's-end, or *Kyng-end*, as descriptive of this township, appears very early. In a terrier of the lands of Bicester priory, taken in the last year of Richard II. A. D. 1399, the field attached is distinctly called the field of Burncester Kyng-end, and in the reign of Henry VI. it is evident that the village itself was commonly known by that name; for in the bursar's account of receipts and expenses of the priory of Bicester for the year 1425, one of the items is, " And four pounds four shillings and four-pence received for the rent of fourteen tenements in Burcestre Bury-end and Kyng-end, as paid by the rent-roll." It is however clear, from the

---

[6] On examining the foundations which still remain in Mr. Coker's close, one of the most intelligent inhabitants of Bicester remarked that they seemed to intimate that the old town of Berencestre stood on both sides of a road, which led, in nearly a straight line, from the Akeman-street, near Graven-hill, into the Bucknell road, above the stone-pits.—And that the fosse and vallum, which for a short distance are parallel with the brook, and run in the direction of those in the Horse-close, seem to have joined them, and formed a part of the ancient fortifications.

care of Sir John de Worth, lord of Bigenhull, to obtain the grant of a fair and weekly market for his manor, and the spot on which it was held, that great part of this township was accounted a part of the ancient manor of Bigenhull, even down to the middle of the following century; when Humphrey Duke of Buckingham obtained letters-patent to confirm the weekly market and St. James's fair. It is not improbable that the honours of Bigenhull were finally cropt by the estate falling into the hands of the lords of *Nonnes Place*, who, when they condescended to part with it, stripped it of all its ancient splendour, and simply disposed of the farm.

It is said that the manors of King's-end, Bigenhull, and the neighbouring village of Kirklington, are part of the domains of the Dutchy of Lancaster, and that in consequence the inhabitants are privileged to attend markets and fairs without paying toll, by a charter granted at some distant period [7]. I have not been able to discover any such charter; but the circumstance of their claim of exemption being allowed in the market and fairs of Bicester Market-end, is a proof that the bailiff considers it well founded.

It is customary for the inhabitants of this parish or township to attend the *court leet* held under the steward of the

---

[7] The late Mr. Egerton, steward to the former and present lord of the manor, informed me that one day a stranger exposed his goods for sale in King's-end fair, but refused to pay the toll, asserting that he was an inhabitant of the domains of the Dutchy of Lancaster, and producing a paper, which he affirmed was a copy of a charter, granting to all the inhabitants of those domains freedom from toll in all markets and fairs throughout England. Mr. Egerton afterwards much regretted that he did not examine the paper; yet he rebutted the claims of the stranger, by remarking that the exemption was limited to places *without* the domains of the Dutchy, and consequently did not apply to King's-end; which the stranger admitted.

If there ever was any connection between the manors of Kirklington, Bigenhull, &c. it must have been anterior to the grant of the manor of Nun's-manor of Kirklington; but the jury are always chosen from among the inhabitants of King's-end, if there are a sufficient number in attendance, and are privileged to sit in a separate room. To this court the inhabitants of King's-end usually pay thirteen shillings and four-pence annually; twenty-pence of which is levied on the lord of the manor; twenty-pence on Bignel farm; and four-pence on each cottage. To ensure a full attendance, the court is accustomed to levy a fine of one penny on every householder absent.

CHAPTER XVII.

Manor of Bigenhull.

THIS manor deserves particular notice, as it anciently included the chief part of what is now called King's-end. It is not however recognised as a manor in Doomsday-book, for in that record two only are noticed, and these defined by Kennett to be Bicester and Wretchwick; a proof that it was then included in the manor of Burchester. At what time Bigenhull was separated is unknown, nor has any account of the tenure by which it was held reached us. The earliest mention is in a grant to Bicester priory, A. D. 1212, in the fourteenth year

---

place to the priory of Merkyate, and then only as members of the same fee. According to Plot, the manor of Kirklington originally belonged to the kings of England, from whom it proceeded to John of Gaunt, Duke of Lancaster. This information Plot professes to derive from an old charter in the possession of Sir T. Chamberleyne, lord of the town. But Dugdale traces the property from John de Hemetz, constable of Normandy, in the reign of King John, through the Bassets to Thomas of Woodstock, who died possessed of the manor, 20 Richard II. Was Plot's account correct, and could the manor of Nun's-place be proved to have once belonged to the same fee, it would be easy to trace the name of King's-end, and the title of the township to the aforementioned privileges.

of King John, when James Le Bret, lord of Bigenhull, and Amable his wife, are noticed as generous benefactors to that infant institution [1]. In the same century it passed into the family of the *Langleys*; and Walter, Alice, and John de Langley are successively mentioned as owners of the lordship. The *folios* remaining give an accurate account of the rents and services as they existed in the time of the latter, A. D. 1325, 19 Edward II. Thirteen years after (1360) Sir Richard le Vache of Bigenhull, a descendant of the Le Vaches mentioned in the folios, together with Sir Miles Stapleton of Middleton, were among the commissioners in the great treaty of peace concluded with Edward III., by which that monarch received many provinces without homage. It is not quite so clear that he was lord of the manor, indeed the probability is against it. How long the family of *De Worthe* had obtained possession before John de Worthe obtained the charter for the market and fair is not known, nor yet into whose hands it passed before it came into the joint possession of *Humphry*, Earl of Stafford, afterward Duke of Buckingham, and John Felmersham, the former of whom obtained *Letters Patent* to confirm the weekly market. No further accounts have reached us of Felmersham; but the whole life of Buckingham seems devoted to the cause of Henry VI. In the battle of St. Alban's he lost his eldest son (1455), and by the sacrifice of his own life in the fields of Northampton proved his enmity to the house of York. Bigenhull came afterwards into the possession of John Stokeys, Esq. and was sold by him to William Staveley, a benefactor to the priory, in whose family it remained for several generations. The body of this gentleman lies buried in the chancel of Bicester parish church, and a brass plate, the oldest monument therein, still perpetuates his memory. His eldest son George is distinguished by his donation to Uni-

---

[1] Kennett, p. 176.

versity College, Oxford. He gave fifty pounds to purchase land of the yearly value of fifty shillings, of which he provided that two shillings and eight-pence should be paid to one of the fellows in holy orders to say mass as often as he pleased at the south altar of the chapel, for the souls of George Staveley, Isabel his wife, John Staveley, and their friends. Of the remainder three shillings and four-pence should be allowed on the anniversary of his death to the master and fellows to increase their commons; two-pence to the manciple; two-pence to the head cook; four-pence to the bible-clerk; and the overplus to be divided on the same day between the masters and the scholars. George Staveley died 17 Henry VIII. A. D. 1523[2].

How long the manor of Bigenhull remained in the hands of the descendants of the Staveleys I have not been able to ascertain. The names of his son John and his grandson Thomas occur, the latter of whom was in possession at the heralds' visitation in Oxfordshire in 1574[3].

The lordship of Bigenhull and the estates connected with the ancient demesne, had been alienated some time before Kennett published the Parochial Antiquities (A.D. 1695), for he says the " name alone of Bigenhull or Bignell remains in a farm-house, which tradition speaks of as the seat of the lord of the manor, now belonging to the daughters and coheirs of Mr. Samuel Lee, and hath been some time in the occupation of John Willson[4]."

The honours formerly annexed to this estate led Sir Robert Dashwood, early in the last century, to commence a law suit with Mr. Coker for the manor &c. of King's-end; which was finally adjudged to the latter, in whose possession all the ori-

---

[2] Kennett, p. 681.
[3] Harleian MS. No. 1095. Brit. Mus.
[4] Mr. Lee is supposed to have made the largest collection of Alchester coins ever known.

ginal documents relative to this manor and township then were, and with whose descendants they still remain.

Passing through several hands, it was at last purchased by John Coker, Esq., who sold it to Mr. Forster.* This gentleman has lately repaired or rebuilt the mansion: part of the walls of the chapel are standing, but it has been lately converted into an out-house. There was a small room or vestry attached, apparently for the use of the priest, or as a depository for the vestments and utensils connected with the celebration of the ancient worship[5]. From the architecture of the windows it is not improbable that the chapel may have been erected in the fourteenth century.

CHAPTER XVIII.

Donations to the Parish.

TOWN STOCK. At an early period lands and tenements in the counties of Berks, Oxon, Northampton, &c. were left by some now unknown benefactor, " *For the relief of decayed tradesmen*" (the words of the donor) in Burcester.

In the parish-archives, deposited over the church-porch, are grants of leases of these estates as early as the reign of Henry VII.; and probably, were the whole of the records carefully examined, the original deed of gift might be found.

Among the loose papers in the Wallingford chest (the only one I examined) is the following memorandum of the receipts in the fifteenth year of Elizabeth (A. D. 1572).

---

[5] Some have concluded that this room was designed for the habitation of the priest, from its containing a fire-place.

DONATIONS TO THE PARISH.

	s.	d.
For tenements in Souldern, *per annum*	10	0
One ditto in Woodstock	14	0
Another ditto in Woodstock	0	0
Stratton Audley, for arable land	4	0

This chest contains most of the bills of the parish expenses during the reign of Elizabeth; yet little use can be made of them, as frequently those containing the most desirable information are without dates; among these is one wherein the name and value of the lands belonging to the poor are specified, the sum total of which is twenty-six pounds and threepence three farthings.

A. D. 1598. On the 6th of April, in the forty-first year of Queen Elizabeth, decretal orders were issued by Sir William Spencer, Knt., John Welsborn, Francis Ewer, George Califord, and William Frere, Esquires, as commissioners appointed to direct the application of this charity, of which the following is the substance.

Every aged poor and impotent inhabitant relieved by the feoffees shall be relieved by the knowledge of the vicar, churchwardens, and four of the inhabitants rated highest in the subsidy books.

When all these are relieved, the profits remaining unbestowed are to be applied to the marriage of poor maidens born in and then inhabiting the parish of Bicester; and if there are no such maidens to be married, then with the like assent, to the mending of the highways, which no private person is bound to repair by tenure, prescription, composition, or otherwise.

No lease of any of the lands, tenements, &c., to be let for more than ten years from the date of the agreement.

No land shall be let for less than its yearly value, nor any fine taken, nor any poor person suffered to live on the estate.

If any disbursements are made contrary to these orders, the party making them to incur the loss.

The accounts to be audited in Whitsun week before the vicar, churchwardens, overseers, and other parishioners, and what money remains in hand to be put in the chest for the use of the poor.

It is decreed that in the next conveyance of the land, tenements, &c., to any persons and their heirs, which shall be made within three weeks after there shall be but four feoffees alive, these orders shall be rehearsed and acknowledged, to be for ever hereafter acknowledged and observed, and to be made by the consent of the feoffees of the lands and tenements; and that all former estates made heretofore by Wykins and Moore were made to the uses hereinbefore expressed. If any of the parties having interest in the lands shall not observe these orders, then the conveyance to their heirs and assigns to be void. "To avoid all disputes, ten shillings only are allowed to be spent at the yearly meeting about the account." Should any of them, the said vicar or churchwardens or overseers, disagree from the rest of them for any thing done in the premises, such dissenters shall give a reason for their disagreement (for it shall not be wilful); and if their reason be not allowed by the major part of the feoffees, all things shall be proceeded in according to these articles. Lastly, it is thought fit, notwithstanding any thing to the contrary, that a lease may be made of any dwelling-house to which no land is attached for twenty-one years, if the house be ruinous, and the lessee is bound by this lease to rebuild it.

Agreeable to the above decree, the mode of appointing feoffees is by indenture of bargain and sale of the enfeoffed lands, cottages, &c. by the surviving trustees, for five shillings for one year, to have and to hold by the rent of one peppercorn if demanded, for the use and purposes mentioned in the above decree, copied into a release.

DONATIONS TO THE PARISH.

The release is also by indenture, in which the former feoffees for ever quit claim to the above, and convey them to the persons specified, their heirs and assigns, according to the decretal orders which are copied into it.

The present feoffees are Sir G. P. O. Turner, Sir Henry W. Dashwood, John Coker, Esq., George Osmond, Richard Smith, Thomas Davis, John Blake Kirby, and Thomas Tubb. The enfeoffed lands, tenements, &c. are

	£.	s.	d.
At Lurgessall, in Bucks, one small public-house and premises adjacent, and twenty-eight acres of pasture land, producing *per annum*	120	0	0
Souldern, in Oxon, two cottages, one small close, and two closes of pasture of about twenty-eight acres, producing together	70	0	0
Land in Potter's-pury, Cosgrove, and Yardley, Northamptonshire	24	0	0
Bicester Market-end, a barn, yard, and two closes of arable land, of about twenty-eight acres	25	0	0
Two cottages in the same near the church	2	0	0
Workhouse in the same, let to the parish	16	0	0
Public funds 150*l.* in 3 per cents.	4	10	0
Total per annum £	261	10	0

It is evident the above decree admitted other objects to partake of the benefits of this charity besides decayed tradesmen; yet it is worth inquiry whether it might not be advisable to limit the application to the relief of those inhabitants for whom the donation was intended.

1749. At the audit holden May 18th it was ordered and agreed by those whose names are under-written, that if any poor persons who received any weekly payments out of the trust estate should receive collections from the parish, such weekly payments out of the trust estate should cease from the time of their becoming chargeable to the parish aforesaid. Signed John Coker, John Wilson, Mor. Stokes, John Egerton, &c.

To guard against this donation being in any ways applicable to the reduction of the poor's-rates, and becoming wrested to parochial purposes, the following oath is directed to be taken by one of the feoffees:

" A. B., residing in Bicester, in the county of Oxford, maketh oath and sayeth that the above account, signed by him, is a just and true account of the rents and profits of the messuages, lands, and tenements therein declared, and that the rents and profits arising from the same are wholly applied in the manner stated in the above account; viz. given to the poor of the parish of Bicester, in the county of Oxford, aforesaid, but not applicable to the reduction of the poor's-rates.

" And this deponent further declares that from his office of feoffee to the said charity, he hath a perfect knowledge of the regulation of the said charity, and of the due application of the rents and profits stated in the above account. Sworn, &c. &c."

These accounts are audited every Thursday in Whitsun-week [1].

1685. In the first year of James II. Sir WILLIAM GLYNN, Bart., of Ambrosden, patron of the church, gave for the use of such as are of the church of England, and belonging to the parish of Bicester, Two large flaggons of massy silver; one silver salver; one silver chalice and cover; a large carpet of purple velvet, with gold and silver fringe, for the communion

---

[1] Original records, books, &c. belonging to the feoffees.

table; a purple velvet cushion with gold and silk tassels; and a purple velvet cloth with gold and silk fringe, for the ornament of the pulpit.

There are several DONATIONS payable annually from different estates in the Market-end; but as every writing relative thereto is in the hands of the proprietors only, it is impossible to give any accurate account of the giver or even amount of the benefaction, since it is too often the disposition as well as the interest of the owner of the property not to let the particulars transpire. Hence these donations in a few years may be expected to be forgotten. The following is all I can collect respecting them.

Out of a leasehold estate in Bicester Market-end, held for the remainder of ten thousand years, of the lease granted to Wykins and Clements, 39 Eliz., consisting of Gillet's Slade; Short furlong ground; Long furlong ground; Freebord next to Launton-moor; a stone-built messuage next to Coney-lane, with farm-yard adjoining; a freehold and leasehold pasture called the Dairy ground; St. Peter's meadow and the home closes; is an annual payment to be made of one pound ten shillings for bread to be given to the poor. By an arrangement at a recent sale of these estates (May 21, 1813) the whole sum was agreed to be charged on the land, and accordingly is paid by the purchaser, Mr. John Proctor.

Mrs. MARY CARLTON, by indenture bearing date November 28, 1717, appointed forty-two shillings and sixpence, the rent of some land in Brill, to be paid into the hands of trustees on or before the 14th of February every year; to be by them expended in the following manner:

Twenty shillings to be given to the minister for the time being to preach a sermon in the afternoon of the second day in March in memory of her daughter Sarah, wife of Dr. Kennett, who died March 2, 1693. The clerk to give notice on the preceding Sunday.

Two shillings and sixpence to be given the clerk for *ringing out* the great bell before the sermon, and cleaning the monuments of Mrs. Kennett and her father, Mr. Robert Carver.

And forty sixpenny loaves of good wheaten bread to be distributed after the sermon among forty of the poorest widows, for the time being, inhabiting Bicester; or, if there are not so many, such as the minister and churchwardens shall appoint, so that such persons shall have the benefit during their lives.

To enable the churchwardens to procure this bread, the indenture directs the trustees of the charity to pay the money into their hands two days before the sermon is preached; and for the security of the whole sum being paid unto the trustees by the day appointed, they are directed in case of any neglect "to take the close and keep possession thereof until the same are satisfied."

The trustees are also directed to repair both the monuments as they may decay, and to deduct the expense out of the several sums in proportion to their amount.

To perpetuate this charity and service, the indenture directs that if the same should be neglected by the parish of Bicester, the donation should go to the minister and parish of Brill, subject to the same application, except cleaning the monuments; and in case of *their* not observing the conditions of the grant, it is further appropriated to the parish of Ambrosden, who are directed to apply it to the same purposes.

The above sum of forty-two shillings and sixpence issues out of a close containing three acres of pasture land, in the parish of Brill, conveyed to John Wilson and his heirs and assigns for fifty pounds. The lease bears date 17 and 18 days of September, 1 Ann. and granted by Mary Carver of Wallingford[*].

1734. Sir THOMAS GRANTHAM gave fifty pounds to John

---

[*] This indenture is in the possession of the churchwardens.

Burrows, gent., the interest of which he directed should be distributed yearly, at Christmas, among such poor widows as the churchwardens and overseers appoint.

A bond was accordingly given by John Burrows of Bicester to Thomas Airson the vicar for the same, but the interest only paid up to 1750.

" RICHARD BURROWS gave by will ten pounds per annum for apprenticing poor children.

" Mr. JOHN HART gave also by will ten pounds per annum for the same purpose of apprenticing children.—Both lost.

" In 1738 one Bowell was charged five pounds per annum on some lands for the purpose of apprenticing some poor children of Wendlebury, Bicester, and Chesterton alternately[a]."

1799. The Reverend THOMAS COKER left by will the sum of seventy pounds, to be given to the poor of this parish, which was accordingly given in bread at the town hall by the minister, churchwardens, and overseers, to two hundred and two families.

1811. WILLIAM WALKER, Esq., of Stamford-hill, Middlesex, in pursuance of the intention of his deceased father John Walker, Esq., of Hackney, in the above county, vested the sum of one thousand pounds three per cent. consolidated annuities, on the feoffees for the poor's lands, in trust, that the interest arising therefrom (deducting expenses connected therewith) might be perpetually applied to the following purposes.

Sixteen pounds per annum to be given to the charity-school in Bicester toward clothing and educating poor children belonging to or residing in this parish.

---

[a] Letter of Thomas, Bishop of Oxford, to Mr. Airson, vicar of Bicester, August 28, 1738. See parish papers.—The whole of these papers, including the above indenture, were found by Mr. Cook in a chest in London, and given to Mr. Smith, the present vicar.

Seven pounds per annum to be applied towards the support of the Sunday-school belonging to the same parish-church; and the remaining seven pounds per annum to be given to the Sunday-school supported by the Dissenters at the meeting-house in Water-lane.

The indenture directs that, if either of the latter schools should be discontinued, the sum applied towards its support shall be given to the charity-school in addition to the former donation.

The above grant was intended to have been settled upon the schools by Mr. John Walker, who was a constant subscriber to them for many years; but by some means omitted in his last will and testament. This intention being well known to his son, Mr. William Walker, he with a liberality seldom witnessed piously determined to carry the design into effect.

CHAPTER XIX.

Biographical Sketch of the Lords of the Manors of Bicester and Wretchwic.—Bailiwick of Bicester.

In the days of Edward the Confessor these villages belonged to Wigod, a powerful and noble thane, who, from the place of his usual residence, was known by the name of Wigod de Wallingford. The earliest records introduce him to our notice as a partisan of the Normans, and state that he met the victorious duke on his return from the battle of Hastings, invited him and his army into his castle of Wallingford, and entertained them for several days. That during the entertainment he had the satisfaction of seeing the nobles of the adverse party submit themselves to William, and tender him the crown and government; and that the pleasures of the feast were finally closed by the marriage of his daughter Aldith to Robert de Oilly, or de Oilgi, one of the most eminent of the Norman chieftains, and the particular friend of the king.

The death of Wigod happened shortly after the marriage of his daughter; and by the accession of his vast estates, and the personal favour of the monarch, Robert de Oilly, according to the best historians, became the most powerful man of his time[1]. At the command of his sovereign he repaired or rebuilt the castles of Oxford and Wallingford (A. D. 1071), and actuated by piety he extended similar favours to many churches within and without the walls of Oxford. His munificence built the great bridge, and his charity relieved the wants of many of the poor. But the monks embellish his history in the following manner:—They say that Robert being always supported by the king's favour grew rich, and injured many churches, and particularly robbed the church of Abingdon of a meadow near Oxford. That the prayers of the monks procured him a fit of sickness, and the horrors of a dream so frightened him that he hastened to the abbot, and before the high altar expiated his sacrilege by the donation of ten pounds per annum in Tadmarton, and large contributions towards

---

[1] Soon after the coronation of William he undertook a tour to the north of England; but finding on his approach to Oxford that the garrison resisted his authority and insulted his person, he stormed the city, and, having obtained possession, gave the greatest part of it to Robert de Oilly, who at the survey is reported to have, within and without the walls, forty-two inhabited houses and eight lying waste.

"In the late expedition Robert de Oilly brought over with him Roger de Ivery, a fellow adventurer and sworn brother, for they had mutually engaged by oath to be sharers in the same fortune, which was a sociable practice of that age. According to this compact, when the said Robert de Oilly had two honours given him beside the estate which came by his wife, he freely gave one of them (that afterwards called St. Waleries, of which Beckley was the capital seat, and within which Ambrosden was included,) to this Roger de Ivery." Kenn. p. 56.

rebuilding St. Mary's Church. He died in September 1090[2], 4 William Rufus.

Milo Crispin married the daughter of Robert[3], and on his death succeeded to the estates of Wallingford, Bicester, Wretchwic, &c.; but the honours of D'Oilly, with Oxford Castle, &c. passed to his brother Nigel. Milo died in 1107, and six years after his widow married again.

Brien Fitz Count, her second husband, was the natural son of Alan Fergunt, earl of Brittany and Richmond, who came over with the conqueror, by Lucia, daughter of Diu de Baladon, lord of Overwent in Wales. He is chiefly remarkable for his attachment to the Empress Maud, to whose fortunes he adhered under the most trying circumstances. To enumerate his various services would be to give the whole history of the conflict. His life and fortune he devoted to her interest; armed his vassals in her cause; exposed his castles to the horrors of a siege, and his estates to forfeiture; yet after all had the pleasure of seeing the cause he had espoused finally triumph. His domestic peace was embittered, however, by the recollection that both his sons were lepers, and unable to succeed him in these military enterprises. Placing them, therefore, in the priory of Abergavenny, and assigning lands for their support; in conformity with the superstition of the age he took the cross and departed for Jerusalem. Tired of the world his lady also retired to a convent, and the honour of

---

[2] He left no heirs male: hence Nigel succeeded to the honours of D'Oilly, the capital seat of which was Hooknorton.—Kennett, p. 72.

[3] Milo Crispin married between the survey and 1084. He had large possessions at that period, and generally resided at the castle of Wallingford after his marriage. In his sickness he gave to Fabricus and the monks of Abingdon an inn at Colbrook, with half a hyde of land, and sent Gilbert Pipart, his steward, and Warin his priest, to deliver possession upon the altar of Abingdon. To the abbey of Bec in Normandy he gave all the tithes of the honour of Wallingford and the manor of Swanscomb.—Dugdale's Baronage.

OF BICESTER AND WRETCHWIC.

Wallingford thus reverting into the hands of the king, was for some time retained as a part of the possessions of the crown.

It seems that during the time of Milo Crispin seven knights' fees [4] of the honour of Wallingford were granted to Gilbert Basset, a younger son of Ralph Basset, chief justice of England, and amongst these fees are the villages of Bicester, Wretchwic, and Stratton particulary specified (A. D. 1107). In conformity to the principles of the feudal system Gilbert Basset zealously adhered to his superior lord, Brien Fitz Count, and was present in most of the encounters. Tinctured also with superstition he was a benefactor to the religious; gave lands and tenements at Charing to the Knights Templars, and the tithes of hay and corn in Bicester and Stratton to the monks of Eynsham. He died 8 Henry I. A. D. 1162.

In the 10th of Henry II. Thomas, his son and successor, was sheriff of Oxon, and soon after appointed one of the itinerant justices. Special services in war procured him the grant of the lordship of Hedington, the hundred of Bolendon, and the hundred without the north gate of Oxford: and this branch of the family were henceforward styled "The Bassets of Hedendon." By his wife Alice de Dunstanville he left one daughter and three sons, Gilbert, Thomas, and Alan. The daughter was afterwards married to Albert de Grelle. He died in 1179.

In the history of Bicester his son Gilbert Basset is chiefly remarkable as the founder of the priory; but as a baron he is noticed as one of the attendants at the coronation of King Richard; and as a feudatory tenant of the honour of Walling-

---

[4] These seven fees consisted of the manors of Coleham and Uxbridge, com. Midd. Picheleshorne, com. Buck. Burncestre, Stratton, and Wrechwike, com. Oxon. Ardington, com. Berks. and Compton in com. Wilts.—Kenn. p. 162, 163.

ford, by his adherence to the cause of Earl John, for which he was compelled to purchase the king's pardon at the expense of eight pounds. The remaining incidents of his life may be comprised in the one hundred pound fine which he paid for leave to marry his daughter Eustace to Thomas de Verdon, a baron and lord of Heth, who shortly after died in Ireland;—in the excommunication passed upon him as an adherent of Earl John;—and in his great benefactions to the Knights Templars. It is generally supposed that he died and was interred abroad in 1203; but his wife Egiline de Courteney survived him several years, and was buried in Bicester priory about 1213[s].

On the death of Thomas de Verdon the guardianship of the young widow became a valuable prize to the possessor, and Gerard de Camvil, lord of Middleton, immediately gave one thousand pounds for this purpose and leave to marry her to his son Richard (A. D. 1200). From an inquisition taken on their succession to the honours of her father, the *return* of seven knight's fees is a proof that no part of the original grant had been hitherto alienated; and the fine of two thousand marks and ten palfreys conveys an idea of the nature and extent of a *relief*. It is probable that henceforward the lords of Bicester abandoned the mansion and park of Gilbert Basset for the castle of Middleton, and from that period to the final disposal of the manor there does not appear to have been any edifice in the town sufficiently capacious to afford them a residence.

Nothing has reached these times concerning Richard Camvil, except his confirmation of the charters of the founder and foundress of the priory, and a trifling grant to the same religious house. He died in 1215, and his daughter and heir,

---

[s] Egelin de Courtenai est de do'ne d'ui R. et t'ra ejus valet in Burnestr, lv^{li}.—Testa de Nevil. Record Hen. III. p. 167.

Idonea, was given in wardship to William Longspe, earl of Salisbury (son of the celebrated fair Rosamond), with liberty of disposing her in marriage to William his son.

The extensive possessions accompanying the marriage of Idonea de Camvil enabled the second William Longspe to urge his claim to the earldom of Salisbury with greater force[6]; but the necessity of deterring men of noble birth and splendid talents from joining the ranks of an invader, by despoiling the offender and his posterity of their honours, rendered every application for that dignity unavailing. Yet to convince him that no personal considerations influenced the decision, his sovereign granted him the several manors of Audiberne, Wamberg, and a moiety of Shrivesham, by the service of two knight's fees.

Renowned in the profession of arms, in 1236 Longspe took the cross, and the legend says, " The terror of his name brought peace to the Christian world." Returning the same year, he so materially contributed to the victory of Xantoigne (27 Henry III.) that the king, in the fulness of his gratitude, granted him sixty marks out of the exchequer till he should obtain judgment on the earldom he claimed, which was promised immediately on the king's return to England.

Again disappointed in his expectations, he once more took upon him the cross (A.D. 1247); but his finances having failed him by the time he had reached Rome, he approached the pope and thus addressed him: "Sir, you perceive I am signed with the cross, and about to fight in this pilgrimage; my martial reputation is great, but my estate is slender; for the king of England, my kinsman, hath deprived me of my title and estate; but as he did it judicially and not in displeasure I do not blame him. Involved in distress I am necessitated to have recourse to your holiness for assistance; and observing that Richard earl of Cornwall, though he is not signed with the cross, through the special grace of your highness, has collected

---

[6] His father forfeited the earldom by joining Lewis, son of the King of France.

many sums from those who are, I presume, to solicit the like favour, &c." The pope, considering the elegance of his address and the comeliness of his person, granted his request, and he immediately received above one thousand marks from those who had signed.

Two years however elapsed before he proceeded in this expedition, a part of which time was spent in his native land; but in July 1250, having received the blessing of his mother, Ela, abbess of Lacock, who had obtained a high repute for sanctity, he joined the French forces in the Holy Land, with many of the nobility and two hundred horsemen. The king of France received them with the greatest respect, and their valour was shortly displayed in the conquest of one of the strongest towers near Alexandria.

Their march eastward affording them opportunities of seizing on many caravans, and the success usually attendant on their enterprises, excited the jealousy of the French, and produced such marks of enmity that Longspe and his followers resolved to remain at Acre with the Knights Templars till the arrival of the rest of the English nobles, to whom he designed to represent his treatment from the French. But before the end of the year, passing from Damietta towards Cairo, the Saracens fell upon them with superior forces, and compelled the brave band to risk an engagement. In the desperate conflict Longspe, after killing more than one hundred with his own hand, had the misfortune to be overpowered and fell. His bravery secured him a grave among his enemies, and two years afterwards his remains were removed with due ceremony, and entombed by the Christians in the church of St. Cross, at Acre in Palestine.

Mathew Paris reports that the night before his death (A.D. 1250, 34 Henry III.) " Ela his mother saw in a vision the heavens open, and her son in complete armour, which she knew by his shield, received with joy by the angels, and she asking 'Who is this?' was answered, 'Do you not know your son William and his armour?' she said, 'Yes,' and was answered, 'It is he whom his mother now seeth.' She kept the vision in her mind; and when about six months afterwards his fate was told her, she lifted up her hands and with a cheerful countenance said, 'I, thy handmaid, give thee thanks, O Lord, that out of my sinful flesh thou hast caused such a champion against thy enemies to be born.'" And the same author adds that, "When messengers were sent two years after to the Soldan of Babylon for the redemption of prisoners taken in war, the Soldan said, 'I wonder much at you Christians who reverence the bones of the dead, that you do not inquire for those of the renowned and right noble William Longspe, because many strange things are reported of them (whether true or not I cannot say), namely, that in the dead of night there have been appearances at his tomb, and that to some who have called upon his God, many things have been bestowed from heaven. For which cause, and in consideration of his nobility and worth, we have caused his body to be here entombed.' Whereupon, at the messenger's desire, the body was delivered to them by the Soldan, and from thence carried to *Acre*, and interred in the church of St. Cross."

On the intelligence of this hero's death reaching England, in conformity with the usages of that age, the king seized all his lands, but restored them to his widow Idonea upon her doing homage. At her death William her son succeeded to the estates of Bicester, Middleton, &c. (A. D. 1252); but part of the estates in Stratton and Wretchwic passed to James, baron of Audley, in frank marriage with Ela his wife, a daughter of the deceased William Longspe.

Little is known of the third William Longspe, except his marriage with Maud, daughter of Walter Clifford, with whom he received a dowry of twenty-eight pounds two shillings and eight-pence in land at Galmington, Salop; and that his credit was injured in a tournament at Blythe. Yet he seems to have engaged in military enterprises, for we find him contracting his daughter Margaret to Henry Lacy, eldest son of the earl of Lincoln, at the wars in Gascony (1256); and assigning the homages, rents, and services of Middleton and Bicester manor for her dowry. But it appears that the marriage was not consummated for several years.

Cut down in the prime and vigour of life (A.D. 1257, 41 Henry III.), his widow Maud was compelled by the custom of the realm to promise on oath she would not marry again without the king's consent ere her dowry was assigned her: yet with true female policy, having placed her affections upon and privately married the Baron John Gifford; she made a grievous complaint to the king that he had taken her by force from her manor-house at Kaneford, and conveyed her to his castle at Brimesfield, and still kept her in restraint. On being sent for, the baron judiciously denied the charge, paid a fine of three hundred marks for marrying her without the king's consent, and, having promised no farther complaint should be made, returned to enjoy the success of the scheme, which had thus secured the estates. In her widowhood she had carefully provided for the weal of her departed husband, by the gift of the lordship of Cavenby, Lincolnshire; four additional canons being appointed to Barlings in the same county, to pray for the souls of William and Maud Longspe.

The wardship of the youthful heir and heiress was in the hands of the king and queen, till Alice, the mother of Henry Lacy, obtained the grant of her husband's lands, and guardianship of her son, for the fine of three thousand seven hundred and fifty-four pounds[7]. By his marriage with Margaret Longspe he acquired the earldom of Salisbury, together with all her father's lands. In 1272 he was knighted with Edward, son to Richard king of Almain, then made earl of Lincoln, and the same year appointed governor

---

[7] Kennett, p. 271.

of Knaresborough castle. At this time his influence with King Edward procured charters for fairs and markets at his manors of Dunnington, Leicestershire; Buckby, Northamptonshire; Wainfleet, Wrangel, and Torreney, Lincoln.

The martial spirit of Lacy first displayed itself in a quarrel with Earl Warren, respecting a pasture near Crendon, which both parties proposed to settle their right to by battle. Forces were raised; but the King interposed, and from an inquiry it appeared justice was on the side of Lacy. Fortune had reserved him a more glorious field for his noviciate; and in the 10th of Edward I. he accompanied that monarch in his expedition into Wales. After its conquest he so studied the art of fortifying the north and marches, that the King granted him the land of Denbigh, where he built a town, walled, and erected a castle, calling it by the same name. On the front of the castle was his statue in long robes, and that of Margaret his wife; and anciently prayers were made for Percy and Lacy. His statue still ornaments the entrance, but his lady's has lately fallen down [8].

Having been long married, and doubting whether he should have any children, he surrendered into the King's hands many of his large possessions, on condition of their being restored in case of the accomplishment of that desirable event; and this it seems had taken place before 1291, for on the 28th of December, Edward I. restored them to him at Newcastle. He was, however, unfortunate in his sons; for one of them died in his minority, and the other was afterwards drowned in a deep well in the castle, on which account that structure was left unfinished.

In 1292 he was appointed ambassador to France, to form a treaty for restraining pirates from robbing merchants' ves-

---

[8] Dugdale, p. 104. The statue of the founder over the castle is inclosed in a frame of buds and stalks, and a figure of his wife Margaret on his left hand in a similar niche was lately pulled down. Gough's Camden, vol. 2, p. 579.

sels[9]. The next year he accompanied the King in another expedition into Wales, but received a repulse not far from Denbigh: the expedition, however, terminated favourably. The three following years he fought with doubtful success in Gascony and Scotland; and during the whole reign of Edward was continually employed in wars or negotiations. Such was the high opinion that monarch entertained of his probity and fidelity, that on his death-bed he exacted the promise "to be good to his son, and never to permit his favourite Gaveston's return into England." In compliance with his dying master's request, he with others entered into a solemn league for the defence of the young king's honour, and the rights of his crown. In return he was constituted governor of Skipponcastle, and about three years afterwards appointed governor of the realm in the king's absence, 1310.

In the last years of his life he had the mortification of seeing Gaveston triumph over the king's affections, and by his ill conduct likely to involve the country in the heaviest calamities. The barons had confederated to oppose the favourite, and in the last illness of Lacy he sent for Thomas Earl of Lancaster, who had married his only daughter Alice, and thus addressed him: "Seest thou the Church of England heretofore honourable and free, enslaved by Romish superstitions and the King's unjust exactions;—seest thou the common people impoverished by tribute and taxes, and reduced to slavery, and the nobility vilified by aliens in their own native country! I therefore charge you in the name of God and Christ, to stand up like a man for the honour of God and his Church, and the redemption of your country: associate yourself with Guy Earl of Warwick, when it is proper to debate of the affairs of your country, and fear no opposers;

---

[9] A description of this bloody piratical war may be seen in Hume's England, page 182, vol. 2. Edin. ed. 1803.

thus shall you gain eternal honour." He departed this life at his mansion called Lincoln's Inn, in the suburbs of London, A. D. 1310; was one of the greatest barons in the realm; had possessions in Bucks, Berks, Dorset, Hereford, Derby, Middlesex, Lincolnshire, Leicestershire, Northamptonshire, Nottinghamshire, Staffordshire, Somerset, and Wales. He was in many instances a liberal benefactor to the religious, particularly Bicester, Salcy, &c. To the canons of Bourscough he ratified the grant of Henry Torbock, and Eleve his wife, of a place called Ruddegate, with this proviso, that a leper from the lordship of Wideness should be admitted and maintained in the priory, mass celebrated at Easter, and his name, and the name of Margaret his wife, registered in their Martyrology.

By his interest with Edward I. he procured charters for many markets on his different manors. Among the rest he obtained the appointment of a Monday market, and annual fair on the eve and day of St. Thomas the Apostle, at Middleton (Stoney) A. D. 1293, 21 Edward I. which it is likely was attended by the neighbouring villagers till the establishment of one in Bicester.

After the death of Margaret Longspe he married Joan the sister and heir of William Martin, who survived him; and afterwards without the king's license married Nicholas de Audley.—He left Alice his only daughter and heir contracted to Thomas son and heir of Edmund Earl of Lancaster, A. D. 1282, then only nine years of age.

An inquisition taken immediately on the Earl of Lincoln's death informs us that he held the manor of Bicester in right of his wife as *of the honour of Wallingford,* by military service; that there were within the manor one hundred and sixty acres of land; that the prior of Bicester held of him the site of the priory, four carucates of land, twenty acres of meadow, and one water-mill, with other appurtenances of forty pounds yearly value, together with the church of the said town of thirty marks value, and the manor of Wretchwic of twenty pounds per annum.

Thomas Earl of Lancaster, husband of Alice Lacy, who succeeded in her right to to the estates of Bicester and Middleton, was first prince of the blood; and by the union of the Lincoln estates with his paternal domains, attended with all the jurisdiction and power annexed to landed property in that age, was by far the most powerful and opulent subject in the kingdom. It was no wonder, therefore, that he mortally hated Gaveston, who had concentrated all the regal authority in himself, and treated the ancient nobility with contempt. Lancaster's vast possessions and influence soon made him the chief of the confederate barons; and success attending their cause, he was made hereditary *Steward of England*.

A. D. 1311. When the weak Edward could no longer bear the absence of his minion, and the return of Gaveston lighted up the flames of civil war, the Earl of Lancaster once more put himself at the head of the malcontents, and pursued the king and his favourite from York to Newcastle. On his arrival he found the king had escaped to Tynemouth, and from thence sailed to Scarborough, where he had lodged the favourite in the castle. Besieged by the Earl of Pembroke, Gaveston surrendered on condition of safety till a general pacification. Under colour of fulfilling the conditions, Pembroke conducted him to Deddington castle between Bicester and Banbury, where he left him with a feeble guard under pretence of other business. In his absence the Earl of Warwick, probably as concerted with Pembroke, attacked the castle; the garrison refused to resist; and the unfortunate Gaveston was taken to Warwick castle, where Lancaster, Hereford, and Arundel, ordered him to immediate execution.

Though the anger of the confederates was somewhat appeased by the death of the favourite, their designs were not completed. They repeatedly attempted to impose restrictions on the King, and the kingdom was perpetually subject to outrages from the different partisans. In one of these, Alice the wife of Thomas of Lancaster was taken by violence from his seat at Caneford in Dorset, by the Earl of Warrene, and conducted to Rygate castle. In their journey the party were sadly frightened by a company with banners at a distance, which they suspected were coming to her rescue; and they fled with precipitation: but closer observation proving them only a religious procession, they returned and took the lady. As they passed, a mean crook-backed fellow challenged the countess for wife, alleging he had known her before she was married; which not being denied, she was delivered up to him, and in her right he afterwards claimed the earldoms of Lincoln and Salisbury in the King's court. This event occasioned a divorce between Alice and Thomas Earl of Lancaster.

1317. The estates of Middleton and Bicester remained with Alice after her divorce; but whether she ever married the crook-backed *Richard de St. Martin* is unknown. Stowe says the separation from Lancaster could produce no regret, for they had no regard for each other.

In 1323, having married Eubolo Le Strange, son of John Lord of Knockyn, (for whom she had long had an affection,) without the King's consent, all her estates were seized, and she was obliged to renounce the whole of her property except three thousand marks *per annum* [10]. Bicester and Middleton were surrendered to Hugh Despencer the younger; and Kennett intimates that these forfeitures were imposed by Roger Mortimer Earl of March.

Their property was afterwards increased by the fee of De la Hay, and an annuity for the third penny of Lincoln out of

---

[10] She had originally estates to the amount of ten thousand marks per annum.

the forfeitures of her former husband [11]. And four years after the downfall of Hugh Despencer, the King regranted them many of their estates, among which were Bicester and Middleton.

On the death of Eubolo, occasioned by fatigue in the Scottish wars (1335), Alice married Sir Hugh de Fresnes, a French knight, who shortly after died of a bloody flux [12].

The eventful life of Alice closed the Thursday after the feast of St. Michael, 23 Edward III. at the age of sixty-seven, and is thus entered in an ancient MS. in the Cotton Library: "Moritur Alesia Comitissa Lincolniæ, anno ætatis suæ 67 & anno Gratiæ 1348, circa festum S. Mathæi Apostoli & Evangelistæ, & sepulta est in ecclesia canonicorum de Berlyng, juxta corpus Eubulonis mariti sui, nec reliquit post se hæredem aliquem de suo corpore procreatum, sed in ejus morte sanguis & hæreditaria successio ultimæ progeniei de Lacy (proh dolor) terminatur [13].

The estates of Bicester and Middleton on the death of Alice passed to *Sir Roger Le Strange*, of Knockyn, who had married Joan a daughter and coheir of Oliver de Ingram, a descendant of Isabel daughter and coheir of William Longspe [14].—Sir Roger was eminent in the wars of Edward III. and in the sixth year of that monarch found ten men at arms and sixteen archers.— He died July 29, 1349, leaving Roger his son and heir twenty-two [15] years of age, by Maud his first wife.

This nobleman also was in most of the expeditions against France in the reigns of Edward and Richard II. He died 26th

---

[11] Anciently territorial jurisdiction and official power were attached to the dignity of an earl, and he was allowed the third penny of the pleas of the county for his support. In the reign of Edward III. this dignity became titular: the sheriff is now the king's officer.

[12] Kenn. p. 427. Dugdale's Baronage, vol. i. p.6 68.

[13] Monast. Anglic. tom. ii. p. 190.

[14] Topographer, vol. ii. p. 312. London, 1790.

[15] The manor of Middleton was settled as a jointure on Joan his mother-in-law, afterwards married to Sir Miles de Stapleton.

August, 1382, (6 Richard II.) Bicester and Middleton remained with Aliva, his relict, till her death, A. D. 1386.

After the death of Sir John their son and heir, (1398) his wife Maud [16], daughter and coheir of Sir John de Mohun, held the estate till her decease (5 Henry IV.) September 20, 1403 [17].

1409. The possession of the manor by Sir Richard their son is marked by a trial in the King's-bench for the manor of Middleton, which was adjudged to him on proving his descent from Roger, brother to Eubolo Le Strange the husband of Alice de Lacy [18].

In 1415 [19], on Easter Sunday in the afternoon, *Constance* the wife of Sir Richard Le Strange contended with the wife of Sir John Trussel, of Warmington, Cheshire, for precedency of place, at the sermon in St. Dunstan's church, East-Cheap, London: upon which disturbance the two husbands and all the retinue engaged in the quarrel. In the fray several were wounded, and one Thomas Petwarden, fishmonger, slain. On the affair being reported to the Archbishop of Canterbury, he suspended the church, and caused the sentence of excommunication to be read against the authors of it in all the churches in the city. On the 21st of April the said Archbishop sat at St. Magnus to inquire of the authors of that disorder, when he found the fault to be in the Lord Strange and his wife, who upon the first of May following submitted themselves to penance, which was thus enjoined them: "That immediately all their servants, in their shirts, go before the parson of St. Dunstan's, from Paul's to St. Dunstan's church, and the lord bare-headed with a wax taper lighted, and the lady barefooted; Reginald Kenwold, archdeacon of London,

---

[16] Elizabeth mother of Maud is reported to have begged from her husband as much land as she could walk round barefoot in one day, to give for a common to the inhabitants of the town of Dunster, Salop. Kennett, p. 527, apud Cambden.   [17] Ib. p. 542.   [18] Ib. p. 552.

[19] Stow says 1417, Annales, p. 352.

following them; and at the hallowing of the church, the lady should fill all the vessels with water, and should offer an ornament of *tenne pound*, and the Lord Strange should offer a *pixe* of five pounds."—A good example of discipline and obedience [20].

Notwithstanding the above *irreligious* act, the susceptibility of her mind to religious impressions may be gathered from her last will and testament (8th March, 1438), wherein she bequeaths her body to ecclesiastical sepulture, wherever it should please her husband, granting five pounds for a *placebo*, dirge, and two hundred masses for the repose of her soul [21].

Sir Richard died 27 Henry VI. leaving John his son and heir five years of age, by Elizabeth his second wife, daughter of Reginald Lord Cobham of Sterborough [22].

Joane the sole daughter and heir of Sir John Le Strange, and Jacquet [23] his wife, daughter to Richard Widvill Earl Rivers, married George, son and heir-apparent to Thomas Stanley first Earl of Derby, whereby the manor passed into that family.

Dugdale informs us that this George received the order of the Bath with prince Edward, 18th April, 15 Edward IV.; and was summoned to parliament by the title of *Lord Strange of Knockyn,* from the time of his marriage till the 12th of Henry VII. The fidelity of the Stanleys to the family of Edward IV. was so well known to their uncle Richard, that after he assumed the sceptre, and the children had disappeared, all communication was forbidden with the Earl of Richmond, who then was considered the head of the adverse party. To gain their favour the father was appointed steward of the house-

---

[20] Kennett, p. 560.   [21] Ibid.

[22] The Inquisition recites " the manor of Burcestre held of the King as part of the honour of Wallingford by the service of the thirtieth part of one knight's fee. Ib. p. 662. Dugdale, vol. iv. p. 666.

[23] Sister to Elizabeth, wife of Edward IV. Dugdale, vol. i. p. 666.

hold, constable of England, and knight of the Garter. Suspicion, however, so preyed upon the mind of the king, that he refused Lord Stanley permission to retire into the country, till he had given up Lord Strange as a pledge for his fidelity [24]. But even this did not finally prevent his acting against that monarch. On the evening of the fatal battle he took the doubtful post of *Atherstone* (nearly at an equal distance from both parties), and this ambiguous conduct induced some of Richard's courtiers to advise the immediate sacrifice of the Lord Strange [25]. Nothing but the hope of preserving the father's allegiance, by this invaluable prize, till victory over his enemies placed him in a fearless state, withheld the King from following their advice: nor till the armies had joined battle did the Lord Stanley deem it prudent to join his friends; and the disastrous issue of the fatal battle of Bosworth for ever prevented Richard's resenting the desertion.

To reward Lord Stanley's important services, the victor created him Earl of Derby on the day of his coronation; but no additional honour was bestowed on Lord Strange.—Dying during his father's life-time, his son Thomas had livery of his lands 9th July, 19 Henry VII. and succeeded to the earldom of his grandfather in the reign of Henry VIII. Of the latter nobleman little has reached us, save his accompanying Henry into France, when he won Theroune and Tournay; and that by will he requested to be buried at Bourscough, Lancashire; Syon Monastery, Middlesex; or Asherrugge College, according to the county in which he might die. Departing this life at Culham, 24th May 1521, he was buried accordingly at Syon.

The life of Henry, his eldest son and successor, abounds in incidents. He was one of the principal persons in Wolsey's

---

[24] Lord Stanley's having married the mother of the Earl of Richmond naturally led Richard to suspect him. See Dugdale, vol. ii. p. 248.

[25] He had a private interview with the Earl of Richmond the day before the battle. *Ibid.*

embassy to France, and was afterwards employed to demand the liberty of Pope Clement on the Duke of Bourbon's sacking Rome (22 Henry VIII.). He was one of those peers who subscribed the declaration sent to the Pope, stating the danger of his supremacy if he did not favour Henry's divorce. He was afterwards employed to raise forces to oppose the insurrection of "the Pilgrimage of Grace," a name assumed by the rebels who endeavoured to support the ancient religion (28 Henry VIII. A. D. 1536). He also attended the Duke of Norfolk, with many others of the nobility, in the Scottish wars (1542), though he did not long remain there. In the commencement of the reign of Edward VI. he was made knight of the Garter, and in the fourth year of the same reign witnessed the ratification of peace with France and Scotland.

Enrolled among the partisans of Mary, he was constituted High Steward of England at her coronation, and seems to have remained in her favour. By Elizabeth he was appointed a privy counsellor, and doubtless continued in that honour till his death, which happened at Latham in 1572, when he was buried in the parish church of Ormskirk, where by will he directed that a chapel[26] and tomb should be erected; the monastery of Bourscough, which was the burial-place of his ancestors, having fallen in the general wreck of religious houses.

... Henry, his son and heir, who succeeded him, was summoned to Parliament in the eighteenth year of Elizabeth, and afterwards employed in many important affairs. In 1585 he was sent with a numerous suite to carry the ensigns of the Garter to the king of France. The following year he was one of the peers who sat at Fotheringay upon the trial of the Queen of Scotland; and two years afterwards was sent with other commissioners to treat with the Prince of Parma, general of the king of Spain's forces in the Netherlands.

---

[26] Dugdale, p. 249, 250.

32. Elizabeth.—Dugdale describes the last important office which he filled as that of Lord High Steward of England, upon the trial of the Earl of Arundel. He died the 25th of September 1594, and according to his will was buried in his chapel of Ormskirk.

By his countess Margaret, daughter to the Earl of Cumberland, he had three sons, two of whom, Ferdinand and William, were successively Earls of Derby.

Ferdinand his son outlived him but a short time, and is chiefly remarkable for the manner of his death, thought by physicians to have been occasioned by a surfeit taken from violent exercise in Easter week; but firmly believed by the common people to have been effected by witchcraft. Stow has detailed every circumstance connected herewith at length; and as it affords a curious instance of the credulity of that age, an abstract of the account may not be unacceptable.

1594. The first of April, the Monday before His Honour fell sick, a woman presented a petition to him, requesting him to grant her a dwelling near his residence, that she might speedily reveal those things which God showed her for his good. The petition was thought vain, and refused.

April 4. He dreamed his Lady was sick unto death; was troubled in sleep in consequence, but awaking and finding her well was comforted. Divers grave men had strange dreams or divinations concerning him about this time.

April 5. There appeared suddenly in his chamber at Krönstey, about six o'clock at night, the figure of a tall man, with a ghastly and threatening countenance, who seemed to cross him in his chamber; and when the Earl approached the part where the spectre appeared, he fell sick. His secretary however saw nothing. The same night he dreamed he received several stabs in fighting.

April 10. About midnight one Master Halsal found in the bed-chamber of the earl a spotted image of wax with hair similar to His Honour's, twisted through the body. This image Halsal says he cast into the fire before it was viewed, thinking thereby to burn the witch, and relieve his lord; but the contrary fell out, for he declined daily afterwards.

April 12. One Jane, a witch, demanded of Master Goborne whether His Lordship felt pain in his lower parts, and whether he made water as yet; and that very night, notwithstanding all help, it stopped, and so remained till he died.

Several justices examined certain witches; one of whom they conjured in the name of Jesus, that if she had bewitched His Honour she should not be able to say the Lord's Prayer: accordingly she never could repeat the petition '*forgive us our trespasses,*' though often repeated to her.

A homely woman, about fifty years of age, was found mumbling in a corner of His Honour's chamber; but what, God knoweth. Sometimes she seemed to ease His Honour; but whenever she did she seemed to suffer his pains, and partake of his complaint. While mixing and blessing certain herbs, one of the doctors who attended the Earl turned her out of the room; yet afterwards she said she could ease but not perfectly help him, His Honour was so strongly bewitched. All physic wrought well, but procured him no ease. His pulse remained good, and as perfect as when in his best health till one quarter of an hour before he died. During the whole time of his sickness he cried out the doctors laboured in vain, for he was certainly bewitched. Twice when he would have taken physic he fell into a trance. In the end he often cried out against all witches and witchcraft, reposing his only hope of salvation on the merits of Christ Jesus, our Saviour [27].

Dugdale, with much probability, supposes him poisoned, though he does not hint that suspicion fell upon any one. According to his will he was buried at Ormskirk. He left

---

[27] Stow's Annales, p. 767-768.

issue by Alice his wife, daughter to Sir John Spencer of Althorpe, Northumberland, three daughters; Ann, married to Grey Burges Lord Chandois; Frances, to Sir John Egerton, Knight, afterwards Earl of Bridgwater; and Elizabeth, to Henry Lord Hastings, afterwards Earl of Huntington.

William, his brother, succeeded him in his honours; but was speedily involved in a dispute with the daughters of his deceased brother, relative to his title to the Isle of Man, under pretence of its harbouring the queen's open enemies and many English runagates. Elizabeth committed the protection of it to Sir Thomas Gerrard till the controversy was determined. After much delay the commissioners for the inquiry declared that the Earl of Derby had no good title, because Henry IV. on the outlawry of W. Scrope (then Lord) bestowed it on the Earl of Northumberland; and upon the latter's rebellion, six years after, granted it to John Stanley for life, Northumberland not being attainted, nor his possessions adjudged confiscate: that this title being found defective, about a month afterwards, the king and Stanley agreed those letters-patent to him for life should be surrendered and cancelled, and the estate be granted in fee: so that, considering the grant being made before the earl was legally attainted, they pronounced the king could not pass unto him any estate for life, and the other could not be valid. The matter was settled by the earl's paying to the widow and daughters of the late earl several sums of money, to quit their claims; and afterwards the sovereign granted it to him and his heirs [28].

The manor and estates, comprising nearly the whole of the town and parish of Bicester (except the grants to the dissolved priory), had passed in regular descent through several females, but strictly according to the laws of primogeniture, from Gilbert Basset the elder to the present Earl of Derby.

---

[28] Dugdale, vol. ii. p. 251.

But in 1596 this nobleman, in consideration of Thomas Wykins of London and Thomas Clements of Burcester paying him the sum of seven hundred and fifty pounds, by indenture bearing date the 29th of June, 39th of Elizabeth, granted for a term of ten thousand years to come all his right and title to the manor and lordship of Burcester, with all its members and appurtenances whatsoever; also all and singular messuages, houses, out-houses, barns, edifices, and buildings of every kind; meadows, leases, pastures, feedings, commons of pastures, heaths, marshes, woods, underwoods, ways, waters, fishings, rents, &c.; courts leet, court baron, frank pledge, profit of court, waifs, estrays, goods of felons, fugitives, and outlaws; knights' fees, wards, marriages, escheats, reliefs, heriots, fines, amercements, &c.; and all profits belonging to the manor of Burcester: together with the woods and underwoods called *Earles Hill*, in Ambrosden, and a close and cottage in Arncott, to be held for their own use and benefit, they covenanting to pay the said Earl of Derby and his heirs every year, at the feast of St. Michael the Archangel, one penny. The indenture further provides for and acknowledges the delivery of all muniments, charters, evidences, &c., to the aforesaid Thomas Wykins and Thomas Clements, relative to the manor and estates, which it describes held by the earl as in fee-simple or in fee-tail [19]. The indenture is signed by the Earl of Derby (Will. Derby) in a very stiff hand, and has a small seal appending; is witnessed by Thomas Ireland, Joseph Sparkes, and Deborah Wymow, and on the back signed by Thomas Clements. The term of ten thousand years commences from the feast of St. Michael following the date of the indenture.

A few years after the date of the lease for ten thousand years Lord Derby conveyed *the reversion in fee-simple* in the

---

[19] The original deeds are in the possession of the present Mr. Coker.

manor, &c. &c. to certain persons in trust, for all the persons interested in that lease. This grant of the reversion is particularly mentioned in the following decree of the Court of Chancery; and the several persons interested in the lease are by that decree declared to be lords of the manor, &c. &c.

BAILIWICK OF BICESTER.

The manor, estates, &c., hereby becoming the property of those gentlemen for ten thousand years to come, was henceforward denominated a bailiwick, and regarded as "purchased for the benefit of those inhabitants, or others who might hereafter obtain possession of parts of the demesne" now offered for sale[30]. Accordingly we find Wykins and Clements soon after disposing of several estates by lease; and in all probability on the same conditions on which they purchased them. But when they had afterwards obtained the reversion of the manor, &c. they wished either to regain or retain the chief part of the manorial rights, which was opposed by the last purchasers, and "various law-suits commenced." To end these, an order was obtained in Chancery for the matters in dispute to be settled by arbitration; and John Welsborne of Fulwell, and James Power of Blechingdon, Esquires; Robert Wincott of W. and Eudulphe Dingley of Yarnton, gents., were appointed arbitrators. These by a decree dated the 1st of April, 3rd of James I. (A. D. 1605), finally ordained that Thomas Clements and his sons (probably Thomas Wykins having no longer interest therein) should resign all claim to the royalty of the manor or town of Burchester, together with the profit of the court-leet and court-baron, which should be assigned in that way which the majority of partisans to the decree should appoint, *for their use and benefit.* "Also in like manner to resign the bailiwick to

---

[30] See a letter from Mr. T. Clements to Mr. T. Coker, when in treaty for the purchase of the estates.

the same persons; and to prevent all disputes respecting the appointment of bailiff, John Lacy should be deputed to execute that office for one year." It was moreover determined, for the settlement of all disputes, that no one shall be permitted to erect any buildings on any part of the market-place; and in consequence a butcher's shop of recent erection was ordered to be removed. There is also an item, " We do order and decree that the mortar-pitts and stone-pitts neare Burcester shall remayne and be to the use and behoffe of the late Earle, his tenants, as in tymes past they have been used and accustomed [31]." Following is an enumeration of the settlement of several houses near the market-place upon different persons and their heirs. Then another item, " We order and decree that the Town Eall, Grarted House, all the soppes and pieces (Town Hall, Guard House, all the shops and buildings), built upon the waste, on or near the market-place in Burcester, and all the cottages in Crockwell, shall remain and be taken as part of the bailiwick, to be disposed of in the committee for the use above mentioned." The decree finally provides, that in case any dispute should hereafter happen among the partisans to the same, the surviving arbitrators have power to settle it.

This decree having thus vested the manor and bailiwick in the inhabitants who had purchased the leases of T. Wykins, T. Clements the elder, and his sons, it is evident no individual could hereafter become lord of the fee, unless it was possible for him to obtain possession of the whole demesne, a case which it is probable will never occur, from the conflicting interest of the parties. That the changes incidental to every kind of property will necessarily give some a greater influence than others, is inevitable: hence we find that when the estates in the possession of a descendant of Mr. Clements came

---

[31] This item clearly proves the right of every Derby-holder to dig stones at the stone pits.

to be added to those already in the hands of Mr. Thomas Coker, in the beginning of the eighteenth century, that gentleman was not inconsiderately regarded as lord of the manor. So when these were afterwards sold to Sir Edward Turner, owner of the priory estates, this accession of property seemed to warrant the transfer of the title, and has even led some authors of respectability to copy the assertions of the uninformed inhabitants.

The market and fairs are held under the bailiwick, which now belongs to Sir Gregory P. O. Turner, John Coker, Esq., Rev. —— Lockhart, Mrs. Cumming, Mrs. Churchill, and others; amongst which are two shares belonging to the poor of Bicester, which are divided annually into five parts, one of which is applied to the use of the poor of King's-End.

CHAPTER XX.

Priory Estates.

THOSE parts of the priory estates contained in the manors of Bicester and Wretchwic were by letters-patent granted to ROGER MORE, a second son of More de la More of Oxfordshire, in the 32d year of Henry VIII. A. D. 1540. Roger More died in September 1551.

By the marriage of Mary, his eldest daughter, the estates passed into the hands of Sir Michael Blount of Maple-Durham, Oxon. The latter gentleman, and probably the former, resided in a part of the dissolved priory.

Whether the estates were disposed of by Sir Richard his son, as the parish papers seem to intimate, I have not the means of ascertaining. They clearly appear to have been the property of the GLYNNES in the protectorate of Cromwell.

Sir William Glynne, who was created a baronet the 13th of

Charles II., was the son and heir of Lord Chief Justice Glynne, who made a distinguished figure in the reign of Charles I. He erected a noble mansion at Ambrosden, enlarged the church-yard and the garden of the vicarage, assisted in the recovery of an estate originally designed to repair the church, gave a noble service of communion plate, and ornaments for the pulpit and altar of Bicester parish church.

Sir William, his son and heir, served in parliament for the borough of Woodstock in the reign of Queen Anne. He considerably improved the glebe lands and ornamented the church at Ambrosden. His only son was the friend of Kennett, and by his interest Sir William presented him to the living of Ambrosden: to which circumstance, connected with the dispute relative to the estate withheld from the purpose of repairing the church, we owe the valuable Parochial Antiquities, perhaps one of the best collections any county can boast. As a tribute of respect, that writer has dedicated one of his plates (the view of the family mansion at Ambrosden) to his young friend. This excellent gentleman died before his father. Sir William departed this life September 3, 1721.

His brother Sir Stephen succeeded him in his dignity and estates; but did not long survive him, dying in April 1729, when his eldest son by the fourth daughter of Sir Edward Evelyn of Long Dutton, Bucks, became possessed of them. His life, however, was not long spared, for he died the following September unmarried.

About 1727 it appears Sir Stephen Glynne was in treaty for the sale of the estates of Bicester, Wretchwic, and Ambrosden. They finally passed into the possession of the TURNERS, a family originally of Leicestershire. On the 24th of August 1733, Edward Turner, Esq. was created a baronet by George II. He married Mary, daughter of Sir Gregory Page of Blackheath, and left one son and successor. He died in Lincoln's Inn, June 19, 1737.

In September 1739 his son, Sir Edward, married Cassandra, daughter of William Leigh of Addlestrope, Gloucestershire, by whom he had issue.

In the election of 1754 Sir Edward and Lord Parker appeared as the candidates for the county of Oxford on the new interest, and Sir James Dashwood and Lord Wenman on the old. To such a height was party spirit carried, that enormities and excesses the most flagrant were committed on both sides. The candidates and their friends visited every part of the county, and expended vast sums to secure the interest of the freeholders. At Bicester Sir Edward endeavoured to increase the number of his partisans by converting many of the Derby-holds into freehold estates [1]. By these and other means the new interest finally prevailed, though not before an appeal to the House of Commons. This election is still remembered by the oldest inhabitants of the county, who frequently amuse themselves and their children by accounts of the Great Election.

The mansion of the Glynnes was partly rebuilt and enlarged by Sir Edward; and the park received considerable additions on the western side by the inclosure of many acres in Merton parish. Numerous gravel-walks, statues, and lodges ornamented its lawns and woods. The young plantations and progressive improvements employed many of the poor, to whom Sir Edward was a constant and liberal benefactor. He died

---

[1] As Sir Edward neither was nor could be lord of the manor of Bicester, and consequently could not be vested with any interest in the leases, it was pretended that the legal heir of the original lessor had relinquished all claim at the instance of Sir Edward. But there seems to be a general suspicion among the inhabitants of Bicester, that some unfair proceedings took place at that time; for great numbers of the parish records were then either taken away or destroyed. Sir Edward is believed to have been too honourable a man to be concerned in the latter transaction, and the crime seems to have been committed by some less respectable agent.

in the midst of his useful career, October 31, 1766, and was succeeded by his son, Sir Gregory.

Tradition has currently reported that on the death of his father, Sir Gregory instantly mounted his horse, and rode round to all the workmen employed about the plantations, walks, &c., and forbad them to proceed;—that every work was stopped, and those employed discharged. Shortly after, great part of the timber in the park and on the estates was cut down; the materials of the lodges sold, and the land disparked and inclosed. Sir Gregory considering the house too large, pulled down a part, but afterwards observing the remaining structure unshapely took down the whole. Thus about 1769 terminated the existence of the mansion of the Glynnes and Turners, after having proclaimed their opulence and grandeur for above a century. Cotemporaries describe the structure raised by Sir Edward as noble and magnificent. Many of the workmen employed in its erection were concerned in its demolition, and it was remarked that the walls were not dry in many places. Two trees planted at its extremities attest its extent, and the reverberation of its hollow vaults, conjointly with the neighbouring solitary moat, serves to remind the contemplative stranger of the mutability of all earthly grandeur.

In August 1795, Sir Gregory on succeeding to the estates of his great-uncle and godfather, Sir Gregory Page, by his will and by virtue of his majesty's signature, added to his own the name and arms of Page. The splendid mansion of Blackheath he sold to John Cator, Esq., who shortly after disposed of it in lots by auction.

Sir Gregory was married January 1783 to Frances, daughter of Joseph Howel, Esq., of Elm, Norfolk, by whom he had

Sir Gregory Osborne, his successor, born Sept. 28, 1785.
Frances Stackpole, born January 15, 1787.
Edward George Thomas, born September 12, 1789.
Ann Leigh Gray, born August 9, 1791, died March 1804.

PRIORY ESTATES.

Francis William Martin, born February 15, 1794.

Sir Gregory Page Turner died at his house in Portland-place in 1805, aged fifty-seven. He was chosen member of parliament for Thirsk, in Yorkshire, in 1784, which he represented till his death. It was said that having stood, and lost, a trial with the maker of an iron bridge over a stream in his garden, which amounted to nine hundred pounds, the chagrin on this event occasioned his death. On examining his secretaire his executors found sixteen thousand seven hundred guineas. His remains were interred in the family vault at Bicester.

By his will he bequeathed five hundred pounds per annum, in addition to the seven hundred pounds settled on Lady Turner at the time of marriage; ten thousand pounds to his second son, and ten thousand pounds to each of his daughters. The bulk of his landed and funded property he settled on his eldest son Sir Gregory, amounting to three hundred and ten thousand pounds. The net produce of the landed property is about twenty-four thousand pounds per annum [7].

CHAPTER XXI.

Annals of Bicester, &c.

CIRCA 634. Bicester founded.

873. Battle fought with the Danes near Graven-hill by Ethelred and Alfred. The Danes gain the victory.

Circa 912. Old Town of Burencester destroyed by the Danes.

---

[7] Gentleman's Mag., March 1805.

1156. Henry II. grants a charter of privileges to the men of the honour of Wallingford, in which Bicester is included.

1182. Gilbert Basset founded the monastery of St. Edburg.

1193. A tournament on Bayards Green. The following is the letter by which King Richard permitted it to be held:—
"Richard by the grace of God, &c. To the Reverend Father in Christ, Hubert Archbishop of Canterbury, &c., greeting. Know that we have permitted tournaments to be held in England in five places; between Sarum and Wilton; between Stamford and Warrenford, between Warwick and Kennelworth, between Brackley and Mixbury, and between Blie and Tytchill, yet so that the peace of the land be not broken, nor damage done to our forests; and an Earl who shall tourney there shall pay us twenty marks; a Baron ten marks; a Knight who has land shall pay four marks; and a Knight who has no land shall pay us two marks. No foreigner shall tourney there. Wherefore we command you that on the day of the tournament you shall provide at each place two clerks, and your two Knights to receive the oath from the Earls and Barons for their satisfaction concerning the said sums, &c."

These tournaments were brought into England during the reign of King Stephen, and much encouraged by the martial disposition of the people, and their tendency to increase the king's revenues. The mischiefs attending them were so great that they were shortly prohibited by the popes, and under the penalty of denying the offenders Christian burial. Though restrained by act of parliament in the reign of Henry, under the penalty of the heirs of the offender forfeiting their estates, the custom was not abolished until the reign of Edward III. Another tournament was held here in the 33d of Henry III.

1215. The tyranny, rapacity, and lechery of John having rendered him odious and contemptible to his subjects, the barons flew to arms, and after several meetings adjourned to Brackley, whither the king sent messengers to learn their demands, which they delivered in a schedule afterwards called Magna Charta. After some opposition and delay the king was obliged to agree and sign. During these negociations this part of the country was the passage between the messengers.

1265. These parishes commanded to send out four or five men each, according to their population, to meet at Oxford three weeks after Easter, and thence to march to Kennelworth against the rebellious barons. The men marched under Robert Gifford.

1326. These parts much concerned in the revolution which finally deposed Edward II. and elevated his son to the throne.

1355. May 25. The king grants his licence for the building and endowment of an hospital in Bicester.

1377. King Richard II. grants a licence to Sir John de Worthe for a fair and market in Biggenhul, in Bicester.

Circa 1400. The parish church built.

Biggenhul market and fair confirmed to Humphrey Duke of Buckingham and John Felmersham, lords of the manor.

Robert Brooks obtains letters-patent for a market in Bicester Bury-end, which afterwards assumes the name of Market-end; and Biggenhul Monday market is discontinued.

1535. Bicester monastery visited.

Circa 1536. Surrendered into the hands of the King, and the Prior and Monks obtain pensions.

1538. The monastery granted to the Duke of Suffolk, the King's brother.

1540. Letters-patent granted to Roger More and his wife, conveying the land, house, and appurtenances of the late priory to them and their heirs. 32 Henry VIII.[1]

1555. On Easter Sunday a priest, sometime a monk of

---

[1] Michaelis Record. Rot. 44.

Ely and of Bicester, named William Branch, *alias* Flower, with a wood-knife wounded another priest as he was ministering the sacrament to the people in St. Margaret's church, in Westminster, for which fact the said William Flower, the 24th of April, had his right-hand smitten off; and for opinions in matters of religion was burned in the Sanctuary nigh to St. Margaret's church-yard [2].

1634. The heralds visit Oxfordshire. Cadwalader Coker's arms are confirmed, together with those of the Oxfordshire gentry: at the same time a special entry is made, that Richard Clements of Bicester is no gentleman, and Richard Clark no gentleman, and that they disclaim arms [3].

During the protectorate Oliver Cromwell is said to have visited Bicester, and slept one night at a house near the market-place, belonging to a Mr. Medcalf.

1666. A summer of excessive drought induces Mr. John Coker, lord of King's-end, to re-open St. Edburg's Well, whose waters flow abundantly.

1678. April 28. "A terrible tempest of lightning, hail, and rain, which continued several hours, burnt much corn, some barns and out-houses, and killed many cattle; also spoyled several persons, and had like to have destroyed the whole town [4]."—The buildings destroyed are supposed to have stood at the back of the house now occupied by Mr. Walford.

1683. October 9. An earthquake felt all over Oxfordshire and the midland counties [5].

1695. Kennett's Antiquities of Bicester, &c. published.

1698. The large gallery in the church built [6].

1704. The small-pox raged so dreadfully in Bicester that it nearly occasioned the ruin of the market; insomuch that

---

[2] Stow's Annales, 626.
[4] Quarto Pamphlet, 1678.
[6] Wardens' book.
[3] Harleian MSS. No. 1557.
[5] Philosophical Trans. No. 321.

grass grew in the market-place, and it bore the appearance of a green meadow. The market has never since recovered its importance[7].

1718. Sir Edward Longueville broke his neck at Bicester races[8].

1724. A sudden and terrible fire, occasioned by the chimney of Thomas Harris and Richard Baker, which in about three hours consumed and destroyed ten dwelling-houses, beside ware-houses, malt-houses, stables, and out-houses, in all about one hundred and fifty-nine bays of buildings, and containing great quantities of malt, barley, beans, oats, tobacco, flax, hemp, hay, candles, household goods, wearing apparel, &c.; the loss whereof, as near as can be computed by able and experienced workmen, amounted to two thousand two hundred and thirty-one pounds fifteen shillings and eightpence. Several of the sufferers obtained relief by a petition presented to the gentry in the neighbourhood[9].

1730. A large fire in King's-end, which consumed many houses.

1744. Mr. Raymond (a hemp-dresser) raised a company of volunteers to oppose the progress of the Pretender, which are supposed to have cost that gentleman five hundred pounds[10].

1752. The Pest House built for the accommodation of those infected with the small-pox[11].

1754. Meeting of the candidates Sir E. Turner and Sir

---

[7] Communication by Mr. T. Harris.

[8] Lysons's Buckinghamshire, Art. *Wolverton.*—Sir Edward's estate in that village had been sold to Dr. Radclife about six years before.—The races were held in King's-end field.

[9] Petition now remaining in the hands of Mr. T. Harris, a descendant of one of the sufferers.

[10] The residence and manufactory of Mr. Raymond was on the site of the house now occupied by Mr. Davis.

[11] Communication by Mr. T. Harris.

James Dashwood at Bicester, for the purpose of canvassing for the county representation[11].

1758. Bicester Field enclosed.

1763. The King of Denmark passed through Bicester.

June 19. Began raining and continued mostly wet weather till the beginning of February 1764, and a perpetual flood from November to the beginning of February, a period of fifteen weeks[12].

1765. August 3. A dreadful storm, and the church on fire by lightning.

1774. November 21. Bowden, a shoe-maker, barbarously murdered by his journeyman George Strap, who beat out his brains with a hammer as he sat at work late one evening. Strap was executed at Oxford, and his body given to the surgeons[13].

1789. The town illuminated, and great rejoicings on the King's recovery.

1793. The French revolutionary Government having countenanced seditious and treasonable practices among the disaffected in every part of the kingdom, a public meeting was held on January 8, and an association entered into by the inhabitants of the town and neighbourhood, for the purposes of " holding out in their own practice an example of respectful submission to the laws; endeavouring to bring to punishment all who by their writings or actions should in any manner disturb the public peace; and assisting the civil power on every occasion that should require their interference." And to show

---

[11] In the ensuing election the numbers of votes stood as follows:—Wenman 2033, Dashwood 2014, Parker 1313, Turner 1892. It seems that Mr. Coker supported Wenman and Dashwood with the votes of twenty-one inhabitants of Bicester.—Seven of Sir Edward Turner's votes in Bicester were struck off on scrutiny.—Gough's Pamphlets, Bod. Lib. Oxford,

[12] Memorandums on the lid of the Parish Register,

[13] Inscription on Bowden's grave-stone,

their detestation of seditious writers, the day was closed by the burning of the effigy of the celebrated Thomas Paine on the Market-hill.

1794. Bicester King's-end Field enclosed.

1795. The first stage-coach from Bicester to London.

1798. This country being threatened with domestic faction and foreign invasion,—in conformity with the example of the principal towns in England, the most respectable part of the inhabitants formed themselves into a Company of Volunteers, for the protection of the government and maintenance of tranquillity. The establishment consisted of a captain, lieutenant, ensign, three serjeants, and sixty privates; the arms and accoutrements only were found by Government, but every other expense was either defrayed by themselves or drawn from a fund raised by subscription. At the peace of Amiens this company was dissolved; but when in 1803 the country was again menaced by invasion, the inhabitants once more resumed their arms, and a more effective company was formed, consisting of one captain-commandant, two lieutenants, one ensign, six serjeants, six corporals, and one hundred and twenty privates. Each of the volunteer corps were commanded by Henry Walford, Esq., and they had the honour of receiving publicly the thanks of the inspecting field-officers for their regular musters and proficiency in military tactics. Their permament duty was marked by similar honours, and they were reported " fit to join troops of the line." This company was dissolved in 1807 [14].

1803. Bicester Bank established, under the firm of Kirby and Tubb.

1810. The eastern gallery in the church erected.

---

[14] Communicated by Mr. W. Ball.

AN INQUIRY
INTO
THE HISTORY OF
Alchester,

A MILITARY STATION OF THE *DOBUNI:*

The Site of which now forms a Part of the Field belonging to the Parish of Wendlebury, in the COUNTY of OXFORD.

———

In Oxfordshire, by Graven-hill Wood,
Stood Alchester so fair and good;
Allectus' walls are brought full low,
Where once they stood now corn doth grow.

MS. History of Alchester, apud Kennett.

ALCHESTER.

THERE is a natural curiosity in the mind of man to become acquainted with the history of the neighbourhood in which he first drew his breath or Providence has fixed his residence; and if any particular spot is rendered memorable by vestiges of ancient magnificence or traditionary splendour, his curiosity is excited in a greater degree. But in proportion to the distance of time in which these remains flourished, the paucity of writers and the want of authentic documents increase the difficulty of obtaining information, and too often after an extensive reading and laborious investigation, the mind of the inquisitive is thrown into the wild regions of conjecture.

These observations particularly apply to those ancient relics of Roman greatness found in the meadows of Wendlebury Field, at a short distance from Bicester, which revolving centuries have universally regarded as the remains of a once flourishing city, known by the name of ALCHESTER.—To investigate this opinion—to afford a view of the various conjectures of those writers who have professedly treated, or incidentally touched upon this subject, and to endeavour to ascertain the most probable period when the station rose to eminence, and fell to ruin—is the object of the present inquiry.

Passing over every supposition relative to the appearance of the face of the country in which Alchester was situated, either as it presented itself to the aborigines, or the Roman armies, it may be remarked that the first historical notice which can be relied on is, that the inhabitants of the principal districts now denominated Oxfordshire and Gloucestershire, at the time of the Roman invasion in the reign of Claudius, (A. D. 43,) were called Bodunni, or Dobuni, a name descriptive of their low or deep situation, and said by Kennett to be derived from the British word *bodun* signifying deep [1]; but according to Camden coming from Duffen (*Dwfn*), a word in the same language of similar signification; because, inhabiting for the most part a plain, and valleys encompassed with hills, the whole people took their denomination from thence. The word *Dob* is observed in a late ingenious treatise to mean stream, and in the same work *en*, land, is shown to have been often varied to *an* or *un*. Thus the compound term *Dobuni* may be inferred strictly to signify a race possessing land on river-sides, or a people who are stream-borderers [2].

The Dobuni are introduced to our notice as a nation subjugated by the *Cattieuchlani*, a warlike people who inhabited part of the counties of Buckingham, Bedford, and Hertford. The distance of the Cattieuchlani seems to intimate that the Dobuni were few in number, or distracted by divisions, so that their more powerful neighbour was enabled to subdue and tyrannize over them [3]. While in this wretched condition, and unable to regain their independence, Bericus a British chief, supposed to be a person of distinction among the Dobuni, was expelled his native country for some factious intrigues, and fled to Rome [4], where he endeavoured to excite the Emperor Claudius to attempt the conquest of Britain, perhaps secretly offering the alliance and assistance of that people. This

---

[1] Paroch. Antiq. p. 5.   [2] Beauties of Oxfordshire, p. 3.   [3] Camden.
[4] Carte supposes that Beric was deprived of his estate and expelled his country by the Cattieuchlani when they subdued it. History of England, vol. i. p. 100.

ALCHESTER. 189

enterprise being resolved upon, a numerous army was ordered to be conducted out of Gaul into Britain, by Aulus Plautius, a wise and valiant general of consular dignity, with orders to acquaint the emperor, if he met with great opposition, that he might come to his assistance. When the soldiers first understood the object of their destination, they expressed much reluctance, and objected to making war beyond the limits of the world; so little was Britain known: nor was it without difficulty that their general prevailed upon them to follow him.— Their army was finally embarked in three divisions, and landed without accident on the British island.

No opposition appearing from any of the states on the seacoast, Plautius marched his army up the country; and immediately the Dobuni (who are said to have declared they considered none enemies but the Cattieuchlani) submitted themselves, and were received under the Roman protection; and as a proof of their new masters' favour, Cogidunus their prince was not only confirmed in the government, but his territories extended. Thus early did this tribe further the views of the masters of the world, in contributing their assistance to enslave their native country; though it must be admitted with regard to themselves, that they only exchanged one slavery for another [5].

The policy of the Romans, as much as the necessity of defending their friends against the attacks of the hostile nations, led the Proprætor to select and fortify permanent stations for his troops; and it is likely some of these were chosen in or near the British towns, for the double purpose of preserving the property and securing the fidelity of the inhabitants [6].

---

[5] Henry's History of Britain, vol. i. p. 31. London, 1805.

[6] Carte supposes that, from the early submission of the Dobuni, and the immediate necessity of leaving a garrison to protect the country, this place was the first station in Britain occupied by the Romans, and thence denominated Alchester. History of England, vol. i. p. 101.

190   ALCHESTER.

The presumption is therefore very fair, that such was the origin of Alchester, originally a British town belonging to the Dobuni, on the frontiers of the Cattieuchlani, and selected by Aulus Plautius as a convenient station, whereby he might be able to repel the incursions of that people, and pursue them with success as far as Buckingham, or the banks of the Ouse. This conjecture will be found more plausible on reflecting that the usual fortifications of a British town [7] would afford the Roman soldiers an immediate security against the assaults of an enemy in an unknown country: it also accounts for their choice of such a low situation, so contrary to their usual stations, and agrees with the opinion of Kennett in ascribing its origin as a Roman fortress to Plautius [8].

The name of Alchester, by which the ruins of this station or city is known, was imposed by the Saxons—written in that language Ealdceaster, and signifies an old town or Roman military work [9].

The difficulty of fixing the precise situation of the stations mentioned in the Roman Itineraries, has produced many disputes among antiquaries who have endeavoured to ascertain these points: it is therefore no wonder that Alchester is not without its difficulties;—but the following may be regarded as the chief opinions advanced on the subject.

I. Mr. Salmon attempts to prove from the Itinerary of Antoninus that this station was the Roman *Isanavatia*; and the arguments which he adduces in support of this opinion are drawn from the different statements of the number of miles and stations between *Lactodorum* and *Benonis*, in the second

---

[7] What the Britons call a town is a tract of woody country surrounded by a mound and ditch, for the security of themselves and cattle against the incursions of their enemies. Cæsar de Bell. Gall. l. v. c. 21. There can be little doubt of the surrounding country answering this description at the time of the Roman invasion.

[8] Paroch. Antiq. p. 5.   [9] Camden's Britannia.

and sixth journeys of Antoninus. This variation he considers impossible to be accounted for, unless it be allowed that there were two branches of the road, which passed through different stations and met at those points; and this opinion, he says, is countenanced by the Iters themselves, one of which (Iter 2) only mentions the intermediate station of *Bennqvenna*, and describes its distance from *Lactodorum* as twelve miles, and from thence to *Benonis* as seventeen, making the whole distance twenty-nine miles; whereas the other (Iter 6) describes *Isanavatia* and *Tripontium* as intermediate, and makes the distance to be thirty-three miles. Hence, though he grants that there is no demonstration that Alchester was ever called *Isanavatia*, yet its distance from *Lactodorum* nearly agreeing with the numbers of the itinerary, and the certainty of there having been a military way leading from that place into Oxfordshire pointing towards Alchester, has induced him to form the conclusion, notwithstanding the objection of those who, content to travel in the old road, have agreed with Camden, making *Isanavatia* the same station as *Bennavenna*, though thereby they are obliged to expunge four miles from the Itinerary [10].

II. Dr. Stukeley considers this place as the " undoubted *Alauna* of Ravennas," and that even the original name is preserved in the neighbouring village of Launton [11]. The Doctor adds, " whether the present name be Alcester as retaining any thing of the Latin, or Aldcester signifying the old city, I dispute not, but think it has no manner of relation to Allectus."

[10]. Salmon's Survey of England. Oxfordshire, p. 449.

[11] Stukeley's Itinerarium Curiosum, vol. i. p. 41, London, 1776. It is surprising that a writer so intelligent as Mr. Brewer should assert that "Dr. Stukeley warmly supports the notion of this place deriving its appellation from Allectus, and is desirous of finding an allusion to Carausius himself in the neighbouring district of Caversfield." (Beauties of Oxfordshire, p. 536.) Nothing is more incorrect: the fact is, Mr. Brewer found the above passage in Gough's Camden, and instantly transcribed it into his own manuscript, without once consulting Stukeley's opinion on the subject.

—Richard of Cirencester [12], Baxter, and Horsley [13], seem to have agreed with Stukeley in considering this place as the Alauna of the Romans.

III. The anonymous author of the History of Alchester supposes this place to derive its origin and appellation from Allectus who slew the Emperor Carausius, in the neighbouring plains of Caversfield: and that having fixed on it as the chief seat of his government, he called it after his own name *Allecti-Castrum,* or the city of Allectus. Hence he supposes that the present name is only a corruption of the former, occasioned by the introduction of a strange language and the lapse of ages [14].

From the foregoing opinions it is evident that nothing decisive can be obtained on this subject. The conjectures of Salmon appear deserving of attention, as they are founded on the distances of the Itinerary; yet it must be remarked that the site of most of the stations is still disputed; and even admitting Stoney-Stratford to stand on or near the spot of the ancient *Lactodorum,* the distance from thence to Alchester is much more than twelve miles, except they are allowed to be computed miles, and varied according to the custom of the country; and even then it is difficult to account for the subsequent stations of *Tripontium* and *Benonis.* Stukeley's opinion is sanctioned by such respectable names that it cannot fail of creating attention, especially when it is recol-

---

[12] Iter 18. From *Eboracum,* York, through the middle of the island to *Clausentum.*

Benonnis, Cleycester, by High Cross, Northamptonshire.
Tripontium, Showel near Lutterworth, Leicestershire, 1 ħ.
Isannaria, Towcester, Northamptonshire, 12.
Ælia castra, Aldcester near Biceter, 16.
Durocina, Dorchester Episcopi, *Durinam Stipendaria,* Oxon, 15.
Tamesi, Stretley on Thames, by Goreing, Berks, 6.—Stukeley, vol. i. p. 137.

[13] Ravennas. Secunda pars Britanniæ. *Tamese,* Dr. Gale supposes Kingston. *Alauna,* Aulcester.—Horsley, p. 492.

[14] History of Alchester, printed at the end of Kennett's Antiquities.

lected that Richard of Cirencester might have access to documents not now in existence. But it must be admitted, notwithstanding the above opinions, that the conjecture of the anonymous author has been generally treated with respect. Yet were it even possible to establish either of the former; still, if this place was any particular favourite of Allectus, its name might be changed by him to *Allecti Castrum*. It is however no more than justice to add, that the latter conjecture is more ingenious than probable; that it has no historical support, and entirely rests on a presumed affinity of names.

During the long period of the Roman power in Britain, the Dobuni appear to have remained in quiet subjection[15]; a presumptive proof of the paternal care of that government. Availing themselves of the opportunities of receiving instruction, these provincials made rapid progress in civilization, and considerably improved in the arts and sciences. Their huts were succeeded by handsome and convenient habitations— their towns and cities formed into regular streets, and defended by strong fortifications. In these improvements we are warranted to conclude Alchester had its share, and without doubt had attained some consideration before the days of Allectus, A. D. 294. However, the anonymous writer is of a different opinion, and ascribes both the building and fortifying of the place to Caius Allectus, immediately on his rebellion against Carausius; "that in case he should be put to the worst at the sea-side, either by his late master, or by Constantius who was coming to reduce Britain to the Roman government, yet he might have where to reinforce himself in the main land;" for which purpose he is supposed to have previously secured a

---

[15] Henry, vol. ii. p. 120. A. D. 80. Agricola endeavoured to civilize the Britons by accustoming them to a more pleasant way of living: he exhorted them to build houses, temples, courts, and market-places; and was so successful that in a short time every town and city abounded with them.

communication with the sea, through the towns of "Allsford, Allinton, and Allingham [16]."

The same writer says, "In the forefront of Allchester Allectus built a sconce or watch-tower, the ruins of which still appear in a plot of meadow ground, where in our days (A. D. 1620) hath been digged up much Roman money, brick, and tile, and pavement of curious and wrought tile, of about the bigness of sixpence, being delicately laid there. Before the tower was an inward hollow place," (perhaps a foss or ditch,) "called a *Tyslanicum* [17], in which a military engine called *Rulla* was kept, made broad-headed like a plough staff, and designed to beat off the enemy from the walls." This engine imparted its name to the tower.—"To guard his city and sconce without, and to break the incursions of horses, Allectus reared up a bank of earth some two or three miles in length on the south-west part of the city, that the enemy might not draw back wings upon him; a good part whereof may still be seen in Wendlebury parish [18]."

Perhaps it is impossible to present a more accurate idea of the form and extent of the city than that which is suggested by the learned Dr. Stukeley, who explored the site with the utmost attention, and thus describes it: The city was fenced with a bank and ditch all round. It is a square of one thousand feet, each side standing on the four cardinal points, these sides are easily discernible at the corners, at each of which the country-people say stood a tower to defend it; and that the brook also originally ran round it. The street that passed from north to south is still visible, as is the other that ran in the contrary direction, meeting the Akeman in its way from

---

[16] History of Alchester, p. 686.

[17] Kennett says, "What the writer means by Tyslanicum I apprehend not, nor can I be informed." p. 7.   [18] History of Alchester, p. 683, 684.

Langford. Without doubt there were other streets; but they have not left sufficient vestiges to be distinguished. Great foundations are known to be in the meadows all around, especially north and eastward, on both sides of the Akeman-street. On the west of the city, a little distance from the city ditch, is an artificial hill, called Castle Hill, full of Roman bricks, stones, and foundations. I attentively considered the place— the circuit is very plain and definable; it was a square of one hundred feet. I guess there has been originally some considerable building in the middle of an area or court,—whether a prætorium or temple might probably be ascertained by digging. The edge of the area is very distinct on the meadow, by the difference in the colour of the grass, the one of which is grey, the other green; but the main body of the building did not reach so far, but lies in a great heap of rubbish, much elevated and of less extent. Before it, to the south, has been another area, paved with a bed of gravel, at least one hundred feet broad, and I doubt not but a curious person who would be at the expense of digging this plot would find it well worth his while [19].

In the spring of 1766 a very considerable opening was made into this mount by Mr. Penrose the proprietor of the meadow (perhaps in consequence of Stukeley's observations); and the following is a minute account of the discoveries made at that time. "The workmen began in the south-western part; and after digging through one foot and a half of old bricks and tiles, and through four feet of ashes mingled with human bones, came to a paved ground covered with fine gravel. Pursuing this for seven or eight yards, they reached the walls of the Prætorium: these were standing about three feet in height. Going

---

[19] Stukeley's Itin. II. vol. i. p. 42. Strangers may find the ruins in a meadow on the left-hand side of the high road leading from Bicester to Oxford; and on the eastern bank of a small rivulet which crosses the high-way about half a mile from Wendlebury, and one mile and three quarters from Bicester. The city extended over the rising ground on the east.

along the outside of the wall about twenty or thirty feet towards the north-western angle, they came to an opening in it which appeared to be a door-way, and was about eight feet in breadth. At this opening they began to enter the building, and immediately discovered a Roman pavement, raised about four feet from the level of the meadow, and appearing to extend through the whole compass of the building. This pavement consisted of tessellæ about one inch and a half in the square, bearing different colours, neatly cemented together, and laid upon a bed of mortar.

" Beneath and on one side of the discovered pavement was found a Roman hypocaust. It was a low room of one foot and a half in height, floored with small pieces of cemented brick, and supported with a great number of little pillars. These were two or three feet distant from each other, and had heaps of ashes between them."

The same writer says, "The site of the castrum is a very damp triangular meadow, bounded by a curving brook on the west and south: the mount rises about eight feet in height, nearly covers half an acre of ground, and seems originally to have been surrounded by a slight ditch.

"The station and town of *Ælia-Castra* was placed upon a very disadvantageous site,—a low ground, and a damp soil. The site of the city has been considerably raised by the foundations beneath, and the adscititious earth above. This appears sufficiently evident from the level of the meadows around it, particularly of the neighbouring station. They are all above one yard and a half lower in the level than the other. The site of the city, damp as it is at present, must have been much damper formerly, and nearly as much so as any of the swampy meadows in its neighbourhood[10]."

The closest investigation at the present day can add little to the foregoing accounts. With copies of the engravings illus-

---

[10] Whitaker's Manchester, vol. i. p. 60.

trating Stukeley's Description of Aldchester in his hand, the present writer carefully examined every spot mentioned (in the month of June 1814); and, as far as he had the means of ascertaining, found the statements generally correct. The land had been lately inclosed, and the divisions occasioned by the planting of new hedges had rendered the appearance of the streets much less conspicuous than formerly. They are, however, still discernible by the elevation of the ground. That which led from north to south may be traced by a hedge planted on its western side. The street which crossed it about the centre of the city, and ran from east to west, may be known by its elevated site, and the circumstance of a new hedge on the south side. The ditch in front of the hedge is cut through the foundations of several brick edifices, but whether they formed parts of small streets cannot be ascertained. The wall on the eastern side of the city passed through the middle of this field: the site is quite evident by the change in the colour of the soil; that without the walls being of a reddish cast, while that within is extremely rich and black, probably from the nitrous particles and animal salts lodged in it. Part of the foundation of this wall may be seen in the ditch before mentioned, which is cut through the angle of some building projecting beyond it. These foundations, from their age and exposure to the weather, are become quite rotten, though in many other parts single bricks may be found as sound and perfect as when first made. The earth abounds with broken pieces of pots and vessels formed of various sorts of coloured earth, red, green, and blue, as when viewed by Dr. Stukeley; nor is it unfrequent for the plough to draw up large bricks and stones, though the spot has formed part of Wendlebury common field for centuries. Great numbers of coins are still found [21], known in the neighbourhood by the name of Al-

---

[21] Many of the inhabitants in this neighbourhood have at different periods

chester pennies;" the inscription on many is very legible. The mount presents a considerable elevation, and perhaps for many years to come will afford the inquisitive stranger the best means of ascertaining the spot once distinguished by the abode of Roman power and magnificence.

The author of the History of Alchester says, "In the midst of that ploughed field, *Alchester*, one Fynmore a husband-man of Wendlebury, ploughing very deep, lighted upon a rough round stone, which being digged out was found to be hollowed within, and seamed and cemented together; and being opened there was nothing found therein but a green glass of some three quarts, full of ashes close stopped up, with lead over the mouth, which warrant it to be the *urna* or burnt ashes of some great man." This person the author supposes to have been Carausius, "slain hard by." At the time of Stukeley's visiting Alchester, this stone was used as a pig-trough at Wendlebury, and, as he says, "had remained so ever since Dr. Plot's time." The cavity he describes as one foot in diameter and nine inches deep. It was afterwards placed in the garden wall of the rectory; but, having been removed some years ago, is now lost, though some of the present inhabitants perfectly remember it [22].

---

obtained considerable numbers of these coins. Mr. Bond, sometime rector of Wendlebury, was furnished by his parishioners with great numbers. Kennett himself says he had nearly one hundred; but the largest collection ever made was by Mr. Lee, once proprietor of Bignal-farm: perhaps the best collection at present is in the hands of Mr. Howse, the landlord of a small inn at Wendlebury.

[22] The same writer says, "A piece of the mouth of the glass was sent me this year, 1622," together "with a piece of brass money found in Alchester, bearing the name and stamp of DOMINICAN. AUG. GERMA."—In another place he says, "George Maund of Chesterton, gentleman, brought me a piece of money there found bearing the picture and name of Constantine, who was second from Allectus; on the right side whereof was this inscription, CONSTANTINUS AUGUSTUS, and on the other side the portraiture of a castle, having the sun and stars in chief above it, and having some word on the coin by

ALCHESTER.

As the situation of the city was low, probably it was surrounded with considerable ditches, which at once secured it from inundations and the assaults of an enemy. Dr. Stukeley says, "It deserves to be called *urbs prætensis*, and may be supposed rather a city of pleasure than strength." It is evident from the extent of the walls that it was not large; unless we suppose that an unfortified suburb surrounded it: and this supposition may receive some countenance from the Doctor's assertion of "the adjoining meadows still remaining full of foundations [23]." But after all, it is much safer to receive no further idea of its extent and importance than the definable site will warrant.

The Akeman-street, the principal vicinal way in this county, passed close by the north side of this city; and, together with the other roads, afforded a free communication with every part of the country. These roads, the work of the Roman legions in times of peace, present to the admiration of succeeding ages a matchless proof of their strength of discipline and their habits of industry. The Akeman-street appears to have been constructed in different parts of the country, either with or without a raised bank, as the nature of the soil demanded. Its progress is described by Kennett as follows :—" Coming down the hill from Tuchwic-ground, it passes along the common road from Aylesbury, over the vale which gives name to the village of Mersh, leaving some traces of a stony ridge, visible and useful. Crossing the rivulet at Steanford [24], or Wordenpool, it enters Oxfordshire by Ambrosden, then ascending Blackthorn-hill ran in the present Bicester road, till in

---

the side of the castle,—to my judgement it was GALLITAS; it is at this day the arms of the castle of Wallingford. P. 695. Kennett supposes the latter inscription was written GALL....ITAS, for GALLENA CIVITAS, the city of Wallingford. p. 12.

[23] Itin. vol. I. p. 41.

[24] So called from the passage being pitched or paved with stones.

Wrechwic[25]-green (which was formerly the common field in that manor) it turns to the left-hand, and proceeds by the north side of Graven-hill wood, in the way leading to Langford, bearing close to the north-side of Alchester, and from thence proceeds to Chesterton and Kirklington town's-end; passing the river Charwell near Tackley, and thence in a straight line till it enters Blenheim-park, which it quits in a direction for the village of Stunsfield, on a raised bank. Here altering its form, though still (even traditionally) retaining its name, it goes over the river Evenlode, and passes near Wilcot and Ramsden; then to Astally, over Astwel-bridge, and through the fields to Broadwell-grove, where it is scarce visible. Passing Broadwell-grove the outlines are more bold and perfect, and the road proceeds in a straight line into Gloucestershire, and thence towards Bath, the old Akemancestre."

He proceeds: " The city of Alchester having had for a long time a fixed garrison of Roman forces occasioned other roads to be formed for a convenient communication with other stations." Of these the most apparent leads over Otmore, which has been (as observed by Plot) evidently paved; and points towards Calleva or Wallingford: hence the country-people succeeded in persuading Camden that this road was the original Akeman-street. Another branch may be traced " declining from the Akeman-street at Chesterton, and passing through Middleton Stoney, (where there is a large barrow, probably a tumulus or sepulchre for the dead,) whence falling into Wattle-bank or Avesditch, this road might lead to Banbury. Another of these streets left the Akeman-street on the east side of the brook; then passing through Langford-ground, cutting the lane which leads to Bicester on the south side of Candle-meadow[26], thence passed through the lower

---

[25] Anciently written Wrechroych.
[26] A meadow so named from its being charged with furnishing a candle or lamp for one of the altars in the conventual church in Bicester.

end of Dunkin's-ground [27] (where upon the late digging of a pond has appeared the plainest evidence of a paved way), and continued its course through Lanton, went on to Stratton [28], and from thence to Buckingham, till it reached the old *Lactodorum*, or Stoney Stratford."

Such appear to be the best accounts which at this distance of time can be collected relative to the station of Alchester, and the different roads by which it was approached. Were it required to affix the period in which it is probable that the city attained its greatest prosperity, it would be proper to select that which intervened between the reign of Carausius, A. D. 284, and Constantine the Great, A. D. 337. At that time historians represent the British province abounding in cities and towns, possessed of elegance, wealth, and power. The loss of its revenues and the boldness of its fleets, while separated from the empire by the rebellion of Carausius and Allectus, might induce the Romans to magnify its importance; but the circumstance of its monarch being able to defy the whole power of the emperors, proves that those representations are not unworthy of credit.

In the long period of tranquillity which followed the suppression of that rebellion, the castles, forts, and walls which had been erected for the defence of the British province, were so much decayed that they afforded little defence against the inroads of the Scots, Picts, and Saxons, who penetrated into the interior in the reign of Valentinian, A. D. 364. Various generals having failed in expelling these invaders, Theodosius was appointed commander; and his success and subsequent policy attest the wisdom of the appointment. Hearne sup-

---

[27] Formerly this ground was a part of the possessions belonging to the ancestors of the writer, who for many ages had a considerable estate in the neighbouring village of Merton, and lie buried in that church.

[28] Stratton is so called from being placed on a Roman street. Kenn. p. 18.

poses that "he garrisoned Alchester, A.D. 367, then a large and well-fortified city, with a considerable number of well-disciplined men. That he also set guards upon the frontiers, ordered divers watches on the highways, and fixed small garrisons or camps at Stunsfield, Round Castle near Bladon, and at Coombe." In another place the same author asserts that Alchester was occasionally honoured with the presence of Theodosius during the time he governed Britain, and that a subordinate officer had a hall or palace erected at Stunsfield. These observations arose from a tessellated pavement having then been lately discovered at that place [29].

The opinion of Hearne was afterwards controverted by a Mr. Pointer, in a pamphlet in which he maintained that Alchester never was the station of Theodosius, but of the different generals who commanded in these parts subsequent to the defeat and death of Allectus. He also ascribes the Stunsfield pavement to a general of the latter [30].

However there may be a disposition to regard the period of the Roman power with complacency, their maxims of policy and government were not ultimately beneficial to the provinces. Professedly a military government, their first object was to deprive the inhabitants of their arms, and commit the defence of the province to the valour of the legions. The numbers of the latter were daily recruited from among the flower of the youth, who when once enrolled were taught to consider the camp as their home, and their only hope of advancement to rest on implicit submission to the will of their commanders, and a strict attention to military discipline. Hereby they became alienated from the peculiar interests of

---

[29] Hearne on the Stunsfield Pavement, published with Leland's Itin. vol. viii.
[30] Pointer's Account of the Stunsfield Pavement, Oxon. 1713.—From these writers it appears that the coins found at Alchester have chiefly been those of Claudius, Probus, Allectus, and Diocletian.

their country, and desirous only of supporting the government. The arts of luxury also which were introduced among the provincials, tended to depress and enervate; and the daily exhibition of strangers raised to the highest honours and offices in the state, while they were studiously depressed, introduced a carelessness of the welfare of their country, and a desire of personal gratification only. So that when the irruption of the barbarians rendered it necessary for the Romans to recall the distant legions, without spirit to defend their possessions the provincials became the prey of the first daring invader.

The period of the Roman government in Britain, from the invasion of Aulus Plautius (A. D. 43) to their final departure in the reign of Honorius (A. D. 420), comprises the space of three hundred and seventy-seven years, during which Alchester attained and preserved some degree of consideration. That day now, however, fast approached which would reduce it to its primitive insignificance:—To mention the circumstances connected herewith, as far as our scanty materials will admit, is all that remains.

The immense hordes of barbarians which assailed the empire on every side, together with the perpetual calls of the government for new levies of troops, which were immediately destroyed, announced to the unhappy provincials the speedy destruction of the Roman power. But in no part of that vast state were these portentous appearances regarded with greater terror, or their effects more speedily felt, than in Britain. The inhabitants beheld the retiring legions with dismay and despair; and before they had finally abandoned the island, trade had ceased, and every mechanical pursuit was given up; so that in a few years the necessary art of masonry had so much decayed, that the Britons were unable to rebuild the broken wall of Severus, or repair their decaying cities, without Roman skill and assistance.

When the mistaken policy of the Britons invited the Saxons

to assist them in repelling the incursions of the Scots and Picts, and these allies afterwards treacherously sought to seize upon the country, the British cities afforded their inhabitants some security against the first attacks of the enemy, and allowed them time to recover from the surprise occasioned by this perfidy. Perceiving that the successive multitudes which continually reinforced the Saxons could aim at nothing less than the entire conquest of the country, they nobly resolved to defend it, or perish in the attempt. Committing their cause to the sword, they engaged in several desperate conflicts, and the prosperous or adverse state of the war daily added discipline and experience to their valour.

For nearly one hundred years the Britons, under various leaders, maintained a vigorous struggle against the numerous hosts of Saxons who assailed them on every side. The British fortresses for a long time retarded their progress; and the natives perceiving their desperate situation, took every local advantage of hill, forest, and morass. Success at first was extremely doubtful: the brave Ambrosius (A. D. 490) performed prodigies of valour, and long sustained the fortunes of his country. His courage was only equalled by his perseverance; and from his assumption of the command to the battle which terminated his life (A. D. 508) his exertions were crowned with success. To encourage the Britons, he visited every part of the country liable to the attacks of the enemy, and animated their resistance by his eloquence and example. In these military excursions it is probable that Alchester was not neglected, and Kennett supposes the encampment of his army on the rising ground of Ambrosden is still preserved in the name of that village.

A. D. 516. The renowned King Arthur served under this prince, and succeeded to his honours and dangers. In twelve successive battles the discomfited Saxons felt the severity of British vengeance; but their final success attests that they gradually gained ground. Cerdic laid the foundation of the West Saxon kingdom; Oxfordshire and the adjacent counties were occupied by the Angles (A. D. 560), not however until the country was entirely desolated, and the cities and fortresses destroyed. The few Britons who remained were reduced to abject slavery; and desolation and barbarism spread itself over the face of a land lately highly cultivated and polished.

Historians represent in strong colours the various cruelties exercised by Pagan Saxons on British Christians. Their priests are described as slain before the altars; their bishops as driven from their flocks; and their churches as entirely demolished. The whole mass of the original inhabitants is said to have been exterminated, and their language eradicated: indeed, the whole country was so much depopulated and desolate, that a few years after the Saxons were settled it bore the appearance of one newly discovered and colonized, so much had these thrown every thing into a state of uncultivated nature[31].

The ruins of some of the strongest edifices in Alchester remained until after the settlement of the West Saxon kingdom, when these were demolished by Birinus the Bishop of Dorchester, and the materials used to build and fortify a town near its site, on the frontiers of the kingdom, which was named, after its founder, *Burin-ceastre*. Time has gradually softened its name and improved its buildings, but Bicester must ascribe its origin to the strong and massive walls of the Roman city[32].

What scattered fragments remained were used by succeeding ages as a quarry to furnish bricks and stones for the construction of their wretched huts and villages. Wendlebury, Chesterton, and the neighbouring hamlets, all conspired to blot out its existence from the earth. The lapse of ages

---

[31] Gibbon's Decline and Fall of the Roman Empire, vol. vi. p. 323-337, 18mo, London 1807. Henry's Britain, vol. i. p. 125-133. Id. vol. ii. p. 314.
[32] Kennett, p. 28.

silently crumbled its scattered masses to atoms, the inundations of the adjacent stream washed away its banks and filled up its ditches, and the efforts of husbandry eradicated all traces of its streets; thus leaving the memory of its former state to be preserved by the tradition of a strange people, entirely ignorant of Roman greatness, and perfectly careless of Roman arts.

The uncertainty that must attend all conjectures respecting the population of a British Roman city, as well as the nature of its edifices, public and private, has induced the writer to pass over the subject [33]. It ought however to be remarked, that as two British churches are mentioned in Oxfordshire [34], previous to the invasion of the Saxons, the small number of stations in that county might render it probable that one of them was built in Alchester.—But on this subject further information cannot be obtained.—No event of sufficient importance occurred in this part of the country to introduce the semi-barbarous historians of a strange language and distant æra to the knowledge of Alchester. All the Roman monuments of learning of a local nature perished in the general ruin; or, if any manuscript survived till learning shed a dim ray on the gloom of the Saxon monasteries, the lazy monk suffered them to decay untranscribed.

---

[33] Those who wish to obtain a description of a British Roman city may consult Dr. Henry, who has collected most of the descriptions given by the Roman writers on that subject, vol. ii. p. 118 to 123.

[34] When Augustine came into the county of Oxford, to a village called Cumpton, i. e. Long Cumpton, Warwickshire, at the edge of the county, the parish priest waited upon him, and complained of the lord of the manor refusing to pay his tithes, upon which Augustine reproved him, and convinced him by a miracle of a dead body raised from the grave; who confessed himself to have been patron of the church in the time of the Britons, and to have been excommunicated for the like default above one hundred and fifty years before.—Kenn. quot. Brompton, p. 136.

HISTORY OF CARAUSIUS AND ALLECTUS.

The neighbourhood and city of Alchester having been supposed to bear some relation to Carausius and Allectus, a short account of these distinguished individuals is subjoined, though it ought to be recollected that there is no authentic history which identifies any of their transactions with these places.

The birth of Carausius is doubtful. Dr. Stukeley asserts that he was born at St. David's, and descended of the old British blood royal: while Gibbon declares he was a Menapian of the meanest origin. It is agreed that he was a brave man, and rose by his merit; that he had served in Britain and Gaul, and was afterwards raised to the important station of Count of the Saxon shore, the duty of which was to guard the seacoasts from the descent of the northern pirates.

Gibbon states that the integrity of the new admiral was immediately warped by his interest; that he suffered the pirates to commit their depredations, and then intercepting them on their return, obliged them to resign a part of their spoil, which he appropriated to his own use. That these circumstances coming to the knowledge of the Emperor Maximian, orders were issued to put him to death; but that the execution of them was eluded by his liberality to the fleet and armies which he commanded; and that these supported the provinces in the revolt, and saluted him emperor. But a more plausible and favourable account of the conduct of this hero is given by Dr. Stukeley:—according to him, the jealousy of Maximian was excited by the reputation of Carausius, after he had defeated the Burgundians and Alemains; and secret orders being issued for his destruction, no other means of escape offered than assuming the purple, in which he was supported by the fleet and the Britons: and after Maximian had tempted the fidelity of his troops, and hazarded an engagement on the sea, that emperor deemed it prudent to respect his claim, and acknowledge him as a colleague, on condition of his continuing to defend the sea-coasts.

The reign of Carausius is generally represented as beneficial to Britain. He secured the friendship of the Picts and Scots, repaired the foss dyke, founded Granta, now Cambridge, and projected many public works. But Diocletian having refused to ratify the treaty which Carausius concluded with Maximian, and on the great festival of Mars (March 1) appointed Constantius Chloris Cæsar and governor of Britain, the honours of Carausius became insecure, and he was obliged to prepare for war.

The friendship of the Franks enabled Carausius to baffle the whole power of the empire, and for seven years his fleets rode triumphant from the Pillars of Hercules to the northern sea. Yet he must feel a secret dismay at the hourly accounts which he received of the preparations of Constantius. The stupendous mole which occasioned the fall of Boulogne, and threw a part of his fleet into the enemy's hand, while it materially increased his danger, showed the perseverance and ability of his foe. However, his courage did not forsake him : he applied himself with great diligence to prepare every thing necessary to resist the threatened invasion. But while thus engaged at York, he fell a sacrifice to the treachery of Allectus, one of his chief officers and confidents, who immediately assumed the government and the purple.

The abilities of Allectus were unequal to the difficulties of his station; yet the three years which intervened between the death of Carausius and the descent of Constantius were diligently employed in fortifying the cities and securing the coasts. The preparations being at length finished, Constantius divided his forces into two parts, which he purposed to land at opposite points of the coast, that the attention of Allectus might be distracted. The command of one of the squadrons was given to the Prefect Asclepiodotus, and the other reserved for himself. The former, setting sail, passed the fleet of Allectus near the Isle of Wight, by favour of a thick fog; and landing on the coast of Britain without opposition, immediately burned his ships, that his troops might have no hope of safety but in victory. No sooner was the intelligence communicated to Allectus, who had posted himself near London, than he hastened to meet and give him battle. This forced march, however, had so fatigued and dispirited his soldiers, that they were speedily overcome, and Allectus himself slain. Destitute of a leader, the province immediately returned to the obedience of the Romans, and Constantius was received with pleasure and surprised with acclamations.

Such appears to be the genuine and authentic history of Carausius and Allectus; but it is varied by the anonymous author of the History of Alchester in the following way.

It is said that Allectus, being envious of his master's honours, determined upon a revolt; and, having collected his partisans, built and fortified Alchester as an inland town, "that he might have where to reinforce himself in the main land." That Carausius, being desirous of crushing one enemy ere another landed, marched an army into this neighbourhood, and formed an entrenched camp on Bayard's-Green. That the armies soon after met, and a desperate battle ensued, on a plain about two miles from Alchester, in which Carausius was slain, and the place obtained the name of Caraus-field or Caversfield. That immediately after the battle, Allectus assumed the purple, and proceeded carefully to fortify the cities, and place the country in the best state of defence against Constantius, who was preparing to invade it. That among the inland fortresses Alchester occupied his utmost attention, and was frequently honoured by his presence and court; but that much of its consideration was lost after he was slain by

Asclepiodotus at the fatal battle of Elsfield, which closed the independence of the British province.

Both these statements are submitted to the judgement of the reader. The writer of the anonymous History of Alchester was evidently a man of learning, and the History itself is the best specimen of his talents. Some credit is certainly due to the ingenuity which so plausibly adapted the names and events to these obscure places: but the attention which his story has gained among succeeding writers may serve to caution future antiquaries against being led away by a coincidence of names.

APPENDIX.

APPENDIX.

No. I.

Life of Rosamond Clifford.

WILLIAM LONGSPE, the grandson of the fair and unfortunate ROSAMOND CLIFFORD, having obtained possession of the Manor of Bicester, together with the circumstance of this neighbourhood having been immediately connected with her eventful story, renders some account of her life particularly interesting.

This lady was the daughter of Walter Lord Clifford, who in conformity with the practice of that age placed her as a boarder in Godstow nunnery, for the purposes of education. According to ancient writers, the females resident in that religious house were allowed considerable indulgence: they were even permitted to spend one day in the year at Godstow fair, and occasionally to visit *Medley* and *Binsey*. It is supposed that Henry first saw Rosamond when she was about fifteen years of age (A. D. 1149), and the prince himself very young. Now if this account of the discipline of the nunnery be correct, opportunities of overture were abundant: nor is it improbable that Henry softened the fall of his victim by promises of honourable retribution :—but the love-promises of a prince depend for performance on political expediency. The repudiated Queen of France, Eleanor of Guienne, held a sceptre in her hand; and the pretensions of ensnared beauty and subdued innocence weighed trivially on the opposite side.

As the circumstances attending their connexion were either treated with indifference or studiously thrown into shade by the writers of that æra, an impenetrable doubt involves the whole affair. But according to the best accounts it appears, that, after Henry had succeeded in seducing Rosamond, he constructed for her reception a bower or retired dwelling at a short distance from Woodstock palace. This building is described by Chaucer (who is supposed to draw the scenery of his poem entitled "The Dream" from that park) as a white castle seated on an eminence and adorned with maples. It is probable that the adjoining gardens consisted of the topiary work so usual with the fanciful gardeners of that period: and perhaps the remains of these twisted and unnatural alleys, together with Henry's amour, gave rise to those tales which have passed from father to son, or rather from mother to daughter, touching a bower erected by King Henry for the reception of Fair Rosamond, round which he constructed a labyrinth so artfully contrived that no stranger could possibly untread its mazes. That here Rosamond was concealed from the jealous Queen, till in a luckless hour that dreaded personage discovered the beauty at the outward door of the labyrinth. Rosamond fled; but in her haste dropped a ball of silk, a part of which adhering to her foot or garment acted as a clue. The Queen penetrated the recess; and, though at first struck by her beauty into amazement, compelled her to swallow poison.

Such is the legendary account. But none of the ancient writers countenance the story; and there is no ground whatever for believing that Rosamond died out of the ordinary course of nature. Brewer is of opinion that she renounced all intercourse with Henry soon after the arrival of Queen Eleanor in England, and retired to the nunnery in which her happiest days had passed, and lived there in penitence and seclusion several years.—This however is directly contradicted by Brompton and Knyghton, both of whom say that she died soon after the splendid apartment was built for her reception at Woodstock [1].

[1] Decem Scriptores, p. 1151. p. 2395.—In the Gent. Mag. is the following extract, published from a book written in the fourteenth century: "It bifel that she (Rosamond) died and was buried whyle the Kynge was absent. When he came agen he wolde se the body in the grave. And whanne the grave was openned there sate an orrible tode on her brest bytwene her teetys, and a foul adder begirt hir body about hir midle, and she stanke so that the Kynge ne none other might stand to se the orrible sight. Thanne the Kynge dyde shette agen the grave, and dyde wryte theese two veersis upon y⁶ grave: *Hic jacet in tomba*, &c." Vol. 54, p. 970.

Rosamond had two sons by that monarch, William Longspe, or Longsword (so called from the sword he usually wore), afterwards married to Ela daughter and heir of the Earl of Salisbury; and Geoffery Plantagenet, elected Bishop of Lincoln and afterwards Archbishop of York.

The body of Rosamond was interred by her parents before the high altar at Godstow, and round a costly monument were lights directed to be kept continually burning; but in 1191 they were removed by order of Hugh Bishop of Lincoln, and her body buried in the Nuns' Chapter-house. At the Reformation her bones were again disturbed and her tomb destroyed, which is said to have had on it *interchangeable weavings*, decked with red and green roses, and the picture of the cup out of which she drank the poison. This cup, however, Gough conjectures to have been a chalice, often found on the coffin-lids of ecclesiastics [a]. When a boy I accompanied my father to Godstow to view a large stone coffin, said to have been Rosamond's, but apparently designed for two bodies, as it was divided by a ridge of stone running from head to foot. This was afterwards engraved from a drawing by Grose, and inserted in the Gentleman's Magazine for Nov. 1791.

No. II.

An account of the Tenants, Rents, and Services within the Manor of Berencester. 1325. 18, 19, Edward II.

(TRANSLATION.)

Berncester.—Persons holding hereditarily by free tenure.

JOHN LE VECHE and Agnes his wife hold one messuage and its curtilage, which is between the land formerly of Emma Bartlett and the land of John le Bakere. They also hold one acre of land; whereof one half acre lies under Buchamwey, between the land of Hugh Eylot and the land of William Hamond; and the other half acre lies in the land which is called Grascroft-furlong, and extends

---

[a] Oxfordshire: Beauties of England and Wales.

towards Cesterton between the land of Walter de Langleye and the land of William Hamond; and pay rent per annum one halfpenny, at Easter; which messuage and its curtilage and land the said John and Agnes have by the demise of Nicholas le Rede and Anne his wife, by their deed, paying rent for the same to the chief lord one halfpenny as aforesaid. And they hold by form of the statute, as in the court held at Berencester on Tuesday next after the feast of Saint Dionysius, in the ninth year of the reign of King Edward son of King Edward, is more fully contained; on which day the said John performed fealty. The said John also holds one messuage and a half yard land by homage and fealty, which Hugh atte Ford Chaplain formerly held, and which the said Hugh had by the gift of Margery atte Ford his mother, who held *in capite* the said land of the lady, paying rent per annum 2s. 6d. at four times of the year; to wit, at the feasts of St. Michael, of the Nativity of our Lord, of the Annunciation of the Blessed Mary, and of the Nativity of St. John the Baptist, by equal portions.

Geoffrey de Langleye, son of the Lord John de Langleye lord of Bigenhull, holds one messuage and one yard land with a meadow in Berencester, which is called le Palmerslond; to wit, that messuage and that yard land with the meadow in Berencester, and pays rent for the same per annum 6s. at the times aforesaid; which messuage and yard land, with the meadow, lie in the field according to the following description; to wit, one acre lies near the Canons' wall, between the land of John the Baker and the land of Nicholas le Grey; and one acre above the Hulle, between the land of the Prioress and the land of Thomas son of William. Also two acres above Longelond near the Wodewey, between the land formerly of the Lord John de Langleye and the Wodewey. Also three acres and a half at the Fish-pond, near the land of Nicholas le Grey. Also two acres and a half above the Croftland, between the land of the said Nicholas and the land of the Prioress and the land of Robert Eylot. Also one acre at the Mulnewey, near the land of the aforesaid Nicholas and of the widow Alice. Also one acre at the Wowelond, near the land of John de la Ford and the land of John son of Walter. Also one acre lying between the land of Alice Heirhiches and the land of Thomas son of William. Also one acre in Bodemore, near the land of the Prioress. Also three acres above Hesneford, between the land of Nicholas le Grey and the land of Simon le Frend. Also three acres at Fishthorne, between the land of the widow Alice and the land of Walter Cavel. Also one acre above Crockwellforlonge between the land of Nicholas le Grey and the land of Ralph, at the upper end of the village. Also two acres above Eldeforde, between the land of Nicholas le Grey and the land of Nicholas Germayn. Also three acres above Hynacre, between the land of the Prioress and the land of Walter Cavel. Also three acres above Imbelowe, between the land of Nicholas le Grey and Kyngesmere. Also one acre above Haggethorn, near the land of Nicholas le Grey. Also one acre above Pudwellforlong, between the land of the Prioress and the land of the aforesaid Nicholas.

The meadow belonging to the aforesaid yard land lies particularly as follows: to wit, Two acres and a half above Rowelowe, between the land of the Prior of Berencester and the land of Nicholas le Grey. Also one acre (Henedacre) lies in Kynsedeham. Also three acres at the Whitbeyes, between Helenesmede and the land of the Lady Prioress. The Prior of Berencester holds two acres of land of the aforesaid yard land, which he had in exchange (*habuit in escambio*) of Walter de Langleye; and they lie together at Eldeford in the North Field, between the land of Nicholas Germayn and the land of Nicholas de Saford.

John son of Thomas Abbod holds by a certain indented writing made to Thomas Abbod and the heirs of his body, in the name of Agnes formerly Prioress, and of her Convent, one messuage with its curtilage, where he dwells, which is situated between the messuage which Robert le Webbe formerly held, and the gable of the capital messuage which H. the Smith formerly held; and pays rent per annum 12d. and suit of court. The said John holds another messuage with its curtilage, where he dwells, by a certain indented writing made in the name of Isabella formerly Prioress, and of her Convent, to Thomas Abbod and the heirs of his body, which is situated between the messuage which Henry the Smith formerly held and the great gate of the Lady Prioress, and pays rent for the same per annum, at the end of the year, 3s. 6d. and suit of court. The same John holds one piece of ground opposite to the ground belonging to his messuage, at the end of the cow-house of the Lady Prioress, where there used to be ingress and egress to the croft of the Prioress from her manor; and pays rent for the same, at the feast of St. Michael, 2d. And holds without a deed, under the name of Matilda and her Convent, and the heirs of the body of the said John lawfully begotten, one messuage with the ground pertaining thereto, which formerly Roger le Mayne held near the messuage of the Lord of Bigenhull, which he holds of the Prioress. They hold also by the same writing ten acres of land of the said Prioress in the Field of Berencester; whereof two acres lie at Eldeford, between the land of the Prior of Berencester, and the land of Nicholas de Saford; and one acre and a half and one rood lie above Morforlong, between the land of Gilbert de Stratton and the land of Nicholas le May; and one rood lies at Levenchesdich, between the land of the Lord of Bigenhull and the land of John Mich; and two acres and a half lie above Lysthynacre, of which half an acre lies between the land of the Earl of Lyncoln and the land of Hamond...; and one acre lies between the land of the said Hamond and the land of John atte Ford; and one acre lies between the land of John Cavel; and one acre called Cuttacre lies above Mangethorn, between the land of John Pines and the land of Agnes le Blake, and half an acre lies near Buchamwey, between the land of John atte Ford and the land of John Mich; and half an acre lies there between the land of William Cavel and the land of Robert Michel; and half an acre lies there between the land of John Knight and William Cavel; and one acre lies above Goldforlong, between the land of the Lord of Bigenhull and the land of Robert Michel, and he pays rent per annum, at four times, 10s. 6d.

Robert son of John le Smith holds one messuage near the court of the Lady Prioress; and pays rent for the same per annum, at the aforesaid times, 3s. and suit of court.

William, son of John Squier, holds one messuage with its curtilage, to himself and the heirs of his body lawfully begotten, by a certain indented writing made in the name of Agnes Prioress of Markyate and her Convent; which messuage with the curtilage belonged formerly to Hugh Coci of Berencester; and he pays rent for the same, at the aforesaid times, 2s. and suit of court.

APPENDIX. 219

John Goldes holds two messuages and four acres of land: whereof one acre lies above Buchamwey between the land of Nicholas de Saford and the land of Robert Thames; and one acre lies at Melleweysend between the land of John Gavel and the land of John de Aston; and one acre lies above Nynacre, between the land of the Lady Prioress which Peter Galewei holds, and the land of Andrew le Rooke; and half an acre lies above the Milleweysend, between the land of John de Aston and the land of Nicholas le Saford; and half an acre extends unto Twyseledwéy, between the land of the Prioress and the land of Andrew le Rooke. And he pays rent for the same per annum, at the aforesaid times, viz. and suit of court.

Sum of the Rents of the Free Hereditary Tenants 34s. 7½d. Whereof 8s. 8¼d. is for the time of St. Michael: 8s. 7½d. for the time of the Nativity: 8s. 8d. for the time of the Annunciation: and 8s. 8½d. for the time of the Nativity of Saint John the Baptist.

Free Tenants of Cottages for the term of their lives.

Matilda the Taylor (le Taillur) holds by Court Roll one messuage with its curtilage, for the term of her life; and pays rent for the same per annum, at the four times aforesaid, 4s. and suit of court.

Isabella Mandi holds one messuage with its curtilage, by Court Roll, for the term of her life; and pays rent per annum, at the aforesaid times, 2s. and suit of court.

John Monekes and Matilda his wife hold by an indented writing, for the term of their lives, one messuage with its curtilage, and pay rent per annum 3s. and suit of court.

John the Baker and Christiana his wife hold by indented writing, for the term of their lives, four houses with the curtilage; and one oven, with customary suit for the same: and they pay rent per annum, at the times aforesaid, 9s. and suit of court. Sum 18s.

Lands of the Domains let for the term of life.

John Abbot holds for the term of his life, by Court Roll, one acre and one rood of land, as they lie in the field in five parcels; whereof one rood lies between the land of Nicholas the Bailiff[a] of Bigenhull and the land of Robert Michell of Bigenhull, and extends as far as Oldedich; and another rood lies between the land of the aforesaid Nicholas and the land of John Rooke above Shottedown, and extends above Longelond; and another rood lies between the land of Robert Michell of Berencester, and extends as far as Longelond; and another rood lies near the land of Nicholas aforesaid of Bigenhull, and extends above Oldedich; and another rood lies at the lower end of Oldedich, near the gap between the land of Nicholas at the bridge and the land of Robert Eylot. And he pays rent for the same per annum, at the times aforesaid, 18d.

The same John holds for the term of his life, by Court Roll, ten acres and one rood of land, which John Faber formerly held: whereof six acres and a half lie in Rydiforlong in the Ridemor near Oxenfordwey, and half an acre lies above Overdemershlond; and one acre and a half and one rood lie together near Cuttacre, between the land of Walter Sebern and the Brodewey, which leads towards Bikenhull; and half an acre lies above Cuttacre, between the land of William Hamond, slave born of the Lady, and the land of William le Blake; and half an acre lies above Magethorn near the land of Nicholas de Saford, slave born of the Lady; and four roods of land lie above the Staneputtes, between Roger le Reve and the land of John James; and one rood lies beyond Overlonglond, between the land of Roger le Reve and ...... and one acre lies in the Netherbrech, between the land of Nicholas le Reve and....

The same John holds by Court Roll one acre and a half of land: whereof one acre lies above Strongforlong, between the land of Walter Sebern and Orcherdeforlong; and half an acre lies near Oldemore, between the land of Hamond atte Nunende and Robert Germeyn, slaves born of the Lady. And he pays rent for the same per annum, at the times aforesaid, 7s. 6d.

The same John holds for the term of his life, by Court Roll, two acres of land at Gibelyng, near the land formerly of John de Bigenhull, on the south side: and he pays rent per annum, at the times aforesaid, 11d.

---

[a] Præpositi.

APPENDIX. 221

John the Baker and his wife hold eight acres of arable land, by Court Roll, at the will of the Lady: whereof two acres lie between the land of Thomas Rook and the land of Thomas William, and extend above Buckamwey; and two acres lie in the Morforlong, between the land of John atte Ford and the land which belonged to Robert Eylot; and two acres lie at Mangethorn, whereof one acre lies between the land of Thomas Williams and the land of William Cavel, and another acre lies between the land of William Cavel and the land of William Frankleyn; and half an acre and one rood lie above Cornhull, between the land of Agnes le Blake and the land of William le Blake, and one rood lies between the land of Simon Germeyn and the land of the aforesaid Nicholas, and one acre lies above Cornhull, between the land of the Lady Prioress and the land of John Wattes. And they pay rent for the same per annum, at the times aforesaid, 4s. 11d.

Nicholas le Blake holds by writing indented, for the term of his own life and that of Agnes his wife, twelve acres and one rood of land: whereof six acres lie above Waterforlong; and two acres lie near the way, to wit the Gores above Shorteforlong, and half an acre at Kyngesmere, and one acre at Longelondes, and one acre at Hangateshull, to wit Foreshete, and one acre and a half above Waterforlong nearer to Berencester, and two roods above Waterforlong in Lallesden, and two acres in Lallesden, and one rood in the Broke beyond Bigenhull. And he pays rent for the same per annum, at the times aforesaid, 7s. 0d.

Simon Germeyn and Matilda his wife hold by writing indented, for the term of their life, sixteen acres of land: whereof one acre lies in Southfeld above Grascroftforlong, and two acres above Lutlemorforlong, and one acre in the Furlong towards Bigenhull, and two acres and a half above Hodesforlong, and half an acre (which is called Brodehalfsacre) in Tachemullewey, and one acre above Merforlong, nearer to Berencester; and three acres in Northfeld above Brokforlong, and two acres above Waterforlong, and one acre in Lallesden, and two acres in the Breche. And they pay rent for the same per annum, at the times aforesaid, 10s.

John de Lacy and Petronilla his wife hold by Court Roll two

acres of land lying together above Overnynacre, between the land of my lord the Earl of Lincoln and the land of John Rooke in the north field. And they pay rent per annum, 14d.

John de Aston holds four acres and a half of land, which John de Bigenhull formerly held: whereof half an acre lies above Overdenyshlond, near the land of John Hargur; and another half acre lies in the same place, near the land of John Whyn; and half an acre lies at Mulleweylonde, near the land of John Goldes; and one acre and a half lie at Cornhull, near the land formerly of John le Bakere holding of the Lady; and half an acre lies at *St. Edburghes Grenewey*, near the land of John Abbot; and one acre in Netherdenyshelond, near the land of Simon Ward. And he pays rent per annum, 2s. 10¼d.

William le Blake, slave born of the Lady, holds at will those three acres which the master William the Vicar sometime held, and after him John Faber and Isabella his wife sometime held: whereof one acre lies in the Morforlong, near Sidenhall; and half an acre lies near Stanfordewey, and another half acre lies ......
.. and another half acre at Eldeford, and another half acre above Overdenyshelond. He pays rent per annum, 2s. 3d.

William Cavel and Nicholas de Saford, slaves born of the Lady, hold four acres of land which Roger Morian sometime held: whereof two acres lie in the Northfeld at Cotemanleye. And they pay per annum, at the times aforesaid, 2s. 8d. And they are held by Roll at will.

William Cavel, slave born, holds four acres of land by Court Roll: whereof one acre lies above Hangeteshulle, near the land of Nicholas le Blake; and one acre between the land formerly of Simon Germeyn and a land of Agnes le Blake, and abutting upon the aforesaid acre and half in Lallesden; and half an acre above Middlefurlong, between the land of Nicholas atte Brigge and Robert Germeyn; and one acre in Middlefurlong, between the land of Nicholas le Blake and the land of Simon Germeyn. He pays rent per annum, 2s. 8d.

Robert le Friend, slave born of the Lady, holds by Court Roll at will five acres of land: whereof one acre lies above Wadforlong, between the land of Simon Germeyn and the land of the said Robert; and one acre lies in the same piece, between the land of Robert Baud and the land .... ; and half an acre lies above the Croftelond, between the land of John atte Forde and the land of John Walter, and extends above the Wodeweye; and half an acre lies above Eldefeld, next to the More between the land of John James and of Walter Sebern; and one acre lies above Netherdenyshelond, between the land of John Knyght and the land ....; and one acre above Shorteforlong, between the land .... He pays rent per annum, 2s. 10d.

Peter Galawar, slave born of the Lady, holds for the term of his own life and that of his wife, six acres of land: whereof two acres and a half lie together above the Netherynacre, between the land of Robert Germeyn and the land of John Goldes; and two acres lie in the Morforlong between the Lord John de Langele and John Erbich; and half an acre lies in the Shorteforlong, *above the old dych* between Robert Germeyn and John Stevene; and one acre extends above Imbelow Grene\Wey between the Lord of Bigenhull and John de Saford, he pays rent per annum, at four times, 4s. 6d. per acre 9d.

Sum of Acres demised for the term of life, eighty acres and a half and one rood.

Robert Elyot Chaplain, son of Robert Elyot lately deceased, who was slave born of the Lady, and who held in villenage[3] two messuages and two half yard lands of the Lady, holds one messuage and half a yard land of the aforesaid two messuages, and two half yard lands, which messuage is situated near the tenement formerly of John Syrech; and the said half yard land contains 29 acres of arable and one acre, one rood, one parcel at Shrofdeles. Two swathes of the said meadow lie as follows:—Half an acre lies in Southfeld in culture, *atte* Spore, near the land of the Lord of Bigenhull: and one rood at Gadewey, near the land of the aforesaid lord; and one rood in Oredoune near the land of William

---

[3] *In bondagio;* in bondage or villenage.

Cavel on the one side, and the land of Nicholas atte Brigge; and one rood above Strongforlong near the land of Peter Gallowar; and at Wowelond half an acre, near the land of the Prioress of Merkyate; and at Godeforlong half an acre, between the land of Peter Galewar and of Walter Sebern; and half an acre *bi Lesemor side*, near the land of the Lord of Bigenhull; and at Funleslo one rood, near the land of Walter Sebern; and at the Foxhal half an acre, near the land of Robert Thames; and in the same place half an acre, near the land of Simon Germeyn; and in the same place half an acre, near the land of John Eylrich; and one acre in the same place, near the land of P. Galewar; and half an acre atte Twiseledewey near the land of John atte Brigge; and half an acre beyond the Twiseledewey, near the land of John le Rooke; and half an acre at Shorteforlong, near the land of John Walter; and half an acre at Brademor, near the land of Robert le Friend; and half an acre in the same place, near the land of Walter Sebern; and half an acre in the same place, near the land of John Walter; and half an acre in the same place, near the land of the Lady Prioress; and one acre at Thoftewellemor, near the land of the Lord of Bigenhull; and in Oldefeld half an acre, between the land of the Lady and of John Walter; also in the Northfeld half an acre, at the Wowelond, near the land of John Walter; and one acre above Crockwelleforlong, near the land of John Walter; and half an acre above Poukwelleforlong, near the land of Simon Germeyn; and half an acre at Isenfordhull, near the land of Robert Wymark; and half an acre at Sidenhal, near the land of Ely Coke; and half an acre beyond the road to St. Edburg, near the land of Robert le Frend; and half an acre at Stanforde, near the land of John atte Ford; and half an acre in the same place, near the land of Robert Thames; and half an acre in the same place, near the road to St. Edburg; and one rood at Cornhull, near the land of Walter Sebern; and one rood in the same place, near the land of Andrew le Rooke; and half an acre at Cotemanlaye, near the land of John atte Ford; and in the same place one rood, near the land of John atte Ford; and at Gatethorn half an acre near the land of John James; and half an acre at Overbrech, near the land of Simon Germeyn; and half an acre at Sagesthorn, near the land of Peter Galewar, and half an acre in the same place near the king's highway, and at Waltersforlong half an acre between the land of John Walter and of Walter Sebern and half an acre in Lallesdon near the land of Walter Sebern, and half an acre at Kyngesacre near the land of Robert Coleyn and half an acre at Middleforlong near the land of the Prior of Berencester and half an acre in the same place near the land of John Cavel and he pays rent per annum at the end thereof one mark and one coming to the court.

Of which meadow half a rood lies *atte Witheyes* near the Prior's Meadow and half an acre *atte Lake* near the land formerly of Simon Germeyn and one rood *betwhene dike* near the land formerly of John at Ford, and one rood *atte Rowelowe* by lot as it shall fall out between the said Robert his brother William, John, Walter, and Peter Galeware, and half a rood and half a *swathe* at Shortedolemede and one parcel at Shrofdolemed between the said Robert and his brother William and containing as it shall fall out by lot, and two *swatkes* at Mathames when it shall fall by lot amongst the community.

Sum of the rents of the Holders of the Domain Lands for the term of their lives 64s. 6¼d. whereof for the time of St. Michael 16s. 1¼d. for the time of the birth of our Lord 16s. 1¼d. for the time of the Annunciation. &c.

Rents and Services of Copyholders.

Robert son of Nicholas Germeyn holds one messuage and half a yard land in villenage at the will of the Lady and is bound to perform one ploughing in winter and one weeding and one wedbedrip[*] at the will of the Lady, and shall have one meal and is bound to perform one mowing for half a day, and a whole yard land of the same tenure shall have *Ivery* at what are called *evenyngs* as much of what is mown as a mower can lift up with his scythe and carry home with the same, and half a yard land of the same tenure shall have livery in the evening with a companion

---

[*] Reaping performed by a tenant for his lord.

as much of what is mown as a mower can lift up with his scythe and carry home, and the mower shall have his breakfast from the Lady Prioress, and the said Robert and all the other copyhold tenants of the Lady having livery are bound to turn the grass which has been mowed in the meadow called Gilberdesham without receiving a dinner and there to toss up the hay and make it into cocks. And he is bound to carry four cart-loads of hay to the yard of the Prioress and he shall have one breakfast from the Lady Prioress. And a yard land of the same kind shall perform three days work in Autumn to wit one day's work without a dinner with three men and one day's work without a dinner with one man and if he be a binder he shall have at the said days work one sheaf of wheat for seed of the last wheat that was bound, and he is bound also to perform one day's work at the will of the Lady with his whole family except his wife and shall dine with the Lady and as often as the binder has his dinner he shall not have the sheaf, and he is bound to carry four cart-loads of wheat in Autumn to the manor of the Lady and he shall have one breakfast and he is bound to be assessed at the feast of St. Michael at the will of the Lady Prioress, nor is he allowed to sell a male horse or an ox of his own feeding, nor to put his son to learning, nor to give his daughter in marriage without the permission and will of the Priotess. But if the Lady Prioress be present the said Robert shall fetch and carry eatables and drinkables to the Prioress during the time that she shall tarry in the county at her will, and he shall also pay rent per annum at the four usual times 2s. 6d. and suit of court.

William Hammond holds one messuage and half a yard land by the same service and pays rent per annum 2s. 6d.

William Cavel holds one messuage and half a yard land in manner aforesaid and pays rent per annum, 2s. 6d.

John Cavel holds one messuage and half a yard land and pays rent per annum 2s. 6d.

The same John holds one messuage at the will of the Lady besides the other aforesaid tenement and pays rent per annum 2s.

Robert Michel holds one messuage and half a yard land by the aforesaid service and pays rent per annum 2s. 6d.

APPENDIX. 227

Robert le Friend holds one messuage and half a yard land by the aforesaid services and pays rent per annum 2s. 6d.

Rose who was the wife of John Knight holds &c. as above and pays rent 2s. 6d.

John Walter holds one messuage and half a yard land and pays rent yearly 2s. 6d.

Peter Galeware holds the same &c.

William son of Robert Eylot holds the same &c.

Nicholas de Saford holds the same &c.

William le Blake holds the same &c.

Alicia who was the wife of Richard le Grey villain and slave born of the lady holds one messuage two acres of land and half an acre of meadow and shall perform one weeding and one wedbedrip and haymaking, and shall find one man to make a haycock as the aforesaid Robert son of Nicholas and shall perform three days work in Autumn without allowance of food and she pays rent per annum 12d.

Nicholas at the Spring holds one messuage with a croft and two acres of land and half an acre of meadow by the same services as the aforesaid Alice and pays rent per annum 18d. and suit.

Sum of the rents of the Copyholders and Villains 34s. 6d. whereof for the time of St. Michael 8s. 7½d. &c.

Sum total of the whole rent aforesaid 7l. 11s 8¼d. &c.

John Abbot holds one messuage and pays rent for it per annum 3s. 7d. at the times aforesaid and suit of court.

The same John holds another messuage formerly Roger le Moyne's and pays rent for it per annum 4s. at the times aforesaid.

The same John and Juliana his wife hold 4 acres of land in fee by deed whereof 2 acres lie at the Cadeford and 1 rood at Liveruchesdich and 2 acres and a half at the Morforlong and they pay rent for the same per annum 3s. 6d. at the times aforesaid.

The same hold 6 acres of arable land in fee by deed whereof 1½ acre lie near Buckinghamewey towards the north side and 1½ acre lie above Overynacre and 1 acre which is called Catacers and 1 acre above Goldfurlong and 4 ends which contain 1 acre &c.

Q 2

The same John holds at the will of the lady 1 acre and 1 rood of land lying in 5 parts whereof 1 rood lies between the land of Nicholas [a] Bailiff of Bygenhull and the land of Robert Michel of Bygenhull and extends as far as Olddich and another rood between the rood of the aforesaid Nicholas and the land of John Rok above Shortdoun and extends as far as Longeland and another rood near the land of Nicholas the bailiff of Bygenhull and extends as far as Oldedich and 1 rood lies at the lower end of the Oldedich near the Scappe between the land of Nicholas at the Bridge and the land of Robert Elyot paying rent for the same yearly 16d. at the accustomed times &c.

Of lands let to farm.

John Squier holds $2\frac{1}{4}$ acres of land of the domain of the Prioress, whereof $1\frac{1}{2}$ acre lie above Overfordeshull and 1 acre above Hodesforlong for the term of his life and pays rent for the same per annum $22\frac{1}{2}d$.

Nicholas le Blake holds 13 acres and 1 rood of land whereof 6 acres lie above Waterforlong and 2 roods near the road, to wit, the Gores above the Shortforlong and $\frac{1}{2}$ an acre at Kyngesmer and 1 acre at Longeland and 1 acre at Hangateshull to wit Foreschetere and $1\frac{1}{2}$ acre above Wateresforlong near Berencestre and 2 roods above Waltersforlong in Lallesdene and 2 acres in Lallesdene and 1 rood near the broke beyond Bykenhull and he pays rent for the same per annum 7s. 6d. at the times aforesaid and holds for the term of his life and that of Agnes his wife.

John de Astone holds 4 acres of land whereof 1 acre lies above Overdencheland and $\frac{1}{2}$ an acre lies at *Seynt Edburges Grene Wey* near the land of John Abbot and $\frac{1}{2}$ an acre at Melesweyende and 1 acre at Cornhull and $\frac{1}{2}$ an acre at Standfordsgreneweye and 1 acre above Netheresdencheland and he pays rent for the same per annum 2s. 10d. &c.

Roger Mortimer slave born of the Prior of Berencester holds 4 acres of land whereof 2 acres lie in Southfeld at Oldediches end

---

[a] Præpositi.

APPENDIX. 229

and 2 acres lie in Northfeld at Colmanleye and he pays rent for the same per annum 2s. 8d. at the times aforesaid and it is held for the term of his life.

Henry by the custom holds 9 acres and 1 rood of land whereof 5 acres lie above Radyforlong and ½ an acre above Overdencheslaud and 1½ acre and 3 roods above Catacre, &c.

No. III.

Charter for the foundation of an Hospital in Burcester.

A. D. 1355.

(TRANSLATION)

The King to all unto whom &c. Know ye that of our special favour we have granted and given permission for ourselves and our heirs as much as in us lies, to Nicholas Jurdan of Burcester Hermit, Guardian of the Chapel of the blessed John the Baptist of Burcester, that he may found a certain Hospital for the reception and entertainment of the poor and sick to the honour of God and of the glorious Virgin Mary his Mother and of the blessed John the Baptist at Burcester and may endow it with one hundred shillings of land and rent per annum with the appurtenances according to their true value, excepting lands, tenements, and rents which are held of us in capite, to have and to hold unto the said Guardian and his successors in aid of the support of the same and of a certain Chaplain to celebrate divine service on every day for ever in the aforesaid Chapel for our welfare and for that of Philippa Queen Consort of England and of Edward Prince of Wales our most dearly beloved son as long as we shall live and for our souls when we shall have been withdrawn from beholding this light, and for the souls of all the faithful deceased, the statute against placing lands and tenements in mortmain notwithstanding, &c.

Witness the King at Westminster 15th day of May.

No. IV.

Account of the outgoings and incomings of the Dairy of Le Brech. 1407, 8, 9, *Henry* IV.

(TRANSLATION.)

WRECHWYKE. Account of Henry Deye and Joan his wife of all outgoings and incomings of the Dairy [7] of the Lord Prior of Burncestre at his close of Le Brech kept by the same from the morrow of St. Michael the archangel in the seventh year of the reign of King Henry the fourth after the conquest unto the same morrow of the same day in the eighth year of the same reign.

Sale of Cows. First; the persons aforesaid are responsible for 7s. received for one cow sold to John Grene butcher of Burncester this year. Sum 7s.

Sale of Calves. For 20d. received for a calf of the aforesaid Cow which was sold to the said John Grene this year. And for 12d. received for a weak calf of a certain heifer [8] sold to the aforesaid John this year. And for 10s. 8d. received for 5 calves of the outgoing of this new year sold to the butcher of Langeton this year. Sum 13s. 4d.

Sale of Skins. In the sale of skins nothing done this year.

Agistment of Beasts. And for 3s. 4d. received for the feeding of sundry beasts within the aforesaid close and out of it this year. Sum 3s. 4d.

Sale of Cheese. And for 67s. 6¼d. received for cheese and butter as appears by a bill of things remaining with brother Richard Albon the Canon this year: and the less on account of the very great plenty of cheese this year throughout the whole parish. Sum 67s. 6¼d.

Sale of Fuel. And for 2s. 2d. received for thorns and branches remaining after the making and repairing of the hedges of the aforesaid close, sold to the men of Langeton this year. And for 3d. re-

---

[7] Dayri. [8] Hekfore.

APPENDIX. 231

ceived for one load of. . . . . . sold to John Grene of Burcester this year. Sum 2s. 6d.

Sum total received as aforesaid 4l. 13s. 7½d.

Allowance. Out of which things are allowed unto the aforesaid Henry and Joan for their yearly salary paid at four times of the year 13s. 4d. And in allowance to the same for five bushels and a half of salt bought this year 3s. 4½d. And for exchange made for one cow remaining in store for one bullock of John atte Mulle 12d. And for a new Cowele[9] bought 9d. And for a new Kevere[10] bought 8d. And there is allowed unto them for one cow with its calf bought of John Okle butcher of Stratton 7s. 6d. And there is allowed to them for two bushels of wheat 10d. And there is allowed to them for carriage of straw by William Holt junior from the rectory of Stratton 11d. And there is allowed to them for the making and repairing of the hedges by sundry men of Langeton 4s. 2d. And for the victuals of the said men 2s. Also there is allowed to them for carriage of white straw for the rectory of Stratton aforesaid 11d. And for William Throcchere threshing for five days 10d. And for the repairing of the Cow-house 11d.—Sum 38s. 11½d.

Costs of a new cart and of new husbandry. And there is allowed to the same Henry for two oxen bought of John Clerk of Langeton 26s. 8d. And for another ox bought of John Yve of Burcester 12s. 6d. Nothing is charged here, because it stands in the account of the Bursar of the Priory of Burncester. And there is allowed to the same for two Turkeys *(Africanis)* bought at Bannebury with their expences 15s. 2d. And in one new plough bought of Hugo Spinan 10d. And for the making of another plough by John Benhull 4½d. And for one share and one coulter and half a beam[11] with one Plowshoe[12] bought 23d. And another share is put down nothing here in money because it was purchased with the working of a plough ploughing the land of Simon Adam. And there is allowed to the same for sundries drawing and driving the plough

---

[9] A tub with ears carried between two persons.
[10] A cover or vessel used for milk or whey.   [11] Toughe.
[12] Plowsho.

with their victuals and expenses this year 17s. 9½d. and for 11 bushels of wheat bought for sowing 5s. 10½d. and for one quarter of pease bought for sowing ...... received from the rectory of Stratton, as appears by the account-roll of Nicholas Alleyn bailiff there this year 2s. 8d. and 2 quarters of barley reckoned here nothing in money because received from the rectory of Stratton aforesaid as appears likewise by the account-roll of the aforesaid Nicholas Alleyn this year. And there is allowed for 18 bushels of oats bought for sowing 4s. 6d. and there is allowed for hay bought for the cows and oxen 6d. and there is allowed for three new harrows bought to harrow 18d. and for one seedlip [13] bought 3d. and for one cart-saddle [14] one collar with one pair of traces bought 14d. and for another collar with whitleather bought 4d. and for the making of drawing-geer [15] by Walter Carpenter of Langeton 3d. and for two other collars bought 2d. and for two hempen halters with whip-cord [16] bought 3d. and for iron bought with three horse-shoes bought at sundry times 7d. and for the expences of William Throcchere .... mowing in the meadow of la Breche 16d. and for one dung-cart [17] bought of Simon Adam with its appurtenances 14d. and for sawing and planing one cart-body [18] by William Pire with his victuals 6d. and for making a cart by Richard Schereman 9d. and for a pair of wheels bought of John Helmenden 3s. 2d. and for fastening the fellies [19] of the same 3d. and for shoeing the same [20] by Laurence Smyth 18d. and for weeding half an acre of land in the crofts 6d. and there is allowed to the same for Richard Plumbar for hanging [21] the waggon for twelve days 3s. and for John Bowdon for hanging [21] the waggon for one day 8d. and for victuals bought for the makers of the Prior's ricks 12d. and John Heyward .... sixteen acres and a half of different grain 9s. 6d. ....
Sum 109s. 2¼d.

Sum total of all the aforesaid expenses 7l. 7s. 5d. and thus the allowances with the aforesaid expenses exceed the receipts 53s. 9½d.

---

[13] Seedcod.   [14] Cartsadel.   [15] Drawgere.   [16] Whippecord.
[17] Dongecart. [18] Cartbody.   [19] Fritting.   [20] Calciatura.
[21] Furcante, fitting the body to hang on the axle or wheels. — Glossary.

Account of Henry Deye and Joan his wife of all outgoings and incomings from the dairy of the Lord Prior of Burncester at his close of Le Brech in the manour of Wrechwyke kept by the same from the morrow of St. Michael the archangel in the eighth year of the reign of King Henry the fourth unto the same morrow of the same day in the ninth year of his reign.

First, they reckon nothing this year from the sale of cows.

Sale of Calves. Also they are responsible for 19d. received for one calf sold to John Grene butcher of Burcester this year.—Sum 19d.

Sale of Skins; nothing this year.

Agisting of Beasts. And 3s. 5d. received for the keep of sundry beasts within the aforesaid close and out of it in the common pasture this year.—Sum 3s. 5d.

Sale of Cheese. And for 57s. 5d. received for cheese and butter sold, as appears by a bill of things remaining with Master Richard Albon Canon this year, and the less on account of the very great plenty of cheese throughout the whole parish, and likewise besides presents of cheese made by the Prior.—Sum 57s. 5d.

Sum total received 57s. 5d.

Allowance. Out of which things they pray to be allowed for surplusage of the account of the year immediately foregoing as appears on the other side of this roll 53s. 9½d. And for their salary for this whole year 13s. 4d. And for salt bought nothing in money, because it was bought with the sale of cheese.

Sum 67s. 1½d. and thus, upon this account there is owing to the aforesaid Henry and Joan 4s. 8¼d.

Account of the aforesaid Henry and Joan for stores remaining within the aforesaid dairy in the year aforesaid.

First; they are answerable for three bulls remaining in store.—Sum 3s. and remain.

No. V.

Priory Accounts. Burcester, 1425.

(TRANSLATION.)

BURCESTER. Account of master Richard Parentyn Prior, and of brother Richard Albon Canon and Bursar there, of all goods received and delivered by them from the morrow of St. Michael the archangel in the third year of the reign of King Henry the sixth after the conquest unto the said morrow in the fourth year of the same king.

Curtlington. First; they are responsible for a red rose received on the day of St. John the Baptist from Henry Bowell of Curtlington aforesaid, for certain lands and tenements which the aforesaid Henry holds there by indenture therefore made.

Newenton Purcell. And for one clove received on Easter day for certain lands and tenements formerly belonging to Roger de Stodele, and some of which are now made over to John Purcell lord of the same to hold to him and his heirs for ever.

Pouhele. From whence nothing this year.

Arrears. They are also responsible for 78*l.* 12*s.* 5¼*d.* remaining of the arrears of the last account of the year immediately preceding, as appears at the foot of the account of the same year.—Sum 78*l.* 12*s.* 5½*d.*

Rent with farms. And for 4*l.* 4*s.* 4*d.* received for the rent of fourteen tenements in Burcestre Buryend and Kyngend, as appears by the rental this year, and for 36*s.* received for the farming of a horse-mill within the priory this year, and not more on account of the bad conduct of the miller, who having occupied it more than half a year ran away without paying any rent. And for 26*s.* 8*d.* received for a water-mill situated there this year. And for 73*s.* 4*d.* received for the rent of tenants in Wrechewyke, as appears by the rental this year. And for 34*s.* received for

APPENDIX. 235

crofts lying there this year. And for 56s. 6d. received for lands meadows and pastures lying in the fields of Wtechwyke aforesaid let to sundry men of Blakethorn and others, as appears by the tally against William Spinan collector of the same rent this year. And for 66s. 8d. received from John Yve for the farm of a new close near Gravenhull per annum. And for 35s. 6d. received from the dairy of La Breche, as appears by the account roll of John Deye and of Margery his wife this year. And for 37l. 8s. received for rent in Dadington, Clyfton, and Hampton, with the farm of the manor and mills of Clyfton aforesaid, with extents of courts, portmotes [96] and the toll of the market, as appears by the account of John Wolfe collector of rent there this year. And for 31l. 13s. 4d. received from the grange of Stratton Audele, as appears by the account of Nicholas Aleyn bailiff there this year. And for 6s. 8d. received for a certain tenement which the same Nicholas holds there per annum. And for 60s. received from the farm of Caversfeld per annum. And for 13l. 6s. 8d. received from the farm of Grymmsbury per annum. And for 4l. 13s. 4d. received from the farm of Westcote this year, and no more on account of the falling off of the rent. And for 26s. 8d. received from the culture and pasture of Blackenhull in the parish of Wodesdon this year. And for 53s. 4d. received for rent in Arncote, with hidage there this year. And for 33s. 4d. received from John Chambre and from John Yve for the site of the manor with the lands and meadows of the domain there per annum. And for 2s. received for rent from Fryngford per annum. And for 18l. 6s. 8d. received from John Donesmore for the farm of Bemount per annum. And for 4l. 4s. 2d. received for rent in Curtlington by tally against William Newman collector of rent there per annum. And for 16l. received for the farm of the Church of Ardyngton this year. And for 4l. 13s. 4d. received for the farm of Letecumbe this year, and no more on account of the falling off of the rent. And 5l. 6s 8d. received from the farm of our part in

---

[96] A convention of the inhabitants, in which some customary dues were paid.

the church of Cumpton Basset, and no more on account of the falling off of the rent this year. And for 18s. received for rent in Wendulburi this year. And for 55s. 4d. received for rent in Takele this year. And for .... received from the farm of Mudlington this year.—Sum 165l. 19s. 6d.

Outgoings of the manor. And for 8s. received for one foal sold by John Deye at Bucks at the feast of the Apostles Peter and Paul this year. And for 21s. 8d. received for ten quarters of pease sold to John Nuttebeme this year. And for 37s. 7d. received for eighteen quarters and two bushels of pease sold to sundry men in lots this year. And for 26s. 8d. received for pease-straw sold to John Trote this year. And for 2s. 4d. received for old hay at Crockwell sold to Robert Grene this year. And for 12s. received for five skins of oxen. And for 4s. proceeding from the cattle store. And 1s. for a certain [97] .... killed at the larder and sold by the cook, as appears by the Journal this year. And for 2s. 7d. received for two cow-skins of the store of La Breche, and which cows were killed in the hostel per week, as appears by the aforesaid Journal of things sold this year. And for 4s. 8d. received for three skins of cows bought and killed in the hostel as above and sold this year. And for 2s. received for sixteen skins of store calves of La Breche killed in the hostel as above and sold this year.—Sum 119s. 10d.

Outgoings of the Sheepfold. And for 4s. received for twenty one lambs sold to John Deye of Wrechwyke this year. And for 9s. received for thirty six skins of Welch tags killed in the hostel, between the end of St. Michael and Lent, and sold by brother William Chestreton cook this year. And for 3s. 3d. received for thirteen skins of store tags killed in the hostel between the end of Easter and sheepshearing time, and sold by the same this year. And for 3s. 1½d. received for fifteen pelts [98] of hoggrels which had been bought and killed in the hostel between the same shearing time and the aforesaid end of St. Michael, sold by the same this

---

[97] Hietto, sheep of two years old. Vide Glossary.
[98] Peltys.

year. And for 2s. 11d. received for fourteen skins. And for 10l. 18s. 6d. received for twenty three tods [99] of clean wool sold to a merchant at Oxon this year at 9s. 6d. per tod. And for 12s. received for refuse wool sold to Nicholas Aleyn this year. And for 2s. for broken wool, viz. locks [30] gathered at sheepshearing sold to John Deye this year.—Sum 12l. 3s. 9d.

Outward Receipts. And for 20d. received for underwood sold by Thomas Seler at Bernewode this year. And for 2s. 7¼d. received in part of payment for the tithe of lambs in Burcester, Wrechwyke, and Bygenhull this year. And for 100s. received from the Vicar of Burcestre, being a donation of the same towards building anew the dormitory this year. And for 20d. received and given by John Tanner towards the same work this year.—Sum 105s. 11¼d.

Letting of Lands. And for 5s. received for a half yard land, with half an acre of meadow in Longedole mede, and with half an acre of meadow in Aylmeres mede, let to Richard Cooke, per copy, for the term of his life, &c.—Sum 17s. 1d.

Sale of Herbage. And for 8s. received for the whole tithe of hay and for headlands lying at Northmede let to Thomas Keep this year. And for 5s. received from Mulneham, with three acres of land formerly arable lying in the Medeacres beyond Langeford &c. And for 9d. &c. for the herbage of the heads of three acres and a half lying together in a certain furlong called Burygate, which John Sellar formerly held, &c. And for Schortdole mede nothing in money this year, because in the hand of the lord. And for the meadow of the Prioress of Merkyate nothing in money, because it remains in the store of the lord this year, &c. And for 6s. 8d. received for two *hammys*[31] of a meadow in the field of Wendlebury sold to Philip Webb this year, &c. And the slade towards Gravenhull nothing in money this year, because it remains in the store of the lord, &c.—Sum 4l. 4s. 10d.

Perquisites of court. And for 6s. 8d. from John Smythe,

---

[99] Todde.   [30] Lokys.   [31] i. e. the herbage of them.

slave-born of the Prior, for a certain fine to have entrance in one messuage with one yard land, formerly belonging to Henry Kyng, lately demised to John Drap by indenture. And for 3d. received for extracts of a court held at Burcestre on the feast of St. Nicholas the bishop this year.—Sum 6s. 11d.

Sum of the whole aforesaid receipts with arrears 273l. 10s. 3¼d.

Re-payments and allowances. Of which things they pray that there may be allowed to the lord Le Straunge for a furlong lying on the outside of the door of the mill of the Priory, 8s. 4d. per annum. And for payment to the lord of Bygenhull for a furlong lying next on the outside of the door leading into the country.... the foot-way 6s. 8d. per annum. And in payment to the same lord for a certain tenement in the *Venella*[a], 20d yearly, and in payment to our lady the queen for a certain tenure at Dadynton 12d. yearly; and in payment to the same lady for a certain *helowe wall* of one house at Curtlyngton 2d. yearly; and in payment to the same lady for a new rent in the same village for a false casting up amongst the tenants there, the present being the 17th current year, 10d. per annum. And in an allowance to the farmer of Clyfton aforesaid for the report of the houses and closes aforesaid of his farm this year, 66s. 8d. &c. And in an allowance to William Newman, collector of our rent of Curtlyngton aforesaid, for his labour this year 4s. And in allowance to the same for irrecoverable amercements this year 6d. &c. And in allowance to the same for two strange oxen valued at the lord's court, but not paid for and unjustly detained, 26s. 8d. &c. And in allowance to the same for the digging of stones at the Prior's quarry there, with the repairing of digging tools, as appears by the account of the same John, 58s. 8d.—Sum 10l. 17s. 9d.

Annual pensions. And in payment to the Abbot of Osencye at two times of the year by two acquittances, 60s. And in payment to the Abbot of Egnesham at two times of the year by two acquittances,

---

[a] Venelle. Fr. *Petite Rue.* Ang. *Street.*

40s And in payment to the Prior of the house of St. Anne of the Carthusian order, near Coventre, for a certain pension of the late Abbot of Aulney in Curtlyngton, at two times of the year by two acquittances, 40s. And in payment to the Abbot of Messenden for a certain freehold farm in Arncote, at two times of the year by two acquittances, 6l. 13s. 4d. And in payment for a certain pension called Schirewyte, 4s. annually. And in payment to John Pepar of Wendlebury for a certain pension 6s. 8d. annually.—Sum 14l. 4s.

Tithes and procurations. The tithe of our lord the king, nothing this year. And in payment for the procuration of the convocation of the clergy held at London before Christmas this year 9d. And in payment for procuration of our lord the pope and acquittance this year 7s. 2d. And in payment to our lord the Archdeacon of Oxford for procuration of the parochial church of Burcestre this year 7s. 7¼d. And in payment to the same for the Easter visitation this year 2s. And in payment to the same for the visitation at St. Michael this year 12d.—Sum 18s. 6¼d.

Debts discharged. And in payment to John Buntyng, citizen and apothecary at Oxford, for sundry drugs bought of the same, &c. 8s. 1d. &c. And in payment for eels and other fresh fish bought at Dadington by John Wulfe in the year aforesaid 2s. 4d.—Sum 11s. 5d.

Cost of ploughs and carts. And in two sets of fellowes for wheels[83] bought at Bemount, as appears by a paper this year, viz. at two sundry times 18s. And in expenses of carriage of the aforesaid two sets of fellowes from thence, with expenses of Richard Dymby at the same place to bargain for the aforesaid fellowes, 23d. And in one pair of wheels called *schozears* bought there, as appears by the aforesaid paper, &c. 7s. 2d. And in six iron *strakys*, &c. 5s. And in cart nails, *gropys*, and other iron articles bought at Oxford of John Mylton, ironmonger[34], 12s. 4d. And in payment to John Pope of Middlington for ironwork for the same 20d. And in ten spikes bought of the same for ironwork for the same

---

[3] Clausis rotarum.   [34] Yrenmonger.

240   APPENDIX.

10d. And in payment for *frytting*[35] five wheels this year, 7d. And in one axletree bought, with putting an axletree to one cart, 8d. &c. And in five yards of *waddemole*[36] bought for horses' collars this year, 2s. 1d. &c. And in three collars, one *basse*, together with three halters bought at Sterisbrugge[37] this year 5s. 10½d. And in one whip bought there this year 2d. &c.—Sum 6l. 8½d.

Necessary stores[38]. And in one large lock bought before the Feast of St. Kalixtus Pope this year 2s. And in parchment bought at the fair of St. Frideswyde 6d. And in paper bought at the same time there 4d. And in one chair bought at London at the feast of St. Thomas Apostle 9d., and in payments to the Sub-prior for copperas and galls bought for varnish at the same time 2d. And in two pounds of candles bought for the Prior's lamp before Christmas this year 12d. And in eight pounds of wax bought at Oxford on the same day to make two torches[39] for Christmas at the Prior's hall 3s. And in repairing a flour-sieve this year 1½d. And in boulting-cloth[40] bought for sifting flour, &c. 10d. And in two horse girths, with more articles bought at the same time for the Prior's table 6d. &c. And soap bought at one time to wash the Prior's hall 1d. &c. And in nineteen ells of linen per ams. bought for making table-napkins for the refectory this year 5s. And in hair-cloth bought there for the bake-house this year 3s. 6d. And in eight snoden of pack-thread bought there for making a net to catch rabbits this year 6s. And in six padlocks bought there 1s. 6d. And in two large locks 2d. And in one pound of bird-lime[41] bought there 3d. And in one hair-sieve[42] bought for the bake-house there 10d. And in two hand-scuttles bought there 7d. And in five scuttles[43] of a smaller kind bought there for other offices 9d. And in four mats bought there this year 13d.—Sum 68s. 1d.

Stores of the inn. And in white bread bought at different times, as appears by the bill, viz. for the Prior and other guests this year 3s. 10d. And in ale, viz. one hundred and thirty-two gallons[44]

---

[35] Fastening with fellows.   [36] Cloth to cover horse-collars.
[37] Stourbridge, or Sturbich.   [38] Munita, from *Munir*, Fr.
[39] Torceys.   [40] Bultercloth.   [41] Byrdlyme.
[42] Heresyve.   [43] Scotellis.   [44] Lagenis.

APPENDIX. 241

and a half, bought of Joan Spinan, Alice Bedale, and other ale-wives, as appears by the bill, &c. 4s. 10d. And in thirty-two gallons of red wine bought of Richard Brasyer of Burcestre, at 8d. per gallon, 31s. 4d.[45] And in three gallons and three quarts of sweet wine bought of the same, at 16d. per gallon, 5s. &c. And in canvass[46] bought at London by Richard Dymby, before the feast of St. Osith the Virgin, for making sheets, 3s. And in a bolt of red silk at Steresbrugge, for making a cope[47] (for the priest), 4s. 8d. &c.—Sum 104s. ½d.

Costs of houses. And to W. Hykkedon, mason, hired for four days to make a threshold for the parlour door towards the prior's hall, &c. 16d., and in nails bought of John Bette for the same door 12d. and in rings bought for the same door 8d.; and to John Coventre, with two servants, tiling over the chamber called Clykchambour, towards the court, for four days, 3s. 4d.; and to two sawyers hired for ten days to saw elm boards for making doors and windows, 6s. 8d.; and in six estregbords[48], viz. wainscots bought at Steresbrugge 2s. 3d. &c.; and to W. Hykkedon, hired by the great at the lord's dwelling-house, to smooth and finish the crest over the chancel of the priory there, 24s. &c.—Sum 53s.

Costs of the dormitory-house. And in W. Skern, with his companions, hired by the great to dig walling-stones at a quarry beyond Crockewell, &c. 23s. 4d. &c. And in sundry men hired at two different times to break stones in the priory for making lime, &c. 14d. &c. And in payment to John Chepyn, quarryman, for fitting and making eighteen corbelstones, to be placed in the aforesaid wall, 5s. 4d. &c. And in John Coventre of Banbury, slater, for undertaking by the great to cover the aforesaid house, 4l. 1d. &c. And in iron pipes, weighing twenty-eight pounds, with two weather-cocks, viz. tin vanes[49], bought of the smith of Cherkton, to be placed over each end of the aforesaid dormitory, 5s. 2d. &c. And in sundry men hired to pull down and draw away the old timber, rubbish, and stones, 10d. &c.—Sum 34l. 17s. 4¼d.

---

[45] It should be 21s. 4d. [46] Canvayce. [47] Anabatam.
[48] Boards from the eastern countries, Norway, &c. [49] Vanys de tyn.

Expenses of the kitchen. And in twenty pullets bought by the cook for the feast of St. Kalixtus 20d. And in one quarter of beef bought in Burcestre market, at the feast of St. Thomas the Apostle, to salt, 16d. And in one cade of red herrings bought of Harmand Banbury, 8s. And in hogs'-flesh bought for the clerks of my lord the Archbishop, sitting at a compertorium at Burncestre on Wednesday next before the Feast of the Conversion of St. Paul, 19d. &c. And in one frail [50] of figs, 3s. 4d. &c. And in twelve pounds of raisins bought, 13d. &c. And in three couple of green [51] fish, with one green ling, with three congers, and with one couple of hakets [52], 9s. 7d. &c. And in a large axe, called a flesh axe [53], 15d. And in one hundred of halfwaxfysche, bought at Sterusbrugge by brother Richard Albon this year, 21s. &c. And in fifteen couple of myllewell of the smaller kind, 10s. 6d. And in twenty myllewell of the larger kind, 12s. And in two bunches [54] of garlick, 6d. And in one salt-stone bought for the dove-house, 2½d. &c.—Sum 46l. 7s. 8d.

Costs of the sheepfold. And in the wages of John Colyns, shepherd at Crockwell, and general superintendant as well there as at Wrechwyke, this year, 20d. &c. And in two yards of russet-cloth, bought and given to the same, 2s. 2d. &c. And in twelve sheep-hurdles bought of Nicholas Aleyn this year, 17d. And in payment for lopping and making thirty sheep-hurdles at Midlington-fold, this year, 19d.—Sum 53s. 4½d.

Purchase of grain. And in four quarters of wheat bought at Stratton of Nicholas Aleyn, for making malt this year, 16s. &c.— Sum 62s. 3¼d.

Bought for the store. And in one bay horse bought of William Salt of Burcestre, before Christmas this year, for the prior's stable, 26s. 8d. And in two colts bought of John Ayrsbrook, at Easter this year, 9s. And in three hundred and twenty-four pounds of Spanish iron, bought at Sterusbrugge fair this year, with carriage of the same, 18s. 5d.—Sum 54s. 1d.

---

[50] Frayle.
[52] Hake.
[51] Salted, but which have not had time to dry.
[53] Fleschaxe.
[54] Bonchys.

Weeding, mowing, and making of hay. And in payment of sundry men and women on the first day of the month of July, hired to weed sundry fields of wheat, as appears by a tally against the field-man [55], this year, 14s. 10d. &c.—Sum 74s. 8d.

Costs of autumn. And in thirty pairs of autumnal gloves, bought for divers servants and other labourers this year, 4s. &c. And in Thomas Hamunde, hired by a general consultation to prepare for the cart twenty-nine lands of barley, ten of which extend themselves into the Caversfield Brook, and nineteen lie in the middle furlong towards the white cross, towards Buckenhull, with the ernes [56], viz. 8d. And in given to William Skinner, a lad from the bake-house, one of the company of mowers for ten days, 12d. &c.—Sum 12l. 13s. 3d.

Thrashing and winnowing. And in John Leseby, thrashing [57] forty-five quarters of wheat, as appears by the tally this year, taking 3½d. for each quarter, 9s. 4½d. And in fans hired by the great to winnow all kinds of grain threshed below the priory this year, 10s.—Sum 4l. 15s. 1d.

The chamber of the convent. And in payment to the prior and convent for their clothing, at the terms of the Annunciation of the blessed Mary, and of St. Michael the Archangel, this year, 10l. 13s. 4d. And in payment to brothers Robert Lawton and William Meriton, for their expenses towards the orders existing at Higham Ferrers, before the feast of St. Michael this year, 7s.—Sum 11l. 4d.

Purchase of livery cloth. And in red cloth bought for the esquires and valets of the prior, of John Bandye, of Great Tue, clothier, about Christmas this year, 7l. 15s. 2d.—Sum 7l. 15s. 2d.

Fees, with the salaries of free-men. And in a fee to John Langston, steward, holding the court, 26s. 8d. per annum. And in a fee to W. Saleman, attorney to the prior, at London, 6s. 8d. per annum. &c. And in salary to John Baldwin, valet de chambre to the prior, this year, 13s. 4d. And in salary to W. Puffe, baker, 15s.

---

[55] Agillariqm.—A person appointed to take care of the tillage and harvest-work and pay the labourers.—See Glossary.   [56] Scattered ears.
[57] Trituranti ad taxam.

per annum. And in wages to William Skynner, his assistant, 10s. And in salary to the wife of the same, she being malt-drier this year, 10s. And in salary to William Gulde, barber this year, 6s. And in salary to Katharine Colyns, making towels for the kitchen this year, 20d. And in gift to the same for one apron, 3d. And in salary to the washerwoman, 6s. per annum.—Sum 8l. 17s. 7d.

Wages of the servants. And in wages to Robert Jamys, upper bailiff at the Grange, 13s. 4d. per annum. And in wages to Robert Clerk, field-man, this year, 13s. 4d. &c. And in wages to William Lethnarde, plough-holder, this year, 15s. &c. And in wages to William Erlyche, plough-driver, this year, 14s. 8d. &c.—Sum 7l. 13s. 5d.

Wages of labourers. And in John Leseby hedging at the sheepfold at Wrechwyke and Crockwell, 13d. &c. And in Thomas Soler, cutting down twenty-one cart loads of underwood at Bernwode, 3s. 2d. &c. And in a certain travelling man hired to drive plough and harrow for twelve days, 12d. &c.—Sum 42s. 3d.

External expenses. And in the expenses of John Gyles, of Oxford, with repairing two saddles there, &c. 2d. And in the expenses of brother William Chesterton, at Letcombe, on the feast of St. Leonard the abbot, for back rent there this year, 12d. And in suits to Thomas Takkele, on account of the returning of two writs at Oxford at that time, 4d. &c. And in Richard Dymby riding to London, the second week of the advent of our Lord, for a boy to be made a canon, with two horses for three days, this year, 2s. And in payment to Thomas Takkele aforesaid taking a certain lad, late the servant of John Grene, to Oxford castle, in Christmas week, because he agreed to serve the prior and did not fulfil his agreement, 20d. And in payment to the gaoler there to receive the aforesaid servant before the time into the aforesaid castle, because he had not a warrant at that time, 3s. 4d. &c. And in hurdles bought to re-build Clyfton bridge, in the year last past, 7d. &c. And in old timber bought at Curtlington, with carriage of the same, for new making a pillory at Dadyngton, 2s. &c. And in payment to John Spinan, for making four quarters of capital malt, before Easter this year, 16d. And in the expenses of Richard Bo-

-teler, at Trentham, on the feast of St. John, *ante portam Latinam*, with sealing the letters of visitation of the canons regular, 4d. &c. And in expenses of the prior at the general chapter held at Leicester, this year, 48s. 2d. &c. And in payment for beds of the servants of the archdeacons of Oxfordshire and Bucks, stopping all night at the inn of John Fletcher once, 2d. &c. And in all kinds of expenses of brother Richard Albon, at Sterisbrugge fair, with three horses going and returning, to buy sundry provisions, &c. for five days this year, 12s. 6d. &c.—Sum 6l. 15s. 9d.

Expenses against the parishioners of Stratton for burial there. And in gift to Master John Garton, the prior's proctor, against the same, 3s. 4d. And in the expenses of John Baldwyn, of London, to confer with Master William Howper for taking counsel in the same matter, before the feast of St. Osith the Virgin, this year, 20d. And in the expenses of the prior there for seven days, to prosecute the same cause, 40s. 8d. &c. And in the expenses of John Saleman, carrying rabbits, capons, and other victuals to the prior whilst he was there, 12d. And in gift to the servant of the rector of Wycheford, bringing good news concerning the same cause, on the day of St. Theodore, 20d. And in gift to Thomas Bekyngham, on the day of St. Katherine the Virgin, the prior's attorney, before the Bishop of Worcester, in the same cause, 20s. And in the expenses of the Rector of Whyccheford, at London, for four days, with two horses, before the same bishop, to confer about the same cause, 7s. 8d. &c. And in Richard Boteler riding to London, at the feast of St. Mary Magdalen, to inquire concerning the coming of the aforesaid bishop to Burcestre, touching the same cause, 20d. And in gifts to the four servants of Thomas Beckyngham aforesaid, when he was before the aforesaid bishop, to hear judgement given by the aforesaid bishop, on the morrow of St. Anne, the mother of Mary, concerning the two bodies which were buried in the chapel of Stratton, which were to be taken up again and brought to Burcestre; and concerning the reparation of other injuries done to the prior and his convent by the tenants there, 6s. 8d. And in gift to Thomas Somerton, at the same time, for counsel, 6s. 8d. And in sundry victuals, &c. 27s. 5d. And in gift to the aforesaid bishop at that time pronouncing the aforesaid judgement, 6l. 13s. 4d. And in gifts to his clerks and gentlemen at that time, 46s. 8d.—Sum 16l. 15s. 9d.

Gifts of the prior. And in gift to a certain Carmelite brother preaching at Burcestre before the feast of St. Luke the Evangelist, this year, 3s. 4d. And in gifts to the prior's servants cleaning the fish-pond near the mill, before the same feast, 6d. And in gift to a certain harper at the same feast, this year, 8d. And in gift to a certain boy of London, permitted to be a canon, before the feast of All Saints, 6d. And in gift to a certain man of Chestreton at the same feast, who brought to the priory a certain deer which strayed from it, 2d. And in gift to a certain minstrel of the Lord Lestraunge at the same feast, 12d. And in gift to a certain servant belonging to the forest, who brought venison to the prior on the morrow of the same feast, 12d. &c. And in gifts to sundry persons playing at football on the feast of St. Katherine, Virgin and Martyr, 4d. &c. And in eight woodcocks bought and given to the Lady Lestraunge on the eighth day after Epiphany, 12d. And in gift to the shepherd of Crockwell on the day of St. Valentine the Martyr, 2d. And in gifts to the messenger of the Lord Bishop of Lincoln on the day of Saints Perpetua and Fælicia, 20d. And in one pair of gloves bought and given to Master Thomas Beckyngton, 20d. And in twelve pairs of gloves bought and given to sundry men of the Bishop of Worcester, 5s. And in gifts for distribution to the poor on supper-day this year, 3s. 6d. And in gifts to two shepherds, 2d. &c. And in gift to the minstrel of the Lord Tallebotte on the feast of St. Edburg the Virgin, 12d. And in gifts to John Donesmore and other tenants and parishioners of Missenden to repair the bell there, 6s. 8d. And in gifts to two servants belonging to the forest, who brought venison to the prior on the feast of the Dedication of the Church this year, 5s. And in two pair of best hose given to the same at that time, 20d. And in sundry gifts to the poor at various times, as appears by a paper this year, 2s. 4d.—Sum 53s. 7d.

Sum total of all the aforesaid expenses .... £218 9 2¼.
And thus the receipts exceed the expenditure £ 55 12 0¼.

No. VI.

Lease of the Manor of Nun's Place, granted by the Prioress and Nuns of Merkyate to John Gryffyth, 22 Hen. VIII.

THYS indentyr made the syx and twenty day of May the yer of the reygn off Kyng Henry the viij. the two and twenty; between Dame Jane Souche, Pryoresse of the monasterye of Merkeyate, and the nonnes of the same monasterye, of the oon p'tye and John Gryffyth, gentylman, s'nt to the Lord Cardynall on the other p'tye. Wytnessyth that the said pryoresse and nonnes, by their own assent, consent, and agreement, be taken, granted, and to ferme letten to the seyd John, hys executours and assygnes, all ther man^r, londe, and ten'ts, rentys, statys, and meds meddows, londs and pasturs, with their app'tynn'es lyyng and beyng yn townes and felds of Burcester, alias Burestir, called the Nunnes Place, or by what soever other name or names they be called, except and reserving to the seyd pryoresse and to her successors, both of the wards and releyvs and halfe of the courts there: to have and to hold all the foresayd man^r, londs, and ten'ts, and other the p'mysses, with ther app'tynn'es except before expressed, to the seyd John Gryffyth, hys executours and assygnes, for the terme of twenty-oon y'rs, fully to be complete and endyd, the t'me to begyn at the feste of Seynt Mychyll th' Archangell, whych shall be yn the yer of our Lord God a thousand five hundredth thyrte and fyve, or else to begyne and take effect at any tyme betwen the date of thyes p'ntes and the seyd feste of Seynt Mychyll th' Archangell, when so ev^r yt shall happen the p'mmisses to come to the hands or possessyon of the seyd pryoress or her successors by forfetur, resygnac'on, surrendre, g'unte, by reco'ry or act'on tryed, or by any other means, and so to contynewe to th' ende and terme of oon-and-twenty yers, then next foloyng and fully to be endyd, yeldyng and payeng the for'd yerly to the said pryoresse and convent, and to their successours, ten marks good and lawful money of Ingland, at too tymes of the yer, that ys to sey at the feste of th' Annuncyac'on of our Lady and Seynt Mychyll thArchangell, by evyn porcyons or wythyn twenty days next aftr end'g of the seyd feste duryng the seyde t'me. And yt ys coven'ntyd and agreed betwen the seyd p'tyes that the seyd John Gryffyth, hys executours or assygness shall yerly pay to the seyd pryoresse and to her successours the moyte' or halffendels of all such wards, relyvs, p'ym'nts of courts so before excepted and resyrved to the said pryoresse as shall come to ther hands other by destryes s'nte of the...... or otherwyse may come to ther hands, and yt is coven'ntyd and agreed betwen the seyd partyes that yff the said John Gryffyth or his assygnees do bryng the seyd rents wythyn the twenty days at any time as ys aforeseyd to the seyd monasterye, and ther pey the seyd rent, then the said John Gryffyth and his assynees shall have allowed him for the bryngyng toward hys labour and costs ev'y yer twenty-pence good money. And yff the seyd rent be not brought as ys afforesaid, but that the seyd pryoresse and her successours be dryven to send for the seyd rent, that then the seyd John or hys executours or assygnes shall pay for the cost and charge of the messengers so comyng for the rent for as long tyme as he shall tary for the same rent, and so yerly as often as the seyd rent shall so happen to be unpaid during the seyd tyme. And also yt ys conuen'ted and grantyd that yff the seyd John Gryffyth, his executours or assygness for nonreceypte of the seyd wards, releyvs, or pym'nts of courts or for the recovry of the same be dryven to dyst'ess or to any other acc'n yn the lawe that the pryoress or her successours shall contynnually half the charge for the recovry of the same as oft as need requires during the seyd time. And the seyd half expence yerly shall be alowyd to the seyd John or his assygnees at the accompte, and yt is further agreed that yf the rent of ten marks happen to be behynd onpaid yn part or yn all after the seyd fests aforseyd, by the space of 12 weeks next after any of the seyd fests during the seyd time that then yt shall be lawful for the seyd pryoresse to reent' into the said p'mysses or any part thereoff, and that to repossess and have agen, and the seyd John. Gryffyth, his executours and assygness utterly to expelle, amove, and put-ought, thys indentyr yn any wise notwythstanding. And it is coven'ntyd and agreed between the seyd pryoresse and John that the seyd pryoresse and her successors shall avow and maynten all such actions as shall fortune to be taken yn ther names agenst the occupy'res of the p'mysses at the costts and charges of the seyd John and his assygnes at any time between the dat of thys p'ntes and the seyd yer off our Lord God a thousand five hundred and thyrty and fyve, and the action or actions they shall not dyscharge nor dyscontyne without the assent, consent, and agreement of the seyd John Gryffyth, his executors or assygnees, and all such recoveryes of the premysses with the costs and damyges of the same, the seyd prioress shall suffer the seyd John Gryffyth, his executors and assygnees to take receyve and levye to their own use and p'ffytt, and thus recey'ed and had, then the seyd John Gryffyth with the profytte of the same costs and damages to repayer and amend the said p'mysses in rep'tiones, and the p'myses so repayred to kepe well and suffy'ently repayred, and so to be kept. And the seyd John g'untyth for him, his executors and assygnees, that they shall fynd and br'ng to the receyvor of the seyd prioress and their servants yerly when they come to receyve the rents and proffyt of the p'mysses, horsemete, mannysmete, and lodging, so they tarry ther too days and too nights yn the yer. In witnesse wherofe to the oon p'te of thys indentur remaynyng yn the kepyng of the said John Gryffyth, the seyd pryoress and convent hath put ther comen seale; to the oder part of this indentur remaynyng yn the custodye of the seyd pryoresse and convent, the seyd John have putte his seale. Geven in the Chapt'-house of the seyd monastrie, under the Chapt' aforeseyd, the day and yer aboveseyd [1].

Seal appending—A lady seated on a throne bearing a large crucifix on her breast. Underneath a nun kneeling, her arms in the attitude of prayer, with an imperfect inscription in Roman capitals.

---

[1] Ex orig. penes Johan. Coker, armiger.

APPENDIX.

No VII.

Valuation of the Possessions &c. of Bicester Priory, by the Commissioners at the Visitation of the Monasteries. 1535. 27 Hen. VIII.

Willms Brown Pior.

Prioratus de Burcestur' in com' Oxon' infra Dioc' Lincoln' et Decanat' ejusd'm.

Valor oniu͞ Man'ioȝ Terraȝ et Ten'toȝ R'coriaȝ Pensionu͞ Porc'onu͞ ac cet'oȝ Possessionu͞ tam sp'ual' q̄m temporal' predict' Priorat' pertinenc' ut sequit'.

In primis de Margeria Coplande pro hospicio le Bell cu͞ molend' infra dict' priorat' cu͞ terris et clausuris cu͞ suis pertin' ut pȝ per indentur' sibi dimiss' per annu͞	vj	iiij	—
D' Ric'o Banaster gentilman pro una claus' jux^a pⁱorat' predict' sibi dimiss' ut patȝ per indentur' per annu͞	—	xj	—
D' Joh'e Lambo'ne pro clausura de Crockwell una cu͞ domo columbar' ut patȝ per indentur' sibi dimiss' per annu͞	—	xiij	—
D' quindecim tenentibȝ custumarijs vidȝ pro cotag' in eadem villa tenent' ad volunt' dn̄i redditibȝ per annu͞ iiij	xij	iiij
D' Joh'e Bodycotte de Burcestr' predict' pro le Lampe Acre jacen' in quodam prato vocato Demayne Mede sic sibi dimiss' per annu͞	—	—	xij
S'ma	xiij	x	iiij

D' terris quondam dn̄icalibȝ monast'ij pred'ci et jam ad firmam dimiss' in le hamlett vocat' le Wrechewyk in parochia de Burcestr' predict' ad firmam dimiss' per indentur' pro t'mino annoȝ hijs ho'ibȝ sequentibȝ.

D' Joh'e Lambo'ne pro duabȝ clausuris in eodem hamleto et pro ijbȝ pec' prati in le Kyngesende in parochia predict' per annu͞	filj	xvii	iiij

APPENDIX.

D' Joh'e Bodycote pro ijb3 claus' ib'm cum di' virgat' terr' jacen' in campo de Blackthorn in parochia predict' per annu̅............................—.. iij — —

D' Joh'e Maunde pro una claus' sub silva ib'm vocat' le Gravenhull per annu̅ .... iiij xiij iiij

D' Joh'e Nashe pro ten'to ib'm cum di' virgat' terre cū pertin' per annu'......................... — vj viij

D' ux'e nuper Willi' Walker pro ten'to cum terris et claus' cū pertin' sic sibi dimiss' per indentur' per annu̅.................................— xxxiij iiij

D' Nich'o White pro clausura vocat' le Ov'breche per annu̅ sic sibi dimiss'................... iiij — —

D' Will'mo Bosworthe pro ten'to ib'm tent' ad volunt' dāi cum pertin' per annu̅..............,— vj viij

P' terris jacen' in le campo de le Blakthorne inter tenentes sive inh'itantes ejusd'm man'ij per balliu' dict' prioris annuati' dimiss' per annu .... iij vj viij

S'ma recept'............... xxij iiij —

Deducco'es et Resoluco'es ejusd'm Monasterij sing'lis annis imperp'm solvend' exeunt' de t'ris et ten'ts sup^adict'.

D' quad^am penco'e abbat' et convent' de Osney et successoribu3 suis annuati' et imperp'm solvend' .... iij — —

Solut' dn̅o de Bygenhull pro uno ten'to in fine regali ville de Burcestr' predict' per annd̅............ — — xx

Solut' vicecomit' Oxon' pro le castell' fee per annu — iiij —

Solut' dn̅o principi pro sect' cur' relaxand' apud Burcestre predict' per annu̅.................. — vj* viij

Solut' archidiaconato Oxon' pro procuraco'ib3 et sinodalib3 eccl'ia3 Burcestr' pred'ce per annu̅........ — x vij ob' q'

P' pane et vino ad missas quotidianas celebrand' pro egrot' et mulieribus p'ngnat^s et in festo S'ce Pasche pro om'ib3 inh'itantib3 ut pat3 per composico'em inde fact' per annu̅........................ — xx —

Solut' ball'io vid3 Joh'i Nashe de man'ijs de Burcestr' et Wrechwyk pro feodo suo per annu .... — xl —

APPENDIX.

Elimosina dat'.

Pro ai'a Gilbarti Bassot fundatoris pred'c'i monast'ij in distribuco'ibȝ et elemosinis parochianis Burcestr' pred'ce sing'lis annis solvend' et imperp'm ut plen' patȝ per cartam fundatoris sui pred'ci .... vj — xx

Elimosina data.

It'm in cena dñi vidȝ Sherthursday om'ibȝ et aliis pauperibȝ sive leprosis ad tunc co̅venientibȝ in pane portu piscibȝ et pecunijs annuati' et imperp'm ..xiij — iiij

S'ma deducc'ois .... xii xiij xj o

Stratton Awdeley in com' Oxon, et infra Dioc' Lincoln'.

D' Edwardo Denton et Thoma Denton gent' pro teñt' t'ris et decimis r'corie ib'm illis per indenturam dimiss' per annu̅ ....:................... xvj — —

S'ma recept'.............. xvj — —

Deduc'oes et Resoluc'oes ib'm.

Solut' dño abbat' de Eynsham pro quadam penc'oe eaȝdem decimaȝ pred'caȝ ut patȝ compositionem imperp'm inde fact' per annu̅ .... — xvj —

S'ma alloc' .... — xvj —

Dadyngton Clyston et Hempton in Com' Oxon' infra Dioc' Lincoln' et Decanat' de Dadyngton.

D' ux'e Simonis Mannyng pro firmaria de Clyston et molend' adjacent' cū suis pertin' sibi dimiss' per indenturam pro t'io annoȝ per annu̅ .... x — —

D' Thoma Bryce de et pro uno ten'to in Dadyngton predict' cū pertin' sibi dimiss' per indenturam pro t'io annoȝ per annu̅...................... — lj vj

D' redditibȝ tam lib'oȝ tenenc' q'm custumar' ib'm per annu̅..................................... xix viij viij ol

Sm'a recept'.............. xxxij — ij ob

APPENDIX. 253

Deduoc'oes et Resolusiones ib'm
Solut' dño Regi pro quiet' reddit' exeunt' de molendino
de Clyston per annū.......................... — ij viij
Solut' dño abbat' de Eynsham pro decimis in man'io
de Cliston exeunt' ut patz per compos' inde fact' per
annū .... — xvj —

Elimosina data
In distribuc'oibz et elemosinis in dict' parochia de
Dadyngton sc'd'm antiquas ordinaco'es prius usitat'
pro ai'a Willi' Hayly benefactoris imperp'm et
annuati.. — ij vj
Solut' Laurencio Ov'ton ball'io n'ro in predicto man'io
pro feodo suo per annū.................... — xxvj viij
    Sm'a deducc'ois ib'm......... — xlvij x

Kyrtlyngton et Tackley in Com' p'd' Dioc' Lincoln'.

D' Joh'e Cokks ballio et collector' redd'us ib'm qam
lib'oz tenenc' q'm custumar' ib'm per annū .... viij xiiij iiij
D' Joh'e Andrewes pro uno molendino aquatico sibi
dimiss' pro t'mno annoz solubil' ad iiij^{or} anni t'ios
canonicis Burcestr' pred'ce in distribucoibz Deo
s'vientibz imperp'm per annū .... iij vj viij
    Sm'a recept'................ xij — xij

Deducc'oes et Resoluc'oes ib'm Elimosina.

P' ai'a Nich'i Baker benefactoris monast'ij pred'ci dat'
est canonic^s ejusd'm loci Deo s'vient' pro exequiis
ad iiij^{or} anni t'ios exequen^s pro ejus ai'a et om'iu
defunctoz in elimosinis an^{tim} et imperp'm........ iij vj viij
Solut' dño Regi pro quiet' reddit' certaz terraz et ten'-
toz cū molendino aq^aico ib'm per annū et imperp'm .... — — xxj
Solut' dño priori Cartuens' jux^a Coventre pro porco'e
ib'm prout pz per compos' inde fact' per annū et
imperp'm .... — lj —
    Sm'a deducc'ois............. — lij ix

APPENDIX.

Arnecote in com' Oxon' et in hundr' de Bolyndon infra Dioc' Lincoln' et Decanat, &c.

De Thoma Marshe tenent' ib'm pro ij^{bus} messuagijs
et trib3 virgat^s terre cū quart'na terre cū pertin' sibi
dimiss' pro t'mno anno3 per annū .... — xxx —
Solut' dño p^{r}iori per tenentes ib'm pro le Hedsylver
in dñico predicto per annū .... — — xviij
D' redditib3 in predicto Arnecott tam līb'o3 tenenc'
q^{a}m custumar' recept' et precept' per Joh'em
Cokks ib'm balliv' per annū .... — lvij vi
     S'ma recept' .... iiij ix —

    Deducc'oes et Resoluc'oes ib'm.

Solut' balli'o hundr' de Bolyndon vid3 Edwardo Kyng
pro omn' sv'ic' in Arnecote pred'ct per annū .... — — xij
    S'ma deducc' ....:........ — — xij
    Et rem' .... iiij viij —

Steple Aston in com' predicto infra Dioc' Lincoln' et decan' &c.

D' Roberto Parsons pro uno messuagio et cert' t'ris
ib'm cū pertin' ad firmam dimiss' per indenturā pro
t'mio anno3 per annū .... — xij iiij

Middylton in com' predic'o et dioc' Lincoln' ac Decanat' &c.

D' Egidio Reede gentilman pro uno messuagio cū
terris et suis pertin' ad firmam sibi dimiss' per indenturā pro t'io anno3 per annū .... — x —

Wendylbury in Com' pred'co et pred'co Dioc' et Decanat' &c.

De Joh'e Brice pro uno cotagio cū cert^s t'ris cū suis
pertin' sibi dimiss' per indenturā pro t'io anno3 per
annū .... — x —

    Chesterton in com' pred'c'o.

D' Joh'e Hyde pro cert^s terris ib'm pro copiam cur'
per annū .... — v —

APPENDIX.

Fryngford in Com' pred'c'o.

D' Joh'e Arden gent' pro cert* terris in ead'm villa
pro quiet' reddit' per annu̅............ — ij —
   S'ma rec'............... — lxx iiij

Hayford Waren' in com' pred'c'o et dioc' Lincoln' &c.

D' Novo Collegio in Oxon' pro terris firmar' eidem
collegio pertin' vid; pro penco'e ut pat; per com-
posicione̅ per annu̅ et imperp'm............ — xxvj viij

Cav'felde in com' pred'c'o infra Dioc' Lincoln' et Decanat' &c.

D' Ric'o Langeston armig'o pro dic' man'ij de Cav'-
felde predict' sibi et heredib; suis dimiss' per indentura' solubil' ad ij^os an' t'minos per annu̅.... — liiij iiij

Samford in Com' pred'c'o Dioc' Lincoln' &c.

D' firmario ib'm pro uno messuagio et una virgat'
terre cu̅ pertinen' solubil' tam ad f'm Sc'i Mich'is
canonic' Deo s'vient' in augmentac'oe stipendio;
suo; per annu̅........................ — v —
   S'ma rec'................iiij v —

Deductiones et Resoluco'es ib'm Elemosina Dat'

P' ai'a Godfridi de Bygenhull b'nfactoris mon' pred'ci — vj —
qui dedit canonic' pro salterio davitico dicent' in ejus
adv's sing'lis eo; per se dicent' separati in elemos' eis
distribuend' annuati' et imperp'm.... (*in to° per annu̅*) — — v

Buckenhull in com' pred'c'o et Dioc' Lincoln' &c.

D' Rob'to Stephens pro cert* terris arrabilib; ib'm
per annu̅................................. — v —
   S'ma recept'................. — v —

APPENDIX.

Feod' Annual' Deducc'oes et Resoluc'oes
Solut' Joh'i Cokks de sup'd'c'is terris pro collecto'e
redditus villata⁊ sup'd'ca⁊ per annu̅............ — xxvj viij
    Sm'a alloc'................ — xxvj viij

Ardyngton in Com' Berk' et infra Dioc' Sar' et Deean' &c.

D' Thoma Hobbes pro cert^s terris et r'coria' ib'm sic
sibi dimiss' per indentura̅ ad t'mios anno⁊ per annu̅ xiiij — —

    In eodem Com' Berk'.

D' eodem Thoma Hobbes pro firmario n'ro apud
Letcombe Bassett per indentura' sic sibi dimiss' pro
t'mino anno⁊ per annu̅ .... iiij — —
    Sm'a rec'.................. xviij — —
    Resoluc'oes ib'm............ null'

Grymesbury jux^a Banbury in com' North^{a}mpt' et infra dioc'
    Lincoln' ac Decanat, &c.

D' Anthonio Cope armig'o firmario man'ij ib'm cu̅
firma molendino⁊ et alio⁊ profic' eidem man'io pertin' sic sibi dimiss' pro t'io anno⁊ per annu̅ .... xiij vi viij
    Sm'a rec' ut p⁊

Nethrope in Com' pred'c'o et infra Dioc' Lincoln' &c.

D' Henrico Taye et Will'mo Smythe de eadem te-
nentib⁊ ib'm per copia̅ cur' de ijb⁊ mesuagijs solubil' ad ij°s anni t'ios canonic' in distribuc'oib⁊ Deo
s'vientib⁊ annuati' et imperp'm .... — xxxij —
    Sm'a rec' p⁊

  Deducc'oes et Resoluc'oes ib'm in Elemosinis.

P' si'a Will'i Hayly benefactoris n'ri pred'ci mon'
dat' est canonic' pro una collect' quotidiana dicend'
ad missam B'te Marie Virginis celebrant' vid⁊ is-

APPENDIX. 257

clina d'ne aurem &c. solubil' at iiij^{or} anni t'i'os distribuend' per man' prioris ib'm annuati' et imperp'm— *xxxij* —

Beamonde jux^a Myssenden in com' Buk' et dioc' Lincoln' &c.

D' Henrico Honoure firmario ib'm man'ij cū pertin'
una cū firma rc'orie sic sibi dimiss' per indenturam
pro t'mino annoȝ per annū .... xiij vj viij

D' subboscis ib'm crescent' infra domin' predc'm estimat' videl't ev'y xijth yere per vicinos et honestos
ho'ies ib'm inh'itantes ad valenc' sex libraȝ et quolib't anno estimat^r per annu .... quolib't anno xij
                    S'ma recept' .... xiij vj viij

Deducc'oes et Resoluc'oes ib'm.

Solut' dño abb'i de Magna Myssenden pro man'io de
Arnecote prout pȝ per composic'o'em inde fact'
annuati' et imperp'm .... vj xiij iiij

It'm solut' archidiac' Buk' pro procurac'o'e et sinodalibȝ eccl'ie de P'va Myssenden annuati' et imperp'm .... — x viij

Solut' in eadem parochia in distribuc'o'ibȝ et elemos'
s'cd'm antiquas ordinac'o'es inde fact' et prius usitat'
ad duos anni t'm'nos per annū et imperp'm ...... — vj viij
                S'ma alloc' vel deducc' .... vij x viij

Wescott in com' Buk' et dioc' Lincoln' &c.

Dr Joh'e Latham firmario ib'm cert^s terris et ten't^s
sibi dimiss' per indenturam pro t'i'o annoȝ per annū iiij x —

Blakenhull in com' Buck' pred'c'o et dioc'.

D^s Joh'e Goodwyn gentilman firmario uni^s claus' pastur' sibi dimiss' per indenturam pro t'm'no annoȝ
per annu .... — xx —

Compton Bassett in com' Wiltes' et dioc' Sar'.

D' r'c'ore ib'm pro quadam pensio'e solubil' ad duos
anni t'm'nos prout pȝ per composic'o'em inde factam per annū .... iiij — —

APPENDIX.

Stodeley in com' pred'co dioc'.

D' mag'ro Hung'ford pro reddit' uni⁸ ten'ti cū pertin'
adjacen' in dicto com' Wiltes' per annū vij⁸ tamen
pred'c'us magister Hung'ford negat soluc'o'em inde
(Sed salvo jure monasterij pred'c'i)
S'ma rec'................ ix x —

Terr' D̄nicales Monast'ij pred'ci in manib3 Prioris jam ex-
isten' in Burcestr' &c. cū Decimis.

In terris arrabilib3 ib'm vid3 undecim virgat' terre cū
suis pertin' jacen' in campis Le M'kett ende dict'
Burcestr' jacent' continent⁸ cciiij×× et vj acres ad
iiij^d qualib't acra per annū .... iiij xv iiij
It'm in terris arrabilib3 vid3 di' virgat' t're jacent' in
Le Kyngesende continent' quindecim acres cū suis
pertin' ad qualib't acra per annū iiij^d............ — v —
In terris arrabilib3 videl't una pecia terre jux⁸ portam
Le Graunge continent' duodecim acr' ad qualib't
acra iiij^d per annū .... — iiij —
It'm in terris arrabilib3 in le hamlett' de Wrechwyk
in parochia dic'e Burcestr' vid3 ij virgat' terre et di'
continent' iij×× acr' et quindecim cū quinque lez
butts cū suis pertin' ad qualib3 acra per aᵐ per annū
iiij^d...................................... — xxv x
S'ma acra3 arrabil'.......... xx××j et v butts
S'ma valoris ea3d'm acra3 arrabil' vj x ij
In una separali pastura vocat' le Wynt' pasture ducent'
v'sus le Gravenhull continent' xliiij acres et di' in
trib3 p'tib3 separati' cū sepib3 ad qualib't acr⁸ v^d. — xviij vj ob.
In una separal' pastura vocat' le Weston Heyes cū
sepe in medio ejusd'm pastur' cont' xlj acres et di'
qualib't acra ad xix^d per annū .... iij v viij
It'm in al' pastura separal' voc' le Ov'breche cont' xl
acres qualib't acra viij^d per annū .... — xxvj viij

APPENDIX.

In una pecia prati jacen' in le Westmede cont' quinq;
acr' et di' ad qualib't acra ij⁵ per annū ...... — xj —
It'm in una separal' pastur' vocat' le Horsse Close prope
monast'iū cont' septem acr' et di' qualib't acra ad
viij^d per annū............................... — v —
     S'ma valoris acraʒ predic'aʒ .... vj vj xj
It'm in quodam prato vocat' Longford Mede cont'
iiij^{or} acr' qualib't acr' xij^d per annū .... — iiij —
In ead'm prato vidʒ Longford Mede iiij acr' qualib't
acr' ad xvj^d per annū .... — v iiij
It'm in quodam campo vocat' Blakthorne Felde cont'
ij acr' prati qualib't acr' ad viij^d per annū ...... — — xvj
      S'ma — x vij
      S'ma terr' dñic'
S'ma valoris oñiū acraʒ dñical' cū dec'is et terris ar-
rabilibʒ ib'm .,........................... xiij vij ix
Tot⁵ .... cxlix xvj — ob'q'
It'm proprijs x$^{m'}$s terr' dñic...... xxvj ix ob'q' clj ij x
 ℥ clxxviij xj vij ob'.

Feod' Annual'.

Solut' Ric'o Banaster armig'o pro offic' senescalli per
annū....................................... — liiij iiij
Solut' Xp'ofero Hucvale auditor' ñro pro ejus feodo
per annū................................... — xxvj viiij
    S'ma alloc'................. iiij — —
Joh'es Middleton subp^{l}or ib'm
Will'm's Fynche sexten
Will'm's Cav'felde sellerar'
   Non h'entes aliquas terras neq; ten't' nec offic' in
   monast'io predic'o in successione neq; vad' feod'
   aut annual' stipend' nisi ad voluntatē prioris.

Noīa Canonicoʒ in dicto Mon' vidʒ.

 Will'm's Browne priour ib'm.
 Joh'es Middleton subprior ib'm.

APPENDIX.

Rad'us Latham canon ib'm.
Rob'tus Bignell.
Joh'es Chester.
Robt'us Cav'felde.
Jacobus Brystowe.
Joh'es Burcestur.
Joh'es Lan'nton.
Ric'us Wodstok.
Nich'us Cony.
Will'm's Hampton.

Deduct' xxxj viij ix ob'

The sume of the hole Possession sp'uall and temporall
demaynes and other is..................... clxxvj vij —ob'
The sume of the deduccions and resolucons is .. xxxix viij vj ob'q'
The hole sume declar' is....................... cxlvij ij x
  Decima pars d̄no Regi............... xiiij xiiij iij ob'

We the seide prior and co'vent of the seide priory
mooste humbly beseche the Kyng's moste Graci-
ouse Highnes and his moste honourable councell,
that thois sumes and chargis herafter foloyng may   Fiat Petic'c
be allowed, which chargis byn annuall and perpe-
tuall, and for no lesse necessitie then the fees and
charg' of auditours, receyvours, and bailyffs and
other chargis as hereafter foloithe

Furste for brede wyne and wax erely spente withyn
the seide priory, aboughte the dyvyne s'vice according to their foundacion..................... vj — —

It'm for the costs and charges of the auditor and re-
ceyvour gen'all in the audite tyme .... vj xiij iiij

It'm the same prior desirethe allouanc' of the visita-
co'n of the bishopp ev'y iii^{de} yere iij^{l} vj^{s} viij^{d}
which is yerely ev'y yere..................... — xxij ij ob'q

It'm for the cost^s charg^s and expenc^s of the same
bishop and his officers and menyall servants, in and
at the tyme of visitac'on ev'y iij^{de} yere .... vj xiij iiij
which is xliiijs. iiijd. yerly.... cxlvij vj xj q'

By the same Commissioners under the Article Com' Oxon' Lincoln' Dioc' et Decanat' Burcest', Valores omn' et sing'loʒ R'c'oriaʒ Vicariaʒ P'bendar' Cantariʒ et aliaʒ Possessionũ tam Sp'ual' quam Temporal' infra Dioc' et Decanat', *is the following entry :—*

Burcest'

Peres Griffith vicarius perpetuus et vicaria sua valet per annũ cum repris' co'ibʒ annis ex recognic'o'e sua super sacr'm suũ........................ xvj — —.
P¹or et convent' ib'm app¹ator ejusd'm et infra p¹orat' predict' on'ant^r pro eodem   infra p¹oratũ predict' comp^r
S'ma........... xvj — —

Et reman' clar' patʒ
    Alloc'   null'
    Decima pars dũo Regi .... — xxxij [1] —

No. VIII.

Extracts from the Church-wardens' Accounts; and the King's Books.

THE Church-wardens' Bills of the reign of Elizabeth are chiefly without dates, and written on long slips of paper. The following is a specimen of the entries in that of the year 1582.

Paide for ij new lockes		xvi*d.*
—— for mending of a locke		ij*d.*
—— for nayles		
Paide to John Pollex the nynth day of December............	vij.	xj*d.*
—— gyven unto father Jollide		xij*d.*
—— gyven to John Potter 23 Aprile		xxv*d.*
Given unto Margyret Brown on the day of her marriage [¶]		ij*s.*
Payde for the stoppyng of the Town Brook		
Given unto a preacher..................................		20*d.*

[1] From the Valor Ecclesiasticus, vol. ii. p. 187. Lond. 1814.
[¶] Probably she was pregnant, and the sum given as a marriage portion.

APPENDIX.

Given unto Rd Godard at his marriage .... ijd.
Payd for mending father Harris's hose .... vjd.

It is uncertain how long the parish officers continued the practice of keeping their accounts on long slips of paper; but their present book commences with the year 1708, and contains few entries of public interest.

		£.	s.	d.
1708.	Pd for casting the third bell, 3lb. of metal added	7	3	9
	Pd for three hedgehogs, one fox, and a polecat	0	2	2
	Pd the dog-whipper's wages	0	8	8
1711.	Apparitor's fees	0	2	2
	For processioning charges	1	19	10
	Clerk's wages..	2	0	0
1714.	For casting the fifth bell and clapper for her	10	16	6
1716.	Pd for the expenses of the pennance of Eliz. Wootton..	0	3	8
1717.	Pd for six leather buckets	1	10	0
1720.	Pd for thirteen doz. sparrows	0	2	2
1736.	Pd for a new church bible	2	7	6
1744.	Pd for mending the basoon	0	16	3
1766.	Allowed at the vestry by the parishioners towards mending the chimes ....'................	14	0	0

Mem. 24 Feb. 1771. At a vestry held this day it is agreed by the inhabitants of Bicester Market-end and King's-end, that an annual subscription be made to the Oxford or Radcliffe Infirmary, of three guineas per annum, and the same to be paid yearly by the church-wardens for the time being.

JOHN STEVENS, ROBERT SHIRLEY, &c.

| 1772.| Payd Isaac Clarke, Osmond, and T. Stratton, due on balance for the organ .... | 8 | 3 | 0 |

KING'S BOOKS[3].

Burchester is a discharged living.

Clear yearly value £ 49.

Burchester vulgo Bister, V. St. Edburgh Pri., Burchester Propr. Sir John Glynn, Bart., 1719. Sir Edward Turner, Bart., 1752. Sir Gregory Turner, Bart., 1779.

King's Books £ 16.

---

[3] By J. Bacon, Esq. London 1786.

No. IX.

Bicester, Oxfordshire.

At a numerous and respectable Meeting of the Inhabitants of this Town and Neighbourhood, held at the Town Hall in Bicester on the 8th day of January, 1793,

JOHN COKER, Esq. in the chair,

The following Resolutions were unanimously approved of and agreed to.

1st. That the late daring attempts of many disaffected and seditious persons, who by the publication of libels and by treasonable combinations have endeavoured to subvert the established government of this country, and to introduce into it all the miseries of anarchy and confusion, have given occasion of much alarm and serious apprehension.

2d. That under such circumstances it is the duty of all good subjects to come forward and to declare their detestation of such practices, and to interpose their efforts for the preservation of the tranquillity and safety of the community.

3d. That the inhabitants of the town and neighbourhood of Bicester are truly and zealously attached to the present constitution and legislative power of this country, consisting of king, lords, and commons.

4th. That they do acknowledge and approve of the timely, judicious, and vigorous measures pursued by the executive power at this critical juncture.

5th. That they will associate for the purpose of supporting their said constitution, and defending it to the utmost of their power against any violation or attack; that they will hold out in their own practice an example of respectful submission to the laws; that they will use their utmost endeavours to bring to punishment all those who by their writings or actions shall attempt to excite sedition, or in any manner to disturb the public peace; and that they will be personally assisting to the civil power upon every occasion that shall require its interference.

APPENDIX.

J. Coker	W. Phillpot	W. Ball
J. R. Greenhill	F. Jennings	J. Sanders
J. Haley	W. Tredwell	H. Borton
J. Eyre	J. Kent	J. Stratton
G. Lamb	T. Stratton	E. Whale
J. Leigh Barnet	W. Phillips	T. Stopp
Rev. W. Ellis	W. Allen	T. Gough
Rev. W. E. Ellis	J. Kirby	J. Jessop
Rev. E. Turner	J. Stopes Clk	R. Foster
H. Walford	G. Collins	H. Carter
J. Moore	W. Blunt	J. Dagley
T. Potter, jun.	T. Miller	J. Warr
F. Penrose	G. Pavier	S. Bowerman
T. Davis	G. Foster	T. Stevens
R. Shirley	J. Burnard	T. Hicks
M. Heather	J. Stratton	
G. Osmond	W. Potter	*Bicester Band.*
J. Stevens	I. Thomas	I. Clarke
R. Johnson	T. Bailey	T. Blowfield
T. Pardo Brett	R. Jessop	W. Shillingford
T. King	W. Hadland	R. King
T. Westcar	W. Cross	W. Mapelwhite
R. Smith	J. Jagger	W. Field
T. Potter	G. Foster	T. Humphrey
R. Kirby	G. Butler	T. Egerton
T. Reading	J. Coles	W. Foster
M. Browne	J. Shirley	J. Maynard
H. Trafford	W. Clarke	E. Humphrey
R. King	W. Coleman	J. Blowfield
W. Painter	T. Kirby	J. Burroughs
J. Webb	T. Egerton	
O. Busby	J. Jackson	J. Humphreys
W. Westcar	T. Harris	J. Busby
J. Thonger	W. Phillips	J. Wells
R. Earlom	W. Beck	W. Berry
J. Foster	J. Dagley	A. Bradwin
W. Birch	T. Foster	J. Smith
H. Churchill	C. Hadland	W. Watson
R. Slaney	W. Bryan	J. Burrows
R. Kersey	J. Burroughs	E. Tanner
W. Rogers	R. Humphrey	J. Smith
T. Sirett	T. Hawkins	T. Watson
J. King	C. Blunt	J. Egerton

APPENDIX.

H. Coxill	W. Pavier	J. Ball
T. Hicks	W. Inwood	J. Bowden
J. Fenemore	W. Hodges	D. Creed
N. Coxill	W. Pates	W. Knibbs
R. Dumbleton	T. Allard	F. Blewett
J. White	W. Izzard	J. Munden
W. Rollins	T. Jennings	W. Cox
W. Bosley	T. Shephard	J. Heirtage
J. Axtill	W. Butler	W. Whitehead
T. Heritage	J. Higgs	G. Spencer
J. Mealings	W. Coxill	W. Howse
J. Neal	W. Berry	T. Lines
T. Humphrey	R. Grimsley	R. Grimsby
T. Hazell	R. Jessop	T. Bowden
J. Smith	W. Daws	W. Jennings
T. Parrot	W. Spacey	G. Stevens
T. Guntriss	J. Hazell	W. Alley
T. Williams	J. Jagger	B. Archer
J. Heritage	R. Bathe	W. Barrett
W. Elstone	J. Jones	D. Green
W. Holton	W. Tanner	R. Heritage
W. Hunt	T. Croxton	S. Phillips
J. Waddup	J. Bottrill	T. Petty
A. Bradwin	B. Edmunds	R. King
N. Ward	J. Hitchcock	T. Wiggs
J. Elston	E. Penrose	J. Travers
J. Neal	J. Gurden	W. Woodcock
M. Neal	T. Franklin	J. Lamb
E. Foster	T. Carthew	J. Williams
M. Thomas	J. Jessop	W. A. Leverett
W. Foster	R. Maynard	M. Wick
J. Jones	J. Whale	T. Pitts
W. Nevill	J. Hewitt	W. Tooley
W. Crump	T. Stratton	J. Jagger
R. Handcock	T. Gibbons	D. Creed
J. Golden	J. Mewkill	W. Jackson
J. Holland	W. Clifton	J. Stanbridge
E. Coxill	J. Heritage	J. Bosley
J. Nevill	T. Hawkes	J. Clifton
J. King	R. Gunthriss	T. Paxton
W. Adams	N. Poulton	J. Turner
J. George	G. Grimsby	S. Cartwright

APPENDIX.

J. Skinner	R. Edmunds	W. Hawkins
W. Marcey	J. Westbury	J. Harris
T. Bowen	W. Blencowe	T. Prior
P. Crook	J. Harris	J. Edwards
H. Lines	J. Archer	W. Pratt
T. Edwards	J. Edmonds	J. Bullock
J. Marten	T. Woodcock	J. Sirett
J. Kendall	W. Smith	

To this Instrument of Association the following Declaration of the Protestant Dissenters of Bicester was affixed.

Bicester, January 14, 1793.

We his majesty's loyal subjects, the Protestant Dissenters of the town of Bicester, do cheerfully upon the present occasion make public declaration of our constant zealous fidelity and attachment to the reigning illustrious House of Hanover, and to the constitution of civil government of this country, established at the Revolution in the year 1688; and we do hereby declare our abhorrence of all traitorous speeches and publications, and our readiness to aid the civil magistrate in suppressing all seditious attempts to subvert the civil government or to disturb the public peace.

Signed by the consent and direction of the whole congregation,

WILLIAM MILLER, Minister.

No. X.

Sports, Customs, &c. in Bicester and its Neighbourhood.

QUINTAL.—In the days of Dr. Plot it was customary at marriages for the inhabitants of the village of Blackthorn to amuse themselves with running at the quintal. The nature of the sport is thus described by Kennett: "They set up a roll, or that instrument of agriculture used to break the clods in the field, and at the erect end they hang a strong rafter board, which turns on the spindle of the roll: to one end of this moving beam or ballance they nail a slab or broader piece of thick board, and at the other end they hang a leather bag filled with gravel or sand of equal poise, which flies round and smites the inexpert rider."

From his subsequent account we gather, that the player was usually on horseback, and funished with a staff or pole, with which he struck the slab with all his force. If he was not dexterous and his horse swift, he was almost certain of receiving a blow from the sand-bag as the rafter turned round—to his own disgrace and the merriment of the spectators. This sport has been long discontinued, and no tradition of its having been ever practised, remains among the inhabitants of Blackthorn or its neighbourhood.

SPORTS ON SHROVE TUESDAY.—The sports of this day were very considerable before the Reformation, and intended as an indulgence previous to the approaching season of Lent. Their commencement is still announced by the ringing of "the pancake bell" at eleven o'clock, the ancient hour of dinner. At the first sound of this bell the young people formerly left their employments, and after a hasty dinner hied away to their varied amusements, which consisted in the barbarous practice of thowing at cocks, or the more active sports of jumping, wrestling, ringing of bells, &c. On this day the parish-clerk still considers himself entitled to the profits arising from ringing of the bells, and accordingly they are let by the hour to those who prefer that exercise. For a trifling sum others are permitted to walk on the tower or on the leads of the church. But though these as well as most other amusements exist, so much have they declined of late years that at present they are chiefly practised by children, and in a short time it is probable they will be discontinued and forgotten.

MAY DAY.—About a century ago May Day was considered a very great holiday in Bicester and its neighbourhood. Both parents and children felt highly interested in its pleasures, and parties vied with each other to produce the best garland of flowers. A little lord and lady decked in gay ribbons and accompanied by several attendants, with small instruments of music, called on their friends, and went in procession round the town and neighbourhood. The afternoon and evening were spent in the greatest hilarity, and generally concluded with a dance round the *May pole*. This custom is evidently derived from the heathen festival instituted in honour of the goddess Flora, who was imagined to preside over flowers. It has declined many years, and is now regarded by the children of the poor only.

WHITSUN-ALES are of remote origin, and, in common with church-ales, clerks ales, &c. formed one of the chief amusements of the middle ages. The object of this entertainment appears to have been a burlesque on greatness; hence a barn, the scene of their festivity, is called a hall, two of the principal male and female characters are dubbed lord and lady, and others bear the name of my lord's waiting-man, and my lady's waiting-maid. A treasurer who carries a tin box before him, a set of morris dancers, a merry-andrew to clear the ring for dancing, &c., form the remainder of the group; and these fantastically dressed and decorated with ribbons, dance or parade among the spectators. The barn doors are ornamented with an owl and monkey, who bear the appropriate names of my lord's parrot and my lady's lap-dog, and to miscall any of these, or accept of my lord's cake or ale, which are carried about in profusion and offered to every one, subjects the offending party to a forfeiture of sixpence, for which however he is treated with a ride on my lord's gelding [1] (if a man behind my lady, or if a female before my lord,) who of course considers himself entitled to a salute: but if this honour is declined, for an additional sixpence the forfeiting party is privileged to enter my lord's hall, and is entertained with cake and ale. By the sums collected in this manner, together with those arising from the voluntary visits

---

[1] A monstrous wooden horse, carried on men's shoulders to a certain distance amidst the shouts of a large company of followers.

of parties to the ball, the expenses of the entertainment, which are very considerable, are defrayed, and oftentimes the surplus is applied to charitable purposes[*]. A towering May pole erected some time before Whitsuntide serves to announce the amusement to the neighbouring villages, and the crowds which usually attend attract great numbers of those itinerant traders who frequent markets and fairs, so that the festival may be considered one of the most entertaining in the country[³].

MEADOW MOWING.—At the mowing of *Revel-mede*, a meadow between Bicester and Wendlebury, most of the different kinds of rural sports were usually practised; and in such repute was the holiday, that booths and stalls were erected as if it had been a fair. The origin of the custom is unknown; but as the amusements took place at the time when the meadow became subject to commonage, some have supposed it originated in the rejoicings of the villagers on that account. These sports entirely ceased on the enclosure of Chesterton field.

HARVEST HOME.—This custom still prevails among the farmers, and nearly according to ancient usage. It simply consists in a supper given to those employed in getting in the corn, some of whom ride to the farm on the last load, shouting " Harvest home!" But if this happens to lie through the town, their merriment is frequently interrupted by the pails of water which the

---

[*] At Bicester in particular this has been the case. A few years ago a funeral pall for the use of the poor was purchased in this way; and a similar object was contemplated by the projectors of the last Whitsun-ale; but through the unfavourable state of the weather the expenses of the amusement were realised only: yet on representation of the circumstance to Mr. Coker, he carried the design into effect. This handsome pall is now kept at the workhouse, and lent to any applicant.

[³] At the neighbouring village of Kirklington is a similar amusement held annually on Lammas-day, and from thence denominated a *Lamb-ale*. The common people say, if the latter were discontinued in that village, the inhabitants of Bicester King's-end would be privileged to establish it in that township.

sportive inhabitants endeavour to throw on them from their windows. The harvest home is a relic of servile customs; and in ancient times was considered a part of the reward for customary services. The present mode of hiring labourers and servants has certainly rendered the custom unnecessary; yet it remains for the farmer to consider how far the prospect of the merry-making stimulates the exertions of the workmen.

A similar supper was given by the late Joseph Bullock, Esq. of Caversfield, at the close of the season for gathering hops.

PAYMENTS.—It was formerly usual for many of the inhabitants to pay sums for rents, &c. in the parish-church, or in and over the church-porch; and to lodge copies of their leases, &c. in the parish-chests, many of which still remain in those depositories. An indenture stipulating payments as above is given by Kennett[4], made 1352, 26, 27 Edward III., between Sir John Trymnel and Thomas de Panton and Camerona his wife, for the conveyance of the enfeoffment of two cottages, with their appurtenances, which were held by John Spaygne and John de Langton in Bicester, for the yearly rent of twenty-nine shillings sterling, to be paid in the parish-church on Sunday after the octaves of St. Michael. In the church-wardens' chest are also several leases of the estates given for charitable purposes, which expressly stipulate for the payment of rents on a certain day into the hands of Mr. John Coker, in the room over the church-porch.

MUMPING.—But perhaps the most singular custom is that which has long obtained on the morrow after Christmas-day, and is usually denominated *Mumping.* Immediately after breakfast many of the poor assemble together, and in a body visit the gentry and tradesmen to solicit a Christmas-box. As they expect a certain sum per head, none of the family are left at home, and the number of men, women, and children collected together for this purpose sometimes amounts to one hundred. This imposition on the

---

[4] Paroch. Ant. p. 476.

more industrious is generally reckoned at one penny for every grown person, and a halfpenny for a child. To guard against a second demand from the same individuals, many of the inhabitants detain them at their doors till the whole are assembled, and then admit them into a yard or court, where they receive their customary dole, and are then re-admitted into the street. The circuit of the town generally occupies them from ten in the morning till three in the afternoon, during which the most active collect from about ten to eighteenpence, which enormous sum is usually spent in some refreshment in the evening.

The other sports and amusements are those which are common to the whole country.

ADDENDA.

The following account of the confinement of several Protestants in Bicester Priory having been omitted in its proper place, the Reader will excuse its insertion here.

In the year 1521 numbers of the inhabitants of Chesham, Uxbridge, and the surrounding towns, were accused of heresy before John Longland, bishop of Lincoln[1], and many being intimidated by ecclesiastical threatenings, were induced to abjure their opinions and submit to penance. These were severally committed to the abbeys and monasteries of Bicester, Tame, Nuttley, Asherugge, Eynsham, Oseney, and others, there to be kept and found of alms all their lives, being prohibited from passing the precincts of the different monasteries without the bishop's dispensation. They were all enjoined this penance— On a particular market-day to go

---

[1] From the last will and testament of Isabell Staveley widow, of Burcester, it seems that she married the father of this prelate.—Kenn. MS. Collec. Lansd. MS. vol. ii. 292.

thrice about Burford-market, stand on the highest greece of the cross bearing a faggot,—again to bear the same faggot both at Burford and their own parish-church during the celebration of high mass, and at the burning of an heretic,—every Sunday and Friday during life to say Our Lady's Psalter,—on no account to attempt hiding the mark imprinted on their cheek, or converse with suspected persons on pain of relapse[2].

The same writer says that in the reign of Queen Mary the Earl of Derby so far degraded his rank as to engage in the prosecution of heretics, that he several times examined G. Marsh at Latham, and materially contributed towards committing him to the flames[3].

Amount of the Subscription in aid of the Sufferers at the Battle of Waterloo.

Collected from pew to pew in the parish-church after
   a sermon preached by the Rev. J. Markland, July 23,
   added to a donation of 10*l.* by J. Coker, Esq..... £43 13 0
Collected among the Dissenters[4].................£ 4 10 0

---

[2] Fox's Martyrology, p. 838. Lond. 1583.   [3] Ib. 1562.
[4] Times Newspaper, August 31, 1815.

A GLOSSARY

TO EXPLAIN

The ORIGINAL, the ACCEPTATION, and
OBSOLETENESS

OF

WORDS AND PHRASES;

AND TO SHEW THE RISE, PRACTISE, AND ALTERATION OF
CUSTOMS, LAWS, AND MANNERS.

By WHITE KENNETT,

VICAR OF AMBROSDEN.

GLOSSARY.

The authorities to which the letter K is affixt will be found in the PAROCHIAL ANTIQUITIES.

ABUNDA. A mete or Bound.—*Juxta ripam de Charwell usque ad metas et Abundas ibidem per me concessas*, K. p. 208. From Sax. Banꝺ a bond, from Binꝺan to bind. Hence hat-Band, wrist-Band, neck-Band: to Bound, to reBound. A Ban, an enclosed field or limited piece of ground. The Ban of a house or a mill, the close or back-yard adjoining to it. A Bandog, a mastiff kept close, or tied up. A Bandore, or veil of a widow to bind over or cover her head and face. A horse-Bin, which in Kent is that apartment of a stable where the chaff and cut meat is secured by a partition of boards. A Bin or Bing, a safe, an aumbry or cupboard in a buttery or lardar. The kiln of the furnace wherein they burn their charcoal for the melting of mettals, is commonly called the Bing. And the cistern into which they throw their crystallized allom for the water to drain from it, is called a Bing at Whitby in Yorkshire. A Bind of eels is a string or stick of eels. A Binne of hides or skins is in some countries a quantity for common sale, consisting of thirty-three skins or hides.

ABUTTARE. To Abutt, *vid.* BUTTES. *Abuttat super prædictam terram*, K. p. 399. In a terrier, or description of the site of land, the sides on the breadth are said to be *adjacentes*, lying or bordering, and the ends only in length are *abuttantes*, abutting or bounding. Which in old surveys they sometime expressed by *capitare* to head, or the head-land so bounding. As in the rental of Wye in Kent belonging to the abby of Battel in Sussex, *Tenent octo acras juxta Goreswall capitantes ad prædictam wallam*, Custumar de Bello, f. 241. Hence to go About was properly to go round by the end, instead of striking cross the middle.

ACOLYTHUS. An Acolite, who in our old English was called a Colet, from which office came the family of Dean Colet founder of Paul's School. An inferiour church-servant, who next under the sub-deacon waited on the priests and deacons, and performed the meaner offices of lighting the candles, carrying the bread and wine, and paying other servile attendance. *Vacante ecclesia de Ambresdon, rector et conventus de Asherugge Johannem de Capella Acolythum præsentarunt,* K. p. 346.

ACRA. An Acre, from Sax. *Æcen* a field. The word at first signified not a determined quantity of land, but any open ground, especially a wide campagne: and that sense of it seems preserved in the names of places, Castle-acre, West-acre, &c. *in com.* Norf. When the word was applied to the measure of ground, the quantity was still various, but determined by the statutes of 31 Edw. I. and 24 Hen. VIII. c. 4: one acre to consist of eight score perches, fourty in length and four in breadth, or so in proportion. Though the perch still differed in different counties, *vid.* PERCH. At the great Doomsday inquisition the common pasture seems measured by hides, the arable land by carucates, and the meadow by acres, K. p. 65.—*Exceptis virgis et buttis, quarum quatuor virgæ faciunt unam acram, et aliquando plures, similiter aliquando quatuor buttes, aliquando quinque, aliquando sex, aliquando septem, aliquando octo faciunt unam acram, videlicet secundum quantitatem earundem in longitudine et latitudine,* K. p. 534.

ACQUIETARE. To Acquit or discharge, or to testifie the receipt of a debt by giving an Acquittance. *Pro ista donatione et concessione acquietaverunt fratres prædicti de quinque marcis argenti,* K. p. 126. It was the common form in deeds of gift and other conveyance.—*Nos autem—warantizabimus acquietabimus et defendemus in perpetuum.—Pro hac autem warantia acquietantia et defensione.*—Hence to Quit any claim or pretension. To get Quit of any danger or trouble. Quite, perfectly, entirely, as Quite dead, &c. Quotted, satisfied and cloyed, as his stomach is quite Quotted.

ACTIONES. The whole process and transaction of a gift and charter, and other formal rites and solemnities of a publick conveyance. So in the donation of Musewell in Ambrosden to the abby of Missenden,—*Affuerunt hiis actionibus præsentes et testes,* K. p. 76.

ADRAMIRE, *Adrhamire, Arramire, Arramare.* To Arrain, *i. e.* to appeal to the law, to offer proof for the claim of right, to proceed to an assise or trial, and stand to the verdict of a jury. So, To Arraine a writ of novel disseisin, *i. e.* to prefer such an action, and prosecute the issue of it. To Arraign an assise, *i. e.* to make plaint, to open the cause, and sue for justice. To Arraign a criminal, *i. e.* to indict and bring him to his trial. Dr. Cowel would derive this term from the French *arranger,* to dispose or set in order, which conjecture is approved and justified by the latter editor of that interpreter. But the more learned Sir Henry Spelman refers it to the old French word *arramir,* to swear or take a solemn

GLOSSARY.

oath. As if *Arramire assisam* were to appeal to the oaths of witnesses, and to the verdict of a jury. But indeed I rather think that *Adramire* was at first a contraction of *Ad arma ire*, because the old legal trial both for the title of estates and the charge of crimes was by solemn combat or duel, when *Arramire* or *Arramare* was to alarm or call the accused person to a decisive trial at arms. And because the champions were upon the first challenge to swear that they would put themselves on this military issue: and at the time and place of combat were again to take formal oaths to observe the stated laws of the camp; therefore *Arramire* was to swear, but in a secondary sense, as solemn swearing did attend and relate to their solemn fighting. When this barbarous custom of determining a cause by arms and blood, was succeeded by the more civilized way of assise or trial by jury, *temp.* Hen. II., then the word was continued when the method was altered, and *Arramire versus aliquem* was to appeal for justice against a person, and to sue for the benefit of a publick trial. And *Arramire reum* was to arraign a criminal, and offer proof for the conviction of him.—*Thomas Abbas de Egnesham in curia hic Adramivit versus eos de advocatione ecclesiæ de Sulthorn,* K. p. 351.

ADVOUSON OF CHURCHES. No church legally consecrated without an allotment of manse and glebe, made generally by the lord of the mannor, who thereby became advocate or patron of that church, K. p. 222. So as the lordship of the mannor and patronage of the church were rarely in different hands, till advousons were unhappily given to religious houses, K. p. 276. During a controversie for the right of patronage, the diocesan presented to the church *salvo jure utriusque.* So in a suit depending between William earl of Sarum and the abbat of Barlings, for the advouson of the church of Midleton, K. p. 192. So Hugh bishop of Linc. presented to the church of Godington, in a dispute of title between Thomas de Camvill and the abbess of Alveston, K. p. 193. When two several persons presented their respective clerk, an inquisition was directed from the archdeacon to be executed within the parish, and returned into the court, K. p. 346. No such inquisition if the right were apparent, *Nulla inquisitione in hac parte capta, quia domino constabat de jure patronatus,* K. p. 507. When the king presented a clerk upon a false title, the bishop instituted the other's clerk, but with great deference to the king's pretended title, and obliging the clerk so instituted to an oath of resignation if the king's right should afterward appear. *Post institutionem suam prædictam juravit tactis sacro sanctis Evangeliis quod si contigerit dictum regem evincere jus patronatus ecclesiæ memoratæ* (*i. e. de Ambresdon*) *illam sine coactione aliqua resignaret,* K. p. 347.

If the patron presented not within six months, there was a lapse
to the bishop, *Dicunt etiam quod tempus semestre nondum elapsum est*, K. p. 351. The king and other guardians presented in
the right of wards, K. p. 192, 193. When the right of advouson was determined by law, a writ lay to the bishop to admit the
right clerk, *Concessum est quod prædictus Thomas abbas habeat
breve episcopo Lincoln. quod ad præsentationem ipsius abbatis ad
prædictam ecclesiam idoneam personam admittat*, K. p. 351. The
Advouson of churches in such mannors, as were held of the king
in capite, not to be given by the lords to religious or charitable
uses, without inquisition *Ad quod dampnum*, and license of the
king, K. p. 352. Trials for right of advouson were in courts Christian, K. p. 642. To prevent litigious suits for the title to benefices, the rural deans took an account of the names and number of
the parish churches within their respective districts; what the
Christian name and sirname of the several incumbents, the time of
their collation to such benefices, by what title they held them,
whether by institution, commendam, or custody; of what age they
were, and in what orders; whether beneficed in more than one
church; the name and quality of the patrons; and the value of
every benefice by the last taxation. This register was distinctly
transcribed, and a fair copy delivered to the diocesan, by him transmitted to the metropolitan in the next provincial council, K. p. 647.
Vid. PATRON.

ADVOUSON OF RELIGIOUS HOUSES. As those who built and
endowed a parish church were by that title made patrons of it,
so those who founded any house of religion had thereby the advouson or patronage of it. Sometime the patrons had the sole
nomination of the prelate, abbat, or prior; either by investiture or
delivery of a pastoral staff, as William Mareschal earl of Pembroke
to the abby of Noteley, *com.* Buck. K. p. 147. Or by bare donation or presentation to the diocesan; as Reginald earl of Bologne
in his charter to the priory of Cold Norton, *Non hoc autem prætermittendum est, quod domus illa de nostra donatione est, et nos ibi
priorem apponere debemus*, K. p. 163. If a free election were left
to the religious, yet a *congé d'eslire* or license of electing was
first to be obtained from the patron, or in his absence out of England, from the seneschal or steward of his barony. So in the
nunnery of Stodley, the founder Edmund earl of Cornwall thus
provided, *Nec est prætermittendum, quod quotiescunque priorissam
eligere contigerit ad eundem prioratum, de seipsis priorissam de assensu meo vel seneschalli mei, si in Anglia non fuero, eligere licebit.
Cum autem electa fuerit, ad præsentationem meam vel seneschalli
mei si in Anglia non fuero domino Lincoln. episcopo debet præ-*

sentari, K. p. 165. When the title of patronage was in dispute, the religious applied themselves to which they pleased of the contending parties : so the monks of Notley asked license of electing their abbat from the Lady Maud de Mortimer, whom they presumed to be their patroness, though the earl of Glocester claimed that right, K. p. 314. The patronage lapsed to the lord of the honour, if the family of the founder was extinct : so Edmund earl of Cornwall became patron of the nunnery of Goring, by no other title than as that house was situate within the honour of Walingford, K. p. 329. On the death of the prelate or governour the lands escheated to the patron as lord of the fee, and were to be compounded for by relief, heriot, and other burdens of military service : unless their endowment was frank-almoin, or such right in the fee was expressly renounced : as Edmund earl of Cornwall in his charter to the college of Bonhommes at Asherugge.—*Ita quod cedente vel decedente rectore ecclesiæ de Esserugge prædicta, quod nos vel hæredes nostri—nullatenus habeamus ingressum in prædictis maneriis seu Advocationibus ecclesiarum prædictarum sive in aliquibus suis pertinentiis quicquam nos intromittamus tempore vacationis quo carebunt rectore, sed semper in manibus ipsorum fratrum tam tempore vacationis quam aliis temporibus remaneant, ne statum suum in aliquo mutent,* K. p. 311. In the vacancy of any religious house the patron presented to the churches of which the religious had the advouson.—*Lucia de Arderne recognovit advocationem illam (i. e. ecclesiæ de Souldern) esse jus prædictæ abbatiæ de Egnesham et post mortem cujusdam Gilberti abbatis vacante prædicta abbatia quidam Richardus de Gravesend quondam Lincoln. episcopus loci illius ordinarius, et advocatus prædictæ abbatiæ contulit illam ecclesiam cuidam Galfrido de Stokes clerico suo,* K. p. 351. When an abby of royal foundation was engaged in great debts, at the next vacancy the king took the abby into his hands, and committed the custody to some steward, to receive the profits and discharge the said incumbrance, K. p. 359.

AFRICANA. A Turkey, either from Africa the country from whence they were brought into these northern parts; or perhaps from the old Latin *Afra*, a Bird.—*Afras aves esse aiunt,* Lat. Gloss. MS.—*Sex Africanæ fœminæ,* K. p. 287. A certain number of this sort of fowl was frequently reserved among the provisions paid to the lord from his customary tenents.

AGILLARIUS. A Heyward, *i. e.* A Herd-ward or keeper of the herd of cattel in a common field, sworn at the lord's court by solemn oath, of which the form is delivered by Kitchin, Of Courts, f. 46.—*Quoddam pratum viride quod vocatur Heywardsmere, eo quod pertineat ad officium Agillarii domini Lestraunge,*

GLOSSARY.

K. p. 534. Which *pratum viride* was I believe the same with what is now called Tadbury balk or The Edburg way balk, in the field of Bisiter King's-end, of which the grass or herbage is still the right and profit of the tithing-man of King's-end. 'The office of *Agillarius* was of two sorts, first, the common Heyward of a town or village, to supervise the greater cattel or common herd of beasts, and keep them within their due bounds; he was otherwise called *Bubulcus*, Cowward, (which is turned into a name of reproach, a pitiful *Coward*) who if he was a cottager or other servile tenant, he was exempted from the custumary works and labours, because he was presumed to be always attending on his herd, as a shepherd on his flock, who had therefore the like privilege.—*Sunt ibi* xvi. *Cotarii, quorum alii sunt Bubulci domini, alii sunt Pastores, qui si non essent, deberet quilibet unum opus singulis septimanis per annum*. Cartul. Glaston. MS. f. 40. Secondly, the *Agillarius* of the lord of a mannor, or of a religious house, who was to take care of the tillage and harvest work, to pay the labourers, and to see there were no encroachments or trespasses committed, &c. The same in effect with that officer who is called the Fields-man and the Tithing man.—*Et in solutis diversis hominibus et fœminis primo die Julii conductis ad sarculandum diversa blada ut patet per talliam contra agillarium hoc anno* xvi. *sol.* x. *den.* K. p. 576. His wages in 3 Hen. VI. was a noble,—*Et in stipendio Roberti Clerk agillarii hoc anno* xiii. *sol.* iv. *den.* K. p. 576.

AGISTATOR. The Agister in a forest, from the French *gister* to lie and feed for a certain *giste* or rate paid to the king. *Agister* in the modern French *adjouster*, to receive in cattel to be so pastured or *gisted*, to keep them within their bounds, and deliver them to the owners upon the payment of such terms for their feeding. *Agistare forestam* was to take in cattel to pasture within the bounds of the forest, for one month, *viz.* fifteen days before Michaelmas, and fifteen days after, when the running of cattel would be no prejudice to the game. *Agistator* was the forest officer, who was to take account of the cattel so *agisted*, whether they belonged to tenants within the forest, who had free *gistment*, or to neighbouring inhabitants who paid a common rate. The *Agistatores* in an old version of *Charta de foresta* are called *Gyst-takers* or *walkers*. *Omnium regardatorum et agistatorum forestæ prædictæ*, K. p. 209. *Homines sui reddent pannagium dicto manerio cum agistamentum acciderit*, K. p. 229. *Eorum animalia agistata fuerunt per duos annos jam elapsos, et solvent Joh. Appulby pro agistamento* xiii. *sol.* iv. *den.* K. p. 497. Hence our graziers now call the foreign cattel, which they take in to keep by the week, *gisements* or *juicements*, (pronounced like the *joices* in building, corrupted from the French *adjoustment*, the cross pieces of timber that are adjusted or fitted to make the frame of the floor.) And to *gise* or *juice* ground, is when the lord or tenant feeds it not with his own stock, but takes in other cattel to *agist* or feed in it. All glossographers agree to derive this word from the French *gister* to lie, *gest* a bed, &c. But I rather think *agistamentum* bears relation to *ager*, the field or feeding place of cattel, and might be the same as *agrarium*, *agerium*, *agroticum*, the profit of feeding cattel upon such a ground or field. Unless it were so, I cannot imagine why the duty or levy for repairing the banks and walls in Romney-marsh was called *agistamentum*, and the laying such a proportion of this duty upon the several estates was called *agistatio*,—*Tunc sequitur numerus omnium acrarum infra dictum mariscum.—Et etiam agistatio tam in magna wallia de Apuldre quant in parva wallia ad quantitatem terrarum. Ordinatio Marisci de Romney*, K. p. 20.

ALTA VIA. A Highway or common road. *Item alta via et generalis inter Brehull et Pidinton maneria Domini Regis omnino esset astopata:* which was adjudged a trespass against the king and county, K. p. 250. Criticks might dispute whether the Latin *altus* gave name to or was borrowed from the British *al* high, or *alt* the ascent of any mountain, as *Alpen* the *Alps*, from *al* high, and *pen* a head or top. Whence *Alpes* past into an appellative for any mountainous or rising places. As High gave a common to a Highal or Hill.

ALTARAGIUM. The profits arising to the priest from the people's offering at the altar. Out of these customary dues the religious assigned a portion to the vicar : so the prior and canons of Saint Frideswide,—*De præfatæ ecclesiæ nostræ (i. e. de Oakle) et capellarum ejusdem altaragiis, ut tenemur, congruam portionem reservatam eidem vicario de qua valent commode sustentari*, K. p. 455. Sometime the whole Altarage was allotted to the vicar, *Habebit vicarius de Cestreton totum altaragium*, K. p. 543. The regulars and secular priests invented a great many pretty arts to augment the altar-offerings. Among other this one was so ludicrous, and conveyed such thoughts of impurity, that it was expressly prohibited by the great reformer of his age Bishop Grosthead.—*Audivimus autem, unde non mediocriter dolemus, quod quidam sacerdotes hujus lucri plenas injungunt pœnitentias, quales sunt, quod mulier cognita a viro post partum ante suam purificationem deportet deinceps oblationem ad altare cum qualibet muliere purificanda in eadem parochia;—quod penitus inhibemus.*—Constit. Roberti Episc. Lincoln. MS. f. 3.—Since the Reformation several disputes arose what dues were comprehended under the title of *Altaragium*, which were thus remarkably determined in a trial in the Exchequer in Michaelmass term, 21 Eliz. on Thursday November 12 Upon the hearing of the matter betwixt Ralph Turner, vicar of West Haddon, and Edward Andrews, it is ordered, that the said vicar shall have by reason of the words *Altaragium cum manso competenti*, contained in the composition of the profits assigned for the vicar's maintenance, all such things as he ought to have by these words, according to the definition thereof made by the reverend father in God John bishop of London, upon conference with the civilians, viz. David Hewes, judge of the Admiralty; Bartholomew Clerk, dean of the Arches; John Gibson, Henry Joanse, Laurence Hewes, and Edward Stanhope, all doctors of the civil law: that is to say, by *Altaragium*, tithes of wool, lambs, colts, calfs, piggs, goslings, chickens, butter, cheese, hemp, flax, honey, fruits, herbs, and such other small tithes, with offerings that shall be due within the parish of West-Haddon.

And the like case was for Norton in Northamptonshire, heard in this court within these two or three years, upon the hearing ordered in the like manner.

Which judgement I presume was grounded on these and the like authorities. *Vicarius de Colingham habeat totum altaragium, exceptis decimis feoni et nutrimentorum animalium provenientium de dominico domini regis.* Mon. Ang. tom. 3, p. 139.—*Ita quod prædictus vicarius—prædictis oblationibus et obventionibus, non bladis aut garbis nisi plantatis aut pede fossis ad altaragia communiter spectantibus contentus, &c.* Will. Thorn, cap. 30, § 4 &c. Yet it seems to be certain that the religious when they allotted the *Altaragium* in part or whole to the vicar or capellane, they meant only the custumary and voluntary offerings at the altar, for some divine office or service of the priest, and not any share of the standing tithes, whether predial or mixt.

AMASIA. A mistress or concubine, *ab amando*, as amorous, amiable, &c. *Henricus primus filius Willielmi Bastard dedit Editham filiam Forne amasiam suam Roberto de Olleio secundo in uxorem,* K. p. 88.

AMERCIAMENTUM. A pecuniary punishment imposed upon offendors, *a la mercie*, at the mercy of the court, and therefore in our law cases is frequently called *Misericordia*; and therefore this difference is commonly stated between fines and amercements. Fines are punishments certain and determined by some statute. Amercements are arbitrary impositions proportioned to the fault, at the discretion of the court. If the amercement were too grievous, there was a relief to be sued by a writ, called *Moderata misericordia*. The amercements in county courts or the assises held by itinerant judges were sometimes granted by the king as a special profit and privilege to a servant or favourite: so King Hen. III. to his brother Richard earl of Cornwall, K. p. 219. The amercements in the view of frank-pledge or court-leet were due to the lord, and received by his bailiffs: *Ballivi comitis Gloucestriæ venient quolibet anno semel ad tenendum visum franci plegii in eodem manerio, et asportabunt omnia amerciamenta inde provenientia*, K. p. 319. A common privilege that persons should be amerced by their peers or equals. So in the lords court within the mannor of Hedingdon,—*Quoties contigerit aliquem prædictorum hominum pro aliquo delicto quoquo modo amerciari in eadem curia, per pares suos et non per alios amercientur, et hoc secundum modum delicti*, K. p. 320. *Amerciamenta illevabilia* were such amercements, as through poverty or escape of the persons became desperate debts, and were deducted in the accompts of the bayliff or steward, or collector of rents and dues. The prior and canons of Burcester to the receiver of their rents at Kirtlington,—*In allocatis eidem pro amerciamentis illevabilibus hoc anno* vi. den. K. p. 573.

ANABATA. *Anaboladium, à Gr.* ἀναϐάλλεσθαι, to cast over or cover. A cope or sacerdotal vest to cover the back and shoulders of the priest. *Et in bolt rubei say apud Steresbrugge propter anabatam faciendam*, iv. sol. viii. den. K. p. 574.

ANCA. A goose, generally female in distinction from the *gander*, which in the north they call a *steg*. *Anca* seems a corruption from *Anserina*,—*Cum decima ancarum et ovorum—porcellos, ancas, ova*, K. p. 455. *Anca, Ancus*, was the thigh or hind legg.—*Affer quatuor panes, affer ancum porci, i. e.* a leg of pork. Hence a Hanch of venison, up to the Hanches in dirt. And hence with some allusion to have a Hank upon, to Hanker after.

ANNIVERSARIUM. An Anniversary, called by our forefathers a Year-day and a Mind-day, *i. e.* a memorial-day. The yearly return of the day of death of any person, which the religious registred in their Obitual or Martirology, and annually observed in gratitude to their founders and benefactors. It was sometime made an express condition in a charter: Yoland Countess of Dreux to the abby of Brueil,—*quod singulis annis post obitum meum Anniversarium solempniter celebrabunt*, K. p. 190. Reginald de Pavelly founder of the abby of Lisle-Dieu in the diocese of Rhemes had his anniversary there observed October 29, which practise of the religious was a great advantage to the history of men and times. A *pietance* or portion of meat and drink was sometime granted for this purpose. Henry vicar of Weston gave six shillings yearly rent to the abby of Oseney,—*Quos quidem attornavi ad unam pietantiam faciendam in conventu Osneiensi annuatim in perpetuum in die Anniversarii mei obitus pro anima mea*, K. p. 263. This was one of the trading arts of the religious, who frequently sold the purchase at very considerable rates. Edmund Rede, esq. gave largely to the abbat and convent of Dorchester for their sale of this privilege,—*Unum Anniversarium novem lectionum videlicet Placebo et Dirige semel in anno*, K. p. 626. Whatsoever was given to this use was forfeited to the crown by Stat. 1 Edw. VI. cap. 16.—The surviving relations made customary offerings at the altar, at every return of such anniversary, in gratitude to the memory and in charity to the soul of their departed friend. This the religious did sometimes assign for a part of the vicar's maintenance: *Omnes oblationes in nuptiis, purificationibus, Anniversariis, in cera, pecunia, ovis, aut fructibus*, K. p. 455.

ANTECESSOR. The word not so often applied to the ancestor of a family as either to the prepossessor of an estate or the predecessor in an office. *Sicut Antecessores sui tenuerunt melius de me et Antecessoribus meis*, K. p. 73.—*Alexander episcopus Lincoln.— Sicut Antecessores nostri eam præfatæ ecclesiæ de Egnesham dederunt et concesserunt*, K. p. 90.

APPENDICIA. The same as *Pertinentiæ*, the appendages or appertinences of any estate. So Simon earl of Northampton gave to the Knights Templers *Meritonam cum omnibus Appendiciis suis*, K. p. 110. Hence our Pentices or Pent houses, *Appendicia domus*, a Pent-stock, &c.

APPELLATIO. An appeal from some sentence or jurisdiction to a presumedly higher judicature, which appeals were frequent, both from the civil magistrates to ecclesiastical powers, and again from the courts Christian to the common law. This liberty of appealing was expresly renounced to make some compacts the more firm and unalterable. So the prior and convent of Burcester, upon a bargain with the abbat and convent of Oseney,—*Renuntiantes in hoc facto omnibus impellationibus super hoc habitis, appellationibus, in integrum restitutioni, regiæ prohibitioni, et omni alii remedio juris canonici et civilis*, K. p. 344. Appeals to Rome when made common, were so great an interruption of all justice that they were forbid and severely punished. So when Gilbert de Segreve archdeacon of Oxford in 34 Edw. I. appealed from the king's court to the pope, he was summoned to Westminster, and obliged to renounce his appeal by oath, and to find pledges for appearing at the next parliament, K. p 353.

APPROPRIATIO. The granting a parochial church or the great tithes and better profits, *ad proprios usus*, to the proper uses of some religious house, to enjoy for ever: whence they called it *perpetuum beneficium*. The prior and convent of Burcester had two parts of the great tithe in Compton Basset appropriated to them, *nomine perpetui beneficii*, K. p. 205. In this manner was the illegitimate birth of most appropriations ; the lay-patrons devoutly and, as they thought, innocently resigned their right of advowson to religious houses, who by their interest and money procured from the popes and bishops the annexion of all tithes and profits to themselves, K. p. 312. They had many artificial pretences to alledge to the pope and the diocesan, to extort their consent, K. p. 481. The methods of appropriating and the fatal abuse of thus robbing church and clergy discoursed at large, K. p. 433. The appropriators often encroached upon the remnant of the vicar, for which invasion of right the stout vicar of Ellesfeld, in 24 Edw. I. entered an action against the prior and canons of St. Frideswide, K. p. 326. A canon or other religious who was not a monk, by the pope's indulgence could hold a vicarage with his station in the convent.—*Proviso tamen quod ecclesia (scil. de Acle) per idoneum canonicum domus vestræ prædictæ (scil. S. Frideswidæ) prout sede apostolica vobis est indultum, et antiquitus extitit consuetum, deserviatur: qui quidem canonicus tanquam vicarius perpetuus a loci diocesano curam animarum recipiet*, K. p. 375. *Unum de canonicis nostris ut olim fuisse dignoscitur rite electum et ad ejusdem ecclesiæ vicariam legitime institutum accepimus*, K. p. 455. The religious took advantage of the vacancy of a church, and then prevailed with the patron to appropriate and give them immediate possession. So Robert Gait in the time of Hugh Wells bishop of Lincoln gave the vacant church of Hampton Gay to the abbat and convent of Oseney, and then notified it to the bishop, desiring him to give them admittance.—*Noverit discretio vestra quod defuncto G. persona ecclesiæ de Hampton me eandem ecclesiam vacantem dedisse et concessisse in perpetuam eleemosinam abbati et conventui de Oseney*, K. p. 404. At other times the religious obtained leave to appropriate a church of their own patronage, when it should next be vacant, and then, impatient for their prey, bought out the incumbent, or got it void by resignation or exchange, K. p. 407. One great mischief of appropriations was this: In the ordination of a vicarage the altarage or voluntary oblations were often divided between the vicar and the religious, which soon lessened the charity and piety of Christian people, who grew less free in their offerings when they found a great share must go away from the parish priest, to whom they designed that bounty, K. p. 455. The religious very apt to oppress the vicar, by throwing procurations and other burdens on them, and particularly when they had covenanted to maintain a capellane in some chapel of ease within the parish, they shifted off that charge and cast it on the vicar, K. p. 588. That the bishops might not loose by granting their assent to appropriations, they sometime compounded with the religious for an annual pension to answer the dues that might otherwise arise to their see from the succession of rectors. So in the appropriating of Merton to the abby of Egnesham,—*Reservamus insuper nobis et successoribus nostris episcopis Lincoln. nomine recompensationis indemnitatis et commoditatis quæ de dicta ecclesia obvenire solebat in singulis vacationibus ejusdem, et poterit similiter obvenire, pensionem annuam viginti solidorum ex causa consimili*, K. p. 483. One great and popular pretension of appropriating benefices to the use of the religious, was to enable them the better to relieve the poor, and in the form of appropriation it was sometimes expressly ordained that a perpetual portion should be allotted at the discretion of the bishop to relieve the indigent parishioners. So when the church of Charlton upon Ottmoor was given to the nuns of Henwode *com.* Warwic.—*Et etiam pro recreatione pauperum parochianorum ipsius ecclesiæ alia perpetua portio moderanda arbitrio diocesani loci deputari debet.* K. p. 522, 524. After the Statute of Mortmain the religious still carried on their gainful trade, by obtaining a dispensation from the king. So in the appropriation of Merton to the abby of Egnesham, K. p. 482, *Vid.* VICARAGE.

APPROPRIARE *ad honorem.* To bring a mannor within the extent and liberty of such an honour. *Petrus de Asherugge tunc seneschallus honoris Sancti Walerici appropriavit dictum manerium ad honorem Sancti Walerici*, K. p. 336.

APPROPRIARE *communam.* To separate and enclose an open common, or part of it.—*Quod possint sibi appropriare et includere pro voluntate sua tres acras prædictæ placiæ, i. e. in communi pastura*, K. p. 336.

APPRENTICIUS. An Apprentice or young person bound by indentures to a master, who upon such covenants is to teach him his mystery or trade. In 12 Edw. III. *Confirmavi Willielmo fratri meo apprenticio apud London*, K. p. 449. This I think is the oldest authority for the name of a servile apprentice: at least I have met with no mention of them till the beginning of the next reign, when Henry de Knighton, *sub an.* 1381, *Apprenticii quoque relictis magistris suis illuc accurrebant.* And Thomas Walsingham in Ric. II. p. 301, *De Londoniis multi apprenticii, plures servi, sumptis albis capuciis, invitis magistris et dominis sunt profecti.* The students and professors of the common law had the appellation of *apprentitii ad legem, apprentitii ad barras, juris regni apprentitii.* Of which titles see Selden's Notes on Fortescue, p. 2.

ARCHIDIACONUS. Archdeacons were at first employed by the bishops in more servile duties, and always in subservience to the urban or rural deans of Christianity, to whom they were as much inferiour as their order of deacon was to that of priest. Till by the advantages of a personal attendance on the bishop, and a delegation to examine and report some causes, and a commission to visit some remoter parts of a diocese, their power and dignity was advanced above the arch-presbyter or dean, K. p. 638. Archdeacons within the diocese of Lincoln collected the spiritualities of the bishop, and paid him some pensions or portions out of their office :—*Summa redditus de quo archidiaconi respondent episcopo Lincoln. per an.* ccxvil. xvis. viiid. K. p. 350.

ARGENTUM ALBUM. Silver coin or current money. By Doomsday tenure some rents to the king were paid *in argento albo*, common silver money, others *in libris ursis et pensatis*, in the metal and full weight. So the king's mannor at Brehull *reddit per annum* xxviii. *libras de albo argento, et pro foresta* xii. *libras ursas et pensatas*, K. p. 165. Hence in the next age that rent which was paid in mony was called *blanch-fearm*, now the *white-rent*: and what they paid in provision was termed *black-mail*.

ARIETUM *levatio*. An old sportive exercise, which seems to have been the same with running at the quintan or quintal, which was to fix a post perpendicularly in the ground, and place on the top of it a slender beam turning on a spindle, with a slob or flat board at the one end, and a bag of dirt or sand on the other; that while the rider strikes at the shield or board, he must shew his strength and dexterity to escape a blow from the turn of the other end. This sport might be called *Arietum levatio*, because such violent manner of riding at and striking did seem to resemble the Roman ways of playing their battering rams: or rather because the shield or board upon the striking end was made in the fashion of a ram's head: or because they fastened the horns of a ram at the returning end, to make the blow more comical. This custumary English sport, practised usually at weddings, was either so ludicrous or so dangerous that it was often forbid by ecclesiastical authority. Among the inquiries to be made by the archdeacons within the diocese of Lincoln, an. 1233. *An alicubi leventur arietes, vel fiant scotalla, vel decertetur in præeundo cum vexillo matricis ecclesiæ.* In the synod at Worcester, an. 1240, can. 38. a strict command was given, *Ne intersint ludis inhonestis, nec sustineant ludos fieri de rege et regina, nec arietes levari, nec palestras publicas.* There be two other authorities that seem more directly to imply it was the same with the quintan. A constitution of that great preserver of church discipline Bishop Grosthead commands that in every church should be published a prohibition, *Ne quisquam levet arietes super rotas, vel alios ludos statuat, in quibus decertatur pro bravio, nec hujusmodi ludis quisquam intersit.* And another constitution of Walter bishop of Durham, an. 1255. *Insuper interdicimus levationes arietum super rotas, et ludos quibus decertatur ad bravium exequendum.* In both which injunctions the expression of *levare super rotas* seems to determine it a versatile sport, like a beam or rafter turning equilibrious upon a pole or post erect. And the bravium or prize which was to be given to the victor. is so described in the quintal by Mat. Paris, *sub an.* 1253. *Eo tempore juvenes Londinenses statuto pavone pro bravio, ad stadium quod quintena vulgariter dicitur, vires proprias et equorum cursus sunt experti.* From whence I am apt to conclude that *quintana* and *arietum levatio* were the same manly exercise, or at least that the latter was but a varied improvement of the former, K. p. 21.

ARMA DARE. To make a Knight. An. 1144. 9, 10, King Steph. *Ego Brientius filius Comitis quem bonus Rex Henricus nutrivit; et cui arma dedit et honorem,* K. p. 101.

ARMA CAPERE. To be made a Knight. An. 1278. 5, 6, Edw. III. *A die quo dictus Comes (scil. Henricus de Lacy) arma militaria a Domino Henrico Rege patre nostro cepit,* K. p. 289.

ARMIGERI. Not only a title of dignity but the common appellation of servants, especially in convents. I suppose the better sort of servants, yet such as wore liveries in the priory of Burcester, where in 4 Hen. VI. the prior and bursar accounted,—*Et in blodeo panno empto pro Armigeris et valectis Prioris de Johanne Bandye de Magna Tue,* K. p. 576. This is the same servile office which by Sir Henry Spelman is called *quædam species armigerorum,* in the abby of Battle, *com.* Suss., where the abbat and convent granted to Hugh Fraunceis *armigero suo,* a yearly pension or wages, and a custumary livery, *ac etiam liberaturam nostram, de secta armigerorum nostrorum, quotiens nos liberaturam generalem dare contigerit.—Necnon tabulam suam infra idem monasterium in aula nostra prout alicui armigerorum nostrorum ibidem deservitur seu deservietur, dum tamen idem Hugo Fraunceis nobis et successoribus nostris suum congruum servitium medio tempore, corporis sui valetudine durante, realiter exhibeat.* Possibly these *Armigeri* of the religious (like the military armour-bearers) might be their retinue of the better rank, who carried their banners in any public procession, and attended in some other of the more gentile offices. As our *bedelli Armigeri,* Esquire bedels.

ARREARAGIUM. Arrears or debts unpaid within the due time.

From the French *arrier*, a *retro*, behind.—*Faciatis habere feodum suum una cum arreragiis suis*, K. p. 289.—*Omnimoda computa et arreragia computorum ac relevia exitus et alias forisfactas sive forisfacturas et alia debita quæcunque*, K. p. 475. *Respondent de arreragiis ultimi compoti*, K. p. 570. Hence the Rere of an army, the Rier-band; the Rier-county, or some place appointed by the sheriff after the end of his office to receive the king's arrears.

ARTICULUS. An Article or complaint exhibited by way of libel in a court Christian.—*Possint eos et eorum successores per omnem censuram ecclesiasticam ad omnium et singulorum præmissorum observationem absque articuli seu libelli petitione, et quocunque strepitu judiciali compellere*, K. p. 344.

ARURA *pro Aratura*. Ploughing. *Una arura*, one day's work at the plough,—*Tenet in bondagio et debet unam aruram in yeme, et unam sarculaturam*, K. p. 401. Hence in Wiltshire to Ear is to plough, and Earing is a day's ploughing.

ASSARTUM, *Essartum, Exartum*. A piece of land within the limits of a forest, grubbed up or divested of the wood and trees, and converted into tillage. Manwood derives it from an old French word, *assartir*, to make plain. Spelman thinks *Essartum* was from the Latin *exertum*, pulled or rooted up. Some derive it à *sarriendo*, weeding of fields. Skinner runs into more fanciful conjectures, à Lat. *exarturare*, *i. e. artus seu ramos arboris descindere, arborem detruncare, vel si malis* a Lat. *exsaltuare*, (*i. e.*) *saltum in agrum cultum transmutare, facili sane* 1 in e *transitu*. Mr. Somner is much more rational and happy, who thinks *exartum* to be a contraction of *exaratum*. To which opinion the learned Du Fresne inclines. *Alii denique ab Exaro, unde Exaratum, ager exaratus, præscissus, et per contractionem Exartum, uti scribi passim in vetustioribus chartis observare est. Quam ultimam sententiam fulciunt tabulæ veteres in Chronico Besuensi*, an. 5. Ludov. Imp. p. 513, *ubi Exaratum scribitur. Ædificiis desuper positis, campisque, pratis, sylvis, exaratis, pomiferis*, &c. Simon de Gerardmulin confirmed to the abby of Missenden the chappel of Holy Cross in Pidington, *et totum assartum quod adjacet*, K. p. 108.—*Reddendo pro prædicto assarto unum denarium*, K. p. 178. Land not to be assarted within the bounds of a forest without license from the king, nor could that be obtained without a previous inquisition *Ad quod dampnum—Jurati dicunt quod foret dampnum et valde nocumentum forestæ, si tres acræ assartæ essent in quoddam planum quod vocatur Fernhurst in foresta de Bernwode*, K. p. 249.

ASSISA, *ab Assidendo*. Originally a court wherein the judges as Assessors did bear and determine any cause. Thence the word Assisa was translated to signifie an ordinance or statute-law, a trial, a jury, a writ, &c. We now apply the word to no other court of judicature but the county courts held by the itinerant judges, called the Assises.

ASSISA MAGNA. A more solemn trial by a jury of twelve or more knights, to be elected and returned by four other knights, to give their verdict in a cause, prosecuted *per breve de recto, i. e.* where the dispute lies not of the bare possession, but of the right and property: distinguished from the *assisa parva* or *minor*, where the question is only of possession, in which the jury were twelve ordinary legal or free-men returned by the sheriff. Roger de Amory quit claimed to the abbat and convent of Oseney, two knights fees in Weston,—*Unde eos implacitavit in curia domini regis per breve de recto, et prosecutum est quousque dictus abbas et conventus posuerunt se super magnam assisam*, K. p. 257. *Johannes de Handlo defendit jus suum, et ponit se in magna assisa domini regis*, K. p. 415. In a great assise the sheriff returned four knights of the same county by the king's precept,—*Vice comiti Oxon. per breve nostrum de judicio praeceptum fuit quod venire faciat coram vobis quatuor milites de com. praedicto*, K. p. 446: which four knights were to appear in court at a day prefixed, and there in presence of the plantiff and defendant, or their attornies, were to elect out of themselves and others, twelve, thirteen, or sometimes sixteen knights, to be summoned against another day of hearing,—*Quatuor milites in propriis personis suis venerunt et super sacramentum suum in praesentia partium praedictarum elegerunt de seipsis et aliis sexdecim milites*, K. p. 485.—*Ponunt se in magna assisa domini regis—et offerunt domino regi dimidiam marcam pro inquisitione seisinae praedictae,—dies datus est partibus praedictis,—ad audiendam electionem magnae assisae dom. regis, et tunc venerunt quatuor milites ad faciendam electionem illam,* K. p. 480. The twelve or more knights elected by the first four were to be all such as held lands and tenements within the county, or else incapable to serve on the jury,—*Quidam illorum de terris et tenementis quae tempore electionis praedictae in com. praedicto habuerunt, se totaliter dimiserunt*, K. p. 446. If between the election of knights and the time of trial any of them were dead or sick, or dispossest of estates within the county, others by the king's precept to the sheriff were to be elected in their room,—*Si vobis constiterit aliquos de praedictis militibus sic electis mortuos esse, sive de terris et tenementis suis praedictis se dimisisse, sive perpetuo languidos esse, ut est dictum, tunc loco eorum alios legales milites ejusdem com. eligi et ulterius in eodem negotio facere, &c.* K. p. 446. If the jurors so elected refused or negected to appear, the sheriff was commanded to distrain their goods and chattels, and arrest their persons and bring them into court.—*Precipimus tibi—quod distringas Edmundum de Cornubia, militem &c. electos in curia nostra—per omnes terras et catalla sua in balliva tua—et quod habeas corpora eorum coram justitiariis nostris apud Ebor.* K. p. 446.

Assisæ *judicium.* Judgement of the court given against plantiff or defendant upon default,—*Ipsi non veniunt ad hunc diem, unde Judicium Assisæ capiatur versus eos per eorum defaltam,* K. p. 351.

Assisa *Forestæ.* The laws or particular orders of the Forest establisht in an Assise or court held by the forest officers,—*Johannes filius Nigelli habet in bosco domini regis Housbote et Heybote cum omnibus feodis forestario pertinentibus secundum assisam forestæ,* K. p. 266.—*Priorissa de Littlemore devastavit boscum suum de Shottore contra assisam forestæ,* K. p. 498.

Assisa *ultimæ præsentationis.* Assise of darrein presentment. A trial for the right of patronage by enquiring who took the precedent turns of presentation, for the more easie discovering and fixing the property of the advouson.—*Thomas abbas de Egnesham per attornatum suum optulit se versus Luciam quæ fuit uxor Thomæ de Leuknore et Petrum de Schevyndon quod essent hic ad hunc diem audituri Assisam ultimæ præsentationis,* K. p. 351.

Assisa *panis et cervisiæ.* The power or privilege of Assising or adjusting the weights and measures of bread and beer. As the weight of bread prescribed by the vice-chancellor, and supervised by the clerk of the market, is still called the Size of bread: So half a crust or a farthing bread in Oxford is in Cambridge called a Size of bread. And a servitor is there a Sizar, or one who is to live upon such an Assized allowance. Hence to Size, *i. e.* to match cloath, silk, &c. to get more of the same Assize or proportion. Hence Size for height and stature, of a middle Size. Sizely in the North is proud and coy, &c.—Sir Ric. D'Amory in 18 Edw. II. was Sysor, or had the assize of bread and beer within the city and suburbs of Oxford for the yearly rent of one hundred shillings: but on complaint of the university and city, the king granted back that privilege to the mayor and vice-chancellor, K. p. 393.

Assisus. Dimised or firmed out for such an assise or certain rent in mony or provisions. *Terra assisa* was commonly opposed to *terra dominica:* this last being held in demesne or occupied by the lord; the other let out to inferiour tenants. So among the lands of the Knights Templars belonging to their preceptory of Sandford,—*Apud Covele de dono Matildis reginæ habentur quatuor hidæ, quarum duæ sunt in dominico, et due assisæ ab hominibus,* K. p. 141. *Apud Meritone duæ in dominico, et quinque assisæ ab hominibus,* ib. Hence *redditus assisus,* the set or standing rent.

Sunt ibidem de redditu assiso, xls. K. p. 314. *Summa reddituum assisorum de manerio*, K. p. 355. Hence to Assess or allot the proportion and rates in taxes and payments by assessors in assessment.

ASSOCIATION. On the death of King Edw. I. Henry Lacy earl of Lincoln, Anthony Bec bishop of Durham, and divers others barons, entered into a solemn association to defend King Edw. II. and the rights of his crown, K. p. 355. In 5 Edw. II. Thomas earl of Lancaster and several peers associated by solemn oath to relieve the oppression of Holy Church, and to recover the just liberties of the kingdom, K. p. 364.

ATTACHIARE. To Attach or seize upon. *Attachiare bona*, to distrain goods. *Attachiare personam*, to arrest a person. From the Fr. *attacher*, to attack or take into custody, which the learned Du Fresne supposes derived from the old Gallic *tasca*, *taschia*, the rent of land or tenement, from the British *tasc* tribute, *tascyd* collector of the tribute, (whence our *tasque* or imposed labour. A *tasquer* or day labourer. A *tasque*-master, &c.) So as *attacher* was no more at first than to gather rent or collect tribute, or else upon refusal to take it by force, as a debt and forfeiture to the state.—*Tibi præcipimus quod ipsum Ychelum attachies, ita quod corpus ejus habeas coram baronibus*, K. p. 328. *Robertus Frere et Joshua Phillippes attachiati fuerunt, quod transierunt cum carectis suis ultra pratum domini de Langeford*, K. p. 458.

ATTACHIAMENTA *bonorum*. A distress taken upon the goods of persons sued for personal estate, by the legal *attachiatores* or bayliffs, and kept in their custody as a security to answer the action. It was a privilege granted to the abbat and convent of Oseney, to have the Attachments of all their tenants quit-claimed or released,—*Omnia attachiamenta hominum nostrorum et plegiorum suorum habenda quieta clamata sunt*, K. p. 196.

ATTACHIAMENTA *Forestæ*. All timber toppings and other vert felled or cut within the liberties of a forest without the view of the verdor and license of the king, were forfeited and to be Attached by the forestar,—*Nichil de boscis prædictis capere potuerunt nisi per liberationem forestarii—absq. attachiamento et impedimento forestarii prædicti*, K. p. 370.

ATTACHIAMENTA *de spinis et bosco*. The privileges granted to the officers of a forest to take to their own use thorns, brush, and windfall trees within such precincts. So John Fitz-Nigell forestar of Bernwode,—*debet habere feodum in bosco domini regis videlicet attachiamentum de spinis de bosco suo, et de bosco qui ventus prostituitur*, K p. 209.

ATTORNARE *Rem*. To Attourn or turn over mony and goods,

i. e. to assign and appropriate them to a certain use,—*quos quidem quatuor solidos—attornavi ad unam pietantiam faciendam in conventu Oseneiensi,* K. p. 283.

ATTORNARE *Personam.* To depute a representative or proxy, as in trials at common law, the plantiff or defendant retained *attornatum suum, positum in loco suo ad lucrandum vel perdendum,* K. p. 405.

AVERIA. Cattle. Sir Henry Spelman deduces the word from the Fr. *ovre* (work), as if chiefly working cattle. But more probably from *avoir*, to have or possess; the word sometime including all personal estate, as *catalla* did all goods and chattels. But commonly taken for all kind of stock or feeding cattle,—*Ad introitum et exitum cum averiis meis et suis,* K. p. 189. *Communem pasturam ad averia sua,* K. p. 227. *Propriam habet communam ad omnia averia in sylva dictorum prioris et conventus,* K. p. 489. In Northumberland they now say, a false Aver, for a sluggish horse or lazy beast, perhaps from *averia,* yet the honoured Spelman rather derives it from the old Lat. *affri* or *affra,* (country horses,) and cites the proverb, A false Aver or Afer. In the north they likewise use average for what in Kent we call the gratten, in other parts the eddish, in Wales the adlodh, the roughings, the stubble and pasture left in corn-fields after the harvest is carried in. From *averia* comes *averare,* which Spelman interprets to carry goods in a waggon or upon loaded horses, but it seems rather to drive cattle to a fair or market,—*Omnes homines (i.e. de Kyngston) debent ter averare ad Bristoliam.* Cartul. Glaston. Abbat. MS. f. 40.

AVER-CORN. A reserved rent in corn paid to religious houses by their tenants or firmers, which Mr. Somner deduces from the Fr. *ovre* or *ovrage* (work), as if corn drawn to the lord's granary by the working cattle of the tenant. But it seems more natural (like *averia*) from *avoir*, to have or receive such a quantity of corn. I suppose it owing to the Sax. Cýpıc-ꝛceat or Church-scot, a measure of corn brought to the priest on St. Martin's day; as an oblation for the first fruits of the earth. Under this title the religious had a reserve of corn paid yearly, as in an inquisition of the estate of the abby of Glastonbury, an. 1201, 2 King John,—*Waltone reddit in gabulo assiso* iv. *lib.* xvi. *sol.—de Churchscet* ii. *summæ et dimid. frumenti.* Cartul. Abbat. Glaston. MS. f. 38. Which *curchscet* by a Norman epithet might easily be called *avercorn.* Possibly from hence the Northern word *havers* oats, the like asperate as in *haver de pois* for *avoir du poids*. But more probably from a German original, *habern* oats in the High Dutch.

AUDITORES. Those religious in a convent who were deputed to state, examine, and pass the house-accompts,—*Computavit co-*

ram dominis—Auditoribus deputatis, K. p. 287. Hence the Auditors, Auditory, Audit-house, Audit-time, in cathedral and collegiate bodies.

AVES DICH. A corruption of Offa's Ditch, which seems to have been at first the boundary between the West Saxon and Mercian kingdoms, and afterward maintained to keep off the incursions of the Danes into these parts, from Northampton and other quarters. It appears to have been continued from Wansdike in Wilts, to Mixbury, *com.* Oxon. p. 40. A Dike in the north is a ditch to a dry hedge, where the wet ditch is called a Sough. From Dike comes the southern Doke, a deep furrow in arable land or any sudden fall of ground.

AUXILIUM *petere.* To pray aid in a suit or cause, *i. e.* when an inferiour tenant is impleaded and not capable to defend the right in his own name, he prayeth aid of the superiour lord to assist and justifie his plea,—*Johannes de Handlo implacitatus de manerio de Pidington—dicit quod ipse non potest prædicto priori sine ipso domino rege respondere, et petit auxilium de ipso domino rege,* K. p. 414.

AUXILIUM *Curiæ.* A precept or order of court for the citing or *sub-pœnaing* a party,—*Vocat inde ad warantiam Johannem Sutton de Dudley chevaler et Isabellam uxorem ejus, ut habeat eos hic in octab. S. Michaelis per auxilium curiæ,* K. p. 477.

AUXILIUM *facere alicui in curia regis.* To be another's friend and solicitor in the king's court, a fiduciary office solemnly granted by some courtiers to their dependants in the country.—*Sciant præsentes et futuri quod ego Bernardus de S. Walerico concessi Rogero de Bercheley et hæredibus suis auxilium et consilium meum in curia domini mei regis Angliæ,* K. p. 126.

AUXILIUM *Regis. Vid.* SCUTAGIUM.

AUXILIUM *Vicecomitum.* The aid or customary dues paid to the sheriff for the better support of his office. Prior de Kime *com. Linc. tenet duas carucatas terræ in Thorpe per servitium* xl. *denariorum per annum ad auxilium vice comitis.* Mon. Aug. tom. 2, p. 245. a.—An exemption from this duty was sometime granted by the king as a special privilege. So King Henry II. to the priory of St. Osith of Chich in Essex,—*Sint ipsi et omnes homines sui liberi et quieti de auxiliis vicecomitum et præpositorum hundredorum,* ib. tom. 2, p. 184. So King Henry II. granted to the tenants within the honours of Walingford and Bercamsted,— *ut quieti sint de auxilio vicecomitum et servientum,* K. p. 114.

AYSIAMENTA. Easements, from the Fr. *aisé,* easie: or from the Sax. Eıð, Easie or ready, which Chaucer calls Eith and Eth: and the Northumbrians still use Eeth, the Welsh Esmwyth. In grants of conveyance and dimise Aysiamenta did include any liberty of passage, high-way, water-course, or other customary benefit for the ease and accommodation of the owners or inhabitants of any house, or the tenants of any land.—*Quiete bene in pace et jure hæreditario in omnibus aysiamentis infra villam et extra ad dictum messuagium—pertinentibus,* K. p. 194.—*Cum omnibus pertinentiis suis valoribus et aysiamentis,* K. p. 229. Hence a house of office is called an Easement, commonly a house of Ease.

AXATIO *carectæ.* Putting on the axle-tree of a waggon,—*Et in uno axe empto cum axatione unius carectæ,* K. p. 574.

B.

BAIUS *Equus.* A Bay horse. From Lat. *Badius.* Gr. Βαΐδιος à Βαΐς, *et* Βαΐὸν, a bough or branch of a palm-tree; so as *Badius* was *coloris phœnicei.*—*Et de uno equo baio empto de Willielmo Salt ad stabulum prioris* xxvi.*sol.* viii.*den.* K. p. 576. Hence Baiard an appellative for horse. Prov. None so bold as blind Bayard.—Or in Chaucer's phrase,

" Ye ben as bold as is Bayard the blind."

Hence Bayard's-watering, Bayard's-green, &c.

BALLIVA. A Bailywick. From the Fr. *bailler,* to deliver or commit. *Ballivus* was the person to whom an authority and trust was committed within such a district. *Balliva* was the whole district within which the said trust was to be executed. A whole county was so called in respect of the sheriff. A whole barony in respect of the lord or baron. A hundred in respect of the chief constable. A mannor in respect of the steward. A circuit of villages and hamlets, with respect to the capital mannor, where the religious held their court or had a mansion-house. So the abbat and convent of Oseney had their *balliva de Weston,* which contained Weston, Blechesdon, Burcestre, Chestreton, Wrechwike, Bucknell, Audley, Arncote, and Northbrook, K. p. 60. The circuit within the liberties of the constable of the castle of Wallingford, called by him *Balliva mea,* K. p. 112. The sheriff of every county had two itinerant bayliffs, who were to execute writs and judgements, &c.—*Johannes Laundels vicecomes Oxon. dilectis sibi Johanni de Baldindon et Roberto Louches hac vice ballivis suis itinerantibus salutem,* K. p. 487. The secular clergy sometimes took these mercenary offices, prohibited by a constitution of the excellent bishop Grosthead,—*Ad amputandum quoque omnem cupiditatis speciem inhibemus firmiter non solum ordinaria sed speciali auctoritate apostolica, ne beneficiati vel ad sacros ordines promoti sint vicecomites vel justitiarii seculares vel ballivas teneant, unde laicis potestatibus obligantur ad ratiocinia de ballivis eisdem reddenda.* Constit. Rob. Episc. Lincoln. MS. *Vid.* FRÆPOSITUS.

BARROW. A large hillock or mount of earth raised or cast up, which may seem to have been one of the Roman tumuli or sepulchers, K. p. 18. From the Sax. Boeŋʒ, a raised heap of earth, or rather from Beaŋu, Beoŋa, which was commonly taken for a grove or toft of trees on the top of a hill. From the old Gallic *Bar*, a high place, from whence several towns in Italy and France from their lofty situation had this name of *Bar* and *Bari*. One of the most noted mountains in North Wales is called Berriw. Hence the Bars, properly a partition set upon rising steps. The Bar or gate of a city, as Temple Bar in London, Bootham Bar in York. The Barriers or mound to fence off the croud in military sports.

BAS-CHEVALIERS. Low or inferiour knights, as distinguished from barons and bannerets, who were the chief or superiour knights, K. p. 378. Hence we now call our bare simple knights, inferiour to baronets, Knights Bachellors, *i. e. Bas-Chevaliers.* Which in all likelyhood gave name to the academical degree of Bachellors, as a quality lower than that of masters and doctors. So in France they call the suburbs the *Bas-ville,* or the inferiour town. The learned Spelman very rationally derives the opprobrious name of Bastard from the Fr. *Bas,* and Sax. ᵹteoꝑt, rise or original, as a person of a base and vile extract. The same termination remains in Upstart, a fellow of a new and late rise.

BASSE. A collar for cart-horses made of flags,—*In tribus coleris, uno basse, cum tribus capistris, emptis apud Sterisbrugge,* K. p 574. Hence the round matted cushion of flags used for kneeling in churches is called Basse, in Kent a Trush.

BATELLUS. A boat or small marine vessel. It is a very frivolous conjecture of Dr. Skinner,—*Nescio an nostrum* Boat *ortum sit a* Teut. *Bott nuntius q. d. cymba internuntia classis.* It is more certain the Lat. *Batus,* Hispan. *Batel,* Ital. *Batello,* came from the Sax. Bat, and that from the old Brit. *Bâd,* which in present Welsh and Irish is a boat.—*Possessiones, naves, batellos, ac bona et catalla sua quæcunque,* K. p. 657. Hence a Bottom, which is still a common word for a marine vessel of burden, a good Bottom: whence the naval term of Bottomry, when the master of a ship borrows mony upon the credit of his vessel, or a safe voyage. *Botellus,* the lower part of the belly, which we now call the Bottom of the belly,—*Si stomachus vel botellus perforatus fuerit, ita ut stercus per vulnus exierit.* Leg. Frison Tit. 22.

BEAUMONT. *Bellus Mons,* Fair Mount. Several places of ascent and fair prospect were so called by the Normans. As the king's house in Oxford: the plat of an old fortification at Mixbury, &c.

BEDELLUS. A Bedell or cryer. Sax. Býðel á Býðbe, to publish, as to Bid and forBid the banns of matrimony, Bidding of prayers. Hence the university Bedels, the Bedell of beggars. The rural deans had their Bedels, which we now call apparitors and summoners, to cite the clergy and church officers to visitations, and execute the orders of the court Christian, K. p. 648.

BEDRIP, *Bedrepe, Wedbedrip.* From Sax. Biððan, to pray, and Repe to rip or cut corn. So as Bedrepe was the custumary service which inferiour tenants paid to their lord in cutting down their corn, or doing any other work or labour in the field. It chiefly related to the days of work in harvest,—*Tenentes de Ewel debent venire in autumpno ad precariam quæ vocatur a la Bedripe.* Placit. 10 Hen. III. *Ernaldus carectator tenet unum messuagium et duas acras terræ in duobus campis (scil. de Pidington) et reddit per annum duos solidos et alias consuetudines ad bedrepium in autumpno,* K. p. 496. From the Eng. *Bidding* or praying, it was called in Lat. *Precaria,* which did likewise comprehend any days or season, when the said servile tenants as Beadsmen were to perform any duty or labour for their lord, which were commonly called Bind-days, *i. e.* Bidden-days, when *ad preces domini,* at the beads, or petition of the lord or his steward, the tenants were to give their custumary attendance and labour,—*Debet venire quolibet anno ad duas precarias carucæ cum caruca sua.* Custumar. de Bello, f. 60. Called also *Precatura* and *Preces,* which were at any indefinite time,—*Quilibet carectarius manerii debet arare tres acras et dimidiam inter festum sancti Michaelis et sancti Martini: et in vere debet arare bis ad precaturas, et in æstate, &c.*—*Quilibet debet arare ad duas preces in hyeme, et ad duas preces in vere.* Cartul. Abbat. Glaston. MS. f. 40. And therefore the more solemn Bedrip in harvest was called *Magna Precaria,* to distinguish it from the other Bidden-days in any different season, and different work,—*Johannes Boyland tenet unum cotagium—et debet invenire unum hominem ad magnam precariam in autumpno.* Custumar. de Bello, f. 97. It was likewise called Wedbedrip, from the Sax. peð, a covenant or agreement, (whence to Wedd, Wedding, Wedded husband, &c.) as if a league or compact made between the lord and tenant,—*Robertus filius Nicholai Germayn tenet unum messuagium et dimidiam virgatam in bondagio ad voluntatem dominæ, et debet unam aruram in yeme, et unam sarculaturam, et debet wedbedrip pro voluntate dominæ,* K. p. 401. *Alicia quæ fuit uxor Ricardi le Grey—faciet unam sarculaturam et unam wedbedripam et levationem feoni,* K. p. 402. Hence a Bedde-ale or

Bid-ale was an assignation made for neighbours to meet and drink at the house of new married persons, or other poor people, and then for all the guests to contribute to the house-keepers.

Bellum Duellum. Duel or combat. An old customary way of trial by arms, wherein the appellant or challenger and the defendant or accepter were at a fixt time and place to engage in single combat, either by themselves or by their deputies, and the cause was adjudged to the conquerour. This fierce practice was allowed and confirmed by the laws of William the Conquerour, cap. 68, 69; and those of Hen. I. cap. 45, 49, and some new orders prescribed for the regulation of it. Leg. Hen. I. cap. 59. So that it is an evident mistake in the late ingenious author of An Introduction to the History of England, that " William the Conqueror endeavoured to abolish two ancient forms of trial used among the Saxons with great reverence, even during their Christian worship. —These were the trials ordeal and of camp fight, K. p. 246.— Both these sorts of trial this king abolished as unchristian and unjust, and reduced all causes to the judgement of equals, or of a jury of twelve neighbours, and by legal forms," K. p. 249. When it is certain the trial of camp-fight or duel was no custom peculiar to the Anglo-Saxons, but was the practice of most northern nations, especially of the Franks and Normans, and was indeed introduced by William the Conquerour, not found here as an ancient usage, much less abolished by him. He made no one order to cancel or to restrain it, but made an express law to license and authorize it. Before the Conquest not one law or one example of this practise, but after the Conquest some publick laws, and very many precedents *Hoc genus* (i. e. *duelli*) *a Normannis* (cum *Anglis illis antiquioribus antea ignotum erat*) *invectum est.* Antiq. Britan. p. 103. *Duellum, singulare certamen intellige, quod genus examinis, cum in Anglo Saxonum monumentis, quod sciam, non occurrat, Normannis eorum successoribus, ut verisimile est, debemus, a quibus a Normannia post Conquestum, ut vocant, huc adductum reor.* Someri Gloss. in voce *Duellium.* I wonder Sir W. T. could fall upon such an ignorant errour; but thus it is to write history without stating any times or producing any authorities. This is to invent not to relate. Alas, history is a very sacred subject; and though matters of opinion may admit of desultory essays, yet matters of fact must be delivered with great integrity and judgement. This camp-fight or duelling was of two sorts, either by court military in cases of felony or treason ; or by court civil for the trial of estates: both these are antiquated, but never really abrogated. Of the latter sort there was a solemn allowance, an. 1571, 13 Eliz., in the case of Simon Low and John Kime plaintiffs, and Thomas Paramore defendant, for the mannor and lands in the Isle of Hartie, near Shepey in Kent. Of the former kind the last example was in 6 Car. I. between Donald lord Rey appellant, and David Ramsey, esq. defendant. But in both these instances, after a great many formalities, the matter was referred witout proceeding to actual fight. In the ninth of King Steph. Brien Fitz-Count lord of Walingford, sent a challenge to Henry bishop of Winchester, wrote in red letters, and concluding thus,—*Ea quæ in hoc scripto assero contra Henricum nepotem regis Henrici episcopum Wintoniæ præsto sum probare vel bello vel judicio per unum clericum vel per unum laicum,* K. p. 101.

BENEVOLENTIAM *Regis habere.* To purchase the king's pardon and favour, and be restored to honour and estate.—*Thomas de S. Walerico dat regi mille marcas pro habenda benevolentia regis, et pro habendis terris suis unde disseisitus fuit,* K. p. 172.

Beopn. A Saxon epithet of dignity and eminence. Bernwode, com. Buck. seems to have been so called as a forest of the greatest remark, K. p. 28.

Bepn. A Barn, granary, or grange. The learned Fr. Junius judges it to be compounded of Bepe, barley; and Epn or Eapn, a place or repository: and asserts it to be so wrot, where it frequently occurs, in the Saxon Gosples, Bepepn, and sometimes separately Bepe-epn, which Spelman writes Bepeun. So Bepe-pic, a grange or the tillage of corn; Bepe-ɀapol, a tax on corn; Bepston, a name given to those villages where the religious had a common granary. But it is a fond conjecture of Dr. Skinner that Burcester, com. Oxon. was Bepn-ceaptep, or Barn-cestre. When, though I inclined to believe, it bore some relation to the first bishop of Dorchester, and might be possibly *Birini-Castrum.* Yet I rather think it was originally *Buri-Castrum,* or *Castrum ad Burum,* from the Bury or rivulet on which it stands, and which still retains the name of the Bury, though commonly the Rea; especially because the east-end of the town, now called Market-end, before the grant of a new market by Hen. VI. was always called Bury-end.

BERCARIA, *Berqueria, Berkeria,* A sheep-fold, sheep-cote, sheep-pen, or other inclosure for the safe keeping a flock of sheep. Abbreviated from *Berbicaria,* from *Berbex,* detorted from *Vervex.* Hence Lat. *Berbicus* a ram, *Berbica* an ewe, *caro Berbecina* mutton. *Berbicarius, Bercarius,* Fr. *Berger,* a shepard.—James le Bret of Bigenhull gave four short ridges or butts of land to the priory of Burcester,—*ad faciendam berkeriam sive quicquid eis melius placuerit.* K. p. 187. John de Charlton and Christian his wife gave to the abby of Oseney a piece of land in Hokenorton, upon which stood the Berchery of Sutton, K. p. 348. *Summa redituum porcoriarum et bercariarum si fuerint ad firmam* vs. vid. K. p. 354. *Et in Johanne Leseby faciente sepes apud bercariam de Wrechwyke et Crokewell,* xiii. *den.* K. p. 577. *Quidam bercarius de Ambresdon tenet terras in Wrechwyke,* K. p. 470. Hence the word *Bercen* or *Barken,* which is now commonly used for a yard or Back-side in Wilts, and other counties. But it first signified the small croft or close where the sheep were brought up at night, and secured from danger of the open fields.

BERIA, *Berie.* Most of our glossographers in the name of places have confounded the termination of Berie with that of Bury and Borough, as if the appellative of ancient towns. Whereas the true sense of the word Beria, Eng. *Berie,* is a flat wide campagne, as from sufficient authorities is proved by the learned Du Fresne in his Glossary, *voce Beria,* and in his Notes on the Life of St. Lewis, p. 89, where he observes that *Beria S. Edmundi,* mentioned by Mat. Paris, sub an. 1174, is not to be taken for the town but for the adjoining plain. To these and other his remarks on that word, may be added, that many flat and wide meads and other open grounds, are still called by the name of Berie and Berie-field. So the spacious mead between Oxford and Ifley was in the reign of King Athelstan called Bery. B. Twine MS. c. 2. p. 253. Such were the Berie-meadows, which though Sir Henry Spelman interprets to be the Demesne meadows or Mannor-meadows, yet were truly any open flat meadows that lay adjoining to any vill or firm. The same with Berras in that plea between the bishop and prior of Carlisle, 18 Edw. I.—*Et quod rex in foresta sua prædicta (scil. de Inglewood) potest villas ædificare, ecclesias construere, Berras assartare, et ecclesias illas cum decimis terrarum illarum pro voluntate sua cuicunque voluerit conferre.* Where *berras assartare,* must be to assart or plough up the plain, open heaths, or downs. Hence our warrens were called cony-Berries. A flat threshing floor is in the north called a Berry-sted and Berrying-sted; Berrier a thresher. As Bersted in Kent was Beri-sted or an open flat place. Hence the termination of many places that are so situate, as Mix-Berie, AcornBerie, now CornBerie, &c.

BEZANTINE, *Bizantin.* A piece of mony coined by the western emperours at Byzantium or Constantinople, of two sorts, *Bisantius aureus et albus,* gold and silver, both which past in England. The monks of Oseney, in consideration of the mannor of Hampton, gave ten marks of silver to Robert de Gait, and one Bezantine to his wife, K. p. 97. The silver Besantine was the value of two shillings, K. p. 109. Chaucer represents the gold Besantine or Besannt, to have been a ducket in weight.

BIDENTES. Two-yerlings: tags or sheep of the second year.—
William Longspe granted to the prior and canons of Burcester,—
*pasturam ad quinquaginta bidentes cum dominicis bidentibus meis
ibidem pascendis,* K. p. 216. The wool of these sheep being the
first sheering, was sometime claimed as a heriot to the king on the
death of an abbat. *Vid.* HERIOT.

BIGA, *Bigata.* A cart with two wheels, drawn often with one
horse, King Hen. III. confirmed to the priory of Repingdon,
com. Derb.—*unam bigam cum unico equo semel in die in bosco suo
de Tikenhale errantem ad focale ad usus suos proprios portandum.*
Mon. Ang. tom. 2, p. 280. So King John to the abby of Noteley,
com. Buck. *Concessimus eisdem canonicis duas bigas singulis annis euntes et redeuntes pro bosco ad focum eorum,* K. p. 160. The
prior and canons of Burcester allotted to the vicar of that church,
*duas bigatas boni foeni—et quatuor bigatas lignorum pro focalibus
de silva prioris vocata Priorswood,* K. p. 670. The two paps or
teats of a female are called in Essex the Bigges. A cap with two
long ears worn by young children and girls is now called a
Biggin.

BLADUM. Commonly taken for all sorts of standing corn in
the Blade and ear,—*Quilibet eorum (i. e. tenentium de Hedingdon)
animalia habens metet in autumpno unam acram bladi de blado domini ibidem,* K. p. 320. *In autumpno metent blada domini,* ib.
But in our old charters the word *Bladum* did include the general
product of the ground, fruit, corn, flax, grass, &c. and whatever
was opposed to living creatures. So when Joan de Pidington gave
or confirmed the hermitage of Musewell to the abby of Missenden,
she granted all the tithe of her demesne lands in Pidington,—*de
blado et de omnibus fructibus terræ, et de ovibus et porcis,* K. p. 76.
—*Decimam de dominio suo tam in blado quam in agris et porcellis,*
K. p. 77. Hence Germ. *Blatt,* Island. and Dutch *Blad,* Eng.
Blade of corn or grass, Blade of a knife, shoulder-Blade, and by
farther metaphor a fine Blade or brisk young fellow. The word
was sometime applied to all sort of grain or thresht corn,—*Tria
quarteria frumenti, tria quarteria avenarum, et unum quarterium
fabarum,—erunt quieti de solutione prædicti bladi in perpetuum,*
K. p. 291. Sometime appropriated to bread corn, or wheat, in
Fr. *Blè.* So the Knights Templars granted to Sir Wido de Meriton's
wife,—*duas summas bladi,* K. p. 120.

BLODEUS. From Sax. Bloð, Island. Blooð. Of a deep red
colour, or what we call as red as blood. The old phrase of Blae
and Bludie, what we now call Black and Blew. *Siquis verberan-
do aliquem fecerit blas et bludie, ipse qui fuerit blae et bludie prius*

debet exaudiri. Leg. Burg. Scot. cap. 87. Hence Bloat coloured and Bloated, *i. e.* sanguine and high coloured: which in Kent we call a Blousing colour, and a great Blouse is there a red-faced wench. Hence to Blush or turn red in the face; to Blote herrings, or by smoak to make red herrings; a Blot or Blotch and Blur, a spot of deep tincture. The prior of Burcester gave his liveries of this colour,—*Et in blodeo panno empto pro armigeris et valectis prioris de Johanne Bandye de magna Tue,* K. p. 576.

BLODEWITE. From Sax. Blod blood, and pite a fine or penalty. It was a customary amercement paid as a composition for the shedding or drawing blood. And sometime a privilege or exemption from this penalty was granted by the king as a special favour. So King Henry II. granted to all tenants within the honour of Walingford,—*ut quieti sint de hidagio et blodewite et bredewite,* K. p. 114. Hence we say a bloody fine, a Bloody sum of mony.

Bodu, *Bodun, Bod.* Brit. *Deep.* Hence the *Dobuni dofn* were called *Boduni, Bodunni,* from the deep fat soil where they inhabited in Glocestershire and Oxfordshire. And thence probably *Bodicote* or *Boducot, com.* Oxon. Hence the Lat. *Bodia, Bodium,* the flat or level ground: and sometimes for a low cottage. Hence our Eng. *Body,* which in some parts of Lincolnshire they use only for the belly or lower part. Hence the Bottom of any thing opposed to the top. Bodmin or the deep bank in Cornwall. And Pliny mentions the old Gall. *Bodincus* for Bodennag or Bottomless.

BONCHYS. Bunches. Fr. Junius derives it from the Dan. *Buncker,* the tops of hills. But I rather believe it from the old Lat. *Bonna, Bunna,* a rising bank for the term or bound of fields; whence *Bonnarium* a fence, or hedge, or wall, and *Bonnagium* mony or service paid for the maintaining of mounds or boundaries of ground. Hence the word Bown is used in Norfolk for swelling or rising up in a bunch or tumour. A Bun is a copped cake. The Bun or upper part of a barrel, the Bun-hole or Bung-hole. A Bunting or round bird. A Bonnet, a little cap or hat, or other covering for the head.—*Et in duobus bonchis allei* vi. den. K. p. 575.

BONDAGIUM. Villenage, servitude, bondage. From Sax, Bond, Bonds or fetters. Hence Prov. I will be your Bond-slave. Vid. ABUNDARE.—*Filius Roberti Elyot nuper defuncti nativi dominæ qui tenuit in bondagio duo messuagia,* K. p. 399.—*Robertus filius Nicholai Germeyn tenet unum messuagium et dimidiam virgatam terræ in bondagio ad voluntatem dominæ,* K. p. 401. Tenants in bondage paid heriots and did fealty, K. p. 456, were not to fell trees in their own gardens without license of the lord, ib. Widow of a tenant in bondage held her husband's estate, *quamdiu vixerit sine marito*, K. p. 458. *Vide* VILLENAGIUM.

BORDARII. Some derive it from the old Gall. *Bords*, the limits or extreme parts of any extent. As the Borders of a country, and the Borderers or inhabitants in those parts. Whence the Bordure of a garment, and to imBorder, which we corrupt to imbroider. But our old *Bordarii*, Bord men, were rather so called from Sax. Boɲð, a house and sometimes a table. Hence our English Boarders, who board or lodge and table at such a house or such a Boarding-school. A cup-Board, a side-Board-table: and Boarding was an old word for facetious table talk. The *Bordarii* often mentioned in the Doomsday Inquisition were distinct from the *Servi* and *Villani*, and seem to be those of a less servile condition, who had a boɲð or cottage with a small parcel of land allowed to them, on condition they should supply the lord with poultry and eggs, and other small provisions for his board and entertainment. Hence *Bordlode* was the firm or quantity of food which they paid by this tenure. *Bordlands* were the small estates that were so held. As in latter times Bordage and Board-half-penny were the dues paid in fairs and markets for boards or tables, booths and standings. The old Scots had the term of *Burd* and *Meet-Burd* for provisions: *Burden-sack* for a sack full of provision. From whence most probably comes our Eng. *Burden*, at first only a load of meat and drink, which we seem still to retain in the Prov. He has got his burden, *i. e.* He has got as much drink as he can beare or carry.— *Robertus de Oilgy tenet Berncestre, sunt ibi*—5. *servi, et* 28. *villani, cum* 14. *bordariis*, K. p. 65.

BORDEL. Lat. *Bordellum*. A Sax. Boɲð a house. At first it signified any small cottage, which growing infamous for a licentious ale-house, and the common habitation of prostitutes, a Bordel, or by metathesis a Brothel and Brothel-house, was a lewd publick house, a stews, from which *femme bordelier* a common whore. Hence in Chaucer a Borel-man a loose idle fellow, and Borel-folk drunkards and epicures, (which the Scotch now call Bureil folk). Goddes hous is made a tavern of gluttons, and a Bordel of lychours. K. p. 613.

BOTHAGIUM. Boothage or customary dues to the lord of the market for the pitching and standing of Booths: of which Dr. Skinner (as in most other words) gives this very ill account. *Minsevus deflectit ab* A S Boðe *tentorium tumultuarium, quod nusquam lego. Potius a* C. Br. Broth, *tugurium, derivarem, nisi quod suspicor hoc sit nostræ originis. Mallem igitur deducere a* Belg. Boade, Bode, *domuncula, casa, vel* Dan. Bood, *taberna ;*

illud fortasse a Belg. Bouwen *ædificare, hoc ab* AS. Buban *manere,* Bigan *habitare.* I rather think our Eng. *Booth* came from the old Lat. *Bota, Buta, Butta,* a vessel for any liquid, from the old Gall. *Bouts,* which the learned Du Fresne says were leather jacks or vessels to carry wine cross the mountains, whence Butta and Buttis signified any larger continent of wine, as our Butt of wine, and the *Butellus* or *Botellus* was a less vessel, as our Bottle of which the most ancient was the leather-Bottle. Hence the cellar or place where they set their wine was called *Buthe* and *Botha,* whence our Buttery, and *Botharius* was the Buttler who had custody of the wine. *Bothagium* was the tax or duty laid on wine. From all which it is easie to imagine that the publick place in a market or fair where they exposed their wine to sale was called a Booth, and the custom paid for such liberty of standing and selling was *Bothagium,* Boothage.—19 Hen. VI. *Rex concessit Roberto Broke —picagium, stallagium, bothagium, et tollagium una cum assisa panis et cervisiæ de novo mercato infra villam de Burcester,* K. p. 680. From the same old Gallick *Bouts,* leather continents of wine, came our Eng. *Boots,* of the same substance and same similitude. So as there was more wit than is commonly apprehended in the repartee of Erasmus to Sir T. More, *Bibitur ex ocreis.* This makes me think of a country proverb, Such a man has got in his Boots, *i. e.* He is very drunk, or has been at a drinking-Bout.

BOUCH *of Court.* From the Fr. *Bouch* a mouth, or rather from the Fr. *Boughs,* Lat. *Bulga,* Eng. *Budget,* of British original, for the present Welsh use *Bolgan,* and the Irish *Bolg* for a belly, and by metaphor for a pair of bellows. Hence a big fat belly is called a Bulge-belly, and Bulging-belly, and any thing prominent is said to Bulge out: from whence Bulke or bigness, a Bully-fellow, Bully-rock, a Budge-fellow. Bouch of Court (or as it commonly occurs) Bowge of Court, which was an allowance of diet or belly provision from the king or superiour lord to their knights, esquires, and other retinue that attended them in any military expedition. Thomas earl of Lancaster retained Sir John de Ewre to serve him with ten men at arms in time of war, allowing them Bowge of court, with livery of hay and oats for their horses, K. p. 378.

BOVERIA. A Cow-house.—*Idem Johannes tenet unam placeam terræ ex transverso curtilagii sui ad capud boveriæ dominæ priorissæ,* K. p. 395.—*Computat de quatuor solidis provenientibus de stauro boveriæ,* K. p. 571.

BOVELLUS. A young steer or bullock castrated.— *Unus bovettus mas. quatuor boviculæ fœminæ,* K. p. 287.

BOVICULA. An heifer or young cow, which in the east riding of Yorkshire they call a Whee or Whey, and a spoiled heifer is called in Oxfordshire a Martin.—*Possunt sustentari sexdecim vaccæ et unus taurus cum boviculis*, K. p 495.

BRASIUM *præparare.* To make Mault (Island. Malt), which was a service paid by some tenants to their lord,—*In manerio de Pidington quilibet virgatarius præparabit domino unum quarterium brasii per annum, si dominus inveniet boscum ad siccandum*, K. p. 496.

BREVE *perquirere.* To purchase a writ or license of trial in the king's court: whence the present usage of paying 6s. 8d. where the debt is 40l., 10s. where the debt is 100l. and so upward in suits of mony due upon bond, K. p. 168.

BREVE *de Recto.* A writ of right, by which a person ejected sues for the possession and fee simple of an estate detained from him. So the abbat of Egnesham impleaded Bernard de S. Walery for the mannor of Erdinton,—*Per breve de recto in curia Roberti episcopi Lincolniæ*, K. p. 133. Roger D'Amory quit claimed to the abby of Oseney two knight's fees in Weston,—*Unde eos implacitavit in curia domini regis per breve de recto*, K. p. 257. Any writ or precept from the king was called *Breve*, which we still retain in the name of Brief, commonly used for the king's letters patent to authorize the collecting of charity for poor sufferers. And the minutes of a cause given for the direction of a pleader is called a Brief or Breviat.

BREDEWITE. From Sax. Bpeod bread, and pite a fine or penalty. So as Bredewite were the amercements arising from any default in the assise of bread. To be exempt from this penalty was a special priviledge granted to all the tenants of the honour of Walingford by King Henry II.—*Ut quieti sint de hidagio et Blodewite et Bredewite*, K. p. 114.

BRIGA. A quarrel, suit, or controversie. From Goth. BRIKAN, German. *Brechen*, Sax. Bpecan and Bpittan, to break or divide. Thence our Breach and Brangle, or quarrel. A Brack or hole. A heart-Breaking or dividing. A Brace or division into two parts. A Bracket or small piece of board to support a shelf. A Break in Norfolk is land ploughed or broke up the first year after it has lain fallow in the sheep walks. To Britten beef in the North is to break the bones of it: thence Brittle, which in Cheshire they call Brichoe, whence our Bricks in building seem so called from their frangible quality. A Brake is an instrument with which they break flax or hemp. Brake and Braken, fern. The Breech or divided part of the body, (the same reason gives

hame to the Twist) covered with Breeches. The Brink or edge
of a hill, &c. where the ground breaks off. A Brisket of beef, or
piece cut off the breast. Hence the old Lat. *Bricia panis*, a piece
of bread. *Bruscia, bruscus*, brush or brittle wood. *Brisin* in the
present Irish is to break.—*Pro dicta briga sive discordia inter eosdem sedanda*, K. p. 410.

BRUERIA. Briars, thorns, heath, à Sax. Bpæp.—*Tantum de
roboribus et brueriis quantum pro vestura indiguerit*, K. p. 620.
Lat. *Brolium, Broilum, Briulum, Brullium*, a hunting chace or
forest. *Bruillus, Brogillus*, a wood or grove. Fr. *Breil, Breüil,
Breüille*, a wood or thicket in a forest. Hence the abby of
Bruer.in the forest of Whichwood, and Bruel, Brehul, or Brill, in
the forest of Bernwode, K. p. 41.

BULTER-CLOTH. A linen or hair cloth for sifting or siercing of
meal or flower. From German *Beutel* a sive, *Beutelen* to Bolt or
sift. The versatile engine for sifting with more ease and expedition, is now called a Bolting-mill, and the cloath round it the
Bolter,—*In emendatione unius cribri pistrinæ hoc anno i.den. ob. et
in Bulter-cloth empto ad pistrinam*, x.den. K. p. 574. Hence
the old Gall *Beluter, Bluter*, to sift, which Menagius fancies to
bear affinity to the Lat. *volutare*. The modern Fr. *Blutter*. Hence
the Lat. *Bolendigarius, Bolengarius*, Fl. *Boulen*, Fr. *Boulenger*, a
baker or bread maker. On which word the learned Du Fresne
has a trifling conjecture, much below his gravity and judgement,
—*Videntur pistores ita appellati, quod panes in formam globorum,
quos Boules dicimus, conficiant*. When they were evidently so
called from Bolting or sifting their flower. From hence by metaphor to Bolt out, or rush upon, as He Bolted out upon me. To
Bowlt a cony, to start or put her up. Bolting or jutting out, as
a piece of timber that overlays upon a beam, has the end Bolting
out: and any such prominence in architecture was called a Boltel.
The Bolt of a door that runs into the staple. The Boltspirit of a
ship, *i. e.* the spiret or mast that Bolts out. Pease-Bolt in Essex
is the pease-straw, when the grain is thresht or sifted out. In the
same county Bullimong is several grains mixt or sifted together.
Hence possibly the old word, a Bolt of silk or stuff, a long narrow
piece,—*Et in Bolt rubei say apud Sterebrugge propter anabatam
faciendam*, iv.sol. viii.den. K. p. 574.

BUNDA. A Bound. *Includendo forestam ex parte dextra per
omnes bundas et metas subscriptas*, K. p. 323. *Vid.* ABUNDĀRE.

BURGAGIUM. A sort of quit rent paid to the chief lord for the
houses and tenements in a town or borough,—*Summa reddituum
assisorum de burgagio in Thame*, lxxvs. K. p. 354. As Burgbote

was the tax for repairing the common buildings of the town. **Burgbrech** was a fine imposed for the breach of peace within the town, &c.

BURSARIA. The Bursery or place of receiving and paying mony and rents by the *Bursarii*, Bursers or officers of accompt in religious houses,—*Computaverunt fratres Radulphus de Meriton et Stephanus de Oxon de bursaria domus Berncestre coram auditoribus*, K. p. 288. The conventual Bursar was to deliver up his accompts yearly on the day after Michaelmass, K. p. 570. From Bursa, which gives name to our English Burse, and hence the same officer who is called Boursar in a college, is in a ship called the Purser. A Pursy man is one who breathes with difficulty, because his breast and belly are fat and extended like a Purse. To disBurs or expend, disBursements or expences. Formerly all exhibitioners or stipendiary scholars at Paris were called Bursars, as they lived on the *burs* or fund, or endowment of founders and benefactors,—*In ea universitate* (scil. Oxonia) *sunt clara collegia a regibus, reginis, episcopis, et principibus fundata, et ex stipendiis eorum scholastici plurimi aluntur, quos Parisii bursarios vocamus*, Jo. Maj. Gest. Scot. l. 1. cap. 5. Which *Bursarii* were most properly those novices or young scholars who were sent to the university and maintained by the religious out of their publick *burs* or stock. *Nomasticon Cistertiense*, K. p. 645.

BUSCHE, *Buscagium, Boscagium*. Brush-wood, fire-wood, under-wood,—*Salva libertate pannagii porcorum et busche in charta Matthæi derani contenta*, K. p. 240. From the German *Busche*, wood. Whence the device that is wore by women to keep in their belly is called a Busk, because made of wood, though now generally of whale-bone. Hence apparently our Eng. Bush and Bushes in a wood or hedge: and the coronated frame of wood hung out as a sign at taverns, is called a Bush.

BUSSELLUS. A bushel, from *Buza, Butta, Buttis*, a standing measure of wine. *Bulticella, Bussellus*, a less measure: from the old Fr. *Bouts*, which were properly leather vessels to carry wine, whence our leather Boots and leather Buskins, and leather Boudget. *Bussellus* was therefore first used for a liquid measure of wine, eight gallons,—*Octo libræ faciunt galonem vini, et octo galones vini faciunt bussellum London quæ est octava pars quarterii. Composit. Mensuarum*, an. 51. Hen. III. *apud Spelmannum in voce Galo.* The word was soon after transferred to the dry measure of corn, of the same quantity,—*Pondus octo librarum frumenti facit bussellum de quibus octo consistit quarterium*, Fleta l. 2. cap 12. §1. —*Quælibet acra poterit seminari tempore suo duobus bussellis frumenti*, K. p. 495.

d 2

BUTTES. The ends or short pieces of land in arable ridges and furrows. Gilbert Basset gave to his priory of Burcester, *viginti acras in Heile-furlong et buttes apud Ymbelowesmere,* K. p. 136,— *quatuor selibnes terræ qui vocantur Buttes,* K. p. 187.—*Johannes Abbod et Juliana uxor—tenent quatuor butta quæ continent unam acram,* K. p. 402. *Vid.* ABUTTARE.

BYRDLYME. From *Bird* and *Lime,* Island, *Lym,* Dan. *Lïm,* glew or any viscous matter,—*Et in* 1. *libra de Byrdlyme empta ibidem* iii. *den.* K. p. 574.

C.

CADE of herrings,—*Et in uno cade rubei allecis empto de Harmando Banbury,* viii. *sol.* K. p. 575. The quantity is thus determined in the accounts of the celeress of the abby of Berking. "Memorandum that a barrel of herryng shold contene a thousand herryngs, and a Cade of herryng six hundreth, six score to the hundreth," Mon. Ang. tom. 1. p. 83. In Kent a Cade of beef is any parcel or quantity of pieces under a whole quarter. Hence in the North to Cadge is to carry, and a Cadger is a butcher, miller, or carrier of any other load: and Cadge-belly or Kedge-belly is a full fat belly.

CALCEA, *Calceia, Calcetum.* A high-way maintained and repaired with stones and rubbish: from the Lat. *Calx,* chalk, Fr. *Chaux,* whence *Chaussée,* Eng. a Cawse-way, or way raised with mould and paved with chalk, stones, or gravel. *Calcagium* was the tax or contribution paid by the neighbouring inhabitants toward the making and repairing such common roads. And *Calcearum operationes* were the work and labour done by the servile tenants, from which duty the tenants within the honour of Walingford were exempted by King Hen. II.—*Ut quieti sint de operationibus castellorum—et calcearum,* K. p. 114.

CALCIATURA *Rotarum.* The shoeing of wheels or straking of them, or nailing iron strakes round the fellows, by which the wheels are shod and made fit to travel,—*Pro uno pari rotarum—et pro calciatura earundem per Laurentium Smyth,* K. p. 550. Hence no doubt comes the Calking or Cauking of horse-shoes, *i. e.* to turn up the two corners, that a horse may stand the faster upon ice or smooth stones. And the Cauking of a ship or vessel, to make her ride or sail the more safely.

CALUMPNIA. Claim or challenge, *Ut hæc eleemosina rata sit et absque calumpnia in posterum,* K. p. 77.—*Ita quod neque ego neque hæredes mei regressum habeamus vel calumpniam aliquam versus aliquos de præfato manerio,* K. p. 127.

CAMERA. From the old German *Cam, Cammer*, crooked, whence our Eng. Kembo, arms in Kembo, a Comb in the North Camb, the present Irish use *Cama* for a bed. *Camera* signified at first any winding or crooked plat of ground.—*Tres cameras ad vineam—unam cameram terræ, &c. apud* Du Fresne *in voce*. The word was afterward applied to any vaulted or arched building, especially to a shop for the sale of goods; and seemed at last appropriated to an upper room, or what we now only call a Chamber. —Robert Clerk granted to Robert le Taillur, *Quondam cameram cum pertinentiis—dictam cameram cum placia terræ*, K. p. 258.

CANON. Not the Mass-book, as mistaken, K. p. 307, but a Book wherein the religious of every convent had a fair transcript of the rules of their order, frequently read among them, as their local statutes: which book was therefore called Regula and Canon. The publick books of the religious were these four: 1. *Missale*, which contained all the offices of devotion. 2. *Martirologium*, a register of the Christian saints and martyrs, with the place and time of passion. 3. *Canon* or *Regula*, the institution and rules of their order. 4. *Necrologium* or *Obituarium*; in which they entred the death of their founders and benefactors, to observe the days of commemoration for them. But as the two first, so likewise the two latter were sometime joined in the same volume.

CANTARIA. A chantry, a small chappel single, or annext to some parochial church, founded and endowed for the maintenance of one or more chantors or chantry-priests, whose office it was to sing masses, and perform other memorials for the soul of the founder, or such other friends whom he had nominated,—*Dominus Walterius Blankett capellanus perpetuus Cantariæ Sanctæ Trinitatis in ecclesia omnium sanctorum Oxoniæ*, K. p 566. In which the capellane or chantor was instituted and inducted, and took an oath to observe the statutes of the founder, K. p. 567. Several of these Chanteries were annext to cathedral churches, and no less than forty-seven to that of St. Paul's in London. Those that escaped the act of 37 Hen. VIII. were all dissolved 1 Edw. VI. cap. 14.

CANTREDUM. A Cantre or Cantred. From Brit. *Cant*, a Hundred, and *Trè* or *Tred*, a Village. The same division of counties in Ireland and Wales as our hundreds in England. *Hundredus Latine dicitur, Wallice et Hibernice cantredus, et continet centum villas*, Jo. Brompton *inter X. Script.* col. 957.—*Castrum et cantredum de bualt cum pertinentiis Wallia*, K. p. 427. Hence the Cantons of Switzerland. To Canton out, *i. e.* to divide into parcels. A Canton or corner in heraldry. To sell by Cantell was an old custom of selling by the lump without tale or measure, which *Cantellum*. Sir Henry Spelman thinks to be *velut quantillum*; but it seems more probable from *Cant*, a hundred, or Cantoning, dividing into hundreds, and was the selling about a hundred weight of goods, or a hundred in tale by guess, as we now call the taking of a hundred pound by content, when we take one hundred pound bag sealed up, without telling the mony. Hence a Cantel is still retained for any indefinite number or dimension, as in Kent we say a Cantell of people or cattle: a Cantel of wood, timber, bread, cheese, &c.

CANVOYS. Canvas. Coarse hempen cloath, à Lat. *Cannabus*, à Gr. Κάνναζις, hemp. Whence a Canopy or Cannoby, an umbrello, made usually of such linen,—*Et in canvoys empto Londin. per Richardum Dymby pro lintheaminibus faciendis*, iii sol. K. p. 574. Hence by metaphor (as Skinner fancies) to Canvass about, and to Canvass for votes, as bearing allusion to the beating of hemp or making canvass. Though perhaps it might be as wise a conjecture to say that *Canna* was a cup or can, whence *Canava* or *Cannava* was the buttery, especially in religious houses, and *Cannavasare* was to promote drinking, which I am sure is the present method of Canvasing in elections.

CAPELLA. A chappel, or what we now call a chappel of ease, built within the precincts of a parish for the benefit of one or more families who lived remote from the parish-church, and made subservient to the said mother church. Such a chappel was often granted in the court or mannor house of the patron, as a privilege to himself and family. So Robert de Grosthead bishop of Lincoln to William de Clinton patron of the church of Eston, *com*. Buck. K. p. 221. The same prelate to Roger de Hida at his mannor-house at Whitchurch, *com*. Oxon. K. p. 233. At the consecration of a chappel there was often some fixt endowment given to it, for its more light and easie dependance on the mother-church. So at Stratton Audley within the parish of Burcester, Gilbert Basset gave to his new priory,—*Capellam de Strattun et in eadem villa de Strattun unam virgatam terræ collectam de terra rusticorum, quæ data fuit in dote prædictæ capellæ*, K. p. 136. The institution and dependance of chappels and their capellanes, with the dignity and liberties of mother-churches discoursed at large, K. p. 585.

CAPELLANUS *liberæ Capellæ*. The chaplain to a chappel of ease, maintained by the parish priest, or by the appropriators, or by the inhabitants, or by joint contribution of them. His stipend was five marks *per an*. in the year 1280, K. p. 588. He was bound by oath to pay due reverence and obedience to the parish priest, K. p. 599. He was sometime called *Serviens de Capella*, as in a charter of King John,—*Dedi et concessi Waltero Borstard Servienti de Capella nostra manerium nostrum de Brehull,* K. p. 164.

CAPELLANUS *Baronis.* A lord's or baron's chaplain. Those who had a chappel allowed them at their court or mannor-house, had the privilege of maintaining a domestic chaplain to officiate in the said chappel without prejudice to the parish priest. By the council of Claremont, an. 1095, can. 68, No lay-man was to retain a chaplain without consent of the bishop.—Warine, chaplain to Milo Crispin baron of Walingford, 7 Hen. I. K. p. 78. The present rights of the nobility for retaining and qualifying of chaplains, are determined by Stat. 21 Hen. VIII. cap. 13.

CAPELLANUS *Sacerdotis.* A curate priest or deacon, retained by the parish priest to assist him in the offices of his church, and the care of souls.—*Willielmus senex sacerdos de Burcester cum Willielmo capellano suo,* K. p. 76.—*Testibus Rogero decano de Pire, Mattheo capellano de Ambrosden... Fulcone capellano de Meriton,* K. p. 121. In large parishes the incumbent was obliged to keep two or more capellanes to assist him, K. p. 122. who were obliged by an oath of fidelity to their masters the parish priests, K. p. 600. Yet no parish priest could take such a curate without the license or approbation of the bishop by the synod of Poictiers, an. 1280, can. 3.

CAPUT *Jejunii.* Ash-Wednesday, being the head or first day of the Quadragesimal or Lent fast, K. p. 132. So *Caput anni,* New-year's-day, upon which was observed the *Festum Stultorum,* to deride the rite of Circumcision, in contempt and hatred of the Jews, forbid by an express constitution of Bishop Grosthead, because there was a great levity in the observance of it, and because it ridiculed the circumcision to which our Saviour submitted. So *Caput kalendarum Maii,* May-day.

CAPUT *Baroniæ.* Head of a Barony. It was the capital village of a barony, where the baron had his principal seat and common residence. So in the barony of St. Walery, com. Oxon. the *Caput Baroniæ* was Beckley, where Richard king of the Romans and baron of St. Walery, had his court or pallace, K. p. 62. The same with *Caput Honoris,* in the barony of Giffard, com. Buck.—*Caput illius honoris Crendon,* K. p. 167. This head of a barony could not be settled in dowry, nor divided among female co-heirs as coparceners, but in default of issue male it passed entire to the eldest daughter.

IN CAPITE *tenere.* To hold immediately from the king, or of his crown in gross, without dependance upon or annexion to any honor, castle, or mannor. Called sometimes *In Capite Coronæ,*

Bernard de S. Walery gave the site and advouson of the abby of Godestow to King Hen. II. *Ita ut præfata abbatia de cætero habeatur libera, et In Capite coronæ regis sit, sicut abbatia sancti Edmundi, et aliæ regales abbathæ,* K. p. 127. No tenure *In Capite* could be alienated or transferred without the king's special license, but upon any such conveyance it escheated to the king without express pardon,—*Pardonavimus dilecto et fideli nostro Johanni de Handlo transgressionem quam fecit adquirendo sibi, et hæredibus suis ballivam forestariæ—quæ tenentur de nobis in Capite, nostra super hæc licentia non obtenta,* K. p. 356.

CAPITALIS *Honor.* The chief honor or prime barony of the whole county, com. Buck—*Willielmus Mareschallus comes de Pembroke habet ibidem capitalem honorem, scil. honorem Giffard,* K. p. 167.

CAPITALIS *Dominus.* The lord of the fee from whom the estate is held by inferior tenants,—*Solvendo tres denarios erga Capitalem Dominum,* K. p. 220.—*Faciendo inde servitium Capitali Domino feodi,* K. p. 162.

CAPITALIS *Curia.* The chief mannor-house or place-house, or court of the lord of the mannor, which in Kent is now often called the Court lodge. Robert earl of Dreux confirmed to the abby of Oseney *Manerium de Mixbury cum capitali curia,* K. p. 191. The same with *Capitale messuagium,—dicunt per sacramentum suum quod capitale messuagium valet per an. cum tota inclausa,* iis. K. p. 314.

CAPUT *Loci.* The end of any place. *Ad caput villæ,* at the end of the town, K. p. 394. *Ad capud boveriæ,* at the upper end of the cow-house, K. p. 395. *Alia roda jacet ad inferius capud del' Oldedich,* K. p. 397.

CAPITALIA *Agri.* Head lands.—*Canonici concesserunt hominibus de Wrechwike duas acras prati pro capitalibus suarum croftarum secus rivulum versus molendinum fluentem ad faciendum stagnum,* K. p. 137. *Vid.* HAVEDELOND.

CAPITULA *Ruralia.* Chapters held by the rural dean and clergy within the precincts of every distinct deanery, at first every three weeks, then once a month, and more solemnly once a quarter, K. p. 640.

CARUCA, Fr. *Carrué,* a plough, from the old Gallic, *Cqrr,* which is the present Irish word for any sort of wheeled carriage,—*Qui carucas habuerunt, arabunt terram domini in dicto manerio,* K. p. 320. From hence the Sax. Ceopl, a plough-man, the Northern *Karl,* our Southern *Churl,* and in corruption of places *Cherl,* as Charlton, Charlbury, &c. *Carl* in modern Welsh is a rustick or clown.

CARUCATA. A plough-land, or as much arable ground as in one year could be tilled with one plough: which in the reign of Rich. I. was computed at sixty acres, Mon. Ang. tom. 2. p. 107. Yet another charter, 9 Rich. I. allots one hundred acres to a carucate. And Fleta, *temp.* Edw. I., says, if land lay in three common fields, then nine-score acres to a carucate, sixty for winter tillage, sixty for spring tillage, and sixty for fallows. But if the land lay in two fields, then eight-score acres to a carucate, one half for tillage and the other for fallow, lib. 2. cap. 72. § 4. The measure of a carucate was different according to time and place. In 23 Edw. III. one carucate of land in Burcester contained one hundred and twelve acres; and two carucates in Middleton were three hundred acres, K. p. 471. *Caruca* was sometime used for *Carucata,* Robert de Ver confirmed to the monks of Thorney,— *Decimas de quinque carucis quas pater concessit in Islep Draitune et Edinton,* K. p. 82. In Doomsday inquisition the arable land was measured by carucates, the common pasture by hides, and the meadow by acres. In some countries the word is still preserved a Carve of land, and the imposition on land *carucagium et carcagium* is called Carvage.

CARUCATA BOUM. A team or draught of oxen, which in some Western parts is still called a plough of oxen. Gilbert Basset, founder of Burcester priory, grants to it—*Pasturam in mea dominica pastura ad tres carucatas boum trahentium una cum bobus meis trahentibus,* K. p. 135. Called *Boves de Caruca* in a charter of Aubrey de Vere to the abby of Noteley, K. p. 155.

CARUCATARIUS. He that held land in soccage or plough tenure, —*summa reddituum carucatariorum si fuerint ad firmam,* xxiis.—*Summa gallinarum carucatariorum et cotariorum* cxiv. *gallinæ.* K. p. 354.

CARECTA. A cart or carriage or waggon. From the same Lat. *Carrum,* Brit. *Carr,* which signified any sort of vehicle by land or sea. Thence a Carrac, Lat. *Carraca, Carrica,* a small ship, the cargo of a ship, Lat. *Carracagium.* A Carrat. or Carect, used formerly for any weight or burden, though now appropriated to the weight of four grains in diamonds.—*Nullus vice comes vel ballivus noster vel aliquis alius capiat equos vel carectas alicujus pro caragio faciendo, nisi reddat liberationem antiquitus statutam scilicet pro carecta ad duos equos* x. *den. per diem, et pro carecta ad* iii. *equos,* xiv. *den. per diem.* Mag. Char. cap. 22. Gilbert Basset gives to the priory of Burcester, in his foundation charter,— *Decimam carectam ligni mei, ut sicut venitur de bosco, attrahatur in curiam canonicorum sicut in meam,* K. p. 135.—Thomas de S. Walery gave to the nuns of Stodeley—*Qualibet septi-*

mana unam carectam ligni mortui in bosco de Horton, K. p. 170.
*Homines de Hedingdon foenum curiabunt usque ad curiam prædicti
manerii, illi videlicet qui carectas habuerunt, et qui carectas non
habuerunt venient cum furcis suis ad dictum foenum levandum et
thassandum*, K. p. 320. The Brit. *Carr* was Sax. Cpæt. Thence
a Cradle or little carriage for children, applied to some other
utensils that carry or bear any thing. As in the North a dish-
Cradle, for the setting up wooden dishes or trenchards. And in
Kent a sithe-Cradle, or rack of wood fastened to a sithe for carrying the mowed barley clean into the swath. Thence a Cratch or
Critch, a rack in a stable. And hence Crutches to bear up or
carry lame persons. In the North, especially at Shefield in Yorkshire, they call a kennel the Carr-sick, from *carr* and *sike*, a furrow
or gutter, q. d. *carr-gutter*. A Carr is in other places a wheel-
trade or wheel-rout, or any such hollow trench where water
stands. Hence to the Carrs or Carviers of a spinning-wheel. Nor
is it impertinent to observe that Carr a gutter is in Lincolnshire a
Gool, in Kent a Guzzle, in Wiltshire a Gushill and Gooshill, which
is the reason why the Southern goosberry is called in the North
a Carrberry. And Carter is the name of a spinning insect like a
spider. Hence again the Lat. *Carpentum*, in the present Irish a
Carbad, or waggon covered with a Carpat or Carpet, as our wag-
gons now with tilts. A Carpenter, &c. Hence the Charge or
carriage of a gun. And a Char to be Charr'd in the North, *i. e.*
a task or labour to be discharged.

CARECTATA. A cart-load or waggon-load. The prior and
canons of St. Frideswide gave the vicar of Oakle—*duas carectatas
feoni, et duas carectatas straminis*, K. p. 455.

CARECTARIUS. A carter. *Hugo filius Eliæ carectarii de Berencester*, K. p. 325

CART-SADEL. The saddle that laid on the fillar-horse,—*Pro
uno cart-sadel, uno colero, cum uno pari tractuum emptis*, xivd.
K. p. 549. Saddle is from the Sax. Setl, a seat or place. Hence
the frame of wood to support the barrels in a buttery or cellar, is
called the Seddle and Settle. So a Settle or couch, a Settle-bed or
truckle-bed. In Kent to Sessle about is to change seats very often.

CART-BODY. The wooden body of the cart or waggon. *Et
pro sarratione et delatione unius Cart-body* vi d. K. p. 550. In
Sussex it is called the Buck of a Cart, *i. e.* the belly of a cart:
from Sax. Buc, a belly, used by metaphor for a jug or big-bellied
pot, thence a Bucket or less measure of the like shape. From the
Teuton. *Bucken*; Sax. Bugan, to bend: whence Bucksome flex-
ible, or of a pliable body, Bonny and Bucksome lass. Hence to
Buckle or to bend. A Buckle, a Buckler. To Budge or move

about, whence Budge and Budgy is the same as Bucksome, brisk and jocund. A Buck or Belly is in some places called a Budge, thence by metaphor a bag or sack, and a Budget or little bag. A Budge-barrel, a Budge-bellied or big-bellied fellow, &c. A Budger or Badger, *i. e.* a carrier or retailer of Bodges or bags of corn.

CARRARIA, *Carrarium.* Now corrupted into Quadraria and Quadrarium, a quarrey or stonepit. The Irish retain the true original a *Carrie*, and the French *un carriere*,—*Una acra jacet in furlungo prædicto in quo prior habet quarreram*, K. p. 529. Corrupted farther into *Quadrarium*,—*Concessi eisdem liberam viam ultra pasturam meam de quadrario suo usque ad prædictam ripam ad stagnum dicti molendini emendandum*, K. p. 208. Hence the old word a Querrour or digger of stones. By the like change of *c* into *qu*, we say a Quarrey or prey, as the Quarry of a hawk, which no doubt was Carrey, or the prey carried off.

CASULA *quasi Capsula.* The Chesible or loose upper vestment of the priest officiating in divine service: like our present surplice, *Vestimentum principale scilicet casula alba*, K. p. 598.

CASTELLORUM *operatio*. Service of work and labour to be done by inferiour tenants for the repair and building of castles. Toward which some gave their personal assistance, and others a contribution. This was one of the three necessary taxes from which few persons were exempted,—*Liberi ab omni servitio, exceptis pontis et arcis constructione et expeditione contra hostem*. This occurs in several of our royal charters. But an immunity from this burden was sometimes granted. So King John to the nunnery of St. Catharine without the city of Exeter,—*quietas esse de operationibus castellorum et pontium*. Mon. Ang. tom. 1. p. 503. b. So King Hen. II. to the tenants within the honour of Walingford,—*Ut quieti sint de operationibus castellorum*, K. p. 114.

CASTELLORUM *custodia*. The service of keeping and defending, or watching and warding in any castle. The barony of Coges, com. Oxon. was held *per serjantiam custodiæ castelli de Dover*, K. p. 324.

CELLARIUM. A Cellar.—*Istud cellarium et illud solarium quæ sito sunt intra domum meam*, K. p 325. From the Lat. *Cèlla*, Eng. *Cell*, or little place or repository. Hence the old Latin *Celdra*, a certain measure, which the Scotch call Chalder, and we retain in the measure of coals a Chaldron.

CESSARE *in solutione.* To fail in payment. *Quoties prior et conventus Burncester in prædictorum sexaginta solidorum solutione terminis prædictis cessaverint*, K. p. 344.

CHALENGIA. A claim or challenge, from Fr. *Challonger*, which Menagius derives from the Gr. Καλεῖν.—*Ita quod ego et hæredes mei nullam chalengiam poterimus habere de futuro*, K. p. 125.

CHARTA. Not only a charter or deed in writing, but any signal or token by which an estate was held,—*Willielmus filius Nigelli tenuit custodiam forestæ de Bernwode de domino rege per unum cornu quod est charta prædictæ forestæ*, K. p. 73.

CHEMINUS, *Chiminus*. A high-way, from the Fr. *Chemin*, or rather from the Sax. Cýman, to come,—*Quinquaginta acras terræ cum cheminis suis et omnibus aliis pertinentiis*, K. p. 428. Hence a Chimney or Cheminey, a way or passage for the smoke.

CHIRCH-SCOT. Cýpuc-ɼceat, *i. e.* church-payment or contribution. The Latin writers have commonly called it *Primitiæ seminum*, because it was at first a quantity of corn paid to the priest on St. Martin's day, as the first fruits of harvest: enjoined by the laws of King Ina, cap. 4, and King Canute, cap. 10. But it was afterward taken for a reserve of corn rent paid to the secular priests or to the religious. So in the reign of. Hen. III. Robert de Hay rector of Souldern claimed from the abbat and convent of Oseney a certain measure of corn under the title of Churchscet for their demesne lands in Mixbury, K. p. 187. It was sometimes a general word, and included not only corn but poultry or any other provision that was paid in kind to the religious. So in the inquisition of the rents of the abby of Glastonbury, an. 1201. *Manerium Glaston. reddit per an. in gabulo* vii. *lib.* vi. *sol.* ii. *den.*—*In Churchscet* lx. *gallinas et semen frumenti ad tres acras*. Cartul. de Glaston. MS. f. 38.

CHOP-CHURCHES. Those secular priests who drove a trade or made an advantage by exchanging of their benefices, against whom some constitutions were expresly made to restrain that mercenary practise, K. p. 541. From Sax. Ceap, goods or vendible wares, thence Ceapan, to buy or to cheapen. Thence a Chapman, a Cheap price: this word gave name to several places of market and trade, as Cheapside in London, Chepstow in Wales, Cheping-Norton in Oxfordshire, &c. Hence likewise to Chaffer or to barter, to Chop or to change, Chopping, vendible or valuable, as a Chopping-horse, a Chopping-boy: both which have been corrupted into Swop and Swopping: and in the North into Coup and Cowping, which in Norfolk and Suffolk is Cope and Coping.

CHOSA. From the Fr. *chose*, a thing or small matter. The Knights Templars gave to Simon son of Sir Wido de Meriton *marcas centum ad quasdam chosas emendas*, K. p. 120. Fr. *quel*₋

que choses corrupted into Kickshaws, thence to Choose or take one thing out of several others: to Chouse or to take more than is just and due.

CHOREPISCOPI. Rural bishops delegated by the prime diocesan, their authority restrained by some councils, and their very office by degrees abolished. After whom the rural deans were so commissioned to exercise episcopal jurisdiction, till inhibited by Pope Alexander III. and the council of Tours, K. p. 639.

CHYROGRAPHUM. Any publick instrument of conveyance attested by witnesses was in the Saxon times called Chirographum, which the Normans stiled Charta. Of which Ingulph gives this good account,—*Chyrographorum confectionem Anglicanam, quæ antea usque ad Edwardi regis tempora fidelium præsentium subscriptionibus cum crucibus aureis, aliisque sacris signaculis firma fuerunt: Normanni condemnantes chirographa, chartas vocabant, et chartarum firmitatem cum cerea impressione per unius cujusque speciale sigillum sub instillatione trium vel quatuor testium adstantium conficere constituebant.* Histor. Ingulphi, p. 901. But to prevent frauds and concealments they made their deeds of mutual covenant in a script and rescript, or in a part and counter-part, upon the same sheet of paper or parchment, and in the middle between the two copies they drew the capital letters of the alphabet, or sometime the word SYNGRAPHUS in the like great letters, and then talliated or cut asunder in indented manner the said sheet, which being delivered to the two parties concerned, were proved authentick by matching with or answering to one another. Like the tallies in wood, or like our present indentures in writing. When this prudent custom had for sometime prevailed, then the word Chirographum was appropriated to such bipartite writings,—*Et in hujus rei testimonium huic scripto in modum chyrographi confecto vicissim sigilla nostra apposuimus,* K. p. 177. —*Ut autem ista conventia rata et inconcussa perpetuo permaneat, præsentis scriptis serie et utriusque monasterii sigilli testimonio una cum sigillis abbatum diviso inter eos chirographo confirmata est.* K. p. 223. Such alternate writings were called likewise *Scripta Chirographata,* K. p. 234: and *chartæ divisæ,* Mon. Ang. tom. 2. p. 94.

CHRISTIANITATIS *Curia.* The Christian or ecclesiastical court opposed to the civil court or lay court, or *Curia Domini Regis.* These courts of Christianity were not only held by the bishops in synods, and the archdeacons and chancellors in consistories; but they were also the rural chapters, where the rural dean or dean of Christianity presided, and the clergy were assessors and assistants, K. p. 641. *Justitiam Christianitatis facere* was to prosecute and censure a criminal in the ecclesiastical court, as 28 Hen. I. *Alexander Lincoln. episcopus Guidoni de Charing parochiano suo salutem. Mando tibi et præcipio ut cito reddas ecclesiæ de Egnesham et Waltero abbati ecclesiam suam de Meritona,—quod ni cito feceris, præcipio ut Walterus archidiaconus nobis justitiam Christianitatis faciat, donec reddas,* K. p. 90.—Osbert vicar of Merton impleaded in the king's court by Thomas le Camvil and Elizabeth his wife for proceeding in a cause before the court Christian against the king's prohibition, K. p. 289. So ·Ichel de Kerwent rector of Bucknel to be arrested and impleaded before the barons of the exchequer by the king's precept to the sheriff,—*quod idem Ychelus ipsum abbatem (de Oseney) jam in curiam Christianitatis coram officiario diocesani prædicti trahit in placitum, ipsum multipliciter ibidem inquietando in nostri contemptum manifestum*, K. p. 328.

CLADUS, *Clades, Clada, Cleta, Clida, Cleia.* From the Brit. *Clie*, the present Irish. *Clia*, a hurdle: whence Dublin was formerly called *Baile cliet, i. e.* the town of hurdles. A hurdle for sheep is still in some counties called a Cley. *Et in* xii. *cladis ovilibus emptis de Nicholao Aleyn hoc anno* xviii. *den. et in solutis pro putatione et factura triginta cladorum ovilium apud parcum de Midlington hoc anno* xix. *den.* K. p. 575.—*Et in cladis emptis ad pontem de Clyfton de novo faciendum*, K. p. 577. A Hurdle is from the Sax. Ɖypƌl, Teuton. *Hurde*. Whence a basket made of twigs interwoven like a hurdle, was in some places called a Hurd, thence a Hoard or Store, to Hoard up. A Hurdle is in some northern parts called a Fleak, and in Kent is sometime called a Riddle, Raddle, or Ruddle: from the rods or twigs of which they are made, as a Riddle-wall, a Riddle-basket, &c.

CLAMOR. Complaint for want of justice. Alexander bishop of Lincoln to Wido de Charing,—*Ne pro recti vel justitiæ penuria amplius audiam clamorem*, K. p. 90. In the same sense as now to Clamour, and to make a Clamour.

CLAMOR. A crie by a publick cryer.—*Mandatum est majori et ballivis Oxon. quod per totam villam Oxon. clamari faciant, quod omnes publicæ meretrices et concubinæ clericorum infra octo dies post hunc clamorem factum exeant villam Oxon.* K. p. 217.

CLAUDERE. To enclose or turn a common into closes and enclosures.—*Dedi et concessi totam culturam ad claudendam et faciendam quicquid inde dictis canonicis placuerit*, K. p. 236. Hence a Closet, a Cloister, a Clod, Clotted-blood, a Clout, Clouted-shoes, a Clouterly fellow. Hence the Sax. Club, a rock. Clough in the North is a vally enclosed between two hills. A Clodge in Kent, a lump of clay or dirt. Clodgy and Cledgy stiff and dirty.

CLAUSTURA. Brush wood for hedges and fences. King Henry III. gave to the prior and canons of Chetwode,—*quinque carucatas clausturæ ad prædictæ terræ clausturam sustinendam,* K. p. 247. This sort of wood is called Teenage, from Sax. Týnan, to enclose, thence to Tine the door, *i. e.* to shut the door; the Tines of a harrow, *i. e.* the teeth of it; the Tines of a buck's-horn, &c.

CLAVUS. A clove, as *clavus gariophili,* an aromatick clove, *clavus allii,* a clove of garlick.—*Reddendo mihi et hæredibus meis unum clavum cariophili tantum,* K. p. 294. Hence the Sax. Cleofan, to divide or to Cleave, a Cleft, a Clift, a Cleaver, and in the opinion of Skinner to Club or divide a reckoning, Club-law, *i. e.* by equal division.

CLEPUD, *Iclepid.* Called or named.—An old man that is Clepud Jon Butforde, p. 412,—that is Iclepid Rich. Davyes londe. *ib.* From the Sax. Cleopan, Clýpian, to call or name. Hence too to Clip or Clép a word, *i. e.* to miscall or pronounce it wrong. Prov. To Clip the king's English. To Clap or make a noise. The Clapper of a mill or of a door, a woman's Clapper, &c.

CLERICUS. A secular priest in opposition to a religious or regular. King John committed to William de Cornbull and Gerard de Camvill,—*Omnes terras et res abbatum et priorum et omnium religiosorum, et etiam clericorum de episcopatu,* K. p. 171. The benefit of the clergy was an immemorial part of common law, confirmed and abridged by several statutes: but perverted from the first intention, which was, that the privilege should extend only to those in sacred orders, afterwards for the encouragement of literature to any offendour who could read like a clerk, and now at last to the most ignorant wretches, by the favour of the judge, and the collusion of the ordinary. The word Clerk was by degrees in general attributed to every scholar, and at last was common to every scribe and notary, whence so many of our law offices, Clerk of the peace, Clerk of the assises, Clerks in the chancery; but these latter were commonly in holy orders before the Reformation.

CLERICUS *Sacerdotis.* A parish-clerk, who was to take an oath of fidelity to the parish priest, and was sometimes maintained by the appropriators as a menial servant to the vicar. So in all the churches appropriated to the abby of Oseney,—*Canonici vero clericum ei (i. e. vicario) et ecclesiæ ministerio, et ejus obsequio devotum invenient, qui juramentum fidelitatis ipsi vicario præstabit,— Ubi autem non fuerint canonici residentes, clericus, qui ut supradictum est expensis eorum procurabitur clavem eorum deferet in domo eorum, et curam habebit liberam, ut per ipsum vicario sufficienter in victualibus et honorifice omnia ministrentur,* K. p. 304. The parish clerks were formerly to be men of letters, and to teach a school in the parish, and were sometimes elected by the parishioners, upon whose alms they were supposed to live. So John Peckham archbishop of Canterbury, an. 1280, ordained in the church of Bauquell. and the chapples annext to it,—*Volumus insuper ibidem esse duos clericos scholasticos per parochianorum, de quorum habeant vivere eleemosinis, industriam eligendos, qui aquam benedictam circumferent in parochia et capellis, diebus dominicis et festivis in divinis ministrantes officiis, et profestis diebus disciplinis, scholasticis indulgentes.* Mon. Ang. tom. 3. p. 227. Parish clerks were to be school-masters in country villages by the constitutions of Alexander bishop of Coventry, an. 1237, and by the synod of Cologne, an. 1280. It would be a good service to the church and nation to restore this ancient practise, especially in remote country villages; where the clerk would do more to the service of God and the benefit of the people if he were able to instruct the children in reading and writing, and rehearsing the Church Catechism, that they might be bred to some sense of Christianity and good manners.

CLOERE. A prison, I believe of some Brit. original, which might give name to the old Lat. *Cloeria,* which Du Fresne conjectures to have been a corruption of *clauseria,* a Close place of restraint. The dungeon or inner prison in Walingford castle was called *Cloere-Brien,* K. p. 97. Hence the Lat. *Cloaca,* which was originally a dungeon, or the nastiest part of a prison, called by the French *Basse-fosse,* and afterward by an easie allusion applied to a jakes or house of office. The old *Cloacerius* is interpreted in a MS. Gloss. *Carceris custos.* The present *cloacarius* or keeper of the house of ease, is an office in some religious houses imposed on an offending brother, or voluntarily chose by him for an exercise of humility and mortification, and in some of our English convents beyond the seas, this sweet office is called Count of Holt.

CLYK. A bell, Lat. *Cloca, Clogga, Glogga,* Sax. Clugga, Teuton. *Glocke,* German. *Gloggen,* Fr. *Cloche,* Welsh, *Cloch,* (possibly from Brit. *Clywed,* to hear, whence *Clyst* an ear) Irish, *Clug,* perhaps all derived from the sound. As from the like sound, the Clicking of clock or watch, the Clucking of a hen, the Clinking of chains, the Clapping of hands, the Clattering and Cluttering of vessels or other moveables, the Clatting or Cutting of the finger-nails with scizzers, or Clatting of wool with shears, the Cnacking or Knacking of the tongue, *i. e.* affecting to speak finely, a word in the North applied to such as love to speak in the Southern dialect,—*Super cameram vocatam Clyk-chambour versus arriam*, K. p. 575. So that our Eng. Clock is plainly so called from striking on a Clyk or bell.

COCK-BOAT. A small boat that waits upon a larger vessel. Dr. Skinner keeps to his habit of trifling in the origination of this word,—*Nescio an a rostro quod aliquo modo Galli cristæ simile est: vel ut optime monet Doctor* Th. H. *à* Fr. G. Coque, *concha marina, hac credo etiam deflexum a concha eliso* n. To which fancy the learned Sir Henry Spelman does incline, *Coqua, Linter. à Gall.* coque; *i. concha, testa. Ang.* a Cock-boat. But certainly what we now call a Cock-boat, was formerly a Cogge-boat, and simply a Cogge. As Chron. MS. an. 15 Edw. III. cited by Spelman *in voce Cogones*. Many Cogs and ships were taken. And Chaucer:

" He found Jason and Heracles allso
Shutte in a Cogge to lond were ygoe."

which word occurs in the stat. 23 Hen. VIII. cap. 18, and is still preserved upon the sea coasts in Yorkshire, where they call a small fisher-boat a Coggle, and in some places by corruption a Cobble: from the German *Kogge*, a ship,—*Posuerunt magnam navim, vulgariter dictam Kogge, cum armatis viris.* Histor. Archiepisc. Bremens. *citot. apud* Du Fresne *in voce* Kogge. Hence the Lat. *Coqua, Cogga, Coggo, Cogo*.—*An.* 1066. *Venit ad hoc in Angliam (Rex Noricorum) trecentis coggonibus advectus,* Mat. West. *sub an.*— *Præparatis cogonibus, galleis, et aliis navibus onerariis,*—600 *naves et* 24 *coggas bene paratas.* Mat. Par. *sub an.* 1218. Hence *Cocula* or *Coculum*, a Cogue or little drinking cup in form of a boat, used especially at sea, and still retained in a Cogue of brandy. The Coges or Cogs of a mill-wheel, are those slobs or broad pieces of board, that like Cogs or boats are drove along by the stream, and so turn round the wheel, and axis, and stones. Hence our old Sax. Cocρeὸe, a seaman, called in the Laws of King Hen. I. cap. 29, *Cotseti,* and cap. 81, *Cothseti.* The old Glossary to these laws made in the reign of Edw. III. interprets Cocsade, *Cocarius*, which the learned Du Fresne seems to understand *Coquus*, a Cook, but *Cocarius* is indeed a Boatman, from *Coca* or *Coquia*, a Boat. As with little variation a Coʒʒe-rpane, a Cock-swain, now a Coggeson or Coxon, is an officer in a ship. Hence the old Lat. *Cogcio, Coccio*, a wandering and begging seaman, which Sir Henry Spelman believes to have been so called from the Gr. κωκύω, *lugeo, ploro*; *Cotyones,* Fr. *Coquins,* but the true name and original was *Cogciones,* Cog-men or Boat-men, who after ship-wrack or losses by sea, travelled about to beg and defraud the people, restrained by many civil and ecclesiastical laws,—*Ut isti mangones et cogcio-*

e

nes, qui sine omni lege vagabundi vadunt, per istam terram non sinantur vagari, et deceptiones hominibus agere, vid. Spelman *in voce* Coccio, *et* Du Fresne *in voce* Cociones. From this Lat. *Cogciones,* Fr. *Coquins,* comes our Eng. Cockquine or Cockquean, an impudent beggar or a cheat : whence no doubt to Cokes or impose upon by lies and stories, like seamen with their pretended losses and sufferings. And a Cokes is an easie credulous person deluded by such shams and false tales. In our sea terms we have still several words that are owing to the obsolete Cogge, a boat. As the certificate given to mariners for having paid custom and other naval dues is called the Cocket. The hard sea bisket is called Cocket-bread, the beach or pebbles with which they ballast a ship are Coggle-stones and Cobble-stones. Fisher-men's great boots with which they wade into the sea are called Cokers. Of the same etymology is the Lat. *Cocula, Coccula, Cucula,* called by the present Irish *Cochull,* a coarse shagged mantle wore at first by seamen, as now by all the poorer people, like our Western Whittle,—*Atque quot jubæ in tua coccula,* (*quod vulgariter vocatur quoddam genus indumenti quo Hibernenses utuntur, deforis plenum prominentibus jubis, seu villis in modum crinium sunt contextæ*) *tot homines per te a pœnis perpetuis eruentur.* Vita S. Cadoci in MS. Cod. Landav. Eccles. *citat. a Spelmanno in voce* Coccula. (The Welsh call a Shepard's hood or coul Cochol.) From whence the *Cucullus* or monk's Coul. The present Welsh Cruch is a boat. Hence for a ship to Cruise up and down the sea, a Cruiser. Hence the Lat. *Cocula* or *Cogue,* a drinking dish in form of a boat was called *Crusela, Crusellus,* from which our Eng. a Cruise of vinegar or oil, a Crucible for melting and trying of mettals. And as the wearing *Cucula* or *Cucullus* was in Eng. a Coul, so the vessel Ciccula or liquor continent gave name to our modern vessel a Coul, carried between two persons with a Coul-staff. And the Coccula or sea garment was called *Crusina* and *Crosina.*

COLERUS. A collar or any thing that goes round the neck, which in old English was the Coll or Cull, from Lat. *Collum.* Hence the Collar of a doublet, the Collar of a horse, the Collet of a ring, and perhaps a Collop of meat, the Welsh call a band a Coller, the old Lat. *Colponer,* slices or cut pieces, in Welsh a Gollwith. This possibly is the reason why a great piggin or pail with a wide neck is called a Collock in the North,—*Et pro uno cart-saddle, uno colero, cum uno pari tractuum emptis* xivd. K. p. 549.

COLLUSIO. A fraudulent contrivance and compact between two or more parties to bring an action one against the other for some deceitful end, or to prejudice the right of a third person,—

Requisiti de collusione inter partes prælocuta contra statutum (i. e. Westmin 2. cap. 32.) *ac etiam de valore ejusdem ecclesiæ, dicunt quod nulla est collusio inter partes inde prælocuta*, K. p. 351.

COMBE. A vally or low place between two hills, which is still so called in Devonshire and Cornwall, Sax. Cumbe, from Brit. *Kum* or *Cwm*, any deep or hollow place. The learned Du Fresne conjectures thus, *Anglo Saxonibus* Comb, *Britannis* Kum *vallis, sic dicta, quod cumbæ seu navigii ita nuncupati quod cavum est et longius speciem referat: seu ab alveo navis qui* Cumba *etiam dicebatur.* But I rather think the Lat. *cumba*, melted into *cymba*, like the Brit. *cwmri* into *cymri*, was derived from the Brit. or old Gall. *Cum, Kum* or *Cwm.* For *cumba* signified at first only the keel or bottom of the ship or boat, and thence by synecdoche (like *Carina* and *Puppis*) was taken for the whole vessel. Hence no doubt *catacumbæ* the Catacombs or Caverns of ancient sepulture near to Rome, where the primitive Roman Christians buried their dead *cata cumbas* or *ad cumbas*, at the crypts or hollow caverns. Whence in our old charters *cumba terræ* and *comba terræ* occurs for a low piece of ground. As in England several villages from their low situation in a bottom, or at the foot of hills, obtained the name of Combe and Compton, as in Warwickshire, Oxfordshire, &c. K. p. 109. Hence our country-men retain the word Comb or Coom for the Bin or low place where they keep corn and chaff for their horses. So in Wiltshire the Comb or Coom of a window, is the bottom or lower ledge of the window. Mr. Somner with good judgement confutes the derivation of Cambria or the country now called Wales, from Camber son of Brute, or from Cimri the progeny of Gomer: and then takes much pains to deduce it from the Brit. *cam* and *cambe*, crooked, as if Cambria from its situation among creeks and windings: as a Camber nose, a crooked nose. Arms a Kembo, Kim-kam, &c. But at last he seems to come nearer to the truth,—*Si tamen rectius dicenda sit* Cumbria, *quam* Cambria, *quod per me licet, tum petendum forte nomen a veteri nostratium voce sive verbo* to cumber, *i. e. impedire, molestare; quod, instar* Cumberlandiæ, Cambria *regio sit montibus abruptis, terrarum arduis, saxetis, silvis, saltibus, stagnis, paludibus, impedita, inaccessa, et impervia, saltem viantibus quam moleta.* This learned man would have been more happy if (without resting in the word *cumber*, which is owing to *cumbe* or filling up a deep hollow place) he had proceeded to derive *cumri* from *cwm*, and *brory* a place or country: so as the Brit. *Cwmry*, Lat. *Cumbria*, like our Eng. Cumberland, might be a country where the inhabitants lived chiefly in the Combs or Cloughs, or vallys surrounded by the mountains.

COMMUNA, *Communio pasturæ*. Commons or right of Common in open fields or woods: all the tenants and inhabitants who had this right (now the Commoners) were formerly called the Communance and Comaunce.—The abbat and convent of Missenden in right of their cell or hermitage at Musewell had *communionem pasturæ tam in bosco quam in plano*, K. p. 76.—*Inquisitio fiat utrum membrum illud de manerio de Brehull quod idem Thomas tenet, debet participare de vasto manerii de Brehull ratione communæ ejusdem manerii, in qua communa nihil habent ut dicunt*, K. p. 171. Whence *communare* to enjoy the right of Commoning,—*Talis appropriatio et inclusio non fiat in prato falcabili, sed in tali loco ubi tenentes omni tempore anni consueverunt communare seu communam clamare*, K. p. 336.

COMPERTORIUM. A judicial inquest in the civil law made by delegates, to find out and relate the truth of a cause,—*Et in carnibus porcinis emptis pro clericis domini archiepiscopi sedentibus super compertorium apud Burcestre*, K. p. 575.

COMPUTUM *reddere*. To give up Accounts. Hence the old word a Count or declaration in law. The Contours or Counters were the serjeants at law retained to plead a cause, as Chaucer,

"A Sheriff had he been and a Contour,
Was no where sich a worthy Vavasour."

Hence to cast Accompt, a Counter or table of Counting in a shop, a Counter or piece of brass with which they Counted. The Counter or prison in London where the citizens were secured till they had accounted and paid their debts,—*Adamus de Catmere reddit computum pro Bernardo de S. Walerico*, K. p. 123.

COMPOSTUM, *Compositum, Compost*. Any dung or sullage or other unctuous matter, compounded (in heraldry Componed) to fatten and improve a soil: whence *compostare* to lay on dung or enrich the ground,—*Inter Hokeday et diem S. Martini bene possunt ibidem ducentæ quadruginta muttones sustentari ad opus domini ad terram suam compostandam*, K. p. 495.

CONFESSOR. In 34 Edw. III. the arch-bishops and bishops through their respective dioceses granted indulgence to all those who went to sea against the common enemy, with particular privilege to choose their own Confessor, K. p. 488. For the Confessionar to receive Confessions, was in the old Eng. to Shreve or to Shrive, Sax. rcpiʀan, whence the party Confessed was bercpiʀan, whence our Eng. Beshreved, or looking like a confessed or beshrieved person, who is imposed a penance; to Beshrew is to imprecate or denounce the curse of sin as in Confession. The act of Confession was called rcpirte, whence possibly to Shift or Shuffle in discourse, like people who are ashamed or afraid to tell all their faults. The most solemn time of confessing was the day before Lent, which from thence is called Shrove-Tuesday.

CONSECRATIO. The first form of consecrating churches in England was at a synod held at Celchyth, an. 816, K. p. 609. A solemn consecration of several churches in the diocese of Lincoln, and particularly in the archdeaconry of Oxford, an. 1238, by Robert Grosthead bishop of Lincoln, and William Brewer of Exeter, K. p. 221. No church could be legally consecrated without an allotment of manse and glebe, generally given by the lord of the manor, who thereby became patron of the church, K. p. 222. Several portions given to the church of Chesterton, *nomine dotis ad ejusdem ecclesiæ dedicationem*, K. p. 222. One virgate and six acres of land given at the consecration of the church of Wormenhale, K. p. 327. One virgate, one tothland, and eight acres given at the dedication of the church of Heyford *ad pontem*, consecrated by Wulfwin bishop of Dorchester, who came to that see an. 1046, and died an. 1067, 2 Will. Conq. p. 514. Two marks paid as a procuration to the bishop, for the provision and entertainment of himself and retinue.—*Nos R. Clonens. episcopum vice venerabilis patris R. Dei gratia Linc. episc. ecclesiam de Elsefeld septimo id. Julii, an. Dom.* MCCLXXIII. *dedicasse, et recepisse a procuratore rectoris dictæ ecclesiæ duas marcas, nomine procurationis ratione dedicationis ecclesiæ*, K. p. 515.

CONSERVATOR. A delegated umpire or standing arbitrator, who as a third impartial friend, was chose or appointed to compose and adjust all differences that should arise between two other parties.—*Ego Simon rector ecclesiæ de Hayford-Warine—subjiciendo me coercioni et compulsioni, civilibus judicibus vel delegatis, seu conservatori quem dicti religiosi et eorum successores duxerint eligendum*, K. p. 513. Whence our English Conservatour became a forinsick word, as Conservatour of the truce and safe conducts, appointed by Stat. 2 Hen. V. cap. 6, and 4 Hen. V. cap. 7. Conservatours of the peace or justices instituted by King Edw. III. &c.

CONSISTORIUM. The court Christian or spiritual court, held formerly in the nave of the cathedral church, or in some chappel, isle, or portico belonging to it, in which the bishop presided, and had some of his clergy for assessors and assistants. But this Consistory court is now held by the bishop's chancellor or commissary, and by archdeacons or their officials,—*Cum inter abbatem et conventum Osen. ex parte una, et priorem et conventum de Burcester ex altera, in consistorio Lincoln. aliquandiu litigatum fuisset*, K. p. 343.

CONSTABULARIUS. Constable. *A* Lat. *Comes Stabuli*, the

master of the horse, or prefect of the imperial stables in the decline of the Roman empire. Afterwards applied to any officer who had the guard or custody of any place or persons. Brien Fitz-Count constable of Walingford, 13 Hen I. K. p. 84. *Robertus de Oily constabularius regis*, K. p. 93.

CONSUETUDO. *Dies de consuetudine*, A day's work to be paid as a customary service by the tenant,—*Debent redditum, et præterea quinque dies de consuetudine*, K. p. 229.

CONVENIRE *coram Rege*. To convene or cite a person to appear in the king's court, and answer an action preferred against him.—*Manerium de Erdinthon dominus rex tradidit cuidam Bernardo de Sancto Walerico, quem Godefridus abbas de Egnesham sæpius convenit coram rege de jure suo*, K. p. 133.

COPPIRE *domum*. To Cope a house or to lay on the roof and covering on the top of it.—*Johanni Banbury tegulatori capienti in grosso ad coppiendam prædictam domum* iv. lib. i. den. K. p. 575. From the Sax. Coppe, the height or top of a thing, Cop a head, all from the Brit. *Koppa*, the top or highest part. Hence the Cope or upper covering, as Prov. Under the Cope of heaven. A Cope or upper garment, as the outer vest of a priest, and the cloak or surtout of any other person, as in Chaucer a Cope is used for a cloak. Hence possibly the southern term to Gaincope or cross a field, *i. e.* to strike off the nearest way to the top or head of the land. A hat with a high crown is called a Copped crown hat. A sea Cobbe or Coppe is a bird with a tuft of plumes on the head. A Coppe or Cob-nut is the top or chief or head-nut. A Cobble is a large pebble stone. Coping-stones are laid on the Cope or Coping or top of a wall. Copt in the North is high, as a Copt-man, *i. e.* a proud and high-minded man. Copt-know or Copt-knolle is the conical top of a hill. A Coppice is properly a small wood or toft of trees on the ascent of a hill. A Cop of hay, a Cop of pease, a Cop of straw, &c. are used in Kent for a high rising heap; which the monks turned into Coppa, so to be understood in that passage of Will. Thorn *inter* X. *Script.* col. 1820. an. 1177.—*Pacti sunt homines de halmoto de Menstre in Thaneto—fruges omnes suas coppare extunc et deinceps, et sic per coppas omnes decimas suas ipsi et hæredes sui a modo et in æternum legitime dare.* Which the learned Du Fresne cites *in voce* Coppa: but seems to understand it only of cutting down their corn, whereas it denotes the gathering or laying up the corn in Copes or heaps, (as they do barley and other corn not bound) that it might be the more easily and justly tithed.—*Quere* whether these words are not owing to the same original, a Knob or Knoppe a high swelling bunch. A Knoll of trees or high toft of trees upon a hill. Knolls or round headed roots or turneps so called in Kent. A Knoddle or Noddle a head. A Knot or protuberance in trees, &c. Gold knops or the flowers of the ranunculus. The Knape or Nape, Sax. Neap, in Kent the Nod of the neck. A Cap for the head, the Cape of a cloak, &c.

COPROSE, Copperas, Vitriol. From Copper, à Lat. *Cuprum*, or Dutch *Koper*. The German *Kupfferigt-angesicht*, was an old phrase for what we call brazen-face or copper-face, and *Kupferige-nase*, for what we call a Copper-nose, or a red carbuncled nose, which was exposed as a sign to some *Hospitia*, innes, or houses of entertainment, from whence was the first occasion of Brazen-nose College in Oxford,—*In solutis sup-priori pro coprose et gallys emptis pro encausto* ii.*den*. K. p. 574. The chief places where they made this Copperas in England, are Deptford and Folkstone in Kent, and Brickelsey in Essex. The metalline stones from which the liquor is dissolved are gathered on the coast of the Isle of Shepey, and on the shore near Bright-Helmston in Sussex, and several other parts.

CORBEL-STONES. I think the same with what Dr. Skinner calls Corbets, and from some authority expounds them to be stones wherein images stand. It seems derived from the Fr. *Corbeille*, Lat. *Corbulus*. The old Eng. Corbel and Corbetel was properly a nich in the wall of a church or convent, in which they placed an image, and the Corbel-stones were the smooth and polished stones laid for the front and outside of the corbels or niches. As at present on the south-side of the church of Ambrosden, the said corbels or niches remain, though the images are taken away. But the same niches and little statues or figures in them continue in the walls of very many old churches and steeples.—*Et in solutis Johanni Chepyn latamo aptanti et facienti* xviii. *corbel-stonys potendis in prædicto muro* v. *sol.* iv. *den.* K. p. 575.

COTAGIUM. A Cottage or a Cot, from Sax. Cote, Island. *Ket*, a little house or hut,—*Tenetur per socagium, et non habentur ibidem nisi tria cotagia*, K. p. 305. *Duo messuagia cum uno cotagio*, K. p. 379. Hence a sheep-Cote or sheep-Cot. Cotswold in Glocestershire, &c. and the termination of Cote or Cot in very many villages.

COTARIUS. Sax. Cotɟeƍe, old Eng. *Cotseth, Cottman, Cottyer*, now Cottager, or the inhabitant of any country Cot.—*Summa gallinarum carucatariorum et cotariorum* xiv. *gallinæ*, K. p. 354. Hence a country clown is now called a Meer Cot, as a citizen ignorant of country affairs a Meer Cit.

COTERELLUS. Spelman and Du Fresne make *Cotarius* and *Coterellus* to be both the same servile inhabitants. But I think in the Doomsday Register and other ancient MSS. there does appear a distinction, not only in their name but in their tenure and quality. The *Cotarius* had a free soccage tenure, and paid a firm or rent in provisions or mony, with some customary service. But the *Coterellus* held in absolute villenage, and had his person and goods disposed at the pleasure of the lord.—Edmund earl of Cornwall gave to the Bonhommes of Asherugge his mannors of Chesterton and Ambrosden,—*Una cum villanis, coterellis, eorum catallis, servitiis, sectis et sequelis, et omnibus suis ubicunque pertinentibus*, K. p. 310.

COTLAND, *Cotsethland.* Land held by a cottager whether in soccage or villenage.—*Dimidia acra jacet ibidem inter cotland quam Johannes Goldering tenet ex una parte, et cotland quam Thomas Webbe tenet ex altera*, K. p. 532.

COWELE. A Cowl or Coal, or tub with two ears to be carried between two persons on a Cowl-staff. From *Cucula* or *Cocula*, a vessel like a boat, from Coca or Cogga, a boat, *vid.* COGGE. A Cowl in Essex is the appellative for any tub: whence a Cowler, now pronounced a Cooler, or brewing vessel.—*Pro novo cowele empto* ix. den. K. p. 549.

CREST, *Crista.* Any imagery or carved work to adorn the head or top of any thing, like our modern cornish. This word is now adopted by the heralds, and applied to the device set over a coat of arms.—*Et Willielmo Hykkedon conducto in grosso ad mensam domini ad dolandum et perficiendum le crest super cancellum prioratus ibidem*, K. p. 575.

CROFT, from Sax. Cpoꝼte, Cꞃuꝼte, which Spelman deduces from the Lat. *Crypta* or Gr. Κρύπlω. A close or small enclosure nigh a dwelling house, *Totam terram quæ est inter croftam Gilberti molendinarii, et messuagium quod fuit Adami*, K. p. 135.

CROPPUS. A Crop of corn or the yearly product of arable land. From Sax. Cꞃoppaꞃ, ears of corn, Cꞃop, the top or head of any thing: whence to Crop or cut off the upper part: Crop-eard, a Crop of beef. In Sussex they call darnel Crop, and in Worcestershire buck-wheat goes by this name of Crap. The old Lat. *Cropa* was the buttock of a horse, whence a Crupper.—*Idem abbas ex mera liberalitate sua croppum de dicta crofta præfato priori instanter concessit pro hac vice*, K. p. 298.

CRUCEM *assumere.* To take the Cross, or to engage upon oath to undertake a personal expedition in the Holy War, for the recovery of Jerusalem, and as a badge of their vow to Saunter, to wear a cross on their upper garment. So Brien Fitz Count lord of Walingford took on him the cross, and adventured to Jerusalem, K. p. 111. When persons had taken the cross, they bought an absolution to excuse them from the danger: by which means some of the nobility, when they had formed a crusade of great numbers among their tenants and dependants, they obtained a general dispensation from the Pope, which they sold again by retail, to release and disengage all those who had more mind to stay at home. This project was very beneficial to Richard earl of Cornwall: and therefore the same favour was asked and obtained from the Pope by William Longspe in 30 Edw. III. K. p. 238.

CUPA, *Cuppa.* A Cup or small metalline drinking vessel. Sax. Cuppe, Brit. *Kuppan.* Hence a Cup-bord, a Cupping-glass; an acorn-Cup, and the Italian *Cupulo* was taken from this form. The plate or drinking Cup of bishops and abbats was part of the heriot paid to the king at their decease.—*Abbas de Oseneia obiit anno regni regis Edwardi vicesimo quinto,—petiit eschaetor ad opus domini regis cuppam et palefridum dicti abbatis defuncti*, K. p. 330. *Vid.* Prynne, Histor. Collect. tom. 2. p. 834.

CURIA. Taken sometimes for the persons or feudatory tenants who did their suit and service at the court of the lord. So to a charter of Bernard de S. Walery, 30 Hen. II.—*Hiis testibus—et omni curia mea,* K. p 139.

CURIA *Canonicorum.* The convent or conventual house.— *Juxta rivulum extra curiam dictorum canonicorum,* K. p. 177.

CURIA *Personæ Ecclesiæ.* The parsonage house,—*Omnes obventiones altaris et cœmiterii prædictæ ecclesiæ, et totam terram et curiam personæ,* K. p. 205.—*croftam quæ jacet juxta curiam personæ,* Ib.

CURIA *capitalis. Vid.* MANSUM CAPITALE.

CURIÆ *adventus.* The service of coming to the court of the lord,—*Reddit per annum ad terminum ipsius unam marcam, et unum adventum curiæ,* K. p. 400.

CURIALITAS. Courtesie or pure kindness.—*Et in datis Willielmo Skynner garconi de pistrina ex curialitate falcatorum per x. dies xii. den* K. p. 576. *Curialitas Angliæ* was that custom which we call the courtesie of England, when a man who has had a child by his wife deceased, enjoys her estate during his own life.

CURTILAGIUM. From Lat. *Curs, Curtis,* a coop or pen, or other small enclosure. A *Curtilage,* mistaken by our writers for a garden, when it properly was a yard or back-side adjoining to a house for the running of poultry, the keeping of hogs, &c.—*Curtilagium cum pertinentiis suis,* K. p. 269. *Et dicunt quod infra curiam domini est unum curtilagium ad nutriendos porcellos quod valet per an.* xiid. K. p. 495.

CUSTOS *Abbatiæ.* The person to whose custody a vacant abby

was committed, who as a steward of the rents and profits, was to give account to the eschaetor, and he to the king.—*Mandatum est Waltero de Lutegareshale custodi abbatiæ de Osneia quod occasione dictorum cupæ palefridi et lanarum nichil exigat*, K. p. 330.

CUSTUMARIUS. An inferiour tenant in villenage or soccage, who by custom is obliged to pay such service of work and labour for his lord.—*Ipse Robertus et omnes alii custumarii dominæ*, K. p. 401.

CYRIC-SCETE. *Vid.* CHURCH-SCOT. The original of the custom and continuance of it historically delivered, K. p. 603.

D.

DANE-GELT. A tribute which the Danes upon their frequent incursions imposed on the English, as the arbitrary terms of peace and departure, an. 873, K. p. 38 : first imposed on the whole nation to continue as a yearly pension to the Danes under King Ethelred, an. 991. Alfred and Ingulph report that King Edward the Confessor remitted and abrogated this tax. But it is certain that William the Conquerour, though he would not reduce the annual payment, yet he ordered the raising of it as often as the necessities of invasion or of expedition did require. It was severely exacted and augmented by William Rufus. And in the reign of Hen. I. it was computed among the king's standing revenues. The next successour, King Stephen, promised by oath on his coronation day, that this Danegeld should be for ever remitted, Hen. Hunt. p. 387. From which time some writers have dated the expiration of this tax. Yet it seems rather to have continued upon extraordinary occasions, till it was abrogated by time, or rather swallowed up in tallage and parliamentary impositions The laws of Edw. Conf. cap. 11, rate this tax at 12*d*. on every hide. Hen. Hunt. computes it at 2*s*. on each hide; and Jo. Brompton at 3*d*. on a bovate or oxgang. No doubt it varied according to the different exigencies upon which it was levied. To be exempted from this tax was a peculiar priviledge granted by King Hen. II. to the tenants within the honor of Walingford, *ut sint quieti de geldis et danegeldis*, K. p. 114. In the donation of lands to religious uses, when many other burdens were remitted, this was still reserved ; so in 27 Hen. II. Henry de Oily gave four hides in Chesterton to the abby of Egnesham, *liberas et quietas ab omnibus querelis, exceptis murdredo et danegeldo*, K. p. 184, 403.

DAYERIA, *Dayri, Dairy.* It is derived by Dr. Skinner from the Fr. *Derrier*, as if the Dairy were on the back part or behind the rest of the house. The learned Fr. Junius is no more happy, when he refers it to the Greek—Δαείρα *et per syncopen* δαίρα *Hesychio exponitur* δαήμων ἔμπειρος, gnara, perita. *Non enim cujusvis est curare lacticinia, sed a lacticiniis edulia concinnaturam singulari rusticarum rerum experientia imbutam esse oportet. Omnino interim huc pertinet, quod Gallis Dariole dicitur cibi genus quod iisdem Gallis alias nuncupatur Laicteron vel* flan de laict. *Ac fortasse quoque Danis ab eadem origine Darere dictum est jentaculum, quod septentrionales lacticiniis jentare sint soliti.* Both these are trifling conjectures: the word Dayrie, or Deirie, is originally English, from Day, Deie, Sax. Daʒ, and signified at first the daily yeild of milch cows, or the daily profit made of them. As a Day-work of land was such a quantity as could be ploughed up by one plough in one day. W. Thorn *inter X. Script.* col. 2203, which the French called *Journal*, Lat. *Jornale*. So in Lorraine and Champagne, they now use the word *Doyer* for the meeting of the Day-labouring women to give an account of their day's work, and receive the wages of it. The Dairy-maid is called *Androchia* in Fleta, l. 2. cap. 87. *Androchia pudica esse debet, et laboriosa daeriæ,*—A Dairy in the North is called the Milkness, as the Dairy-maid is in all parts a Milk-maid.—*Wreckwyke, compotus Henrici Deye et Johannæ uxoris suæ de omnibus exitibus et proventibus de dayri domini prioris de Burncester*, K. p. 548.—*Computant de* xxxv. *sol.* vi. *den. receptis de dayeria de la Breche,* K. p. 570.

DAPIFER, *à dapes ferendo*. At first a domestick officer, like our steward of the household, or rather clerk of the kitchen. Then by degrees any fiduciary servant, especially the chief steward or head bayliff of an honor, barony, or mannor.—*Malcolmus rex Scotiæ dapifero suo de honore de Huntingdon*, K. p. 119. Possibly from *Dapifer*, the chief servant of better figure than the rest, comes our present phrases a Dapper-fellow, and Dapperly-done. Hence the Lat. *Dapsilis*, hospitable and generous.—*Dapsilis in mensa frugalia pabula præstans,* K. p. 340.

DECANUS Christianitatis. The dean rural or urban who had the district of ten churches in the country or city, within which he exercised a jurisdiction of great advantage to ecclesiastical discipline. They were sometime stiled *Archipresbyteri*, and were at first both in order and authority above the archdeacons, K. p. 635. They were elected by the clergy, and by their votes again deposed; but afterwards were appointed and removed at the discretion of the bishop, and thence called *Decani temporarii*, as distinguished from the cathedral deans, who were *Decani perpetui*, K. p. 639. The rural dean was sometime simply called *Decanus*, as in a charter of John de'l Osse of Wendlebury, 11 Hen. II. *Hijs testibus—Ro-*

gero decano de Pire, K. p. 121. So likewise the urban or city dean, as in a composition between the abby of Egnesham, and priory of Burcester, 34 Hen. II. *Hiis testibus—Nigello decano de Oxenford,* K. p. 144. Called *Decanus Episcopi* in the Laws of Edw. Confess. p. 633. Deans rural and urban collected the taxes imposed upon the clergy, K. p. 130. The chapter in every deanery were a court Christian for determining the right of tithes, &c. K. p. 123. Robert Grostbead bishop of Lincoln by advice of the predicant fryers, commanded his archdeacons and rural deans to make strict inquisition into the lives of all the nobility and commonalty within their precincts, which was thought such a grievance and imposition upon the liberty of sinners, that upon complaint the king interposed and stopt the proceedings, K. p. 238. The taxation of benefices by Walter bishop of Norwich, an 1254, was done by the bishop's appointing the dean and three rectors or vicars in every deanery, who upon oath were to certifie the just estimate of all church revenues, K. p. 312. All the parochial clergy bound by oath to attend the rural chapters, to which purpose the appropriators were sometime obliged to find a horse for the poor vicar, K. p. 304. It was their office to give induction to clerks after their presentation by the patron, and admission or institution by the bishop. So an. 1220, 5 Hen. III. Richard rural dean of Wodesdon inducted the prior and canons of St. Frideswide into the appropriated tithes of Oakle, and certified it by special instrument concluding thus,—*Ego et plures alii viri fide digni de capitulo de Wodesdon in hujus rei testimonium sigilla nostra apposuimus,* K. p. 407. The same office done by John vicar of Wynchendon dean of Wodesdon, an. 1326, *ib.* The sentence of superiour ecclesiastical judges committed to the execution of the rural dean, K. p. 408. The title of *Decanus Christianitatis* falsely applied to the cathedral dean by the editor of Append. ad Fascic. p. 636. An historical account of deans rural, urban, cathedral, and conventual, delivered from p 631 to p. 653.

DEDICATION of Churches. The wake or feast of dedication kept with solemnity and generous entertainment,—*Et in datis duobus valectis forestæ portantibus carnes ferinas priori in festo dedicationis ecclesiæ hoc anno v. sol.* K. p. 578. Solemn processions on the day of dedication, K. p. 658. Those inhabitants who had the priviledge of a chapel of ease, were to repair to the mother church on that festival, K. p. 595; and there to make their oblations, K. p. 596. The history of the institution and observance of wakes or feasts of dedication, K. p. 610. *Vid.* CONSECRATION of Churches.

DEFALTA, *Defaltum.* From Fr. *Defaut,* default, a neglect or omission of appearance in a court of justice, for which judgement might be given against the defalter.—*Ipsi non veniunt ad hunc diem, unde judicium assisæ capiatur versus eos per eorum defaltum,* K. p. 351. *Ipse non venit et alias fecit defaltum,* K. p. 479.

DEFENDERE *se.* A phrase in the Doomsday Register to be taxt for such a quantity of land. As the mannor of Brill was taxt for twenty hides, *Tunc* xx. *hidæ se defendebant,* K. p. 165.

DEFORCIARE. *Vid.* after DEVOTA.

DEMESNE. From the Lat. *Dominicum,* as that part of a mannor or estate which the lord keeps in his own hands, or to his own use. Or as some pretend from the Fr. *de mesne,* as land which a man holds of himself, and not from a superiour lord. It was generally taken for those grounds that were adjacent to the court or mannor house, which the lord did not let out to feudatory or servile tenants; but either manured himself or assigned to tenants at will. The barons often granted (with consent of ecclesiastical authority) the tithe of their own demesne to religious houses, K. p. 75, 76. In those mannors which our kings held in demesne, they had palaces or royal seats, where by frequent changing of their stations, they made a sort of constant progress through their whole kingdom, K. p. 52.—*Manerium de Brehull fuit antiquum dominicum regis,* K. p. 285.—*Homines de manerio de Hedingdon quod est de antiquo dominico coronæ Angliæ,* K. p. 319. At these demesne mannors the kings had free chappels exempt from episcopal jurisdiction: as at Brill, Hedingdon, &c. *Dominicum pratum,* the meadow grounds not rented out, but kept in the hands of the lord, K. p. 76.

DENARIUS *S. Petri.* Peter-penny, Hearth-penny, *Romefeah, Romescot.* In the North Ream-penny: where they use this proverb, He reckons up his Ream-pennies, *i. e.* he tells all his faults. This levy was at first a penny from every house wherein there were thirty pence *vivæ pecuniæ* of ready money: collected and sent to Rome, which by custom passed into a standing tax, though at first it was only a voluntary contribution, of which one half was to goe for alms to the English school at Rome, and the other to the Pope's use. It was given first by King Ina, and confirmed by King Offa and King Ethelwolph, established by the laws of King Canute, cap. 9, Edgar, cap. 54, Edw. Confess. cap. 10, Will. Conqu. cap. 18, Hen. I. cap. 11. Collected by the bishops, who employed the archdeacons and rural deans to receive it before the festival of St. Peter *ad vincula,* Aug. 1, as appointed by the canons of King Edgar, K. p. 603. The whole sum was by P. Greg. stated at two hundred pounds twenty-six shillings, of which the proportion in this diocese of Lincoln was 42*l.* King Edw. III. an. 1365, forbid the payment of this duty to the Pope. But this was only a bold instance of that prince's displeasure. For the custom soon returned, and continued to the reign of Hen. VIII. when Polydore Virgil was employed here as the Pope's general receiver. No place nor religious house was exempted from this imposition, but only the abby of St. Albans. Some churches and parishes paid a stated composition, as in 30 Hen. II. *Capellæ de Egnesham et de Chersinton, et de Ardinton, similiter etiam ecclesiæ de Stoches et de Cherleviri ab omni onere episcopali ab antiquo liberæ sunt, nec solvent pro denariis beati Petri nisi octo solidos,* K. p. 140. In the diocese of Canterbury the rural deans were the collectors in their respective districts, K. p. 648. The religious often obliged their firmers and tenants to pay a certain proportion towards this tax: as in the rental of the abby of Glastonbury taken an. 1201.—*Manerium Glaston. reddit per annum in gabulo* vi. *lib.* vii. *sol.—in denariis S. Petri* xxxiii. *den.—Pylton reddit in gabulo* xiii. *lib.* iv. *sol.—de denariis S. Petri* iii. *sol. &c.* Cartul. Abbat. Glaston. MS. p. 38.

DENARIUS *tertius Comitatus.* In the fines and other profits arising from the county courts, two parts were allotted to the king and a third part or penny to the earl of the county, who either received it in specie at the assises and trials, or had an equivalent composition paid from the Exchequer. So Eubulo le Strange in right of his wife Alice, daughter and heir of Henry de Lacy earl of Lincoln, had by letters patent 5 Edw. III. *Custodiam et wardam castelli nostri de Lincoln. cum balliva ibidem, et viginti libratas annui redditus pro tertio denario comitatus,* K. p. 418.

DENARII. A general term for any sort of money,—*Solventur hominibus de Hedingdon de denariis domini, singulis annis proximo die quo falcare incipient, quinque solidi,* K. p. 320.

DESPONSARE. To take a woman in marriage. So of Maud daughter and heir of Robert de Oily, sen. *Milo Crispinus desponsavit eam,* K. p. 112. *Mulier desponsata,* a lawful wife. Henry de Fontibus gave his estate to his sister and her husband, in default of issue so lawfully begotten,—*Nisi hæredem habuero de muliere desponsata,* K. p. 115.

DETACHIARE, *Dittachiare.* By a writ of Detachment to seise or take into custody goods or persons,—*Nec nos nec hæredes nostri prædictum Radulphum vel hæredes suos dittachiemus vel disseisiri faciemus,* K. p. 203.

DEVISÆ. The borders or limits of division between lands, parishes, or counties,—*Sic usque Hetheneburn inter Akemanstrete inter devisas com. Oxon. et Buck.* K. p. 324. Hence the Devises or Devizes, a town in Wiltshire, situate on the confines of the West Saxon and Mercian kingdoms.

DEVOTA *Deo.* A woman in her widowhood, or latter part of her life, took a religious habit, and was called a Vowess or Devotee.—So Edith widow of Robert de Oilly, jun. in old age grew penitent, and became *Memorabilis matrona Deo devota,* K. p. 95.

DEFORCIARE, Strictly and properly to turn out by violence, or to keep possession of lands in open violation of the rights of the heir or lawful owner. But it often signified no more than to fence off a suit or action, or to defend the right and property of possession. And therefore in assises or trials, the claimer or plaintiff was called *Querens,* and the possessor or defendant was *Deforcians.* —*Inter Johannem filium Nigelli querentem, et Sampsonem de Adingrave et Mariam uxorem ejus deforciantes,* K. p. 291. *Idem* K. p. 291, 321.

DEFORCIATIO. A distraint or seizure of goods for satisfaction of a lawful debt,—*Nos et hæredes nostros distringere possint per bona mobilia et immobilia et hominum nostrorum, et deforciationem tenere quousque plenarie fuerit satisfactum,* K. p. 293.

DISSEISIRE. To disseise, eject, or turn out of possession. *Rex Richardus* I. *disseisivit Gerardum de Camvilla de castello et vicecomitatu Lincolniensi,* K. p. 152.

DISTRINGERE. To distrain and keep the *districtiones,* distresses, or distraints, till payment and full satisfaction,—*Possint nos et successores nostros et prædictas omnes terras—distringere ad solutionem memoratam, et districtiones retinere quousque—plenarie fuerit satisfactum,* K. p. 344.

DOMESDAY-BOOK. When King Alfred divided his kingdom into counties, hundreds, and tithings, he had an inquisition taken of the several districts, and digested into a register called *Dom-boc, i. e.* the judicial or judgement book, reposited in the church of Winchester, and thence entitled *Codex Wintoniensis,* to which King Edw. sen. seems to refer in the first chapter of his Laws. The general survey taken by King Will. Conq. was after the precedent of King Alfred, and seems but a corruption of, or rather an addition to, the same name, *Domboc* into Domesday-book. And therefore a trifling derivation to impute the name to *Domus Dei,* as if so called from the church wherein it was first reposited. Nor is it any wiser conjecture to ascribe it to Doomsday or the final day of judgement. When the appellation does really imply no more than the Doom-book, or register from which sentence and judgement might be given in the tenure of estates: whence by Latin writers commonly called *Liber Judicialis.* Nor may it be improper to observe (because no notice has been yet taken of so small a matter) that the addition of *dey* or *day,* (*Dom-boc, Domesday-book*) does not augment the sense of the word, but only doubles and confirms it. For the word *dey* or *day* in that composition does not really signifie the measure of time, but the administration of justice. For as Dr. Hammond well observes in his Annotation on Heb. 10, 25. The word *day* in all idioms does signifie judgement. So 1 Cor. 3, 13. Ανθρωπίνη ἡμέρα is humane judgement, &c. And even now in the North a *Deies-man* or Days-man, is an arbitrator, an umpire, or judge. So as Doomsday-book is no more than the book of judicial verdict, or decretory sentence, or dooming of judgement, K. p. 63.

DOMINA. A title given to those women who in their own right of inheritance held a barony. So Maud the daughter of Robert de Oily, sen., who inherited the honour of Walingford, was therefore stiled *Matildis domina de Walingford*, K. p. 78.

DOMINIUM. Right or legal power.—*In sylva dicti manerii sive dominii de Pidintona, aut infra præcinctum ejusdem non habent aliqui extranei dominium aliquo modo in parte vel in toto se intromittere*, K. p. 498.

DOS. It properly signified the portion brought by the wife to the husband, and not the dowry settled by the husband on the wife. Yet it was sometime taken in this latter sense, for the jointure to be enjoyed by the widow after the husband's decease. And if an equal provision had not been made before the husband's death, his relict might sue the heirs at law *de rationabili dote*, for a reasonable share of the estate to be assigned for her maintenance. So Eustace the relict of Thomas de Verdon taking for a second husband Richard de Camvill, she claimed her reasonable dowry of Nicholas de Verdon, her husband's heir, which occasioned a legal fine, *inter Richardum de Camvill et Eustaciam uxorem ejus petentes, et Nicholaum de Verdon tenentem de rationabili dote ipsius Eustaciæ, quam ipsa clamat versus eundem Nicholaum de omnibus tenementis quæ fuerint Thomæ de Verdon quondam viri sui*, K. p. 166. *Vid.* DUARIUM.

DRAW-GERE. Any furniture of cart-horses for drawing a waggon or other carriage: from *Draw* and Sax. ʒeappe, in our Eng. *Geer*, any preparatory utensils or instruments, and especially cloaths and bodily habit, whence ʒeapkın or *jerkin*, a short diminutive coat. From ʒeappıan, to provide or to cloath. This the modern Latin writers turned into *Gerada*, which Du Fresne rightly interperets, *utensilia aut quemvis apparatum*, but seems with some violence to derive it from the German *Ghe-reed*, when it bears more immediate relation to the Sax. ʒeappe, old Eng. *Geere*, as in the obsolete proverb, Ne gold ne geere, *i. e.* neither money nor goods. In no geere, *i. e.* not ready, unprovided: whence the old word *Geerefull* or *Gierefull*, well habited or well fitted with arms, as in Chaucer, Troilus, l. 4, f. 167. "To preve in that thy gierfull violence." Hence the Sax. Geaρᵭ, Eng. Yard, properly *Geard* or Garden, or as now in Lincolnshire *Garth*, a place well fenced and cultivated. Thence Gýρᵭan and ᵹýρᵭl, to girt, a girdle, a garter. In the North to Garre, *i. e.* to make a garment or do any other work. Sax. Geaρn, Eng. Yarn, still in the North called Garn, or wool workt into a thread, Geaρnian, Eng. to Earn, or obtain by labour. The old word Garth is owing to the same original, and signified any work or device, to take or to catch game. As the Fish-garths in stat. 23 Hen. VIII. cap. 18, were nets and unlawful engines for catching fish, used by the Garth-men or poachers, mentioned stat. 1, 13 Rich. II. cap. 9, *et* an. 17, cap. 19. The sound and the sense of the Sax. Geaρρe and ᵹeaρρian are more nearly preserved in the present English *Head-geer*, *i. e.* headcloaths; *Horse-geer*, *i. e.* harness; *Gearish* and *Garish*, *i. e.* spruce and fine. And in the North to *geer* or to *gear*, is to dress; whence prov. Snogly geared, *i. e.* neatly dress'd. As in the South, we say such a person is in his geers, or out of his geers.—*Pro factura de draw-gere per Walterum Carpenter de Langeton* iii d. K. p. 549.

DUARIUM, *Doarium, Dotarium.* The Dowry of a wife settled on her in marriage to be enjoyed after her husband's decease. The English Dowrie is by Fr. Junius rightly referred to the old Eng. to Dowe, *i. e.* to give, as Chaucer, " To whom for evermore mine hart I dowe," whence a Dose or Dows, or portion of any thing given to eat or drink, is as near the old Eng. as the primitive Greek. The same Junius does conjecture that our English Widow is hence owing to the Sax. Ƿeᵭ and ᵭuρe, as if a woman wedded to or by covenant assured of such a certain dowry. To which sense the word Dowager does well agree. The wife with consent of her husband could assign a part of her dowry to religious uses.—*Ego Editha Roberto de Oili conjugali copula juncta consilio et voluntate ejusdem Roberti mariti mei de duario meo de Weston dedi in perpetuam eleemosinam, &c.* K. p. 94.

DYTENUM, *Dictenum.* A Dittany, Ditty, or Song. *Venire cum toto ac pleno dyteno*, to sing harvest home. *Homines de Hedyngdon ad curiam domini singulis annis inter festum S. Michaelis et S. Martini venient cum toto ac pleno dyteno sicut hactenus consueverunt*, K. p. 320.

E.

ELEEMOSINA. Sax. Ælmeʃʃ, Eng. Alms; *Eleemosinaria,* Fr. *Aumônerie*, Eng. Aumerie, Aumbry, Ambry, which in the North they now use for a pantry or cup-board, Welsh *Almari*. *Eleemo-*

f

sinarius, Almoner, *Eleemosina pura et perpetua, et libera.* Pure and perpetual Frank-Almoigne. Lands so given to religious uses were discharged from all taxes and other secular burdens, — *Qualiter extincta sunt feoda domini abbatis quæ ab ipso petita sunt,— profert chartam Roberti de Olleio, et confirmationem regis quod habet—in puram et perpetuam eleemosinam*, K. p. 305.

EMENDATIO *domorum et sepium.* The repair of houses and mending of hedges. To religious houses a privilege was often granted to receive as much wood as was needful for these purposes. So the abby of Missenden in right of their hermitage at Musewell had a grant from Joan de Pidington,—*de bosco quod opus fuerit ad emendationem domorum et sepium suarum*, K. p. 76.

EMENDATIO *Panis et Cervisiæ.* The assise of bread and beer, or the power of supervising and correcting such weights and measures, a privilege granted by the king to lords of manors, which power gave occasion to the present office of Ale-taster, appointed in every court-leet, and sworn to look to the assise of bread, and ale or beer, within the precincts of that lordship,—*Ad nos spectat emendatio panni panis et cervisiæ, et quicquid regis est excepto murdredo et latrocinio probata*, K. p 196.

EPISCOPALE *onus, Episcopalia.* Synodals, Pentecostals, and other taxes and contributions from the clergy to the diocesan bishop. Which burden was remitted by special privilege to some churches, and especially to those free chappels that were built upon the king's demesne. So 30 Hen. II. *Capellæ de Egnesham et de Chersinton et de Ardinton. Similiter etiam ecclesiæ de Stoches et de Cherlebiri ab omni onere episcopali liberæ sunt*, K. p. 140.

ERNES. The loose scattered ears of corn that are left on the ground after the binding or cocking of it.—*Conducto ad præparandum usque ad carectam* xxix. *seliones— ordei cum les ernes viz.* viii. *den.* K. p. 576. From the old Teuton. *hr*, an ear of corn ; *Ernde*, harvest ; *Ernden*, to cut or mow corn Hence to Ern is in some places the same as to Glean, or what in Kent we call to Lease. Hence Ersh in Sussex is the stubble after the corn is cut, what in Kent we call the Gratten, in the North Eddish, from the Sax. Eðıȝc, roughings and aftermaths. The Ersh in Sussex is in Surry the Esh, as a wheat-Esh, a barley-Esh, &c.

ESCAETOR *Regis.* The king's eschaetor, who took into custody and accounted for all escheats to the crown, as forfeitures, lapses, wards, &c. Of which officers there was one commissioned in every county to execute the office for one year, and to certifie his receipts into the Exchéquer. *Thomas Maunsel escaetor regis in com.* Buck. *computat regi* xxxv*s. de manerio de Lutegareshale*, K. p. 246. This officer received all heriots due to the king, and entered upon all vacant sees and abbies held in barony, and accounted for the intermediate profits which arose before the restitution of the temporalities, K. p. 330.

ESPICURNANTIA. The office of *Spigurnel* or sealer of the king's writs. *Spigurnellus*, which word Spelman and Du Fresne recite without interpreting. It seems detorted from the Sax. Spaɲɲaɲ, to shut up, to seal, or to secure : whence the Spar of any mineral, i. e. the outward coat that involves or shuts up the oar. The Spar of a door, i. e. the bolt. To Spar a door in the North is to shut the door. Spars and Sparables are nails to enclose and shut up, &c. The monks of Rochester were to allow a set quantity of provisions to the king's *Spigurnels* at their coming to that city.—*Pro ista autem provisione et concessione debent prior et conventus Roffensis ubicunque dominus rex fuerit quieti esse pro cera ad sigillum.* Spelman, *in voce* Spigurnellus. Oliver de Standford in 27 Edw. I. held lands in Netlebed, *com.* Oxon. *per serjeantiam espicurnantiæ in cancellaria domini regis,* K. p 292.

ESSOIN. Fr. *Essoigne,* Lat. *Essonium, Exonium.* From the old Lat. *Sunnis,* an impediment, let, or hindrance. When a person was cited to appear and answer in any court, upon any just cause or reason of absenting, he was allowed to alledge his *Essoin* or excuse, and if the pretence were just and well approved by the court, he had his *Essoin* or respite of longer time. *Essonium de malo lecti* was in case of sickness of the party summoned, which sickness was to be attested in open court four days successively, when the judges might appoint four knights to attend the sick person, and see him depute a proctor or attorney to appear for him. But this excuse was not allowed to the proctors or attornies themselves, because one deputy could not depute another, K. p. 108. *Essoin* was granted on a non-suit, and the parties suffered themselves to be non-suited to gain this respite. *Predictus Johannes fecit se esse non versus prædictum priorem de prædicto placito, et habuit diem per essonium suum ad hunc diem,* K. p. 414.—*Et prædictus Johannes tunc fecit se essoniari de servitio domini regis et habuit inde diem per essonium suum hic usque a die Paschatis in* xv. *dies,* K. p. 471.

ESTREGBORDS. Eastern-boards or deal-boards brought from the eastern parts for wainscote and other uses.—*Et in sex estregbords, viz.* waynscots *emptis apud Steresbrugge* ii. *sol.* iii. *den.* K. p. 575.

EVENYNGS. The delivery at even or night of a certain portion of grass or corn to a custumary tenant, who performs his wonted service of mowing or reaping for his lord, and at the end of his day's work receives such a quantity of the grass or corn to carry home with him as a gratuity or encouragement of his bounden

f 2

service. So in the mannor of Burcester,—*virgata terræ integra ejusdem tenuræ habebit liberam ad vesperas quæ vocatur* Evenyngs *tantam sicut falcator potest per falcem levare et domum portare per ipsam*, K. p. 401. This gave occasion to the present corrupt and shameful practise of day-labourers in felling and faggoting of wood, who at every evening carry home with them a burden of wood, as great as they are able to bear, though it be no part of their wages or covenanted hire. Now servile tenures and customary services are extinct, this practise of labourers carrying home a load or bundle is no better than pure theft, and ought in all honour and justice to be punisht and reformed.

EXACTIO *secularis*. Any sort of tax or imposition paid by feudatory and servile tenants, from all which the freeholders within the honor of Walingford were exempted by special privilege,—*Ut quieti sint ab omni consuetudine et exactione seculari*, K. p. 114.

EXCOMMUNICATUM *capias*, or a writ *de excommunicato capiendo*. A precept directed to the sheriff from the court of Chancery for the apprehension of a person who has stood obstinately e.communicate for fourty days.—Robert de Pidington and others imprisoned for such contempt of ecclesiastical authority, were at the request of the arch-bishop of Canterbury released to prosecute their appeal to Rome, K. p. 352.

EXERCITUS *bestiarum*. A herd or drove of deer or other forest game.—*Ille locus est magis et maximus exercitus bestiarum totius forestæ*, K. p. 249.

EXHIBITIO. An allowance for meat and drink, such as the religious appropriators made to the poor depending vicar So in all churches appropriated to the abby of Oxeney, *Vicarius habebit sufficientem exhibitionem sicut canonici quoad victualia in mensa canonicorum ubi canonici moram faciunt*, K. p 304.

EXPLICIA, *Expletia, Expleta* The rents or intermediate profits of an estate in trust.—*Capiendo inde explicia ad valentiam quinque solidorum et amplius*, K. p. 414.

EXTENTA. The survey and valuation of an estate made upon inquisition or the oaths of a jury, impanelled by the sheriff by vertue of the king s precept.—*Extenta terrarum et tenementorum quæ fuerunt domini Johannis filii Nigelli defuncti in villa de Borstall*, com. Bucks. *facta ibidem*, K. p 314. *Extenta manerii de Ambrosden per duodecim juratores*, an. 28 Edw. I. K p. 681.

EXTRACTA *Curiæ*. The profits of holding a court arising from the customary dues, fees, and amercements,—*Computant de tribus denariis receptis de extractis unius curiæ tentæ apud* Burcester, K. p. 572.

EYTE. A low wet place or little island, called in some old

writings an *Eight*, which Skinner would have to be a contraction of *Islet*, *i. e.* a small island. But the word bears more immediate relation to the Sax. Eaʒe, Lat *Eia*, an island, which in terminations is *Ey*, the present Islandick appellative for an island; which syllable ends the name of very many of our little islands, as Eley, Shepey, Pevensey, Ramsey, &c. Hence an Eylet, and Eylet- or Ilet hole. The French in Du Fresne's opinion have hence borrowed their *Eau*, water, and possibly the Irish *Ait*, a place.—*Duas placias prati quæ jacent prope Thamisiam quæ vocantur Porters-Eyte*, K. p. 295. So the low mershy tract that lies by the river in Blackthorn, within the parish of Ambrosden, is now called Blackthorn-Eyte.

F.

FALCARE *prata*. To cut or mow down grass in meadows hayned or laid in for hay: a customary service done for the lord by his inferiour tenants.—*Homines de Hedingdon per duos dies prata domini falcabunt, tertio vero die herbam ibi falcatam vertent*, K. p. 320. *Falcatura una* was the service of one time mowing or cutting grass in the demesne meadows of the lord. *Tenet in bondagio, et debet unam falcaturam per dimidium diem.* ib. *Falcata* was the grass fresh mowed and laid in swathes.—*Ipse Robertus et omnes alii custumarii dominæ liberam falcatam in prato vocato Gilberdesham sine prandio debent tornare, et inde fœnum levare, et mulliones inde facere*, K. p. 401. The customary mower had the liberty of carrying away with him at night a bundle of hay, as much as he could take up and carry off with his sithe. *In manerio de Pedinton—quilibet falcator habebit ad vesperam singulis diebus quamdiu falcabit fasciculum fœni quantum potest capere sursum cum falce sua sine auxilio aliorum*, K. p. 496. This liberty was legal, when custom or compact settled it on servile tenants; but in our present labourers who have their full days wages, for them to carry home wood or any other materials whereon they work, is no better than an open theft, which is certainly a sin for the hireling to commit, and as certainly a shame for the master to connive at.

FALMOTUM, *Falchesmota, Folkesmote, Folkmote.* From Sax. Folc, people, and Mote or ʒemoꞇe, a convention or assembly. So as the *Folkmot* was a popular convention of all the inhabitants of a city or town called a *Burgmote*, or of all the free tenants within a county called the *Schiremote*. Which solemn assembly in boroughs or towns upon extraordinary occasions, was to be convened by sound of bell called the Motbell. In the county Folkmote, all knights and free tenants did their fealty to the king, and elected the annual sheriff on Octob. 1, till this popular election was devolved to the king's nomination, an. 1315, 9 Edw. II. after which the city Folkmote was swallowed up in the common council, and the county Folkmote in the sheriff's turn and assises. The word *Folkmote* was sometimes of a less extent, and applied to any populous meeting, as of all tenants to the court leet or baron of their lord So to a charter of Wido de Meriton about 10 Hen. II. *Testes donationis sunt Fulco sacerdos de Meriton, Luvellus de Horsputh, et totum falmotum meorum hominum et suorum*, K. p. 120. Some remains of the word *Mote* and *Gemote* are in the Moot-house or council chamber in some towns. Moot-hall, Moot-case, Mooting, &c.

FANNATIO. The Fawning of does, or casting their young Fawns. From the Fr. *Faön*, a little kid, which Menagius deduces from the Gall. *Fan*, a child. Whence Pierce Ploughman, f. 37, uses the word Fauntekyns for little children.—" And confirmyn Fauntekyns." And to this seems owing the western term to Fang for a child, *i. e.* to be god-father or god-mother to that child: or in Somersetshire by the usual melting of *F* into *V*, to Vang, as He Vanged to me at the Vont. To the same original we may ascribe the word *Fangles* or *Vangles*, properly the baubles or play things of children that are proud to be new Fangled. From the Fr. *Faön* Du Fresne deduces the flesh *Faoneson*, venison, which in the Forest Charter of Rich. I. is called *Foinesun*. *Tempus vel mensis fannationis*, was the Fawning or the fence month, fifteen days before Midsummer and fifteen after: when great care was taken that no disturbance should be given to the does or to their young. —*Accederent ad malefaciendum tam tempore fannationis quam alio tempore*, K. p. 249.—*Tenentes de Brehull, Borstall. et Okle infra forestam prædicti manerii habent communem pasturam omnium averiorum—omnibus temporibus eis placentibus, præter cum capris bidentibus, et porcis ætatis unius anni in mense fannationis, videlicet quindecim ante festum Nativitatis S. Johannis Baptistæ et quindecim post*, K. p. 502.

FELONIA, *Felonum bona*. Felons' goods due to the king, and by him granted to the lords of mannors, &c.—*Cum messuagiis, gardinis, ædificiis, feloniis, eschaetis*, &c. K p. 412. The learned Spelman deduces the word Felon from Sax. Fælen and Felen, Teuton. *Faelen*, to Fail or offend. Or otherwise from Sa Feh or Feah, Fee or estate, and German *Lon*, value or price: as if Felony were the trespass of a vassal against his lord, to be punished by the loss of his fee, or the mulct of his whole estate. For all those offences which now come under the name of Felony, had pecuniary mulcts or *weres* and *weregilds* imposed on the committers, till King Henry I. an. 1108, inflicted death on thieves, and several statutes have since declared what crimes shall fall under the name and penalties of Felony. Hence the old *Fellown* and *Fell* cruel. *Felo de se*, a self murderer. To Feal in the North is to hide any thing surreptitiously gotten : as in the prov. He that feals can find. Our word Fellow seems to have had the worst sense of an associate in felony, which sense is still preserved in the proverb, Ask your fellow whither you be a thief.

FEODUM, *Feudum.* Any Fee, benefit, or profit. Sax. Feo, pea, peoh, stipend, gratituities, and other perquisites of any place or office.—*Johannes filius Nigelli habet in bosco domini regis housbote et heybote cum omnibus feodis forestario pertinentibus secundum assisam forestæ*, K. p. 266.—*Mandamus quod Henrico de Lacy, com. Linc. faciatis habere feodum suum quod percipere debet, et antecessores sui in com. Linc. percipere consueverunt ad Scaccarium*, K. p. 289, *Feoda* sometimes implied all the dues of scutage and other taxes in military service. *Qualiter extincta sunt feoda domini abbatis quæ ab ipso petita sunt patebit inferius*, K. p. 305. *Feodum habere*, to have or enjoy all the customary rights and profits of an office. As John Fitz-Nigel forestar of Bernwode—*debet habere feodum in bosco domini regis videlicet attachiamentum de spinis de bosco suo*, K. p. 209.

FEODUM *Militis vel militare.* A knight's fee, which by vulgar computation contained 480 acres, as 24 acres made a virgate, four virgates one hide, and five hides one knight's fee, for which the common relief was one hundred shillings. Yet no doubt the dimension was uncertain, and differed with times and places. In 3 King Steph. at Ottendon, *com.* Oxon. five virgates made the fourth part of a knight's fee, K. p 93.

FEODUM *Laicum.* A Lay-Fee, or land held in fee by a layman, in opposition to the tenure of *Frank-Almoigne* in religious houses.—*Abbas de Egnesham—pro habenda recognitione utrum duæ carucatæ terræ—sint laicum feodum Thomæ de S. Walerico, vel libera eleemosina pertinens ad abbatiam suam*, K. p. 168.

FEODARY, *Feodatarius.* The seneschal or prime steward, who received the customary fees of the lord, aids, reliefs, heriots, &c. An. 24 Hen. VI. " Robert Power, feodary of my lord the duke of Bokyngham, hath reseyved of Edmund Rede esquire xxv*s*. for a relyf, and v*s*. for a tenable eyde to the marriage of the heldyst daughter of my seyd lord for the fourth part of a knight's fee in Adyngrave," K. p. 655.

FEOFFAMENTUM. A Feoffment, or title by which a person is possest of an estate in fee to himself and his heirs. *De antiquo seu veteri feoffamento* was the tenure of lands held from the crown before the reign of Hen. II. and those lands in which the owners were afterwards enfeoffed, were called *De novo feoffamento.* So Richard de Camvil in 11 Hen. II. held the mannor of Middleton as one knight's fee, *De antiquo feoffamento,* K. p 121. An. 13, Hen. II. Henry de Oily held thirty-two knight's fees and a half of the old feoffment, and the twentieth part of a fee of the new feoffment, K. p. 125.

FEOFFARE *aliquem in terris.* To enfeoff a person or persons in an estate, as feoffees in trust, for a legal method of insuring or conveying the said estate to such persons or uses.—*Edwardus Rex, &c. Licentiam dedimus Johanni filio Nigelli quod de iis quæ de nobis tenet in capite feoffare possit Robertum de Harwedon, et ipsi Roberto ut dare possit et concedere, &c.* K. p. 338.

FERIÆ. Fairs, Sax. Fæʒeɲɲ, at first occasioned by the resort of people to the feast or dedication, and therefore in most places the fairs (by old custom, not by novel grant) are on the same day with the wake, or the festival of that saint to whom the church was dedicated, K. p. 611. And therefore kept often in church-yards, till by authority restrained, K. p. 613. From the solemn feasting at wakes and fairs, came the word Fare, provision, good fare: to fare well: *Farly* things, *i. e.* fine and curious things: *Farant* and *farantly* in the North, specious and handsome, as prov. Fair and Farantly. So *farand* in composition for a jolly festival humour, as prov. He is in a fighting-farand, *i. e.* He is flustred and in a fighting humour. And children when they are pert and witty beyond their years are said to be Aud-farand. And in our language those persons who got a high colour by eating and drinking, were said to have a red fare, as we say a red face.

FICTIO. Old Eng. *Feintise,* fraud or deceit: whence *feignt, faint, i. e.* false and deluding, as in old law terms a Faint action, a Faint pleading, &c. *Absque fictione,* without falshood or knavery, —*Qui carucas habuerunt arabunt terram domini in dicto manerio eodem modo et in tantum quo terram propriam absque fictione arare deberent,* K. p. 320.

FIRMA. A Farm or land and tenements hired at a certain rent. From Sax. Feoɲm, meat or entertainment; Feoɉ man, to feast or entertain. Whence Lat. *Firma,* for the reception and entertainment of the king, or any other lord and his retinue : as frequently in Doomsday book, a condition of tenure was *pro firma per unum diem,* or *pro firma unius noctis.* Whence *firma* signified the rent and profits of an estate, because in the Saxon and part of the Norman times, the rent of lands was paid in provisions, especially to the king, till Hen. II. for better conveniency altered the custom

GLOSSARY. 73

into an equivalent of mony, which pecuniary rent was still called *Firma Regis.* So Henry de Essex sheriff of Bucks. 4 Hen. II. *computavit de* lx *s. de firma regis in Brehul,* K. p. 114. Simon Fitz-Peter sheriff of Bucks. 5 Hen. II. accounted for lii *l.* xi*s.* ii*d, de veteri firma in Bruhella,* K. p. 115. From the Sax. Feoꞃm Fr. Junius does thus ingeniously and evidently derive the diet of sodden wheat called *Furmetie* and *Frometie,*—*Vulgus Anglorum nusquam (quod sciam) frumentie (quasi a frumento) sed receptissima ubique consuetudine* frometie *dicat, plane statuendum videtur cibum hunc propria voce primitus* ꞃeoꞃmetie *dictum a* ꞃeoꞃme *quod prima sua acceptatione olim denotabat edulia omnia ad victum necessaria:* ꞃeoꞃman *est victum præbere. Ab hoc igitur* ꞃeoꞃme *veteribus* ꞃeoꞃmecie *dictus videtur cibus quem prædia rustica facillime uberrimeque suppeditabant ad hospites prandio cœnave excipiendos.* And possibly to this original is owing the French *Fromage,* cheese ; and the Irish *Flummerie,* made of oatmeal.

AD FIRMAM *dare.* To Firm-let, or to let out for a reserved rent. Gilbert Basset concludes his foundation charter to the priory of Burcester—*Prædicti canonici supradictas ecclesias vel possessiones non debent dare vel pro alia ecclesia vel aliis possessionibus commutare, neque ad firmam dare,* K. p. 135. *Ad firmam perpetuam credere,* to let by copy-hold of inheritance at a stated quit rent and other reserves,—*Abbas et conventus Glocester. crediderint ad perpetuam firmam omnes decimationes, &c.* K. p. 223. *Idem* p. 344, 349. *Ad firmam tenere,* to hold a farm : so Robert Fitz-Simon of Meriton gives the Knights Templars *tres acras terræ in manerio de Meriton, quas acras Nicholaus Roc aliquando tenuit de me ad firmam,* K. p. 138. *Firmam reddere,* to pay a covenanted rent. King John let out his mannor of Brehul to Walter Borstard,— *Reddendo inde annuatim antiquam firmam, et de incremento* xl *s. pro omni servitio,* K. p. 194. *Tenere pro hac aut illa firma,* to hold for this or that rent. *Hugo de Plesseys concedit pro se et hæredibus suis, quod omnes homines teneant terras suas in eodem manerio pro eadem firma per quam eas prius tenere consueverunt,* K. p. 319. *Affirmatus,* Farmed out or let for a certain rent,— *Item de burgo affirmato* xxiii *l.*—*Item de hundreto affirmato* ix *l.* K. p. 354.

FIRMARIUS. A Farmer, or he that firmed or rented an estate, the tenant or occupier of it.—*Nigello Travers tunc firmario de Brehul,* K. p. 300. *Si tamen hujusmodi clausuræ in manibus tenentium seu firmariorum extiterint,* K. p. 609.

FIRMARE. To fortify,—*Licentiam dedimus Johanni de Handlo quod ipse mansum suum de Borstall juxta Brehull in com.* Buck. *muro de petra et calce firmare et kernellare possit,* K. p. 363.

FLESCHE-AXE. A cleaver with which butchers cut out their meat.—*Et in magna secure vocata flesch-axe* xv. *den.* K. p. 575. *Flesh* from Sax. Flæɟc, or more commonly ꝑlæc, which was not so properly the flesh of a living creature, as of a dead one when the skin was stript off. Whence to Flea or to Fleak, *i. e.* to pull off the skin. A school phrase, to be fleakt off, *i. e.* to have the skin fetcht off by whipping. A Flake is properly a piece of skin tore off the flesh, whence by metaphor a Flake of snow. Flaks or Flags in Norfolk are the turfs which they pare off from the surface of the earth. A Fleak in the North is a hurdle made of twigs that are shaved or stript of their rind. Fleaky, Flaggy, Flabby, is feeling soft like flesh. A Fleck is properly a sore in the flesh from whence the skin is rubbed off : whence by metaphor they use in Lincolnshire the word Flecked for spotted.

FOCALIA. Fuel, fire-wood. The prior and canons of Burcester allowed the vicar,—*quatuor bigatas lignorum pro focalibus de silva prioris vocata Priors wood,* K. p. 670.

FOENUM vertere. To turn grass or hay, K. p. 321. *Foenum tornare,* to turn grass or hay, K. p. 401. *Foenum levare,* to make hay, K. p. 321. *Foenum cariare,* to carry in hay, K. p. 321. *Foeni mulliones facere,* to make hay into cocks or pouts, K. p. 401.

FORAGIUM. Forage or fodder for horse or other cattle. Fr. *Forage, Forrage.* Lat. *Fodrum, Foderum,* from Sax. Foðꝛe, Island. *Foodur,* German *Futter.* Whence to Fodder cattle, *i. e.* to give them food or fodder : and by metaphor to Fodder a room, *i. e.* to throw things loose about it. To keep a Fodder or Fudder, *i. e.* to fling or scatter about.—The prior and canons of St. Frideswide gave to the vicar of Oakle *duo quarteria frumenti pro prebenda equi sui, et decimam foeni de Lathmede pro foragio,* K. p. 455.

FORERA, *Forreria.* A Foreland or Foreness, formerly called a Heavod-land, now a Head-land, or that part in a field whose end lies abutting on the side of another land.—*Fuit seisitus in manerio domini de una forreria in Alchester,* K. p. 469. Hence our Furrow from Sax. Fýꝛian, to plough : and possibly to this we owe the old word to Fure, to go, as prov. Whither fured you ? *i. e.* Whither went you ? (or rather to the Sax. Faꝛan.) And the Fourm of a hare, and a Form or seat.

FORESTARIUS. Forestar, or keeper of a forest, assigned by the king, or employed by knights and barons, who had lands and woods within the bounds of a forest.—*Rex præcipit quod omnes illi qui boscos habent intra metas forestæ domini regis, quod ponant idoneos forestarios in boscis suis,* K. p. 174. *Item præcipit quod sui forestarii curam capiant super forestarios militum et alio-*

rum, K. p. 174. No sale or waste to be made of the woods within the precincts of a forest without the view or livery of the Forestar,—*Boscus de Ernicote et boscus de Pydington fuerint afforestati post coronationem domini Henrici regis proavi domini regis nunc ad tale dampnum, quod nec ipsi nec eorum antecessores seu prædecessores per tempus prædictum usque nunc nichil de boscis prædictis capere potuerant, nisi per liberationem forestarii et ejus forestariorum voluntatem*, K. p. 370.

FORINSECUS. Outward or on the out-side,—*Excepto uno selione forinseco illius croftæ versus austrum ad faciendam quandam viam*, i. e. the outward ride or furrow for a common path.

FORINSECUM *servitium*. The payment of aid, scutage, and all other customary burdens of military service.—*Salvo forinseco servitio dominorum*, K. p. 229.—*Salvo forinseco servitio quantum pertinet ad dimidiam virgatam terræ*, K. p. 230.—*Salvo mihi et hæredibus meis forinseco servitio debito et consueto*, K. p. 235.—*Pro omnibus servitiis forinsecis, et intrinsecis curiarum sectis et omnibus secularibus demandis*, K. p. 345.

FORINSECUM *Manerium*. That part of a mannor which lies without the burg or town.—*Summa reddituum assisorum de manerio forinseco Banbury cum molendinis forinsecis.—Item de molendinis in Banbury*, K. p. 354.

FORSCHET, *Forescheta*. From Sax. Fop, before, and Sceat, a part or portion. The outer or fore-part of a furlong that lies toward the high way, to the quantity of about half an acre.—*Una acra et dimidia videlicet foreschet jacent ibidem*, K. p. 531.—*Partim inter Goldwell-furlong, et partim inter unam foreschet in Busthames-furlong*, K. p. 532.—*Hæc pecia terræ prioris vocatur Heralds-pece, et habet unam forschetam jacentem proxime juxta prædictam meram*, K. p. 535.—*Inter unam forschetam quam Hugo Bylendon tenet*, K. p. 537.—*Istæ tres dimidiæ acræ sunt foreschets et incipiunt furlong de Long-Cuttesworth*, K. p. 538.—*Hoc furlung incipit cum una forescheta*, ibid. As *Forschet* was a slip or small piece of land: so *Ferschet* was the customary payment for passage over a river, from Fæp, a journey or passage, Eie, water, and Sceat, a scot or tax, or equal part of payment. Whence a Ferrie or Ferry cross a river, Ferry-boat, for which passengers pay their fare. A fellow passenger was called a Fere.

FOSSATORUM *operatio*. The service of work and labour done by inhabitants and adjoining tenants for repair and maintenance of the ditches round a city or town: for which some paid a contribution called *Fossogium*. An exemption from this duty was sometime granted by special privilege. So King Hen. II. to the tenants within the honor of Walingford,—*Ut quieti sint de operationibus castellorum, et murorum, et fossatorum.* K. p. 114.

FRANCIPLEGIUM. *Visus Franciplegii.* From the Fr. *Frank*, free, and *plege*, a surety. The ancient custom for the free men of England at fourteen years of age to find surety for their truth and fidelity to the king, and good behaviour to their fellow subjects. This surety among the Saxons was taken in their Friborg or Tithing-court or Laþ, (which word Lath is still preserved in the court of bayliff and jurates of Romney-marsh convened at Dimchurch in Kent.) After the coming in of the Normans the custom was by them called Frank-plege, and was continued in the court leet of royal jurisdiction, to be held annually on the feast of St. Michael by Magna Charta, cap. 36. So that *habere visum franciplegii*, to have the view of Frank-pledge, was no more than to have the privilege of holding a court leet, the power of which was determined by the stat. 8 Edw. II. and 1 Edw. III.—This liberty granted to religious houses as the pertinence of such a mannor. *Ecclesia S. Georgii data fuit fratribus Osen. et habet ibidem visum franciplegii, et totum regale servitium,* K. p. 60.—Richard earl of Cornwall granted to the abby of Oseney, *Franciplegium de tota villa de Mixbury,* K. p. 211. A right inherent in the crown, and to be conveyed to a subject only by express charter. *Johannes filius Nigelli sen. summonitus fuit ad respondendum domino regi de placito quo waranto clamat habere visum Franciplegii de tenentibus suis in Borstall, qui ad dominum regem et coronam suam pertinet.—Johannes dixit quod ipse et antecessores sui a tempore quo non extat memoria extiterunt seisiti de prædicto visu, et quod ita sit petit quod inquiratur.—Et Gilbertus de Thornton qui sequitur pro rege dicit quod Franciplegium est quædam libertas regia mere spectans ad coronam et dignitatem domini regis contra quam longa seisina valere non debet, unde petit judicium,* K. p. 313. View of frankpledge to be held once a year, by the lord's bayliff or steward. *Ballivi comitis Gloucest. venient quolibet anno ad tenendum visum Franciplegii in eodem manerio,* K. p. 319.—*Ad visum suum tenendum prout mos singulis annis existit,* K. p. 331. At such court, twelve-pence was in some places levied by the steward in full of all dues. So at Knyttinton, *com.* Berc. *Seneschallus honoris S. Walerici tenuit unum visum per annum levando de eadem villata* xii. *denarios de recto visu pro omnibus,* K. p. 333. The place of holding such court was on some open green, except in rainy weather, when it was adjourned to the mannor-house, or the house of any tenant. *Fuit locus tenendi visum ibidem in quadam viridi placea in villa de Knyttinton,—et in tempore pluvioso per licentiam ballivi prioris aliquando seneschallus tenuit visum ibidem in curia prioris, et aliquando in domibus aliorum tenentium*, ib.

FRAYLE of figs. A basket in which figs are brought from Spain and other parts. Minshew derives the word from Lat. *Fragilis*. Skinner from the Italian *Fragli*, the knots and folding of the flags with which it is made. No doubt the name is owing to the language of that place from whence they are brought.—*Et in uno frayle ficuum* iii. *sol.* iv. *den.* K. p. 375.

FRATRES *Jurati*. *Vid*. SWORN-BROTHERS.

FRUMENTUM. Bread corn or wheat opposed to all other grain.—*Tria quarteria frumenti, tria quarteria avenarum, &c.* K. p. 291.—The canons of St. Frideswide allowed the vicar of Oakle, *quinque quarteria frumenti, et quinque quarteria ordei*, K. p. 455.

FRYTTYNG of wheels. Perhaps what we now call the Rinding of wheels, *i. e.* fitting and fastning the fellows, (or pieces of wood that conjointly make the circle) upon the spokes, which on the top are let into the fellows, and at the bottom into the hub.—*In solutis pro fryttynge quinque rotarum hoc anno* vii *den.* K. p. 574.

FUNDATOR. Founder of a religious house. This title was not only given to the first actual founders, but continued to those barons and knights who held the fee of the estates given to those monasteries, and were the patrons of them, K. p. 60. And if after the extinction or long intermission of this title, any person could prove his direct descent from the prime founder, he was assumed by the religious to the name and honour of their founder. So the convent of Augustine friers at Oxford,—*Edmundum Rede et hæredes suos in fundatorem dictæ domus suscepimus ac admisimus de jure sibi adquisito ex præfato lineali descensu*, K. p. 637. And accordingly received him with solemn procession, *ib.*

FURCA. A Fork to gather up and pitch hay and straw; called in old Eng. a *Gib*, whence the *Furca*, gallows, Sax. Galʒa, was called a Gibbet. A nut hook in the North is a Gibbon. A quarter-staff is a Gib-staff. And in Sussex a Gibbet is any great cudgel which they throw up in trees to beat down the fruit. A hanging-coat that was cast over the shoulders, and hung down with two long sleeves, was called a Gipe and a Gippo, and Gippon. The *Furca* in the Roman agriculture was the twist or forked piece of wood, which they set under the rods or fore-part of the *plaustrum* to bear it up, which in the North they now call a Nape or Neap. —*Furcare carectam*, was I suppose to hang a waggon, or to fit the body of it to hang upon the axel and wheels.—*Allocantur eisdem pro Richardo Plumbario furcante carectam per* xii. *dies.* iii *s.*—*et pro Johanne Bowdon furcante carectam per unum diem* iii *d.* K. p. 550.

FURENDELLUS, *Fardella, Ferlingus.* A Fardingel, Fartundel, or Ferling of land, *i. e.* the fourth part of an acre, which in Wiltshire is now called a Fardingale: and in other parts a Farthindale, from Sax. Feorð, fourth, and Del or beal, a part. Whence a farthing or fourth part of a penny. And in the north a Furendel or Frundel of corn is two gawns or gallons, *i. e.* the fourth part of a bushel.—Hugh Richards of Borstall granted to John de Handlo— *unum furendellum prati in Bradmoor,* K. p. 339. Which fourth part of an acre is in the east riding of Yorkshire called a Stang.

FURNUS. An oven.—*Johannes le Baker et Christina uxor ejus tenent quatuor domos cum curtilagiis et unum furnum cum secta custumaria ad eundem, i. e.* one publick oven in a common bakinghouse, with the custumary profits of it. For the tenants were formerly obliged as to grind their corn at such a mill, so to bake their bread at such an oven, and to pay *furnagium,* Furnage, or such a custom for baking, as toll for grinding. The word *Furnus* is now translated from an oven to a Furnace.

G.

GABALUM, *Gabulum, Gablum.* From Goth. ГІБЛΛ. Island. *Gabl,* German *Geehvel,* Dutch *Gevel,* Eng. Gavell and Gabell, the head or end or extreme part of a house or building. As the Gablehead, the Gavle-end.—*Quandam particulam terræ—extra gablum molendini octo pedes in latitudine,* K. p. 201.—*Quæ domus sita est inter gabulam tenementi mei et gabulam tenementi Laurentii Kepeharm,* K. p 286.—*Quod situm est inter messuagium quod Robertus le Webb aliquando tenuit, et gablam capitalis messuagii quod H. Haber aliquando tenuit,* K. p. 395. Hence a wide *gabling* room.

GALLUS *silvestris.* A woodcock.—*Et in octo gallis silvestribus emptis et datis domino Lestraunge ad Octab. Epiphaniæ* xii. den. K. p. 578.

GALLYS, *Galls.* From Sax. Gealla, German and Island. *Gall.* —*In solutis suppriori pro coprose et gallys emptis pro encausto* ii. den. K. p. 574.

GAPPE. A breach or Gap in a hedge.—*Alia roda jacet ad inferius capud del Oldedich juxta le Gappe,* K. p. 397. From Sax. Geapan, to open or to Gape, Dan. *Gaber.* Whence our Eng. to Gabber. *i. e.* to open the mouth without articulate sound. Thence Goth. *Guepstock,* in the northern English a Gobstick, a spoon. To Gobble, to open the mouth wide and swallow greedily any gob, or goblet, or gobbet.

GARBA. A sheaf of corn, of which twenty-four made a thrave. From Fr. *Gerbe* and *Garb.*—*Posito ad caput ejus frumenti mani-*

pulo quem patria lingua Seaf (alias Sceaf) dicimus, Gallice vero Garbam. Mat. West. p. 166. It extended to a cock of hay, a faggot of wood, or any other bundle of the fruits or product of the earth. Manasser Arsic baron of Coges gave to the priory at Coges two garbs of tithe at Fritwell, while the third garb was only paid to the parish priest, K. p. 81. Which two garbs were resigned by the prior of Coges to the prior of St. Frideswide, in consideration of two shillings yearly rent, K. p. 123.—*Custumarius dominæ in autumpno, si sit ligator, ad dictas precarias habebit unam garbam seminis de ultimo blado ligato,—Et quoties ligator habet prandium, non habebit garbam,* K. p. 401. Within the mannor of Pidington,—*In autumpno qui operantur super proprium custum, omnes et singuli ligatores herbarum habebunt unam garbam ad vesperam,* K. p. 496. Hence a Gerbe in heraldry. Garbage, any collection, especially of filth, as guts and Garbage. The dust and sullage of drugs and spices is called the Garbles in stat. 21 Jac. I. cap. 19. The officer whose duty it was to Garble spices or to separate the dregs and refuse, is called the Garbler of spices, 21 Jac. I. cap. 9. And the Garbling of bow-staves was choosing out the best, and throwing aside those which were of no use or service, stat. 1 Rich. III. cap. 11. And possibly from hence by metaphor the choicest garment was called a Garb, from which the person was said to be in a neat or handsome garb. What we call a sheaf of arrows, was formerly a Garb of arrows, which by the laws of Rob. I. king of Scotland, was to consist of twenty-four arrows.

GARCIO. Any poor young servile lad or boy-servant. Fr. *Garcon.* It seems of old Gallick or British original; for in the present Irish *Garsun* is an appellative for any servant. In all the churches appropriated to the abby of Oseney,—*Canonici vicario clericum invenient—et ipsi vicario similiter Garconem invenient ipsius obsequio deputatum, quos in omnibus suis expensis procurabunt,* K. p. 304.—*Et in datis Willielmo Skynner garconi de pistrina ex curialitate falcatorum per x. dies xii. den.* K. p. 576.— *Et in solutis Thomæ Takkele adducenti quendam garconem nuper servientem Johannis Grene ad castrum Oxon. in ebdomeda Natalis Domini, quia convenit servire priori, et non implevit,* K. p. 577.

GELD. Any tax or imposition. From Goth. ΓIΛd, Sax. Gelb, German *Gelt.* In the North they still call the rate paid for the agistment of cattle Nowt-geld or Neot-geld. The mint-master of Walingford had his house free from Geld, while he coined mony, K. p. 54. Whence Lat. *Geldare,* Sax. Gelban, to pay taxes: whence by liquefaction to Yield or pay. To Gelt or extort a man's mony from him: and possibly by metaphor to Geld or castrate.—*Quietum esse a geldis* was a special privilege. So King

Hen. II. granted to the tenants within the honor of Walingford, —*ut quieti sint de geldis et danegeldis*, K. p. 114. Hence the Lat. *Gilda*. Eng. Gild, a fraternity or society, who Gelded or paid all publick charges out of a common stock, and were called *Gildones* and *Congildones*, and made their Gilden or publick feast in a Gild-hall or Guild-hall : of which John Bale in his Preface to the Journey of Johan Leland, 12ᵐᵒ an. 1599, writes thus : "This most worthy commodyte of your countrey, I mean the conservacyon of your antiquytees, and of the worthy labours of your lerned men. I thynke the renown of such a notable acte wolde have much longer endured than of all your belly banketts and table triumphes, either yet out of your newly purchased haules to kepe S. Georges feste, *i. e.* Gylde-hawles."

Gersuma, *Guersuma*. Sax. Geapɲuma, which Mr. Somner derives from the old Sax. Geaɲo, ready, and Sum or ɲome, as if ready mony. *Gersum* signified any expence or payment, but was commonly used for the ready mony or other valuable consideration paid in hand, to bind or confirm any bargain, which we call Ernest. —*Pro hac concessione dedit dictus Richardus duas marcas argenti in gersumam*, K. p. 125.—*Pro hac mea donotione—dedit mihi prædictus Johannes in gersuma quadraginta solidos sterlingorum*, K. p. 178, 194, 225, 325.

Gore. A small narrow slip of ground.—*Duæ rodæ jacent juxta viam scilicet le Gores super sholefurlong*, K. p. 393.—*Una acra et dimidia jacent simul ibidem, et vocantur quinque Gores*, K. p. 532.—*Una acra cum uno Gore*, K. p. 534. The Lat. *Gors*, Eng. *Gort* and *Guort*, which occur in the Doomsday-book, are by Spelman interpreted a narrow part of a river, or weer for the catching of fish. And a Gord of water is by Gouldman explained to be a narrow stream of water. Hence a slip of cloth sewed into any garment we call a Gore, and Gorette and Gusset. The old Fr. and Eng. *Gort, guort,* and *gorz,* Lat. *Gordus,* are by Dû Fresne deduced from Lat. *Gurges*, whence the French and English borrow their *gorge*, a throat, to be Gorged or over-fed, a Gorget, to wear under the throat or round the neck. G..re-bellied, fat and corpulent, &c.

Grangia. A Granary or Grange : commonly taken for the country farm and out-houses where the religious reposited their corn. *Ordinavimus eidem vicario nostro tresdecim quarteria bladi boni percipienda de grangiis prædictæ ecclesiæ per annum*, K p.455. But more properly taken for any barn with a thres ing-floor.—*In hebdomade proxime post festum S. Martini quilibet virgatarius terræ arabit domino tres rodas terræ, et etiam intrabit grangiam domini ad semen dictæ terræ triturandum*, K. p. 496. In Lincolnshire they call every lone-house, or farm that stands alone by itself, a Grange.

GRAS-HEARTH. The customary service for all the inferiour tenants to bring their ploughs, and do one day's work for the lord within four days after Michaelmass.—*Quando autem facient consuetudines sive redditus, venient omnes carucæ infra villam de Pydinton ad arandam terram domini uno die quem eligere voluerit ballivus infra quatuor dies proxime post festum S. Michaelis per summonitionem ballivi vel præpositi quod vocatur* Gras-Hearth, K. p. 496.—*In eodem manerio—præpositus erit quietus ab omni servitio pro labore præter* Gras-hurt, K. p. 497. Goth. ΓΚΛS, Sax. Gæpy and Gρæy, whence what we commonly call Grass is in some northern parts called Gers.

GRAVA. Sax. Gpæy, a Grove.—Thomas de Druesval gave to the abby of Egnesham,—*quandam gravam juxta Epelhanger, et quandam insulam proximam villæ de Stoches, et servitium quod Adam de Wodecote fecit ei in dicta grava et insula,* K. p. 329. Whence a Grovette or Grotte, or Grotto.

GRAVEN-HILL. The hill of graves or sepulture of the dead. Sax. Gpæy, a Grave, Island. *Grafa,* to digg, Goth. ΓΚΛБΛΝ, whence to Grub or digg up. A Gripe or Grip or ditch, which in Lincolnshire is called a Grove, in southern parts a Grippe and a Grindlet, in the North a Grupe. Hence to be Groveling on the ground. To Grave or cut in wood or metal or stone. A Groove or Grove, a furrow or deep line struck by a joiner.

GROPYS. Hooks and irons belonging to a cart or waggon. From Sax. Gρupan, to take or hold: whence to Gripe or hold fast, Griping or covetous, to Grope or feel out, to Graple or fasten with Grapling-irons, in old Eng. Grapenels.—*Et in clavis carectatis gropys et aliis ferramentis emptis Oxon. de Johanne Mylton yrenmonger* xii. *sol.* iv. *den.* K. p. 574. They have an iron hook fastned to the axis with a short chain, to hook upon a stave of the wheel, to keep it from turning round on the descent of a hill, which they call skidding of a wheel, Lat. *rotam sufflaminare.*

GROSSUS, *Conducere in Grosso,* to hire a workman by the great, for performing such a work without computing the time.—*Et Willielmo Hykkedon conducto in grosso ad mensam domini ad dolandum et perficiendum le cresi super cancellum prioratus ibidem* xxiv. *sol.* K. p. 575. *Grossus denarius,* a Groat.

GUERRA. Publick war or private dissension. From Sax. Geρ, arms or weapon.—*Quantum inde habuit ante guerram, et disseisitus est occasione ipsius guerræ,* K. p. 184. Thence to warn, *i. e.* to challenge.

GULA AUGUSTI. The calends or first day of August, the festival of St. Peter *ad vincula*. Durandus suggests a reason of the name from a young lady being cured on that day of a quinsie in her throat by kissing the chains of St. Peter. But perhaps *Gula Augusti* signified the first day of that month only, as *gula* was the mouth or entrance of any thing. As *gula fluvii*, the mouth of a river, &c. *Die sabbati post gulam Augusti*, K. p. 228.

GWAYF, *Waif, Waivium*. Such goods as felons, when pursued, cast down and leave in the high way, which become a forfeiture to the king or lord of the mannor, unless the right owner legally claim or challenge them within one year and a day,—*Recognitum est militibus et liberis hominibus—quod ad nos spectat le Gwayf, &c. Ita et statim redditum est nobis le Gwayf le Ernicot scilicet ii. porci cum v. porcellis*, K. p. 196.

H.

HABUNDA. Abundance, plenty.—*Receptis de caseo et butiro, et eo minus propter habundam casei maximam*, K. p. 548.

HAIA. A Hedge, from Sax. Hegge, bæg, in Lincolnshire a Haok. Hence in Kent a Haw, *i. e.* a small close hedged in. A Haw-thorn, *i. e.* a hedge-thorn. Haws, or in the north Hughes, the fruit of that thorn. The Hagge or Hatch of a door. Hedk a door in the north. The Hatches of a ship. As from the Lat. *Haia*, Hey-bote or Hedge-bote, *i. e.* liberty for taking wood for reparation of fences. A Hay or net to take conies. To dance the Hay, &c. Proverb in Chaucer, "Nether busk nor hay," *i. e.* Neither wood nor hedge.—*Terras et tenementa cum aquis haiis fossatis, &c.* K. p. 274. *Cum gardinis, curtilagiis, pratis, haiis, muris, fossatis*, K. p. 389.

HAKE. A sort of fish dried and salted, called Poor-John. In the west parts, Haket, from Sax. hacod. A prov. in Kent, "As dry as a Hake."—*Et in tribus copulis viridis piscis, cum uno viridi lynge, cum tribus congere, et cum una copula de hake*, K. p. 575.

HAMMA. From Sax. Ham, a house. Hence what we call Home they term Hame in the north, and Hamely for Homely. To this we owe the termination of so many English places in Ham, as Buckingham, &c. Hence a Hamlet, a collection of houses,—*Blakethorn quæ est hamlettum in parochia de Ambresdon*, K. p. 346. But as Haya was both a house, a hedge, and a close; so Ham or Heam had all those acceptations. It sometimes signified a hedge, whence to Hem in or to enclose, the Hem or outward border of a garment. It farther signified a small croft or enclosed meadow.—*Quoddam pratunculum quod vocatur Hamma*, K. p. 195. Qua-

GLOSSARY.

Subr. acras prati in gore juxta hamam Gilberti, K. p. 176. *Dimidiæ acræ prati propinquioris prato nostro quod vocatur Gilberdsham*, K. p. 177.—*quoddam pratum domini mei quod vocatur Kinsith-heam*, K. p. 188. *Computant de sex solidis octo denariis receptis de duobus hammys prati in campo de Wendleburg*, K. p. 572.

HASTA porci. A shield of brawn.—*Johanna de Musegrave tenet terras in Blecherdon de domino rege per servitium deferendi domino regi unam hastam porci pret.* iid, *cum fugaverit in parco suo de Cornburie*, K. p. 450.

HAVEDELOND. From Sax. Heapod. A Head-land, now commonly a Had-land, whence the Head-way or Had-way.—*Item una pecia terræ jacet ibidem cum Havedelonds, et jacet pro duabus acris et dimidia,* K. p. 585. *In superiore fine acræ S. Edburgæ jacent quatuor brode-londs quas alii vocant Prestes-haved-londs,* K. p. 537.

HEKFORE. An Heifer, which in the east riding of Yorkshire is called a Whee or Whey, and in some midland parts a Twinter, i. e. of two winters. And in Oxfordshire a splai'd heifer is termed a Martin.—*Computant de xii. denariis receptis de debili vitulo cujusdam hekfore vendito Johanni Grene,* K. p. 548. *Vid.* BOVICULA.

HELOWE-WALL. The Hell-wall or end wall that covers and defends the rest of the building. From Sax. helan, to cover, Scotch Hele, in north Wales Hilio. Hence in the north of England the Hylling of a bed, *i. e.* the bed-cloaths or covering, which our Oxford bed-makers call the Healings. Whence in Kent to Heal up a child in a cradle, or any other person in a bed: and in some parts to Heal a house is to cover the top. And in the West, the workman who covers a house with slatts or tiles, is called a Hellier or Healer: whence to Heal a wound, *i. e.* to cover it with skin: and by metaphor to Heal any sickness, to be Hail and Healthy. In some northern parts Helow or Helœ is bashful, or close and reserved, with a face covered. To the same original are owing the Hulls, or cods, or coverings of beans, pease, &c. the Hulls or chaff of other corn: Helmet or covering of the head. A Helm in the North, *i. e.* a Hovel or any covered place. Possibly the Healm or Hawm with which they thatch or cover houses. To Sheal or uncover, as the Shealing of beans, pease, &c. A Shel or outward covering. In the North to Shel or Sheal milk is to curdle it, or separate the pasts. Hollen in the North is a wall set before dwelling-houses to secure the family from the blasts of wind rushing in when the block or door is open: to which wall on that side next the hearth is annext a sconce or screne of wood or stone.—*In solutis eidem dominæ pro quodam Helowe-wall unius domus apud Curtlyngton annuatim ii. den.* K. p. 573.

HEN. Old: whence Henshaw in Cheshire is by Leland derived from Sax. Hen, old, and Shaw a wood. Henley in Oxfordshire, which Dr. Plot thinks to be so denominated from Hen and Lley, a place, being the old town of the Ancalites in the time of Julius Cæsar, K. p. 2. So *Gual-Hen, Vallum Antiquum,* now Walingford in the opinion of Humph. Lluyd, K. p. 5.

HERBAGIUM. Herbage or grass, especially to be cut or mowed. *Salvo mihi et hæredibus meis herbagio dicti stagni, et herbagio ex altera parte aquæ, quantum aliquis homo pro profunditate aquæ poterit metere,* K. p. 201. *Herbagium anterius* the first crop, in opposition to after-math. *Dicunt quod est communis via, et sua communis pastura, quum foenum et anterius herbagium amoveantur,* K. p. 459.

HERCIARE. To Harrow. Hercia, an harrow, from *Herpex, Herpicia,* contracted *Hercia.—Homines manerii de Hedingdon solos equos habentes terram domini ibidem herciabunt, et per duos dies in quadragesima similiter arabunt, et herciabunt,* K. p. 320. *In manerio de Pydinton omnes virgatarii terræ arabilis per quatuor dies per totum annum—venient cum uno equo et uno crate ad herciandam terram domini quousque plene perseminetur,* K. p. 496. *Et allocantur pro tribus novis cratibus emptis ad herpicandum,* K. p. 549. Thence to Harry and Hurry, to be Harried and Hurried up and down, Harast.

HEREMITORIUM. A Hermitage, which signified strictly a convent of hermites, or frier minors, who under the institution and discipline of Fr. Paul inhabited desart and solitary places.—*Johannes Stokton prior conventus Oxon. ordinis fratrum heremitarum Sancti Augustini,* K. p. 672. But secondly, this name was attributed to any one religious cell, built and endowed in some private and recluse place, and then annext to some larger abby, of which the prelate or governour was called *Heremita.* So Ralph the Hermite built a hermitage in a close retirement at Musewell, with a chappel dedicated to the Holy Cross, annext to the abby of Missenden, K. p. 74. King Hen. II. gave the hermitage of Finemere, which was of the fee of Rowland Malet of Queinton, to the abby of St. Marie's Noteley in Crendon *com.* Buck. K. p. 118. King Hen. III. gave the hermitage of St. Werburg at Brehul to the prior and canons of Chetwode, K. p. 246. King Edw. III.— *Rex omnibus &c. Licentiam dedimus—Nicholao Jurdan de Burcester Heremitæ custodi capellæ beati Johannis Baptistæ de Burcester quod ipse quoddam hospitale—apud Burcester de novo fundare possit,* K. p. 478.

HERESYVE. From Sax. Ðæp, Island. *Haar,* and Sax. Sȳfe, a Hair-sive. *Et in uno heresyve empto ad pistrinam ibidem x. den.* K. p. 574.

HĒRIETUM, *Heriotum, Hariotum.* SAX. heɲʒeat, from heɲe, an army, and Geat, a march or expedition. For heriots were first paid in military arms and horses: which proportion of horse and armour according to the different quality of the deceased, was settled by the laws of King Canute, cap. 69, and is still commonly the best riding horse of which a tenant dies possest. Heriot-service was a reserve by charter or other conveyance, and made one condition of the tenure of estates in fee simple, which is now for the most part extinguisht. Heriet-custom, when a tenant for life was by custom obliged to such payment at his death; which payment to be made not only by the next heir in blood, (as a relief was only due) but by any the next successor. It was the practise of our devout ancestors to have a heriet paid to the parish priest, which was commonly the best horse of the deceased, led before the corps, and delivered at the place of sepulture, of which piety several instances are given by Dugdale, Antiq. Warwic. p. 680. This no doubt was one sort of soulcheat or legacy to the church, for satisfaction of all tithes and dues ignorantly detained In abbies of royal patronage, at the death or cession of an abbat, his cup and horse were paid for a heriet to the king.—*Cum ex consuetudine approbata et obtenta habere consueverimus palefridos et cuppas episcoporum et abbatum regni cedentium et decedentium,* Prynne, Histor. Collect. tom. 2, p. 834.—*Abbas de Oseneia obiit anno regni Regis Edwardi* 25.—*Petiit eschaetor ad opus domini regis cupam et palefridum dicti abbatis defuncti, et etiam lanas bidentum ejusdem abbatiæ de tempore vacationis,* K. p. 330. Those who held in bondage or villenage paid a heriet. *In manerio de Wrechwyke— Juliana Hardy quæ tenuit de domino unum messuagium et unam virgatam terræ in bondagio diem clausit extremum, et accidit domino nova herieta,* ii *boves, pret.* xvi *s.* K. p. 456. *Robertus Hikes tenens domini de Wrechwyke qui tenuit in bondagio—diem clausit extremum, et accidit domino nova heriota, unus bos pret.* viii*s. et una vacca pret.* v *s.* K. p. 458. *Willielmus Foul qui de domino tenuit— apud Wrechwyke in bondagio, diem clausit extremum, et debentur domino nominibus heriettæ et mortuarii* ii. *vaccæ pret.* xii *s.* K. p. 470. *In manerio de Pidington siquis villanus morietur super feodo domini, dabit domino meliorem bovem suum, ita scilicet, quod sustentabit uxorem ejus in domo et terra quamdiu vixit, si teneat se viduam, sive occasione nemo maritabit filiam suam sine licentia domini,* K. p. 496. The religious appropriators reserved the Live Heriets, *i.e* such as were paid in cattle, to themselves; and allowed the Inanimate Heriets, as of less value, to the poor vicar. So in the endowment of the vicarage of Oakle, the prior and canons of St. Frideswide— *Ordinavimus eidem vicario universa herieta inanimata,* K. p. 455.

And some appropriators exacted a Herlot from every dying vicar, as a badge of servile subjection to them.—*Vicarius de Cestreton post ejus decessum dabit heriettam rectori et conventui domus de Askerugge,* K. p. 543.

HEYBOTE. From Sax. Đay, a hedge, and Bote, repair or emendation. The liberty of cutting so much underwood and bushes within the premises as is necessary for mending and maintaining the fences or hedges. John Fitz Nigel forestar of Bernwode had *in dominico bosco domini regis Husebote et Heybote pro custodia divtæ forestæ,* K. p. 209. *Vid.* HUSBBOTE.

HIDE of Land. Not as Polydore Virgil fancies, from the hide of a beast, as if an English hide of land were like the extent of Carthage, *Quantum taurino possint circundare tergo.* But from Sax. Dyð, a house or habitation, from Dýban, to cover. The word was sometime taken for a house, as we still preserve the word Hutte for a cottage. And what Bede calls *Familias* (which *Familia* seems to have been a circuit of ground sufficient for the maintenance of a family) his Saxon interpreter King Alfred calls Ðybelanðer. The quantity of it was afterwards described to be as much as was sufficient to the cultivation of one plough. *Hida Anglice vocatur terra unius aratri culturæ sufficiens,* whence our term of plough-land. The quantity of a hide was never expresly determined. Gervase of Tilbury makes it one hundred acres. The Malmsbury MS. cited by Spelman computes it at ninety-six acres, one hide four virgates, and every virgate twenty-four acres. And yet the history of the foundation of the abby of Battle (Mon. Ang. tom. 1, p. 313) makes eight virgates go to one hide. But Polydore Virgil blunders most, who reduces a hide to twenty acres. The truth seems to be, that a hide, a yard-land, a knight's fee, &c. contained no certain number of acres, but varied according to different places. In the Doomsday Inquisition the first enquiry was how many hides, K. p. 65. One hide of land at Chesterton 15 Hen II. contained sixty-four acres, K. p. 125. The yearly value of a hide of land in Blechesdon was fourty shillings in 35 Hen. III. K. p. 244.

HIDAGIUM. Any royal aid or tribute to be raised in such a proportion upon every hide of land. Will. Conq. an. 1084, imposed six shillings on every hide; William Rufus four; and King Hen. I. three shillings. To be exempted from this common tax was a peculiar privilege granted to the tenants within the honor of Wallingford,—*Ut quieti sint de geldis et danegeldis et de hidagio,* K. p. 114. When the lord paid Hidage to the king, the tenants paid a proportion to the lord of the mannor,—*Prior et bursarius de Burcester computant de liii. sol. iv. den. receptis de redditu in Arnesate cum hidagio ibidem hoc anno,* K. p. 571.

HILL. Though by this word we now commonly mean any rising ground, yet some would have it restrained to such risings as were occasioned by the burial of the dead, as barrows and tumuli. As the word Hell, which though now appopriated to the place of the damned, yet at first signified no more than a grave, from Helam to cover, K. p. 37. Whence Island. *Hel* is death.

HOBELERS, *Hobelarii.* A sort of light horsemen, who rode on small nimble horses, with light armour, which made them fitter for any expeditious service, like our present dragoons. The word is commonly supposed to come from their Hobbys or small horses; which Casaubon, Fr. Junius, and others deduce from Gr. Ἵππος; yet Sir James Ware, Antiq. Hiber. cap. 7, says they were Irish horses, and so called from their easie pace. Hence we still call a little nag a Hobby, a Hobby-horse, and our plough-men to some one of their cart-horses generally give the name of Hobin, the very word which Phil. Comines uses, Hist. l. 6, cap. 7. And therefore the Hobelers were by the French, or rather by the Armoricans, called Hobiners. Fourty men at arms and thirty Hobelers, K. p. 459. The Lat. *Huba* and *Hoba* signified a countrey-house or small cottage, from Sax. Hope, Teuton. *Hoff*, modern German *Hoëva*, Eng. Hovel. Whence the Coloni, ceorls or clowns, were called *Hobarii*, to which we owe the name of Country-hobs, Plough-hobbers, now Plough-jobbers, Hobbernouls now Jobbernouls, or jolt-headed country fellows. To the same Huba possibly we owe the Hub of a wheel, a Hubbub or confused clamour, &c.

HOKE. A Hook, nook, or corner. *Sic usque le hoke versus le frereslone*, K. p. 324. The Lat. *Huchia*, in Picardy and Scotland *Huche*, Eng. Hutch, was a long wooden box, from whence possibly a Huckster, who carried about goods to sell in such a box; and perhaps things are thence said to be laid or kept in Huggermugger.

HOKEDAY. The Tuesday fortnight after Easter day, celebrated with sports and rejoycing in memory of the Danes being killed on that day, and expelled this island, an. 1002, under King Ethelred. Mr. Lambart makes it Ꝺucxꞇueyꝺeᵹ, *dies Martis irrisorius.* Spelman from German *Hocken*, to besiege or to bind. But possibly Hokeday was no more than Heaᵭæᵹ, high-day. Sax. Ꝺea, Fr. *Haut*, corrupted into Hock and Hog, as *Haut-goust* into Hogo.— *Item inter Hokeday et diem S. Martini bene possunt ibidem ducenta quadraginta multones sustentari ad opus domini ad terram suam compostandam*, K. p. 495.

HOMINES. All sort of feudatory tenants. They claimed a privilege of having their causes and persons tried only in the court of their lord. When Gerard de Canvil, 5 Richard I. was charged with treason and other high misdemeanors, he pleaded that he was *Homo Comitis Johannis*, and would stand to the law or justice of his court; K. p. 152.

HOMAGIUM. The duty of submission and profest dependance made by every *Homo* or feodal tenant, at first accession to an estate held from a superiour lord. The manner of paying this Homage was determined by the stat. 17 Edw. II. If the lord accepted the homage, it was a concession of the tenant's right.—*Optulit ei Bernardus homagium, sed recusante abbate Godefrido. Robertus secundus episcopus Lincolniæ suscepit illud, salvo jure abbatis et conventus de Egnesham*, K. p. 133.

HOSTIÆ. Consecrated wafers in the holy eucharist or Host. Isabel countess of Albemarle confirmed to the convent of Burcester five quarters of bread corn,—*ad hostias faciendas in domo prædicta*, K. p. 270. From this Lat. *Hostia* Mr. Somner deduces the Sax. Dujel, the Lord's Supper, and Dujlian, to administer that sacrament, and old Eng. to Housal, to receive it. And hence no doubt the old word Oste, the altar, and Oste-clothe, the altar-cloth, both which are transferred by metaphor to the top of a kiln for drying malt, and to the hair-cloth on which the malt is laid.

HOSTRICUS. From Lat. *Astur*, a goshawk. The mannor of Broughton, *com*. Oxon. in the reign of Edw. II. was held by John Mauduit—*In capite per serjantiam mutandi unum hostricum domini regis, vel illum hostricum portandi ad curiam domini regis*, K. p. 569.

HUNDREDUS. The word not only used for the division of it self, but for the levy or contribution paid to the *hundredarius* or chief constable of every hundred for better support of his office. From which imposition some persons were exempted by special privilege. So Hen. II. to Bernard de S. Walery,—*ut terræ suæ sint quietæ de scyris et hundredis*, K. p. 123. *Secta hundredi* was to pay a personal attendance, and do suit and service at the hundred court held in some places once in three weeks, and in others once a month. *Bardulphus de Cestreton debet sectam ad hundredum de Chadlinton de tribus septimanis in tres septimanas*, K. p. 318. By the stat. 14 Edw. III. these hundred courts were reduced to the county courts, yet some few hundreds have their old franchises remaining. *Hundredus affirmatus*, the profits of a hundred court firmed out for a standing rent. *Item de burgo affirmato* xxiii*l*. *Item de hundreto affirmato*— K. p. 354.

HUSEBOTE. From Sax. Duy, a house, and Bote, amends or repair. The liberty of cutting as much wood on the premises as is necessary for the support and repair of the farm-house and adjoining buildings.—*Concessi prædictæ Alesiæ heybotum et housbo-*

tum in dominicis boscis meis de Acle, K. p. 259.—*De antiqua consuetudine tenentes de Pidington habent Housbote et Heybote in bosco domini per licentiam domini, et per visum ballivi ejus,—Et si boscus domini abeat in vastum, tum acquietabunt dominum de prædictis Housbote et Heybote,* K. p. 497. We now call it *Estovers,* or *Rationabile Estoverium, quod duplex est ædificandi et ardendi.* Coke on Littleton, f. 41. Whence Stover in Sussex is used for the fodder of cattle. From Sax. Bote comes our Eng. no Boot, *i. e.* no profit. What Booteth it? *i. e.* to what purpose. To give to Boot, *i. e.* to give odds as in compensation. Bote, a remedy, as Chaucer, " Bote of his bale," *i. e.* remedy of his grief.

I.

ILLUSIO *mandati.* An evasion or contemptuous omission of any order or command.—*In nostri contemptum manifestum, et mandatorum nostrorum illusionem,* K. p. 335.

IMPANALARE. To impanel or return upon a jury. From Lat. *Panella,* which, says Spelman, is properly *Pagella, atque inde deducta* g *in* n *transeunte.* More naturally a contraction of *Paginella,* which was the narrow scroll or slip of paper or parchment, whereupon the sheriff wrote the names of the jurors. As Fortescue de Laud. Leg. Ang. cap. 25. *Vicecomes retornabit breve prædictum coram justitiariis una cum panello nominum eorum (Juratorum) quos ipse ad hoc summonivit.* It is a sorry supposition of Sir Edward Coke, Gloss. ad Littleton, sect. 234. " Panel is an English word, and signifieth a little part, for a pane is a part, and a panel is a little part."—*Non ponatur nec impanaletur in aliquibus assisis, juratis, recognitionibus, &c.* K. p. 657. Hence the counter-Pane of an indenture, or the duplicate responding sheet. The cover or counter-Pan of a bed. A Pane and Pannel in glass and wainscote. The brain-Pan. A Pan or broad plate, now commonly an earthen dish. A Pan-cake, not because made in a pan, but in the fashion of a panella: as a marche Pane, *i. e.* a sugar-cake. In the North a Pan in building is a term of architecture for that piece of timber which lies on the top of a wall, to which the bottoms of the spars or rafters are fastned; which in timber buildings is commonly called the Rasen, or Resen or Resening. Thence to Pan, *i. e.* to close or join together. As prov. " Weal and women cannot pan, but wo and women can." Dr. Skinner gives this silly derivation, Pannell *à* Lat. *Pannus, q. d. Pannellus, metaphora a segmento panni ad segmentum ligni tabulati traducta.*

IMPLECTO, *idem ac Implacito.* To implead in a court of justice.

Cum homines de manerio de Hedingdon Hugonem, de Plessey in curia domini regis implectassent, K. p. 319.

IMPORTUNITAS *viarum.* Badness of the ways. *Capellæ parochianis ipsis ex gratia sunt concessæ, quia ad matricem ecclesiam pro importunitate viarum et temporum—accedere nequeant,* K. p. 587.

INCLAUSA. An Inclosure round a house. *Dicunt per sacramentum suum quod capitale messuagium valet per annum cum tota inclausa,* ii s. K. p. 314.

INCREMENTUM. An advance in rent or other payment.— *Reddendo antiquam firmam, et de incremento* xl s. K. p. 164.— *Taxatio spiritualitatis una cum incremento per retaxationem,* K. p. 316. To which was opposed *Decrementum,* abatement, whence Decrements in our buttery books.

INDICTATIO. An Indictment or presentment of those who committed any illegal trespass. The benefit of which indictments in the Swainmote was given to the forestar. So in the forest of Bernwode, John Fitz Nigel had *Indictationes siquæ fuerint de viridi et venatione,* K. p. 209, 265.

INFANGETHEF. A liberty granted from the king to some lords of a mannor to try all thieves their tenants within their own court. As Outfangethef was a liberty of trying forreiners or strangers apprehended for theft within their own fee. Sir John de Molins had a charter for these privileges in his mannors of Brill, Ludgareshale, &c. 11 Edw. II. K. p. 447. From Sax. Def, a thief; and Fangan to take. Whence in the North to Fang is to take, and thence possibly the Fangs or tusks of a boar.

INFIDELES. *Inter infideles connumerare,* to excommunicate. So Henry bishop of Winton threatned Brien Fitz-Count lord of Walingford,—*Et vos nisi correxeritis inter infideles Angliæ connumerabo,* K. p. 100.

INHOC. This word is neither interpreted nor mentioned in any glossary I have yet seen. It signified any corner or out part of a common field ploughed up and sowed (and sometime fenced off), within that year wherein the rest of the same field lay fallow. It is now called in the North an Intock, and in Oxfordshire a Hitching. It seems derived from Sax. Inʒe, a field or meadow, and Hoke, a corner or nook. Whence an Inge now in Lincolnshire signifies any open field or common. The making of such Inhoke or enclosure by any one lord or tenant, was a prejudice to all who had the right of common.—*Frater Walterus prior Berencestriæ fieri fecit quoddam Inhoc in campo waretabili utriusque Ernicote in Mucklecroft sub curia ejusdem prioris per quod abbas Osen. dicebat se de communi pastura ibidem disseisivi,* K. p. 297. *Noverit universitas ventra nos fecisse quoddam Inhokium in campo de Dunthrop sine assensu et voluntate prioris et conventus de Cold-Norton,—unde quorundam fratrum et aliorum amicorum freti consilio prædictum Inhokium volunt depascere,* K. p. 298. This trespass or encroachment was expresly prohibited in some charters.—*Hac ratione quod dominus hayam nec pasturam separabilem faciet ab hominibus infra campum warectabilem,* K. p. 496. The nature of an Inhoke is more plain by this deed. *Anno regni regis Henrici filii regis Johannis quinquagesimo secundo die S. Barnabæ apostoli facta fuit hæc conventio inter fratrem W. abbatem Osen. et priorem de Coges, et dominam Katherinam Lo. l, Robertum de Broc dominos villæ de parva Tywa et alios liberos tenentes ejusdem villæ ex una parte, et Johannem de Pratellis dominum de magna Tywa ex altera, videlicet, cum dictus Johannes seminasset et Inhokam fecisset de quadam cultura quæ vocatur Costowa sine voluntate dicti abbatis et aliorum prænominatorum, et insuper in defensum posuisset communem pasturam totius warettæ inter viam quæ vocatur Wodewey, et parvam Tywam, quam communam dictus abbas et prænominati clamaverunt ex antiquo esse jus suum, &c. Dictus Johannes recognovit illam communam pasturam esse jus ipsius abbatis et aliorum dominorum prænominatorum quotiens a dictis culturis bladum asportatum fuerit, et terra seminata non fuerit. Et obligavit se et hæredes suos imperpetuum per fidem et præsens scriptum quod nunquam de dicta pastura quicunque seminabit nec Inhokam faciet in præjudicium dicti abbatis, &c.* Ex Regist. Osen. MS. *penes Decan. et Capit. Æd. Ch.* Ox. MS.

INLANDYS. Inland was that part of an estate which was held in demesne, or to the proper uses of the lord in opposition to the Outland, which was set to tenants; or rather the inclosures as distinguisht from the common fields. Thomas Billingdon quit claimed his right of commonage in all the Inlandys of Edward Rede lord of Borstall, 15 Hen. VI. K. p. 624.

INQUISITIO. An Inquest on the oaths of twelve or more legal men to give verdict in any cause, for licence of which a fine was paid to the king.—*Thomas de Fekingham debet regi quinque marcas et unum palefridum, sic quod inquisitio fiat utrum, &c.* K. p. 171.

INSECTATOR. A prosecutor or adversary.—*Quod etiam ejus insectatores parvo post tempore duraverunt, imo dira morte perierunt,* K. p. 388.

INSTAURAMENTUM. Store or breed.—*Et de instauramento tria jumenta, i. e.* three store cattel, K. p. 288.

INSTITUTION. A clerk might be instituted in an ecclesiastical benefice, either in person or by proxy.—*Johannes le Fleming præsentatus ad ecclesiam de Ambrosdon et admissus, et rector in persona*

Johannis de Scalleby presbyteri procuratoris sui canonice institutus, K. p. 334.

INVADIARE. To engage or give security. From Lat. *Vadium, Guadium,* a pledge or surety. Thence a Gage, a Wager, a Mortgage, to Wage war or law, Wages, &c.—*Habenda sibi et hæredibus—et cuicunque dare, vendere, invadiare, assignare, &c. voluerint,* K. p. 262.

INVESTITURA *terræ.* Livery of land and tenements from the lord to any inferiour tenant.—*Quando aliquis tenens de Wrechwyke mortuus fuit, et terra sua sit seminata, et uxor ejus non potest invenire plegios ad tenenda messuagia et terras quas ipse et ipsa in vita sua tenuerint, quod erit ad electionem domini quis habebit investituram prædictæ terræ,* K. p. 459.

JURNALE. The Journal or diary of accounts, or receipts and expences in a religious house.—*Ut patet per jurnale hoc anno—ut patet per prædictum jurnale,* K. p. 571. From Fr. *Jour,* a day, whence Journey was properly one day's travel. Journe was in old Eng. one day's work. A Journy-man, or one who works by the day. To Adjourn, &c.

JUSTITIA. Just rights, liberties, and privileges.—*Dummodo diocesani episcopi eis suffragetur assensus, et per novam structuram veterum ecclesiarum justitia non lædatur,* K. p. 594.

JUSTITIARIUS *Forestæ.* Justice in Eyre.—*Testibus Hugone le Despenser justitiario forestæ citra Trentam,* K. p. 339.

K.

KALENDÆ. Rural chapters so called because held on the kalends or first day of every month, as at first every three weeks, and at last only once a quarter, K. p. 640.

KERNELLARE. To build a wall or tower Kernelled or *Crenellé,* with Cranys or notches out of which they shot their arrows. Spelman derives it from the Sax. Cýpnel, a seed or Kernel, from whence says he Cýpnelen, to rise in knobs or bunches. But Du Fresne justly reflects on this violence done to the word, and finds it to be *quarnellus* or *quadranellus,* a four square hole or notch, *ubicunque patent quarnelli sive fenestræ.* This form of walls and battlements for military uses and chiefly for shooting with bows and arrows, might possibly borrow name from *quadrellus,* a four square dart.

"*Nec tamen interea cessat balista vel arcus
Quadrellos hæc multiplicat, pluit illa sagittas.*"

Licentiam dedimus Johanni de Handlo quod ipse mansum suum de

Borstall juxta Brehul in com. Buck. muro de petra et calce firmare et kernellare possit, K. p. 363. Sir John de Molins obtained leave to fortifie his mannor-houses of Stoke-Pogeis and Ditton with walls of stone and kernelled, K. p. 463.

KEVERE. A Cover or vessel used in a dairy house for milk or whey.—*Compotus Henrici Deye et Johannæ uxoris de exitibus et proventibus de Dayri—Allocantur pro novo Kevere empto* viii. *den.* Hence in Devonshire a Keeve is the Vat or Fat wherein they work their beer. And in Kent a Keeler is a broad shallow vessel of wood wherein they set their milk to cream and their wort to cool. The Kevels in a ship are the holes wherein they lay up the shrouds and tackling.

L.

LACRYMATORIES. Small earthen vessels, wherein the tears of surviving friends were reposited and buried with the urns and ashes of the dead, K. p. 13.

LAGÆNA. *A* Gr. Λάγανος. Whence Sax. Flaxa, Eng. Flaggon, and Flesk of wine, Flask for gun-powder, Flasket for cloaths, old Eng. Flash of arrows, &c. Claret was eight-pence and Muscadine sixteen-pence *per lagenam* at Burcester in 3 Hen. VI. K. p. 574.

LARDARIUM. *Lardi Locus.* The Larder or place where the Lard and meat were kept. Whence to Lard with bacon. *Tenentes de Pidington cariabunt salem domini de foro ubi emptus fuit ad lardarium domini,* K. p. 496.

LEGATUM. A mortuary. In all churches appropriated to the abby of Oseney, the perpetual vicars by endowment were to have every second mortuary, if to the value of sixpence: and one half of it if beyond that value.—*Vicarius per abbatem et conventum Osen. præsentandus et instituendus ab episcopo—habebit secundum legatum ad valentiam sex denariorum, et quod ultra sex denarios fuerit, intra ipsum et canonicos dimidiabitur,* K. p. 304. So at Burcester, K. p. 559.

Per LEGEM *Angliæ tenere.* To hold by the law or courtesie of England: when a man is tenant for life to the inheritance of his wife deceased. *Hen. de Lacy com. Linc. tenet manerium de Burcester ad terminum vitæ suæ per legem Angliæ de hæreditate Margaretæ uxoris suæ,* K. p. 361.

LEGALES *homines.* Persons who are legally qualified to serve in a jury, as being neither excommunicate nor out-lawed. *Abbas Robertus implacitavit—et electi sunt duodecim homines legales de vicineto,* K. p. 134.

LEES. A common pasture. From Sax. Læype, whence in the

North Leasow, a meadow. And in Kent most of the wide common heaths or pastures are called Leeses, as Braborn Lees, Rostling-Lees, &c.—*Dimidia acra bi Lese-mor-side*, K. p. 400. One close in Adingrave called Pennie-leys, K. p. 624. Though this latter seems from the Sax. Leag, a field, whence a Lay and Ley of land, and the Laies in a common field.

LEVARE *denarios*. To Lewy or raise mony. *Petrus de Asherugge tunc seneschallus honoris S. Walerici appropriavit dictum manerium ad honorem S. Walerici, et ibidem tenuit visum per annum levando de eadem villata* xii. *denarios de racto visu pro omnibus*, K. p. 333.

LEVARE *foenum*. To make hay, or properly to cast it into windrows, in order to cock it up.—*Debent quinque dies de consuetudine videlicet per unum diem foenum levare, et per tres in autumpno metere*, K. p. 229.—*Homines de Hedingdon venient cum furcis suis ad dictum foenum levandum et thassandum*, K. p. 320. *Una levatio foeni*, one day's hay-making, a service paid the lord by inferior tenants.—*Alicia quæ fuit uxor Richardi le Grey,—faciet unam sarculaturam, et unam wedbedripam, et levationem foeni*, K. p. 402.

LIBELLUS. A Libel or declaration in a court of civil or ecclesiastical judicature. *Petitio Libelli*, the sueing for or taking out such libel.—*Possint eos et eorum successores per omnem censuram ecclesiasticam ad omnium et singulorum præmissorum observantiam absque articuli seu libelli petitione et quocunque strepitu judiciali compellere*, K. p. 344.

LIBERA. A Livery or delivery of so much grass or corn to a customary tenant who cuts down or prepares the said grass or corn, and receives some part or small portion of it as a reward or gratuity. —*Habebit liberam ad vesperas quæ vocatur evenyngs*, K. p. 401. So the Livery of hay and oats, as giving out such a quantity of provender for the feeding horses, K. p. 378. Whence a Livery-stable, Livery-horses, servants in Livery. A white Livered fellow, &c.

LIBERATURA *et seisina*. Livery and seisin given by the superior lord of the fee. When a minor was in ward, and came to age, the estate of military service in the king's hands was delivered up: for which Livery the heir paid a fine or composition. So Gerard de Camvil having married Eustace daughter of Gilbert Basset, gave two thousand marks and ten palfries to the king for Livery of her father's inheritance, K. p. 167.

LIBRA *ad numerum*. A pound in ready mony opposed to *Libra arsa et pensitata*, a pound weight in solid metal. In Doomsday Register the king's mannor of Brill *reddebat tempore regis Edwardi xxiii. libras ad numerum*, K. p. 166.

LIGIUS. Liege, pure, lawful. *Viduitas ligia*, pure widowhood.—*Ysabel Gargat filia mea in ligia viduitate et libera potestate sua*, K. p. 190. *Potestas ligia*, free and absolute disposal,—*Ego Ela de Aldithleia in libera viduitate mea et ligia potestate*, K. p. 280.

LINTEAMEN. A towel or other course linnen cloth.—*Et in canvays empt. Londin. per Richardum Dymby—pro lintheaminibus faciendis* iii. *sol.* K. p. 574.

LITERATURA. Literature, in old Eng. Lettrure. *Ad literaturam ponere*, to put out children to school. Which liberty was denied to some parents who were servile tenants without consent of the lord. So in the lands at Burcester which were held in villenage from the prioress of Merkyate,—*Quilibet custumarius non debet filium suum ad literaturam ponere, neque filiam suam maritare sine licentia et voluntate priorissæ*, K. p. 401. This Julian like prohibition of educating sons to learning, was owing to this reason, for fear, the son being bred to letters might enter into religion or sacred orders, and so stop or divert the services which he might otherwise do as heir or successor to his father.

LOCUTORIUM. A parlour. The religious after they had dined in their common refectory had a withdrawing room, where they met for discourse and conversation: which room for that sociable use they called *Locutorium*, *a loquendo*, and Parlour a Fr. *Parler*, —*Et Willielmo Hykkedon latamo conducto per quatuor dies ad faciendum limen hostii locutorii versus aulam prioris* xvi. *den.* K. p. 574.

LOKYS. Sax. *Loecay*, Locks or flocks of course and refuse wool, which in Kent are called Lucks and Dag-wool.—*Computant de duobus solidis receptis de lana fracta videlicet Lokys collecta in tonsura ovium vendita Johanni Deye hoc anno*, K. p. 572. Whence a Lock of hair, and a hard matted or matted Lock of hair in the neck is called an Ellflock. Thence Lock, a thread, and Lockram, linnen cloath of a courser thread.

LOQUELA *sine die*. A respite in law, or demurr to an indefinite time.—*Si vir tenens fuerit infra ætatem et uxor plenæ ætatis, cum implacitati fuerint, non remanebit loquela sine die propter minorem ætatem viri*, K. p. 210.

LUMINARE. A lamp or candle set burning on the altar of any church or chappel, for the maintenance of which lands and rent charges were frequently given to religious houses and parish churches. So Gilbert Basset gave to his now priory at Burcester, —*unam virgatam terræ in Stratton ad luminare prædictæ ecclesiæ*, K. p. 136. It was sometimes expresly provided that this luminary should burn all night, and in the day at canonical hours, and during divine service. So Richard de Camvil and Eustace his wife gave a virgate of land in Burcester to Robert Clerk,—*Ita tamen*

*quod prædictus Robertus Clericus vel hæredes sui invenient lampa-
dem unam ante altare sancti Nicholai in majori ecclesia S. Mariæ et
S. Edburgæ de Berencester,—qualibet nocte totaliter, et quolibet
die dum divina celebrantur, et ad horas canonicales ardentem,*
K. p. 180. Which virgate of land seems to have been one part
of Candle-meadow, so called from being thus charged with finding
a light or candle in the conventual church, which part of the said
meadow was afterwards resigned to the said prior and convent.—
Philippa countess of Warwick gave seven shillings yearly rent to
the priory of Burcester,—*Ita tamen quod dicti canonici—unam
lampadem semper ardentem coram altari beati Johannis Baptistæ in
ecclesia conventuali de Berencester in perpetuum inveniant,* K. p. 233.
Hugh de Plugenet granted to the Priory of St. Frideswide common pasture in his mannor of Hedingdon, &c. to find one lamp in
the said church of Hedingdon, K. p. 334. A Luminary at the
great altar was sometimes maintained by the rector of the church,
and in vicarages this expence was charged on the appropriators.—
So in the ordination of the vicarage of Meriton appropriated to the
abby of Egnesham,—*Incensum luminare in cancello prædicto dictos
religiosos et eorum successores supportare volumus et ordinamus in
perpetuum suis sumptibus subire,* K. p. 483. By the ecclesiastical
constitutions in Normandy it was ordained that once in a year about
Pentecost, the priest and capellanes should come with their people
in a full procession to the mother church, and for every house
should offer on the altar a wax taper to enlighten the church, K.
p. 598. The rents that were given to this use were sometimes em-
bezled by the parish priest, against which abuse bishop Grosthead
provided in this diocese,—*Præcipimus etiam ut redditus assignati
per devotionem laicorum ad luminaria vel ad alios usus honestos in
ipsis ecclesiis non committantur per ipsos rectores in usus et emolu-
menta eorundem.* Constit. Rob. Episc. Lincoln. MS.

M.

MANERIUM. A Mannor. Skene gives it an affected derivation,
Manerium quasi Manurium, such a circuit of land to be Manured or
cultivated by handy-work. But it is truly from the Fr. *Manoir,* habitation, or Lat. *Manendo,* the place of residence to the chief lord.
This word was brought in by the Normans,—*Galfridus Constan-
tiensis episcopus—dono Gulielmi regis ducentas et octoginta villas,
quas a manendo manerios vulgo vocamus, obtinuit,* Order. Vital. l. 4.
The constitution of a mannor was this, The king granted to some
baron or military man a certain circuit of ground for him and his
heirs to dwell upon and to enjoy, holding some part in demesne to

GLOSSARY. 97

their own use and occupation; and letting out other parcels to free or servile tenants, who were to do their suit and service at the court of the said mannor, now called the lord's court and court baron. *Manerium* was sometimes used simply for the court or mansion of the lord, whence we say the site of the mannor, and the mannor-house, called otherwise *Manerium domus*, as Reginald earl of Bologne and Ida his countess gave to the priory at Cold Norton *Manerium domus sicut sedet et constitutum est*, K. p. 163. Again it was sometimes taken for the mannor-house, and all the demesne land belonging to it,—*Habebit vicarius de Cestreton totum altaragium ac omnes decimas minores et oblationes ad dictam ecclesiam qualitercunque spectantes, decimis tamen quibuscunque de manerio ibidem provenientibus totaliter exceptis*, K. p. 543. In the Doomsday tenure, one village or parish was often held for two or more mannors. So Robert de Oily held Burcester *pro duobus maneriis*, K. p. 65. At present the word Mannor does not so much imply the seat or the land, as it does the royalty and jurisdiction belonging to a court baron. For a man may now have the mannor though he has not a foot of land within the bounds of it, which is called a Mannor in Gross. As the other may be called a Mannor Appendant which goes along with the mannor-house, or site, or other ground.

Mansio *Canonicorum*. The court or chief country-house of the religious upon one of their mannors, where they kept their courts, and sometimes resided for health and diversion. *In Weston virgatam, ubi mansio canonicorum est*, K. p. 198.

Mansum *Capitale*. The chief manse, or mannor-house, or court of the lord. Henry de Oily gave to the abby of Oseney *Capitale mansum meum in Weston cum ejus pertinentiis*, K. p. 150. Called sometimes *Curia Capitalis*.—Thomas de S. Walery gave to the abby of Oseney *totum manerium meum Mixebury cum capitali curia*, K. p. 150.

Mansus *Presbyteri*. The Manse of the parish priest, the parsonage or vicarage-house.—*Habeat etiam dictus vicarius (i. e. de Ambresdon) pro inhabitatione sua illum mansum in quo presbyter parochiæ dictæ ecclesiæ inhabitare consuevit, et duo cotagia eidem adjacentia*, K. p. 431.

Manuprisor. One who was bail, plege, or security for another person Sir Eubulo le Strange in 5 Edw. III. was a Manuprisor for Hugh de Spensar, K. p. 419. Whence Without bail or Mainprise.

Mara. A Moor. Either from Lat. *Mare*, or rather Brit. *Mor*. The word *Mara* was used for any lake, pool, pond, or other standing water,—*Sedens super lacum quem usu quotidiano loquendi Ma-*

h

GLOSSARY.

ram vocamus, Will. Gemet. l. 2, cap. 20.—*Castrum et manerium de Bolyngbroke cum soke mara et marisco,* K. p. 418. Called sometimes Mera from Brit. *Mēr,* Sax. Œeꞃ, watèr, whence a Mereswine, a dolphin, a Mear or lake, Mire or dirt, the Meers or ditches, or Mere-stangs, or other boundaries of land.—*Istud præcedens furlong jacet ab Oxenford-wey usque ad quandam meram terræ dominicæ dom. Lestraunge,* K. p. 530. *A Lousmonger's-path prædicta jacet una viridis mera, et in fine inferiore ipsius meræ descendit quidam sulcus fluens inter medium de Stanford-more,* K. p. 531.—*Incipiendo juxta quoddam parvum more jacens ad finem cujusdam semitæ pedestris vocatæ Seynt Edburgh-wey,* K. p. 531. —*Cum marisco integro qui vocatur Crocwell-moor,* K. p. 187. Hence to Moore a ship, *i. e.* to lay her up in the mud of a haven.

MARINARIUS. A Mariner. *Marinariorum Capitaneus,* the admiral or warden of the ports, which offices were commonly united in the same person. The word Admiral not coming in before the latter end of King Edward I.—*Rex capitaneo marinariorum, et eisdem marinariis—salutem,* K. p. 322.

MARCHIO. From the Lat. *Marchia,* Sax. Œeaꞃc, limit or bounds. Hence the Marches, old Eng. Marchis, or borders of Wales. The March or limited motion of an army, though *this military Marching seems rather from the Brit. and old Gall. *March,* a horse, from whence Sax. Œæꞃe, Eng. Mare. *Marchio* was strictly the governour of the Marches, but any keeper or constable of an eminent castle was called *Marchio.* As *Brientius filius Comitis marchio de Walengford,* K. p. 85. Whence our titles of Marquess and Marchioness.

MARITAGIUM, *dare in maritagio.* To give an estate as a marriage portion to a daughter.—*Concessimus Thomæ Basset terram de Dedinton quam dederat Willielmo Malet in maritagio cum filia sua,* K. p. 102. *Villam de Menelida quam Alanus de Dunstanvill pater ipsius Ceciliæ dedit ad se maritandam,* K. p. 171. *Maritagium Liberum,* frank-marriage; when a baron, knight, or freeholder, granted such a part of his estate with a daughter to her and her husband, and the heirs of her body to hold without any homage or service to the donor. So Maud daughter of Simon St. Liz, gave to the abby of St. Neots, com. Hunt. the third part of the mannor of Cratesfeld, held by her in frank-marriage,—*Dedi tertiam partem totius manerii mei de Cratesfeld quod est liberum maritagium meum,* K. p. 79.—*Willielmus Longspe dedit et concessit Henrico filio Edmundi de Lacy Margaretam filiam suam et hæredem, et cum ipsa in libero maritagio maneria sua de Burncester et Midlington,* K. p. 251. *In libero maritagio suo,* in her pure widowhood, when the relict held the lands which she brought to her late husband:—

GLOSSARY. 99

Post mortem Roberti de Oily Editha in libero maritagio suo plurimas terras dedit canonicis de Oseneia, K. p. 90. In marriage it was a custom for the woman to be endowed at the church door, K. p. 388. *Maritagium habere,* to have the free disposal of an heiress in marriage, a favour granted by the king who was guardian of all wards or heirs in minority.—*Mandatum est vicecom. Oxon. quod habere faciat W. com. Sarum maritagium filiæ Ricardi de Camvill genitæ de Eustachia—ad opus Willielmi sui primogeniti,* K. p. 182. *Pro maritanda filia,* a fine or composition paid to the king by every baron or military tenant, for leave to marry a sole daughter and heir. Gilbert Basset 6 Rich. I. gave one hundred pounds fine to the king, that his daughter Eustace might be married to Thomas de Verdon, K. p. 154. If any person married such an heiress without the king's leave, he lost her whole estate, unless he could compound by a severe fine. So Robert de Peesley paid sixty marks and one palfry to be reconciled to the king for having married Alice de Chesterton, K. p. 161. John Giffard paid three hundred marks for marrying without licence Maud the widow of William Longspe, K. p. 275. Jurdan de Meriton paid twenty marks fine for taking Maud the relict of John le Marsh, K. p. 308. Sir John de Handlo compounded for one hundred pounds upon marriage of Maud widow of John Lovel, K. p. 371. Alice countess of Lincoln and Sarum lost the greatest part of her estate for this trespass of marrying Eubulo le Strange, K. p. 391. Some inferiour tenants were under the same obligations to the lords, as the lords to the king,—*Si homines (de Hedingdon) filias suas extra libertatem dicti manerii maritare voluerint, dabunt domino pro qualibet filia sic maritata duos solidos,—et hoc pro catallis extra libertatem dicti manerii cum ipsa remotis: et si infra libertatem ejusdem manerii eas maritaverint, nihil dabunt pro maritagiis earundem,* K. p. 320. In the mannor of Wrechwyke—*Willielmus Searich ad habendum in uxorem Johannam quæ fuit uxor Willielmi Foul venit hic in curiam, et dat domino de fine pro eadem in maritagio habenda* x s. *et habet inde diem solvendi,* K. p. 470. Among the customary tenants at Burcester King's-End, who held from the prioress of Merkyate—*Quilibet custumarius non debet—filium suum ad literaturam ponere, neque filiam suam maritare sine licentia et voluntate dominæ priorissæ,* K. p. 401. The widow of a tenant in villenage held her husband's estate during her widowhood, *Matilda quæ fuit uxor Roberti Hikkes clamavit totum prædictum messuagium--dum vixerit sine marito faciendo servitia et redditus omnes,* K. p 458. The fine or composition paid by such tenants for the liberty of disposing their daughters was called *Merchetum,* Merchet, from the Scotch Marchet, Marcheta, which was a commutation of mony or cattel given to the lord to buy off the old impious custom of the lord lying with the first night with the bride. Hect. Boet. Hist. Scot. p. 260. Buchan. l. 7. Skenæus *in voce*, &c. From which *Marcheta mulieris* used sometimes for the said commutation, and sometimes by metaphor for a maidenhead, possibly comes the prov. " Such a woman's Marchet or market is spoiled;" more especially applied to her who has lost her Marchet or virginity. Hence in several parts of England the word Merkin is used for *Puhes mulieris*. From the word Marry they use Marrow in the North for a companion or fellow, as gloves and shoes are not Marrows, *i. e.* are not well matcht, or not fellows.

MARTYROLOGIUM, *Martilegium*. A Martyrology or register kept in religious houses, wherein they set down the donations of their benefactors, and the days of their death: that upon each anniversary they might commemorate and pray for them. And therefore several benefactors made this a condition in their charters,— Isabel Gargate covenanted with the prior and canons of Burcester, —*Cum de hac vita migraverimus, facient nomina nostra scribi in martirologio suo*, K. p. 189. Henry Lacy earl of Lincoln was a benefactor to the canons of Burscough *com*. Linc. on this condition, that they should insert in their Martyrology and canon or mass book his name, and the name of Margaret his wife, K. p. 307. The canons of St. Marie Overy in Southwark for the favours of Sir John de Molins covenanted, that as soon as they should hear of the death of him or of Egidia his wife, they would inscribe their name in their publick Martyrology, and make recital of them annually in their chapter, K. p. 425. The religious granted the promise of this civility to their patrons, as a complement of gratitude and respect, — *Nos Johannes Clyfton et conventus canonicorum regularium mon. Dorcestre Lincoln.—voluimus et ordinavimus quod cum contigerit eundem Edmundum (i. e. Rede de Borstal) ab hac luce migrare, ut nomina omnium supradictorum cum obitu eorum in nostro martilegio inserantur, et singulis annis futuris perleganturin die anniversariorum suorum præsenti conventu in domo nostra capitulari*, K. p. 626.

MATTES. Mats made of straw or rushes. From Lat. *Matta*, Ovid. l. 6. Fast.—*in plaustro scirpea Matta fuit*, which perhaps the Romans borrowed from the old Teuton. *Matte*, Sax. Ceatte. To make bed-Mats of reeds or straw was a great employment of the ancient monks. Hence to be Matted or entangled,—*In quinque scotellis minoris sortis emptis ibidem pro cæteris officiis ix. den. et in x. Matts ibid. hoc anno xiii. den.* K. p. 574.

MEDIETAS *Beneficii*. The Moity, or half the annual profits of an ecclesiastical living, which some of the clergy freely contributed to King Edw. I. to maintain a war with France, for which benevo-

GLOSSARY. 101

lence the king granted his special protection,—*Cum dilectus nobis magister Radulfus de Mertival persona ecclesiæ de Ambrosden medietatem beneficii,* &c.—*nobis in subsidium nostrum de anno præsenti juxta taxationem ultimo inde factam liberaliter concessit et gratanter,* K. p. 322.

MERCANDISA. All goods and wares exposed to sale in fairs and markets. *In omnibus burgis et villatis nostris, et etiam in singulis nundinis, et mercatis nostris libere valeant emere et vendere omnes mercandisas absque ullo theloneto seu stallagio,* K. p. 311. And therefore *Mercatores* was not restrained, as it now seems to be, to Merchants or traffiquers in forreign commodities, but extended to all sort of traders, pedlers, buyers, and sellers,—*Omnes homines et mercatores honoris de Walingford,* K. p. 113.

MERENNUM, *Merannum, Merremium, Maremium, Maeremium, quodvis materiamen, unde vocis origo,* called in French *le merrien* and *marren.* Any refuse wood, or old pieces of timber and boards that are left among the rubbish after building or repairing, or pulling down of houses,—*In diversis hominibus conductis ad seponendum et extrahendum vetus merennum massam et lapides* x. *den.* K. p. 575. —*Et in merenno empto apud Curtlyngton cum cariagio ejusdem pro collistrigio apud Dadyngton de novo faciendo,* K. p. 577.

METTESHEP. Perhaps it ought to be Mittenscep, from Sax. Ɯitten, to measure, or Ɯitta, a mete or measure, and Ceap, goods or chattle: for the Metteshep seems to be a fine or penaltie paid by the tenant for his neglect or omission of doing his custumary service. In the mannor of Pidington—*quælibet virgata terræ solvet per an. quinque solidos et quatuor dies de consuetudine, videlicet unum diem ad pratum domini falcandum ad cibum domini, vel domino dabit quadraginta denarios pro Metteshep,* K. p. 495.

MINISTRALLUS, *Ministrellus, à ministrando.* At first any buffoon or actor of ridicule, commonly retained for the diversion of persons of quality, and afterward restrained to a player on musick, a Minstrel. *Et in datis cuidam ministrallo domini Lestraunge in eodem festo* xii. *den.* K. p. 578. These Minstrels or merry fidlers were in several parts of England a sort of corporation, and had a King of Minstrels, for which a charter and a confirmation of it may be seen in Mon. Ang. tom. 1. p. 355.

MISSALE *celebrare.* To say Mass, and administer the sacrament of the Mass. *Habebit de oblationibus ad altare provenientibus unum denarium, missale quoties celebraverit, et denarius provenerit,* K. p. 304.

MOLITURA, *Mulitura, Multura; à Molo* to grind. It sometimes signified a grist or sack of corn brought to the mill to be ground. But more commonly taken for the toll paid for grinding.

So Sir Wido de Meriton in his charter to the Knights Templars,—*Concesserunt mihi fratres unam libertatem ad suum molendinum scilicet molendi segetem pro multura reddenda pro segete quæ est in tremula, et meum brasium sine multura*, K. p. 120. *Molitura libera*, free grinding without paying toll, a privilege which the lord generally reserved to his own family,—*Salva mihi et hæredibus meis molitura libera familiæ nostræ quieta in dicto molendino*, K. p. 236. *Salva mihi et hæredibus meis secta curiæ, et molendini mei de Bigenhull cum omnimodo blado et brasio*, K. p. 296. Our Eng. Mil is from the Sax. Œÿlen, Island. *Mil*, to grind: *in præterito, Mulde*, whence in Lincolnshire a Mill is called a Miln, and in other parts a Muln, as Muln-wey, *i. e.* the Mill-way, K. p 395. Hence the Sax. Œolb, Island *Molld*, Eng. Mould, or what is ground to dust, old Eng. Mulle, pouder or dust. Mouldy, and ready to Moulder away. Mullock in the North dirt or rubbish: and a Mole from casting up the Mould is called a Mould-warp. A Mullet, the stone on which painters grind their colours. Molter in the North the toll of a Mill.

MOLNEDA, *Mulneda*. A Mill-pool. Gilbert Basset in his foundation charter to the priory of Burcester, gave—*quoddam pratunculum quod vocatur Hamma, quod extenditur de crofta Serici de Wrechwic per la Mulnedam usque illuc ubi novus rivulus descendit in veterem rivulum, et ipsam mulnedam ad faciendum ibi molendinum*, K. p. 135. Molta, Fr. *Moulte*, was to be paid for the service of grinding, or the use of a mill. If I should from hence derive our Eng. Malt, Dutch *Mout*, it would be a less absurd conjecture than that of Dr. Skinner, who would deduce it from the verb to Melt, *quia, ut omnibus notum est, aquâ maceratur, donec germina emittat*.

MORTMAIN. Statute made in 7 Edw. I. *de terris in manum mortuam non ponendis*, to restrain the donation of any lands or tenements to religious or pious uses, where they lay in a dead band, without succession or due service to the lord and the king. By any such donation after the said statute, the lands were forfeited to the king, if the more immediate lord of the fee made not his claim within one year after such alienation,—*Accepimus per inquisitionem coram nobis factam quod abbas et conventus de Oseney appropriarint sibi et domui suæ duas virgatas terræ in Chestreton—post publicationem statuti de terris et tenementis ad manum mortuam non ponendis editi sine licentia regis*, K. p. 367. When the kings by special license dispensed with this statute, there was a previous inquisition *Ad quod dampnum*, and a return upon oath, that it would be no prejudice to the dignity and revenues of the crown, K. p. 381. This law is now relaxed by stat. 39 Eliz. cap. 5, of giving lands to hospitals: and 14 Car. II. cap. 9, of purchasing lands and tenements for the poor within the cities of London and Westminster.

MORTUARIUM. A Mortuary. The word was used in a civil as well as an ecclesiastical sense, and was payable to the lord of the fee, as well as to the priest of the parish.—*Debentur domino (i. e. manerii de Wrechwyke) nominibus herietæ et mortuarii duæ vaccæ pret* xii. *sol.* K. p. 470. *Vid.* HERIETUM *et* LEGATUM.

MULLO, *Mullio.* A cock or pout of grass or hay.—*Ut strepitum rugientis aquæ audivit—monticulum foeni quod extra tugurium erat, velociter ascendit.* Impetus autem irruentis et omnia involventis aquæ foenum sublevavit, et de loco illo mullonem huc et illuc fluctuantem longe transtulit.* Order. Vital. l. 13, p. 899.—*Ipse Robertus et omnes alii custumarii dominæ liberam falcatam in prato vocato Gilberdsham sine prandio debent tornare, et inde foenum levare, et mulliones inde facere,* K. p. 401.—*Alicia quæ fuit uxor Richardi le Grey—faciet unam saculaturam, et unam wedbedripam, et levationem foeni, et inveniet unum hominem ad mullionem foeni faciendum,* K. p. 402. Hence in old Eng. a Moult, now a Mow, Sax. ꝏope, of hay or corn.

MULTO, *Mutilo, Molto, Muto, Mutto.* A Mutton or sheep. Several ridiculous derivations are given of this word. Joh. de Garlandia from *Mutus,* dumb. *Et cum sit mutus, poterit bene muto vocari.* Menagius from *Mons,* as if creatures that fed chiefly in the mountains. Ferrarius would fetch it *à Montando,* because forsooth the venereal rams do mount or cover the ews. And Dr. Skinner with like modesty from the old Lat. *Muto,* the yard of a man or beast, as if rams of all creatures were best provided in that member. I suppose the original was British; for Molt in the present Irish tongue signifies a ram, or male wether, to which the Lat, *Multo* is alway restrained, and does not extend to the female sheep or ewe,—*quatuor boves, sex mutilones,* K. p. 287.—*Inter Hokeday et diem S. Martini bene possunt ibidem ducentæ quadraginta multones sustentari ad opus domini ad terram suam compostandam,* K. p. 495.—*In stauro sunt* lii. *matres oves,* xxxv. *multones,* xii. *agni mares, et* xiv. *agni feminales.*—xxxii. *oves lactrices,* iii. *multones,* xl. *oves otiosas, i. e.* thirty-two milch ews, three rams or wethers, fourty barren ews. Cartul. Abbat. Glaston. MS. f. 39. Hence the gold mony impressed with an *Agnus Dei* on one side, were from that figure called Multones, which were common in France, and current in England, as appears by a patent 33 Edw. III. cited by the learned Spelman, though he had not then considered the meaning of it. *Rex tenetur Ottoni de Grandisono in decem millibus mul-*

tonum auri. And hence the military engine like the Roman battering ram is called Monton by Frosart, Hist. vol. 3, cap. 102.

MURDREDUM, *Murdrum, Mordrum.* Murder, from Sax. Moɲð, death, Island. *Mord.* By the laws of Edw. Confess cap. 15. If any person was murdred, the murderer was to be apprehended by the friborg where the body was found, and delivered up to justice. If he could not be immediately taken, a respite of one month and a day was allowed to the said inhabitants; and if he was not then produced, a fine was imposed upon them of fourty-six marks; of which sum, by the laws of Hen. I cap. 91, fourty marks were paid to the king, and six to the nearest relations of the party murdred. So that *Quietum esse a murdredo* was an exemption from this fine, and was a special privilege granted to the tenants within the honor of Walingford,—*Ut quieti sint de murdredis et de variis ad murdredum pertinentibus,* K. p. 114.

MURORUM *operatio.* The service of work and labour done by inhabitants and inferiour tenants in building and repairing the walls of a city or fortress. From which duty some were exempted by special privilege. So King Hen. II. granted to the tenants within the honor of Walingford—*ut quieti sint de operationibus castellorum et murorum,* K. p. 114. For which expence a tax was levied called Murage. Whence those officers who in the city of Chester are to supervise and repair the city walls, are now called Murengers.

MUSIVUM *opus.* Musaic, and corruptly Mosaic work. *Pavimenta tessellata,* Pavements of curious little pieces of brick, or tile, or marble, about the bigness and form of dice, with which the Romans generally paved the place where they fixed the pretorium or general's tent: of which several have been ploughed up in this county, K. p. 12. Fr. Junius cites this account of them from a MS. Saxon Glossary of Laurence Noel,—" Musaike work, which is a kind of ornament made in picture with little square stones like dies of all colours, set together with certain fine cyment upon a wall or floor, so that the forms of things be therewith pourtrayed and expressed as though they were paynted. Also it is more durable than any kind of paynting, by reason that neither by weather, wearing, nor washing, the colour can be taken away, which hath the thickness of the little dies wherewith this work is made. Of this kind of work is little in England. Howbeit I have seen of it, especially upon church-floors before altars, as is to be seen before the high altar at Westminster, although it be but gross. In Italy it is almost every where, and in most churches to be met."

MUTO, *mutare.* To Mew up hauks in the time of their Muting

or Molting, or casting their plumes. Hence the *Muta Regia*, the Mews near Charing Cross in London, now the king's stables, formerly the falconry or place for the king's hawks. The mannor of Broughton *com.* Oxon. in reign of Edw. II. was held by John Mauduit—*per serjantiam mutandi unum hostricum domini regis, vel illum hostricum portandi ad curiam domini regis*, K. p. 569.

MYCHER. A sordid covetous extortioner. "In such feyrs and markets whersoever it be holden, ther ben many theyves, mychers, and cut purse," K. p. 613.

MYLLEWELL. A sort of fish, the same with what now in Lancashire is called Milwyn, which Spelman renders green fish, but it was certainly of a different kind.—*Et in tribus copulis viridis piscis, et in xv. copulis de Myllewell minoris sortis* x. *sol.* vi. *den. et in* xx. *Myllewell majoris sortis* xii. *sol.* K. p. 575.

N.

NATIO. A native place. The jurors of the borough of Walingford return upon oath—*quod nullus de natione istius burgi pro quocunque facto quod fecerit debet suspendi, imo secundum consuetudinem istius burgi debet oculis et testibus privari*, K. p. 258.

NATIVUS. A servant or villane by birth and descent from servile tenants.—*Servi aut nascuntur, aut fiunt; nascuntur autem ex nativo et nativa alicujus copulatis vel solutis.*—*Item nascitur servus, qui ex nativa soluta generatur, quamvis ex patre libero, quia sequitur conditionem matris, quasi vulgo conceptus.* Bracton, l. 1, cap. 6, sect. 4.—*Terram Willielmi Hamond nativi dominæ*—*Nicholai Saford nativi dominæ*, K. p. 397.—*Rogerus Mortimer nativus prioris de Berencester*, K. p. 403.—*Cum omnibus servitiis liberorum hominum et nativorum de Heyford et Caldecote cum corporibus dictorum nativorum catallis et eorum sequelis*, K. p. 514. Hence the old Eng. Neife, a bond-woman, mentioned stat. 9 Rich. II. cap. 2, and 1 Edw. VI. cap. 3.

NAVIS, *Navicula*. A Caster or small silver dish to hold the frankincense, before it was put into the *thuribulum* or smoakingpot.—*Inter ecclesiæ ornamenta—turribulum cum navi*, K. p. 598. It seems so called from the shape resembling a boat or little ship, as a Cogue of brandy from the like reason. *Vid.* COCK-BOAT.

AD NONAM. At the ninth hour by Roman computation, *i. e.* at three in the afternoon. *Vescitur ac nona merenda messor in hora.* —*Illa die comedent iidem homines, et omnes dicti messores cum domino ad nonam, et præfati homines, et non messores eodem die cum domino cœnabunt*, K. p. 320. The monks and other religious had their *Refectionem Nonæ*, or *Biberes Nonales*, properly their dinner.

—*Non licet clericis ante horam tertiam prandere.* Can. *cit. à* Spelman. Which *Biheres* or refection given to school-boys and children about three after-noon, we still call a drinking. It was from this *Nona,* formerly the chief eating time, we take our word Noon, though removed to another hour. And it is from hence that in Kent a Noonchion or Nunchion of bread or any edible is a great piece, enough to serve for the Nooning or dinner of any common eater.

NUCES *colligere.* To gather small or hazle nuts. One of the works or services imposed upon inferiour tenants.—*Homines de Hedingdon uno die colligent nuces nomine domini in bosco qui vocatur Stowode,* K. p. 320. *Homines de Pydinton per unum diem colligent nuces ad opus domini in bosco suo cum uno homine,* K. p. 495.

NUTRIMENTUM. Breed of cattle.—*Quilibet custumarius dominæ non debet vendere equum masculum neque bovem de proprio nutrimento suo,* K. p. 401.

O.

OBLATIONES *Altaris.* Oblations or offerings from the parishioners to the parish priest were solemnly made four times in a year. —*Ordinavimus eidem vicario (i. e. de Oakle) omnes oblationes quæ quater in anno ab omnibus parochianis offeruntur,* K. p. 455. The custumary oblations at Burcester in the ordination of that vicarage about the year 1212, were one penny for a burial, one penny for a marriage, one penny for churching a woman: and the altar or sacrament offerings were three-pence at Christmas, two-pence at Easter, and a penny at the two other principal feasts, besides the offerings at confession, K. p. 569. Among the altar oblations were reckoned the little sums paid for saying masses and prayers for the souls of the deceased. As in the churches appropriated to the abby of Oseney,—*Vicarius habebit de oblationibus ad altare provenientibus unum denarium, missale quoties celebraverit, et denarius provenerit, et quicquid ex devotione fidelium et rationabiliter fuerit collatum,* K. p. 304.

OBLATIONES *Funerales.* If the corps of the party deceased was carried from the mother church to any other place of sepulture, there were custumary offerings due to the parish priest where the party died: of which offerings the sordid appropriators sometimes engrost three parts, and allowed only one to the oppressed vicar.— *Ordinavimus eidem vicario (i. e. de Oakle) quartam partem omnium obventionum funeralium dictorum parochianorum alibi quam apud Acleiam sepultorum quæ de jure vetere vel novo debentur ecclesiæ parochiali,* K. p. 455. At the burial of the dead, it was a custom

GLOSSARY. 107

for the surviving friends to offer liberally at the altar for the pious use of the priest, and the good estate of the soul of the deceased, which the appropriators were sometimes so just as to allow the vicar,—*Omnes oblationes in nuptiis, purificationibus, sepulturis, anniversariis,* K. p. 455. This pious custom does still obtain in North-Wales, where at the rails which decently defend the communion table, I have seen a small tablet or flat board conveniently fixt, to receive the money which at every funeral is offered by the surviving friends, according to their own ability, and the quality of the party deceased. Which seems a providential augmentation to some of those poor churches.

OCTAVUS. The Octaves, in old Eng. the Utas, or eight days after any festival, for the observation whereof Alcuinus gives this reason,—*Octavæ, quas hodie colimus, ideo reverenter celebrantur, quia primis diebus concurrunt sicuti unus dies dominicus ad alterum, qui eadem die celebratur.*—*Infra octavas,* within the said term of eight days. They were only some prime and remarkable feasts which were thus attended with Octaves, which feasts are enumerated in the laws of Edw. Confess. cap. 12.—*Ecclesia de S. Frideswidæ annuatim persolvet ecclesiæ de Coges duos solidos vel Bisantium unum infra octavas S. Michaelis,* K. p. 123.

OFFICIARIUS *Episcopi.* The bishop's chancellor or official in his court Christian.—*Idem Ychelus ipsum abbatem ea de causa jam in curiam christianitatis coram officiario diocœsani prædicti trahit in placitum,* K. p. 328.

OFFICINÆ. Wash-house, brew-house, and what we call out-offices.—*Capitale messuagium valet per annum cum tota inclausa iis. et non plus, salva reprisa domorum et aliarum officinarum,* K. p. 314.

OPERA. Works or services done by vassals or tenants in bondage to the lord.—*Johannes præpositus tenet unam virgatam terræ arabilis de Bardulpho, et debet opera quæ valent quolibet anno xiiis. ivd. ob. q.* K. p. 318. But servile tenants had their wives and their shepbards excused from these labours. *Vid.* PASTOR.

OPERATIO. One day's work performed by such inferiour tenants.—*Hominès de Hedingdon facient Hugoni et hæredibus suis pro qualibet virgata terræ sexdecim operationes, videlicet, uno die inter festum, &c.* K. p. 320.

OPILIO. A poor person or indigent beggar —*Et in datis opilioni de Crockwell in die S. Valentini martyris* ii. *den.*—*et in datis duobus opilionibus* ii *den.* K. p. 578.

ORDEAL. From Sax. Op, great, and Dele, judgement. The old judicial custom of proving the guilt, or attesting the innocence, of parties accused, chiefly by water or hot iron. As Queen Emma submitted to the walking blinded and barefoot over nine hot plough-shares laid at an unequal distance, and thereby purged herself from the charge of incontinence, K. p. 53. This was simply called *Judicium* in opposition to *Bellum*, duel or camp-fight, which was the other customary purgation: and neither of them was abolished by Will. Conq. though Sir W. T. does so assert. *Vid.* BELLUM. Servants or other deputies might undergo this trial in the cause and name of their masters, especially of those lords who were bishops and ecclesiastical men. As in time of Will. Rufus *Remigius episc. Lincoln. de regia proditione aliquando accusatus, sed famulus suus igniti judicio ferri dominum purgans, regio amori restituit.* Mat. Par. *sub an.* 1085.—So Brien Fitz Count in his challenge to Henry bishop of Winchester, *an.* 1144,—*Contra Henricum præsto sum probare vel bello vel judicio per unum clericum, vel per unum laicum,* K. p. 101.

ORDINARIUS. He that has the ordinary jurisdiction in ecclesiastical matters, as the bishop of a diocese, &c. *Richardus de Gravesend quondam Lincolniæ episcopus loci illius ordinarius, et advocatus prædictæ abbatiæ,* K. p. 351.

ORDINES. A general chapter, or other solemn convention of the religious of such a particular order.—*Et in solutis fratribus Roberto Lawton et Willielmo Meriton pro suis expensis versus ordines existentes apud Hygham-Ferrers ante festum S. Michaelis hoc anno* vii. *sol.* K. p. 576.

ORDINUM *Fugitivi.* Those of the religious who deserted their houses, and renounced their orders in contempt of their oath and other duty. The favouring and protecting such fugitives was charged on Thomas earl of Lancaster.—*Ordinum fugitivos, legisque transgressores, ne lege plecterentur, pertinaciter fovere,* K. p. 388.

P.

PAKTHRED. Pack-thread. From old Teuton. *Pack,* a bundle; Packen, to make up a load or burden. Hence a Pack-horse, a Pack-saddle, a Pack-needle, to Pack up, a Packer of cloath, to Pack away, &c. And possibly from hence the Sax. Pocca, Island. *Poke,* Eng. Poke or bag, and Poket or Pocket. In the east riding of Yorkshire Poke is the general word applied to all measures, as a Met-poke, a three bushel Poke, &c. Perhaps from Pack or Packed may come by abbreviation a Pad or bundle, a Pad of straw, to Pad or to bind up. But a Pad or horse, and a Padder or high-way man, are more plainly from the Sax. Paað, a path or way.—*Et in octo snoden de Pakthred emptis ibidem pro quodam reti faciendo,* K. p. 574.

GLOSSARY. 109

PALAFREDUS, *Palfridus*. A Lat. *Paraveredus*, a Palfry or saddle-horse. This was commonly part of the fine or composition with the king for seisiñ or livery of an estate. Richard de Camvill gave two thousand marks and ten palfries for the inheritance of his wife Eustace Basset, K. p. 167. This seemed a remainder of the old custom of paying the relief in horse and arms, as a proper badge of military service, till in 27 Hen. II. there was a commutation of mony for the arms, but the horses or part of them were still delivered *in specie*. A Palfry was part of the fine or penalty imposed for a transgression against the king. So Robert de Peesley paid sixty marks and one Palfry, to be reconciled to the king for the offence of marrying without the king's consent, K. p. 161. A Palfry was paid to the king for license to obtain a trial for the right of lands,—*Abbas de Egnesham debet unum palefridum pro habenda recognitione duodecim legalium hominum*, K. p. 168. At the death of every bishop and abbat who held in barony, a Palfry of the deceased was part of the heriot to the king,—*Obiit abbas de Oseneia, petiit escaetor ad opus domini regis cupam et palefridum dicti abbatis*, K. p. 330.

PARCUS. A Park. From Fr. *Parc* or *Parque*, or rather Sax. Peappoc and Peappuc, an inclosure. John Ross of Warwick asserts the first park in England to have been made by Hen. I. at Woodstock, *an*. 1119, K. p. 87. But Spelman proves from the Doomsday-book and other authorities, there were parks in the time of the Saxons, who called them Deperald, *i. e.* Deer-fold. *Parcagium* was a contribution paid by adjoining tenants toward repair of the walls, pales, or other mounds of a park. *Operationes Parcorum* were so many days work for that purpose. An exemption from this duty was granted as a special privilege to the tenants within the honor of Walingford,—*ut quieti sint de operationibus castellorum et—parcorum*, K. p. 114.

PANDOXATUS, *Pandoxata, Pandoxator, Pandoxatrix*. An Innkeeper, or Alehouse-keeper, from Gr. Πανδοχεῖον, *Hospitium*,—*Et in cervisiis videlicet* cxxxii. *lagenis et dimidia emptis de Johanna Spinan, Alicia Bedale, et aliis pandoxatis, ut patet per bullam* iv. *sol*. x. *den*. K. p. 574.

PARROC. Sax. Peappoc, a Parrock, Paddock, or Puddock, a small Park or enclosure near a house or chief seat for the convenience of securing deer, to be turned out and hunted. In the donation of Gilbert Basset to the priory of Burcester,—*Duæ acræ et dimidia quæ vertuntur in Parroc*, K. p. 136. Whence a Pattock or Paddock-course.

PARCELLA *Honoris vel Manerii*. When one parish or hamlet pertains to another honor or mannor as a part or parcel of it.—*Jo-*

hannes de la Vache—seisitus de manerio de Hokenorton, cum pertinentiis.—Johannes Trillowe seisitus de Chesterton in dominico suo ut de feodo unde prædictus locus est parcella, K. p. 580. *Terra et boscus in Rytherfield Grey tenentur de abbate de Abingdon ut parcellum de feodo de Padenale,* K. p. 617. It was to this Parcelling of baronies and mannors that it now happens we have part of one parish remote and incompast in another; and whole parishes belonging to one county lie out of the common extent, and within the very bowels of some other county.

PAROCHIA. The word to be understood a Diocese not a Parish in that expression,—*Honorius provinciam suam in parochias divisit,* K. p. 586. The beginning and gradual advance of parishes and parish churches, K. p. 587.

PAROCHIANUS. A compellation given by a bishop to any person living within his diocese and jurisdiction,—*Alexander Lincolniensis episcopus Guidoni de Charing parochiano suo,* K. p. 90.

PARTICULA. A slip or small parcel. Simon de Gerardmulin gave to the abby of Missenden the chappel of Holy Cross at Pidington, and—*quamdam particulam nemoris quæ est inter eandem capellam et nemus de Bruhellè,* K. p. 108.

PASNAGE, Pannage, Panonage. Lat. *Pastio, Pastionaticum, Pastimaticum, Pasnagium, Pannagium.* From the Fr. *Pasnag,* Lat. *Pasco,* the feeding of hogs: or from the old Eng. Pawns, *i. e.* the mast of beech and oak, and fruit of other forest trees. Cowel gives it a much harder derivation from Fr. *Panez* or *Panets,* the root of wild parsnip. And it is no less absurd in Dr. Skinner to deduce it from the Fr. *Pain,* or Lat. *Panis,* bread or other food. *Pannagium* had a double acceptation, first for the running and feeding of hogs within a forest: secondly, for the price or rate paid for their so running. *Liberum aut quietum pannagium,* was free Pannage, or liberty of hogs running within the limits of such forest or woods; a privilege granted to some private persons, and to several religious houses. Aubry earl of Damarun confirmed to the abby of Missenden the hermitage of Musewell,—*et pasnagium quietum de suis dominicis porcis,* K. p. 131. Sir William Fitz-Elias granted to Alicia de Maydwell—*heybotum et housbotum in dominicis boscis de Akle ad porcorias suas faciendas ubi sibi placuerit, et ad habendos porcos suos quietos de pannagio,* K. p. 259. Gilbert Basset granted to his new priory at Burcester—*quietantiam de pasnagio,* K. p.135. The price of Pannage within the liberties of the abby of Battle, com. Suss. was two-pence for every hog of full age. So at Estaples in Picardy, two-pence for every grown hog, and two *deniers* for a little hog, (which young hog of the first year we call in Kent a Sheat, and in Sussex a Shote) to be paid on St. Andrew's day.

In Scotland the tithe or tenth hog was paid for Pannage: as in those forest laws,—*Iste autem est modus pannagii, videlicet de qualibet cindre, id est de decem porcis, rex habebit meliorem porcum, et forestarius unum hogastrum.* This custom obtained in England, and was here called Tack,—*Debit pannagium vocatum Tack, videlicet, pro decem porcis unum porcum meliorem, et si non habet decem, dabit domino decimum denarium porcorum suorum cum appretiati fuerint per vicinos suos.* Ex Lib. Baroniæ de Shereborn MS. In 19 Hen. III. the four agistors within the forest of Bernwode were obliged to take care of the running hogs from Holy Rood day to fourty days after Michaelmass, and then to take the Pannage of one farthing for every hog, K. p. 219. If the Pannage were not duely paid, there was a process from the Exchequer, and distraint by the sheriff,—*Quia constat per inspectionem rotulorum de Scaccario—debent de pannagio—Mandatum est vicecom. ut distringat ipsos vel hæredes vel tenentes terras eorum ad reddendas regi portiones ipsos contingentes de prædictis denariis,* K. p. 259. The tithe of Pasnage was sometimes alienated from the parish priest to the appropriators. As the tithe of Pannage at Musewell within the parish of Ambrosden was granted to the abby of Missenden as a part of the endowment of their cell or hermitage of Holy Cross at Musewell, K. p. 75. And so confirmed by William king of Scots, 13 Hen. II.—*cum tota decima de dominio de Pedyngton in omnibus rebus quæ decimari debent, et de decima de padsnagio,* K. p. 124.

PASSAGIUM. A tribute or toll paid by travellers or passengers for the repair and maintenance of some road or passage: from which contribution some were by special privilege exempted. As King Hen. II. granted to the tenants and traders within the honor of Walingford,—*Ut quieti sint de thelonio, pontagio, passagio,—* K. p. 114.

PASSAGIUM. A channel or dike cut for a water course on the side of a river, or a weer for fish. So Wido de Meriton to the Knights Templars,—*Dedi—omnes percapturas quas fratres inceperunt versus me in faciendo passagium suum,* K. p. 120.

PASTOR. A Shepard. When inferiour tenants were obliged to bring themselves and their whole family to do work and services for the lord, an exception was made of their wives and their shepherds, as also of the cow-herds: for this reason, that the first might alway attend their houses, and the other their flocks and herds. So the tenants in Hedingdon,—*tribus diebus autumpno metent blada domini sumptibus ejusdem domini, primo scilicet die cum omnibus famulis suis, exceptis uxoribus et pastoribus suis,* K. p. 320.—*Cum tota familia sua præter uxorem suam,* K. p. 401.—*Sunt ibi sexdecim cotarii, quorum alii sunt bubulci domini, alii sunt pastores, qui si non essent, deberet quilibet unum opus singulis septimanis per annum.* Cartul. Abbat. Glaston. MS. f. 40.

PATRONUS. The advocate or patron of a church, who had *Jus Patronatus* the right of advouson, which was at first acquired by endowing a parochial church at the foundation of it with manse and glebe, which endowment was generally made by the lord of the mannor, to which piety we owe the original of Lay Patrons, K. p. 222. The Patrons for a mark of honour had precedence in their own churches, and in all solemn processions within the limits of the parish, wherein they had a right of carrying the chief flag, or first colours, K. p. 425, 507. No other lay men but the patron only was to be admitted within the bars or partition of the chancel from the nave of the church, in time of divine service. *Ad hæc adjicimus ne laici stent vel sedeant inter clericos in cancello dum divina ibidem celebrantur, nisi forte ob reverentiam vel aliam rationabilem causam et manifestam. Hoc solum patronis permittitur.* Constit. Rob. Episc. Linc. MS.

PAX *firma*. Peace and freedom from arrest, or any other molestation. Henry bishop of Winchester to Brien Fitz-Count lord of Walingford.—*Firmam pacem omnibus ad feriam meam venientibus a vobis et vestris dari quæsierim*, K. p. 100.

PECIA, *Petia*. A Piece or small parcel of ground.—*Cum duabus peciis—dictæ terræ pertinentibus*, K. p. 240. Whence to Piece and to Patch.

PELTYS. Lat. *Pelves*. Pelts or sheep-skins when the wool is off. Germ. *Peltz*. Hence the Pelt-rot, when sheep dye of poverty or ill keeping. Pelt in falconry is the skin of a fowl stuft, or any carcase of a dead fowl thrown to the hawks.—*Computant de tribus solidis, uno denario, ob. receptis de* xv. *Peltys bidentum de stauro necatarum in hospitio inter tonsuram et festum S. Michaelis*, K. p. 572. The Lat. *Peltis* was in Sax. Fæl and pælt, whence our Fellmonger who dresses the skins. A Felt or hat made of courser wool. *Pelvis* in old Eng. a Pelt, was likewise a leathern bag made of sheep skin, in which they carried salt, &c.—*Homines de Dukelechurch debent habere unum baconem de tribus solidis, et duos caseos, et duas pelves plenas salis, et duas summas de ligno.* Cartul. Abbat. Glaston. MS. f. 40.

PENTECOSTALIA. Pentecostals or Whitsun-contributions, that were allotted to the bishops, and are still paid in some few dioceses: of which the first occasion was possibly owing to the oblations made to the cathedral church at that season of the year, K. p. 597.

PERCAPTURA. A wire, a fishery, or place in a river made up for the better convenience of preserving and taking-fish. Of which kind there were several artificially contrived in most waters and streams. So Wido de Meriton granted to the Knights Templars *Omnes percapturas quas fratres inceperunt versus me in faciendo passagium suum*, K. p. 120.

PERTICA. A Perch, which in the reign of King John was the measure of twenty foot, and was the same as *Virga*,—*Quælibet virga, unde quarantanæ mensurabuntur, erit viginti pedum.* Mon. Ang. tom. 3. p. 16. So in 33 Edw. I.—*quadragenas unam acras et unam rodam et dimidiam per perticas viginti pedum*, K. p. 350. But now commonly a Perch, a Rod, a Pole, in Wiltshire a Log, is sixteen foot and a half in length, whereof fourty in length and four in breadth make one acre of ground. Yet there is no such fixt standard, but that it differs by custom in several counties.

PICAGIUM. Picage. A custom or duty paid at fairs and markets for breaking the ground and pitching of stalls and standings. From Lat. *Pica*, Fr. *Pic*, Eng. Pick, Pick-ax, and in Sussex a Pitch, old Eng. Pekois. Whence to Pick, or Peck, a Picker, a Pecker, to Pitch down, to Pitch up, a Pitch-fork, in Wiltshire a Pick, a souldier's Pike, a Peek or high top, as a woman's Peak, the Peak of Derby, &c. To have a Pique or quarrel, to be Piquant, &c.— King Hen. II. granted to the tenants within the honor of Walingford—*ut quieti sint de thelonio, pontagio, passagio, et picagio*, K. p. 114. The profit of Picage was generally granted in charters for the holding a fair or market, 19 Hen. VI. *Rex concessit Roberto Brook*—*picagium, stallagium, bothagium, et tollagium, una cum assisa panis et cervisiæ de novo mercato infra villam de Burcester*, K. p. 680.

PIETANTIA. A Pietance or Pittance, or allowance of bread and beer, or other provision to any pious use, especially to the religious for an augmentation of their commons,—*Quos quidem quatuor solidos*—*attornavi ad unam pietantiam in conventu Oseneiensi annuatim in perpetuum in die anniversarii mei obitus pro anima mea*, K. p. 283. From the Lat. *Pietas* comes our Pitty, which Duglass calls Pietie, thence Petans, Piteous, Pitiful, &c.

PISCARIA. A Fishery, or Were, wear or wire, Sax. Ƿæp. Bernard de S. Walery granted to the nuns of Godestow,—*unam piscariam de Werehama*, K. p. 128.

PLACIA. A Place or plat of ground, commonly the site of a house or other buildings. In Yorkshire and Lancashire a Plack, from Sax. Plæce. Whence the court or principal seat in a village is in several parts of England called the Place, and Place-house. Yngeram de Kirtlinton gave to the prior and canons of Burcester, —*totam illam placiam quæ se extendit*,—K. p. 208,—*cum quadam placia terræ*, K. p. 258.

PLACITUM. A Plea, Suit, or Trial. Whence Pleas of the crown, common Pleas, Pleading, Pleader, &c. *Placitum motum fuit inter dictos religiosos et nos*, K. p 285. *In Placitum trahere*, To prosecute or cite into any court of justice. *Idem Ychelus ipsum abbatem ea de causa jam in curiam christianitatis coram officiario diœcesani prædicti trahit in placitum, ipsum multipliciter ibidem inquietando*, K. p. 328 *Placitum conventionis*, A composition or final agreement of a depending suit by mutual compact,—*Unde placitum conventionis sumptum fuit inter eos in eadem curia, scilicet quod prædicti, &c.* K. p. 286. *Concordia facta in curia domini regis— unde placitum conventionis sumptum fuit inter eos in eadem curia,* K. p. 321.

PLANUM. Plain or open ground, opposed to woods and coppices. —*Communionem pasturæ tam in bosco quam in plano,* K. p. 76. —*In viis et planis, in aquis et molendinis,* K. p. 187. Hence a Plane or instrument of Planing, a Plat, Plot, or smooth place, the Plan or Plat-form of a building. A Plate, Platter, a Plash of water, to Plash or cut down, Plat-footed, &c. And what we now call the Blade of a sword or knife, was formerly termed the Plat.

PLEBANIA. A mother church with depending chappels, thus defined by the old canonists,—*Plebania est aliud genus beneficii, et majus quam rectoria, habet sub se capellas, et dignitatem esse putant interpretes.* Syntag. Juris. l 15, cap. 24 K. p. 589.

PLOWSHO. The plate of iron that is a shoe or defence to the bottom of the plough, as wheels are said to be Shod or Shoed, when they are guarded with iron. - *Pro uno vomere et una cultura et dimidia Toughe cum uno Plowsho emptis* xxiii. den. K. p. 549. A Plough, by the Alemans called *Pluch* and *Plug*, by the Danes *Ploug*, by the Dutch *Ploeg*, by the Anglo Saxons Sul, whence the *aratrum* now in Wiltshire is called a Sullow, and the word Plough is there attributed to any other waggon or carriage. But no question the Saxons had likewise the word *Plucce* for a Plough, and their *Pluscian*, our to Pluck, was originally to draw or pull along the Plough, which by metaphor was applied to any other sort of plucking or pulling. To this we owe a Plug or piece of wood to stop a hole, and to be Plugged or pulled out at pleasure.

PLURALITY of Ecclesiastical Benefices. This corruption so great in the reign of Edw. I. that Bogo de Clare rector of St. Peter's within the city of Oxford, was presented by the earl of Glocester to the church of Wiston, *com.* Northamp. and obtained leave to hold it with one church in Ireland, and fourteen other churches in England, all which benefices were valued at 238*l.* 6*s.* 8*d,* K. p. 292.

PONTAGIUM. Pontage, a toll or custom paid by travellers or passengers over a bridge toward the repair and maintenance of it. King Hen. II. granted to the tenants and traders within the honor of Walingford and Bercamsted—*ut quieti sint de thelonio, ponta-gio, passagio. &c.* K. p. 114. This privilege some donors called *Pontem Liberum*, as to the prior and canons of Burcester at their mill in Kirtlington,—*Concessi etiam dictis canonicis quod habeant pontem liberum ultra aquam ad bladum cariandum*, K. p. 201. It is a good pious custom that still obtains in Ireland, where the natives at passing over any bridge, pull off their hats, or give some other token of respect, and pray for the soul of the builder of that bridge.

PONTIUM *operationes*. The custumary service of work and labour done by inferiour tenants for making and repairing of bridges: from which servile duty some persons were by special privilege exempted, as the tenants within the honor of Walingford were,—*quieti de operationibus castellorum et pontium*, K. p. 114.

PORCUS. A Swine, Sax. Spỹn, a Hog, called a Porker, especially in those counties where sheep of the first or second year are called Hogs, and Hoggrels.—*Dare porcos in bosco*, to grant pannage or free running of hogs in such a wood or forest,—*Ego Ricardus le Bigod de Merston dedi canonicis de Nuttele quadraginta porcos in bosco meo*, K. p. 220.

PORCORIA, called in Lindwood *Porcitecum*. A Hogstie, which in the North is called a Swinhull, and a Swine-crue. In the woods and forests where the hogs run for pannage, there were several of those *Porcoriæ* or huts, where the Swine-herds at night secured their drove of hogs.—*Concessi Aliciæ heybotum et housbotum in dominicis boscis meis de Acle ad faciendas porcorias suas in boscis prædictis*, K. p. 259.—*In manerio de Dorcestre—summa reddituum porcoriarum et bercariarum si fuerint ad firmam* vs. vi d. K. p. 354.

PORTMOTA. Sax. Popt-ʒemote, a Portmote, Port-meeting, or convention of the inhabitants of a port or borough, in which some custumary dues were paid to the lord of the fee. The prior and bursar of Burcester in 3 Hen. VI. accounted—*de firma manerii de Clyfton—cum extentis curiarum, portmotis, et tolneto fori*, K. p. 570.

POSTULATIO. A Postulation made upon the unanimous electing of any person to a dignity or office, of which he is not capable by the ordinary canons or statutes, without special dispensation. So a chapter postulated for a bishop actually possest of another see. And the religious postulated for a prelate to be taken from another convent.—*Johannes supprior de Berencester a canonicis de Chetwode postulatur*, K. p. 257. An election could be made by a majority of votes, but a postulation must have been *Nemine contradicente*.

POTAGIUM. Pottage or liquid broth, of which Porridge and Posset are evidently corruptions, though Dr. Skinner violently fetches Porridge from Lat. *Porrus*, an onion, because forsooth the Romans put leeks in their broth; and Posset from the Fr. *Poser*, to settle, because the curdled or coagulated parts do fix or settle. It is pitty men's wit should be so much above their judgement.—From hence a Porringer or Pottage-dish, formerly called a Pottenger, and the smaller continent which we now call a Pipkin was formerly a Posnet. The appropriators were sometimes so liberal as to allow peas-porridge to the vicar. So the prior and canons of St. Frideswide to the vicar of Oakle,—*unum quarterium pisarum de melioribus dicti manerii sui pro potagio suo*, K. p. 455.

PRATUNCULUM. A ham or little meadow, which word Meadow, Sax. Œbe, Fr. Junius derives from the old Teuton. *Maden*, to mow, and says the Danes call a Mede or Meadow *Meaie*, the Dutch *May-land*, and the old Frisians *Miede*. Gilbert Basset in his foundation charter to the priory of Burcester, gives—*quoddam pratunculum quod vocatur Hamma*, K p. 135.

PRÆBENDA. A Prebend, an endowment in land, or pension in money, given to a cathedral or conventual church *in præbendam*, i. e. for a maintenance of a secular priest or regular canon, who was a *Præbendary* as supported by the said Prebend. Twelve shillings *per an.* was given out of the mannor of Hedingdon for a Prebend in the conventual church of Oseney, and was continued a rent charge upon the whole mannor, K. p. 334. *Ecclesia Præbendalis*, a church appropriated to a cathedral or religious house, the profits whereof were assigned for a prebend either in gross to the whole society, or to some particular member.—*Prior et conventus de Burncester dimiserunt ecclesiam prebendalem de Sotton cum capella de Bokyngham*, K. p. 342. *Præbendu* in profane and common acceptation was any sort of allowance or provender for cattel. As the prior and canons of St. Frideswide gave to the vicar of Oakle *duo quarteria frumenti pro prebenda equi sui, et decimam foeni de Lathmede pro foragio suo*, K. p. 455.—*Vicarius de Burcester habebit foenum et prebendam ad equum unum de prioratu*, K. p. 559.

PRÆCEPTORIA. A Preceptory, or commanderie. As the larger monasteries had their remote country cells which were subordinate to the mother house of religion: so the Knights Templars and Hospitalers sent part of their fraternity to some country cell governed by a preceptor or commandour, and thence called a Preceptorie or Commanderie, all which were subject and accountable to the prime body who had their principal seats in London. So the preceptorie of Sandford *com.* Oxon.—*Hoc factum est tempore fratris Johannis existentis præceptoris de Covele*, K. p. 121.

PRÆPOSITUS *Manerii*. The bayliff or steward of a mannor, who was to collect the rents, to levy distresses, to prevent trespasses, to keep the peace, and to do all the offices of equity and right between the lord and tenants.—*Compuiavit Johannes Canon præpositus de Clifton de manerio de Clifton*, K. p. 287.—*Sibilia filia Walteri filii præpositi de Pyria*, K. p. 327.—*Nicholaus præpositus de Byghenhull*, K. p. 202, 203. This provost or steward of a mannor was elected by all the tenants at the lord's court, and there took an oath of impartial fidelity in his office. So 17 Edw. III. *Omnis status de Wrechwyke elegerunt Hugonem Kyng ad officium præpositi, et juramentum suscepit*, K. p. 456. Part of his office was to take into the lord's hands such lands as the tenant through poverty was not able to occupy,—*Jurati dicunt quod uxor ejus (i. e. Thomæ Bavard nativi domini tenentis domini de Wrechwyke) non potest tenere prædicta messuagium et terram propter paupertatem, ita ut præpositus possit capere in manibus domini prædicta messuagium et terram*, K. p. 458. The clergy or secular priests were sometimes elected into this office, till they were restrained by ecclesiastical authority, as particularly by the constitutions of Robert Grosthead bishop of Lincoln.—*Walterus Hardy clericus est præpositus domini, et præstitit sacramentum ad officium præpositi bene et fideliter faciendum*, K. p. 470.

PRÆSTATIO. A payment.—*Prædicti prior et conventus Burncestræ omnia onera ordinaria et extraordinaria et omnes præstationes ratione dictarum decimarum semper sustinebunt*, K. p. 344.

PRECARIA. A Bedrep, or day of custumary work and labour done to the lord by his servile tenants, especially in the time of harvest.—*Virgata terræ ejusdem conditionis faciet tres precarias in autumpno, videlicet precariam sine prandio cum tribus hominibus, et unam precariam sine prandio cum uno homine*, K. p. 401.—*Alicia quæ fuit uxor Richardi le Grey—faciet tres precarias in autumpno sine cibo*, K. p. 402. The tenants who thus paid their bounden service to the lord, besides their ordinary meals and repasts, had a more solemn entertainment at the end of harvest, when they came to the court or seat of the lord, *cum toto ac pleno dyteno, i. e.* in a full body to sing harvest-home. Which is the original of our now obtaining custom, though the reason of it is altered. This treat given now to the tenants and labourers is in Kent at the end of wheat-harvest, and is called a Whetkin: but in these midland parts it is at bringing in the latest corn, and is termed a Harvest-home. *Vid.* BEDREPIUM.

PRESBYTER. The parish priest in opposition to the capellane or curate.—*Hiis testibus, Waltero capellano de Heyfyrd, Waltero presbytero de Meriton*, K. p. 121. *Fulcone presbytero de Meriton*, K. p. 122.

PRISO-QNIS. A Prisoner. From Fr. *Prendre*. The tenants were sometimes obliged to maintain at their own charge all prisoners who were apprehended within the extent of their own mannor. *Homines de Hedingdon omnes prisones qui infra dictum manerium capientur sumptibus propriis custodient,* K. p. 320.

PROCURARE. To provide for, or to entertain. In all the churches appropriated to the abby of Oseney,—*Canonici ipsi vicario invenient clericum et garconem, quos in omnibus suis expensis procurabunt,* K. p. 304.

PROCURATIO. A pecuniary sum or composition paid to an ordinary or other ecclesiastical judge, to commute for the provision or entertainment which was otherwise to have been procured for him. A procuration of two marks paid to the bishop for consecrating a church.—*Nos ecclesiam de Elsefeld—dedicasse, et recepisse a procuratore rectoris dictæ ecclesiæ duas marcas nomine procurationis ratione dedicationis ecclesiæ,* K p. 515. In 3 Hen. VI. the prior and bursar of the convent of Burcester accounted—*pro procuratione convocationis cleri tentæ London ante natale Domini hoc anno* ix. *den. Et in solutis pro procuratione domini papæ* vii. *sol.* ii. *den. Et in solutis domino archidiacono Oxon. pro procuratione ecclesiæ parochialis Burcester hoc anno* vii *sol.* vii. *den. ob. q.* K. p. 573. The archdeacon's procuration was commonly laid upon the appropriators, yet often injuriously thrown back upon the vicar. —*Cætera onera ipsius ecclesiæ (i. e. de Ambrosden) ordinaria subeat vicarius prædictus, præter procurationem archidiaconi, quam iidem religiosi solvent in futurum,* K. p. 43!.

PROCURATORIUM. The Procuratory or instrument by which a person or persons did constitute or delegate their proctor to represent them in an ecclesiastical court or cause.—*Tenor vero procuratorii dictorum religiosorum,* K. p. 584.

. PROCURATORES *Ecclesiæ Parochialis.* Church-wardens who were to act as proxies and representatives of the church for the true honour and interest of it.—*Johannes Peris sen. et Johannes Baily procuratores ecclesiæ parochialis de Acle,* K. p. 562.

PROCURSUS *bestiarum in foresta* The walk, or range, or running, for deer and other beasts in a forest.—The jury found it would be a prejudice to assart, *i. e.* to grub and cultivate, two acres of land upon Fernburst within the forest of Bernwode,—*quia si essent assartatæ, bestiæ amitterent procursus suos ad transversum forestæ,* K. p. 249.

PROHIBITIO. A Prohibition, or writ from the king in behalf of one prosecuted in the court Christian, upon an action or cause belonging or pretended to belong to the temporal jurisdiction.—John de Pydington had a prohibition against William vicar of the church of Little-Brickhill, 20 Edw. I. K. p. 318. This liberty of suing a prohibition was expresly renounced in some covenants between the religious.—*Renuntiantes in hac facto omnibus impellationibus super hoc habitis, appellationibus, in integrum restitutioni, regiæ prohibitioni, et omni alii remedio,* K. p. 344.

PROVINCIA. A Diocese.—*In provincia Alexandri Lincoln. episcopi,* K. p. 93.

PROTECTIO. A writ of Protection was given to religious houses, and to particular priests for contributing freely to the king.—*Ex hac causa libentius providere volentes suscepimus in protectionem et defensionem nostram specialem præfatum Radulphum et singulos de prædicto Radulpho homines, terras, res, reddituss, et omnes possessiones ejusdem,* K. p. 323, 329.

PULLANUS, *Pullus*. A colt or young horse, by Chaucer called a Stod, as now in the North a Stot, Sax. Steða and Stoð, Eng. Steed,—*duo pullani fœmini* (i. e. two mare colts) *quatuor boves, &c.* K. p. 287. *Tres pulli masculi, unus fœminus,* K. p. 288.— *De octo solidis receptis de uno pullano vendito per Johannem Deye apud Bucks.* K. p. 571.—*Sex pulli et tres equulæ, et unus equulus de duobus annis, et duo pulli de uno anno,* K. p. 38. From the Lat. *Pullus* came the Sax. Folle, old Eng. Phully, now Filly, a young colt, or in some parts only the mare colt. In a team, the horse which goes in the rods is commonly called the Fillar and the Fill-horse. It is a sorry ignorance in Minshew to derive Filly, a colt, from *Filia*, a daughter. And a very learned man could only trifle on this word.—*Fillie, recepto sæpe nomine generosioribus quibusdam Anglis dicitur equa præter cæteras adamata. Fortasse nimirum aliquis equulæ suæ adblandiens* φίλην *olim dixerit, atque inde remanserit hæc denominatio. Fieri quoque potest eos equulam præcipuè in deliciis habitam Phillie nuncupásse, ab illo Phyllidos nomine, quod perdité dilectis amicabus passim tribuunt impotentiores amasii.* Fr. Junius *in voce* Phillie.

PURPARS. Fr. *Pour part, pro parte* A Purparty, or that part or share of an estate, which being held in common by copartners, is by partition allotted to any one of them.—*Inquisitio de hæreditate Margaretæ et Elizabethæ—liberes, habenda in purpartem ipsius Elizabethæ,* K. p. 502.

PUTTA. Sax. Pitte, a Pit, Stone-pit, Chalk-pit, &c. From *Puteus*, a well, or rather *Putus*, little. *Una in Crocwell-furlung quæ jacet ad puttam inter terram Johannis le Palmer, &c.* K. p. 186. This in the broad country tone is still called a Putte. Staneputtes, the Stone-pits, K. p. 397. Hence by metaphor Lat. and Ital. *Putta*, Fr. *Putte*, a whore, and *Putagium*, in old Eng. *Putre*, fornication on the woman's side. As now in London a Buttock or Puttock is a plain dealing whore, opposed to a File or pick pocket whore. In the North a Puttock-candle is the least in the pound, put in to make weight, called in Wiltshire a Pissing candle, in Kent a Make-weight.

Q.

QUADRARIUM. A Quarry, or stone-pit. *Vid.* CARRUM.

QUARENTENA. A Quarentine, a Fourty long, or Furlong. From the Fr. *Quarente*, fourty. A measure of fourty perches. *Quarentana vero quadraginta perticis.* Mon. Ang. tom. 1. p. 313. In which computation the perch was twenty foot. *Quælibet virga unde quarentenæ mensurabuntur, erit viginti pedum.* Mon. Ang. tom. 3. p. 16. In the Doomsday survey, it was the usual mensuration of wood-land. So in Burcester there was—*Silva unius quarentenæ longitudine et unius lat:tudine,* K. p. 65. A Quarentine was also the space of fourty days, wherein any person coming from foreign parts infected with the plague, was not permitted to land or come on shore, till he had performed his Quarentine, or fourty days were fully expired. A Quarentine was likewise a benefit allowed by the law of England for the widow to continue in her husband's chief mansion-house (if it were not a castle) for the space of fourty days after his decease.

QUARTERIUM. A Quarter, a seam, or eight bushels of corn.— *Tria quarteria frumenti, tria quarteria avenarum, et unum quarterium fabarum,* K. p. 291. *Vid.* SUMMA.

QUERELA. An action preferred in any court of justice, in which the plantiff was called *Querens,* and his *breve,* complaint or declaration, was *Querela,* whence our Eng. Quarrel. *Quietos esse a querelis* was to be exempted from the custumary fees paid to the king or lord of a court for the purchasing a liberty to prefer such an action. But more usually to be exempted from fines imposed for common trespasses and defaults. So King Hen. II. to Bernard de S. Walery,—*Terræ suæ sint quietæ de omnibus placitis et querelis, exceptis murdredo.et latrocinio,* K. p. 123.—*Quatuor hidas apud Cestreton liberas et quietas ab omnibus querelis excepto murdredo et danegeldo,* K. p. 403.

QUIETUS. A writ of discharge granted to those barons and knights, who personally attended the king in any foreign expedition, and were therefore exempted from the claim of scutage, or a tax on every knight's fee. So Gilbert Basset had his writ of Quietus in 2 King John for seven knights fees within the honor of Walingford, K. p. 162.

QUINTAN, by the French termed *Quintain,* by the old English Quintane and Whintane, now commonly corrupted into Quintal.

At first a Roman military sport, still retained in those parts of England which lay adjacent to the Roman garrisons and ways; and now made a custumary sport at weddings, K. p. 19.

R.

RAISES. The northern term for the Risings, the barrows or hillocks raised for the burial of the dead, K. p. 37. They use likewise in the northern parts near Scotland a Ram-raise to signifie the motion of stepping backward for the better advantage of taking a leap forward.

REA or Rey, an appellative for a river, whence Suthrey, the county on the south-side of the river Thames, K. p. 27. The small rivulet that runs through Burcester and cross Otmoore, is called the Rea or Rey: which in Lat. was termed *Burus*, whence Burcester Bury-end or River-end, in opposition to King's-end. And in Bury-end feld there was Schort-reye-croft, Nether-reye-croft, and Over-reye-croft, K. p. 536. So St. Marie Overies on the Southwark side of London.

RECOGNITIO. The impanel of a jury, or inquest of twelve or more legal men, who were therefore called Recognitores.—*Habere recognitionem*, to have a trial or verdict of jurors, for liberty of which a fine was paid to the king.—*Abbas de Egnesham debet unum palefridum pro habenda recognitione duodecim legalium hominum de vicineto de Erdinton*, K. p. 168. *Recognitio novæ assisæ*, a new trial.—*Richardus de Camvill et Eustacia uxor ejus debent unam marcam pro habenda recognitione novæ assisæ*, K. p. 173:

RECTUM. Right of inheritance. Brien Fitz-Count engaged to serve Maud the empress,—*Eam auxiliari rectum suum acquirere quod vi aufertur*, K. p. 101. Right and satisfaction to be obtained in a legal course of justice. Alexander bishop of Lincoln to Guy de Charing,—*Ne pro recti vel justitiæ penuria amplius audiam clamorem*, K. p. 90. *Vid.* BREVE DE RECTO.

RECTORIA. The word used for a parsonage-house, even where there was no instituted rector. As at Stratton-Audley a chappel appendant to Burcester and appropriated to that priory,—*Pro cariagio albi straminis a rectoria de Stratton*, K. p. 549.

REGARDATORES *Forestæ*. Those officers who were every year upon oath to make a Regard, or take a view of the forest limits, and enquire into all the damages and trespasses committed, and present them in writing at the next swainmote or forest-court. Manwood refers their institution to King Hen. II. but Spelman believes the name at least was since given, and that in the reign of

Hen. II. they were called *Custodes venationis.—Per sacramentum omnium regardatorum et agistatorum*, K. p. 209.

REGRESSUS. A re-entry upon an estate past away, which was commonly renounced in the charter of conveyance. Bernard de S. Walery gave the site and advowson of Godstow to King Hen. II. —*Ita quod neque ego neque hæredes mei regressum habeamus, vel calumpniam aliquam versus aliquos de præfato manerio*, K. p. 127.

RELEVIUM. A Relief or fine paid to the king by all who came to the inheritance of lands held *in capite* or [by] military service, to Relieve or as it were to redeem their estate, and obtain possession of it. It consisted at first in horses and arms, till by the Assise of Arms, 27 Hen. II. every man's armour was preserved for his heir, and the Relief payable in money, of which the fixt rates were determined by Magna Charta. An earl for his whole county one hundred pounds. A baron for his whole barony one hundred marks. A knight for his whole fee one hundred shillings; and so in proportion, to be paid by every inheritor of an estate, at full age, the heir male at twenty-one, female at fourteen. Thomas de S. Walery lord of Ambrosden indebted to King John one hundred and seventy marks for a Relief, K. p. 159. Sir William Fitz-Elias paid one hundred shillings for his Relief of one knight's fee in Oakle, 11 Hen. II. K. p. 202. The judges determined that William Longspe should pay two hundred pounds for the Relief of two baronies, K. p. 246. One hundred pounds paid for the Relief of one barony by Hugh de Plessets, 47 Hen. III. K. p. 260. One hundred pounds by Theobald de Verdon baron, K. p. 282. If the baron were beyond the seas at the time of his coming to full age, the estate was by the king's special favour surrendered to his use, with security given for paying a reasonable Relief at his return.—*Cum idem Henricus sit in transmarinis partibus, volentes ei gratiam facere, omnia prædicta ipsi reddidimus, accepta securitate de rationabili relevio*, K. p. 469. Reliefs were payable not only to the king as prime lord, but to all barons and knights by those tenants who held under them by military service. This was chargeable on estates of this tenure given to religious houses. As the priory of Poghele *in com.* Berks. at the succession of every new prior paid to Sir Ralph de Chesterton lord of the fee one hundred shillings for the Relief of one knight's fee in Bettreton, K. p. 234.

RELEVARE. To pay such Relief and obtain possession of such estate. Some customary and servile tenants did Relieve or pay a fine for renewment of a tenure on the death of the last possessor, which in one virgate was double the rent, and four shillings over. So in the mannor of Hedingdon 20 Edw. I. *Cum integram virga-*

tam terræ tenens decesserit, hæres ejus per duplicationem sui redditus annualis et per quatuor solidos terminum ultra relevabit, et qui minus tenuerit de una virgata, ultra redditum suum duplicatum, minus det secundum quantitatem tenementi sui, K. p. 319.

RELIGIOSI. The Religious or all regulars of a religious order, as opposed to lay men and to the secular clergy. Before the statute of Mortmain, the nation was so sensible of the extravagant donations to the religious, that in the grant and conveyance of estates it was often made an express condition, that no sale, gift, or assignation of the premises should be made to the religious.—*Tenenda sibi et hæredibus suis, vel cuicunque vendere, dare, vel assignare voluerint, exceptis viris religiosis et Judæis.*

REPASTUM. A Repast or meal. *Unum Repastum,* one meal's meat given by custom to servile tenants when they laboured for their lord.—*Tenet in bondagio, et debet unam wedbedrip pro voluntate dominæ, et habebit unum repastum,* K. p. 401.

REPRISA. The deductions and charges paid out of lands and tenements to be allowed and excepted in the clear value of the estate.—*Capitale messuagium valet per annum cum tota inclausa ii. sol. et non plus, salva reprisa domorum et aliarum officinarum,* K. p. 314.

RESPECTUS. Respite or longer time. *Se ponere in respectum,* To gain a continuance of term, or forbearance, in order to make a better proof or defence in a cause depending.—*Robertus Frere et Joshua Phelippes attachiati—se ponunt in respectum quousque melius poterit per fide dignos probari,* K. p. 458.

RESTITUTIO *in integrum.* A writ of restitution, to put a person into repossession of such lands and tenements as whereof he had been wrongfully disseised. The procuring such writ was expresly renounced in some covenants of sale, the better to secure a title to the purchaser. *Renuntiantes in hoc facto omnibus impellationibus super hoc habitis, appellationibus, in integrum restitutioni, regiæ prohibitioni, &c.* K. p. 344.

RESTITUTIO *Temporalium.* All bishopricks and abbies held in *capite* upon every vacancy or death of a prelate, were taken as a lapse into the king's hands by the eschaetor, who was to receive the intermediate profits, and upon the election and confirmation of a successor, a writ was issued out *De Restitutione Temporalium.*—*Abbas de Oseneia obiit* 25 *Edw. I. et ante restitutionem temporalium dictæ abbatiæ successori dicti abbatis dictæ domus electo factam, petiit eschaetor ad opus domini regis cupam et palefridum,* K. p. 330.

RETINEMENTUM. Reserve.—*Sine ullo retinemento ad me vel hæredes meos pertinente,* K. p. 162.

ROTULUS *Curiæ.* The court roll of the lord, in which the

names, rents, and services of the tenants were copied and enrolled. *Per rotulum curiæ tenere,* by copy hold.—*Matildis le Taillur tenet per rotulum curiæ unum messuagium,* K. p. 396.

ROTULI *Placitorum.* Court records, or the register of trials, judgements and decrees, in a court of justice.—*Dicti homines præmissas conventiones in rotulis placitorum domini regis de anno supradicto ad majorem securitatem inrotulari procurarunt,* K. p. 321.

RUDGE. The back or top of any thing, thence by metaphor applied to a hill or any ascent. As Asherugge, *Mons Fraxineus,* a hill of ashes. From Sax. ₥ŋıʒe, ₥ŋıck, Dan. *Ryc.* Hence a Rack and Rick of hay or straw. A Rack of mutton, *Dorsum ovile.* A Ridge of land. The Ridge of a house. Rugged or high-backed, a Rug, Rough, Roughings, Rigging or cloaths. To Rig or lade a vessel. And in old Eng. the word Rigge was used for the back, as Pierce Plough-man describes the pedlar with "a Pake at his Rigge," *i. e.* a pack at his back.

RUSTICI. Those Corls, Churls, Clowns, or inferiour tenants who held cottages and land by the service of country work or handlabour. The land of such ignoble tenure was called by the Saxons Gaɲollanƌ, as afterwards Soccage tenure, and was sometimes distinguisht by the name of *Terra Rusticorum.* So Gilbert Basset gave to his priory of Burcester—*Unam virgatam terræ in Strattun collectam de terra rusticorum, quæ data fuit in dote prædictæ capellæ,* K. p. 136.

S.

SACERDOS. The parish priest, rector, or vicar, as distinguished from his capellane or curate. So to the donation of the hermitage of Musewell to the abby of Missenden, the witnesses are—*Willielmus senex sacerdos de Burcester, cum Willielmo capellano suo, et Willielmo sacerdote de Ambrosden,* K. p. 76. To a charter of Sir Wido de Meriton to the Knights Templars. *Testes donationis sunt Fulco sacerdos de Meriton,* K. p. 120.

SACRAMENTUM. An oath. The common form of all inquisitions made by a jury of free and legal men: *Qui dicunt super (aut per) sacramentum suum,* K. p. 314. Whence possibly the proverbial offering to take the Sacrament in affirming or denying, was first meant of an oath.

SACRAMENTUM *Altaris.* The sacrifice of the mass, or what we now call the Sacrament of the Lord's Supper: for which communion, the bread and wine was provided by the priest out of the ample offerings, and in appropriated churches this burden was often laid on the vicar.—*Panem et vinum pro sacramento altaris vicarius illius ecclesiæ (i. e. de Meriton) propriis sumptibus exhibebit,* K. p. 483.

SACRILEGIUM. Sacrilege, or an alienation to lay men and to profane or common purposes of what was given to religious persons and to pious uses. Our fore-fathers were very tender of incurring the guilt and scandal of this crime. And therefore when the Knights Templars were dissolved, their lands were all given to the Knights Hospitalers of Hierusalem,—*Ne in pios usus erogata contra donatorum voluntatem in alios usus distraherentur,* K. p. 390.

SALARIUM. A Salary. At first it signified the rent or profits of a *Sala* or house. In Gascoigne they now call the seats of noblemen *Sales,* as we do Halls. It afterwards stood for any wages or annual allowance,—*Qui quidem capellanus et successores sui nomine salarii sui recipient singulis annis in perpetuum omnimodas decimas,* K. p. 661.

SALT-SYLVER. One penny paid at the feast of St. Martin by the servile tenants to their lord, as a commutation for the service of carrying their lord's salt from market to his larder.—*In manerio de Pydinton quilibet virgatarius dabit domino unum denarium pro Salt-Sylver per annum ad dictum festum S. Martini, vel cariabunt salem domini de foro ubi emptus fuerit ad lardarium domini,* K. p. 496.

SARCULARE. To weed standing corn. From Lat. *Sarclum, Surculum,* a weeding-hook.—*Tenentes de Hedingdon per duos dies in quadragesima similiter arabunt, et herciabunt, et uno die postea sarculabunt blada domini ibidem,* K. p. 320.—*Et in solutis diversis hominibus et fœminis primo die Julii conductis ad sarculandum diversa blada, ut patet per talliam, contra agillarium hoc anno* xiv. *sol.* x. *den.* K. p. 576. *Una Sarculatura,* the service of one day's weeding for the lord.—*Tenet in bondagio, et debet unam aruram, et unam sarculaturam,* K. p. 401. —*Alicia quæ fuit uxor Richardi le Grey faciet unam sarculaturam, et unam wedbedripam,* K. p. 402.

SAY. Silk. *A* Lat. *Sericum,* Ital. *Seta,* Teuton *Seide,* Sax. Sibene. Whence our Sattin, which yet Vossius deduces from Lat. and Gr. Σινδων, as that from the Syriac *Sadni.*—*Et in bolt rubei Say propter anabatam faciendam* iv. *sol.* viii. *den.* K. p. 574.

SASSONS. The corruption of Saxons, a name by which the English were formerly called in contempt (as they still are by the Welsh) while they rather affected the name of Angles.

SALICETUM. An Osier-bed, or low moist place on the bank of a river for the growth of osiers, willows, or withies. Sax. Ƿelıȝeɾ, old Eng. Wickers. Thence a Wicker basket, a Wicket or door made of basket work. The Wicket or cross stick to be thrown down by the ball at the game called Crickets, &c. *Molendinum de Kertlinton cum qualam particula saliceti, quæ de meo feodo est*, K. p. 201.

A SCEAP. A measure of corn. Lat. *Schapa, Schaphula, à Scapha*, a boat, or Scipp or Sciff. *Sceppa salis*, a quantity of salt. Mon. Ang. tom. 2. p. 284.—Eight quarter and one sceap of wheat, K. p. 604. Hence a basket is called a Skip or Skep in the south parts of England, and a beehive is called a Beeskip.

SCHOZEARS. They seem to have been plough-wheels, from Sax. Scor, Shoes, and Ɛpian, to plough or ear.—*Et in uno pari rotarum vocat. Schozears empto ibidem* vii. *sol.* ii. *den.* K. p. 573.

SCIREWYTE. An annual tax or imposition paid to the sheriff of the county or shire, for holding the assises or county courts.— *In solutis pro quodam pensione vocata Scirewyte annuatim* iv. *sol.* K. p. 573. *Shire, Schyre*, from Sax. Scýpan, to divide, whence a Share or division, a Shore dividing sea and land, a Skry to cleanse and separate corn, a Skreen or partition in a room. To Shear or to cut with a pair of Shears, a Wheat-shearing in Kent is the time of cutting wheat. A Sciver, now a Shiver or Shavings of wood, a Sceuer for meat, a Schrift or shift, a Schred or shred, a Scheart or shirt, Sceord or short, a Sceort or skirt, &c. In Kent we call a bridle-way a Sheer-way, as separate and divided from the common road, or open high-way.

SCOTELLA. *Scutella, à Scutum.* Sax. Scutel, Scuttel, any thing of a flat and broad shape like a shield : especially a plate or dish, as a shallow platter is still called a wooden Scuttle : and in Kent the shovel with which they turn their malt is called a Scuttle. To the same Lat. *Scutum* we owe the Scuttles of a ship, a weaver's Shuttle, a Shuttle-cock, &c.—*Et in duabus scotellis manualibus emptis ibidem* vii. *den. et in quinque scotellis minoris sortis emptis ibidem pro cæteris officiis* ix. *den.* K. p. 574.

SCRUTINIUM. A view and inquest made by neighbours as select arbitrators to adjust any depending difference.—*Idem prior facto inde per vicinos diligenti scrutinio certioratus per eosdem*, K. p. 297.

SCUTAGIUM. Scutage, from Lat. *Scutum*, a shield, whereon they wore a device or military distinction, whence *Scutum Armorum*, a coat of arms. Fr. *Escusson*, whence our Escocheon or Scutchion. All tenants who held from the king by military service were bound to attend personally in wars and expeditions; or for default of personal service, a Scutage or composition tax on every *Scutum militare* or knight's fee and the proportionable parts was assest and levied for the king's use. In 7 Hen. II. there was a Scutage of two marks on every knight's fee, K. p. 118. A Scutage of one mark in 13 Hen. II. K. p. 124. A Scutage of ten shillings on every fee collected in 3 Rich. I. K. p. 148. A Scutage of twenty shillings for the king's redemption, 5 Rich. I. K. p. 154. A Scutage of two marks in the first of King John, K. p. 160. The same Scutage in 2 King John, K. p. 162. A Scutage of three marks in 27 Hen. III. K. p. 231. A Scutage of twenty shillings on each fee for marriage of the king's eldest daughter in 29 Hen III. K. p. 235. A Scutage of fourty shillings for making Prince Edward a knight in 39 Edw. III. K. p. 249. A Scutage of fourty shillings in 6 Edw. I. K. p. 290. If a baron or knight had paid his personal attendance in any expedition, he had the king's discharge from Scutage to himself or to his heir.—*Rex vic. Oxon.*—*Sciatis quod W. Longspe quondam comes Sarum fuit nobiscum in exercitu nostro Muntgumery. Ideo tibi præcipimus quod de Scutagio quod per summonitores scaccarii exigis a filio—pacem ei habere permittas,* K. p. 200. The barons and knights when they paid a Scutage to the king, had power to levy the same tax of those tenants who held from them in military service. And this was often made an express condition in subordinate grants and conveyances. So Amfride Fitz-Richard gave to the abby of Oseney one hide of land in Chesterton,—*Ita quod quando dominica terra de Cestreton dat scutagium, dicta terra dabit quintam partem unius scuti,* K. p. 126.—*De liberis tenentibus dicunt, quod Robertus Pickerell tenet de octo virgatis terræ cum pertinentiis in Meriton, quæ pertinent ad manerium de Pydinton, et tenentur de domino ejusdem per servitium militare, et quum scutagium currit domino, dabit unam marcam,* K. p. 495. The barons upon other extraordinary occasions obtained the king's precept, whereby they were impowered to tax their inferiour tenants. As when Richard king of the Romans and earl of Cornwall was to visit Rome, upon his own and his royal brother's urgent affairs, the king issued one writ to the said earl, to authorise him to demand, and another to his tenants to oblige them to pay, a certain Scutage to him. And at another time by the king's order a Scutage was imposed on all the tenants of the said Richard, to raise the mony which he had expended for his redemption when a prisoner to Montfort's party, K. p. 268.

SEAL. Sax. Sıȝel, from Lat. *Sigillum.* Those persons who had no proper seal of their own procured the seal of some other private friend or publick officer to be affixt to their acts and deeds. So Margaret le Frankleyn in 10 Hen. III. put the seal of Gerard de Wyzeri, because she had no seal in her own right, K. p. 199. If persons thought their own seal to be obscure and unknown, they generally procured the affixing of some more authentick seal; as in the form of several charters,—*Quia sigillum meum penitus est incognitum—Ideo sigillum—apponi procuravi,* K. p. 442, 663, 666.

SECRETARIUS, *à Secretis,* a Secretary. The word formerly signified any confident, favourite, or intimado.—*Cuncta denique agenda sua ad nutum unius secretarii sui passim committere*, K. p. 388.

SECTA *Curiæ*. Suit and service done by tenants at the court of their lord,—*Homines de Hedingdon facient sectam curiæ domini de sex septimanis, et si breve domini regis in dicta curia attachietur, tunc sectam illam facient de tribus septimanis in tres septimanas*, K. p. 320. This suit or attendance was often remitted to the religious as a special privilege. So Richard earl of Cornwall confirmed to the abby of Oseney their land in Mixbury,—*quæ terra quandoquidem consuevit facere sectam ad curiam nostram de North-Osenei, hanc sectam, &c. relaxamus in perpetuum*, K. p. 212.

SECTA *Schirarum et Hundredorum*. The attendance, suit, and service done by tenants in the county and hundred courts. *Quietos esse de hac secta*, was a privilege to be exempted from such custumary service. So the abbat of Abbotesburie *in com.* Dorset, had this privilege in the hundred of Whitchurch,—*Prædicti abbas et prædecessores sui sunt quieti de secta illius hundredi per concessionem Roberti de Mandevil quondam domini ejusdem hundredi*. Mon. Ang. tom. 1. p. 279. So King Hen. II. granted to the free tenants within the honors of Walingford and Bercamsted,—*ut sint quieti de sectis schirarum et hundredorum*, K. p. 114. The religious had commonly their tenants discharged from this duty for those lands which they held in frank almoigne,—*Eleemosinam liberam et quietam ab omni sectantia et exactione*, K. p. 132.

SEED-COD. A basket or other vessel of wood carried upon one arm of the husbandman, to bear the seed or grain which he sows with the other hand. From Sax. Sæb, seed, and Cobbe a purse, or such like continent. Hence Codd in Westmorland is a bolster or pillow, and in other northern parts a Cushion, as a Pin-cod; *i. e.* a pin-cushion, a Horse-cod, *i. e.* a horse-collar to guard his neck. The Cod of a man or beast, a Cod-piece, a Peas-cod, &c.—*Pro uno seed-cod empto* iv. *d.* K. p. 549. This Seed-cod was commonly by the Saxons called Sæb-Leap, which very word Seed leap is still retained in Essex, but here in Oxfordshire corrupted into a Seed-lip, and in other parts a Seed-lib. The Sax. Leap was properly a basket or pannier made of osiers; whence a Weel made of willows or osiers to catch fish, is now in Leicestershire called a Leap. From this continent they borrowed the Latin word *Lepa*, a Lepe, or measure of about five gallons, as in this citation from an extent of the mannor of Garinges produced by Sir Henry Spelman,—*Debet triturare tres bussellos frumenti, et dimidiam lepæ, vel quinque bussellos fabarum, pisarum, vel vescarum*. And more evidently from an extent of the mannor of Terring in Sussex, 5 Edw. I. quoted by Mr. Somner,—*Willielmus le Cupere tenet ferlingum unius vir-*

gatæ continentem quatuordecim acras pro octodecim denariis solvendis,—et colliget de nucibus in bosco domini tertiam partem unius mensuræ quæ vocatur Lepe, quod est tertia pars duarum busselorum, et valet quadrantem. The words Leap and Lib in Sussex do now signifie the measure of half a bushel, or four gallons.

SELIO. A ridge of ploughed land, or as much as lies between two furrows. In old Eng. a Selion of land, and a Stitch of land: Coke on Littleton derives the Lat. *Selio* from the Fr. *Sellon,* a ridge. But the learned Spelman gives its original to the Sax. Sul, or Sýl, a plough, which in the North is still called a Sull, and in Wiltshire a Sullow.—Joan prioress of Merkyate and her sisters granted to Henry prior of Burcester and the canons—*duas seliones in Hodesham,* K. p. 166.—*quatuor seliones terræ quæ vocantur buites,* K. p. 187. Alice Segrim granted to Sir John de Handlo, —*duas seliones terræ arabilis in Southcroft,* K. p. 347.—*Octo acræ jacent apud le Bowelonde in novemdecem selionibus,—et duæ acræ continent quatuor seliones cum duabus buttis,* K. p. 428.—*Ad præparandum usque ad carectam* xxix. *seliones ordei,* K. p. 576. From the Sax. Sul came the Lat. *Sulinga,* old Eng. Sulinge, a ploughland, which thus occurs in an old charter of King Offa to archbishop Janibert,—*In nomine Jesu Salvatoris mundi, &c. Ego Offa rex totius Anglorum patriæ dabo et concedo Janiberht archiepiscopo ad ecclesiam, aliquam partem terræ trium aratorum, quod Cantianiste dicitur* three Sulinge. From Sull a plough we must derive to Sully, *i. e.* to throw up dirt, and perhaps the looks and colours of Sullen and Sallow; nor is it unlikely our Eng. Soil and to Soil, are rather owing to the Sax. Sul than to the Lat. *Solum.*

SEISINA, *Saisina.* From Fr. *Saisir,* to take or possess. *Ponere in seisina,* to give or put in possession. *Constituo—attornatum meum ad ponendum Johannem filium Nigelli jun. de Borstall nomine meo in seisina de omnibus terris, &c.* K. p. 275. Longa seisina, long and immemorial possession. *Franciplegium est quædam libertas regia mere spectans ad coronam et dignitatem domini regis, contra quam longa seisina valere non debet,* K. p. 313.

SENESCHALLUS. A Seneschal, from the Germ. *Sein,* a house or place, and *Schale,* a servant. The Seneschal of a baron was his chief steward or head bayliff that kept his courts, received his rents, and managed his demesne lands. Hugh de Bochland was Seneschal to Brien Fitz Count lord of Walingford, K. p 100. *Edmundus comes Cornubiæ dilecto et fideli suo Simoni de Grenhull seneschallo honoris S. Walerici salutem,* K. p. 331. When the baron was absent out of England his Seneschal acted all matters as his lord's attorney or proxy,—*Nec est prætermittendum quod quotiescunque priorissam eligere contigerit ad eundem prioratum, de seipsis*

k

priorissam de assensu meo, vel seneschalli mei si in Anglia non fuero, eligere licebit, K. p. 165.

SEPARIA, *Separaria.* A Several or divided enclosure,—*Placia quæ jacet juxta separiam prioris et conventus de Burncester,* K. p. 336.

SEQUESTRARE. To Sequester the profits of an estate or benefice, or detain them from the use of the proprietor or owner. A power of sequestration reserved to the bishop against the appropriators, if they failed in any performance of covenant or pension. As in the ordination of the vicarage of Melton,—*Liceat eo ipso, et non servato alio processu, nobis et succesoribus nostris episcopis Lincolniæ omnes fructus redditus et proventus ipsius ecclesiæ sequestrare, et sub tuto tenere sequestro, donec dicta pensio cum suis arreragiis integre persolvatur,* K. p. 483.

SEQUI. To prefer an action and prosecute a cause, as attorney of the plantiff.—*Gilbertus de Thornton qui sequitur pro rege dicit quod franciplegium, &c.* K. p. 313.

SEQUELA. Suit and service and all other customary duties of those tenants who depended on the lord. William de Longspe confirmed to the priory of Burcester their land in Wrechwick,—*cum villanis et eorum sequelis et catallis,* K. p. 216.—*Villanos cum villanagiis omnibus catallis et tota sequela ipsorum,* K. p. 288.—*Una cum villanis, coterellis, eorum catallis, servitiis, sectis, et sequelis, et omnibus suis ubicunque pertinentibus,* K. p. 310.

SERA *Pendibilis.* A Pad-lock, which Pad Minshew makes to be a contraction of Pendible, but Skinner from the German *Padde, Seræ Latibulum,* the staple into which the bolt runs.—*Et in sex seris pendibilibus emptis ibidem* xviii. *den.* K. p. 574. The Sax. Loc signified not only the Lock of a door, but any sort of enclosure, whence a Lock or restraint of water on the river, a Lock or pen for sheep.

SERJANTIA, *Servientia.* A Serjeantry or service done for the holding of lands, either Grand-serjeantry, some honourable military service paid only to the king, as to carry his banner, to bear his sword, to find him a certain number of men and horses, &c. Or Petit-serjeantry, some inferiour and less noble service paid to the king or any other lord, as reception and entertainment, provender for horses, to give a bow, spurs, gloves, &c.—*Johannes filius Nigelli tenet de rege unam hidam terræ arabilis in Borstall per magnam serjeantiam custodiendi forestam de Bernwode,* K. p. 265. —*Isabella de Handlo tenuit unum messuagium quatuor carucatas terræ, et triginta unum solidatos, et quatuor denariatos redditus in Hedindon a domino rege in capite per magnam serjeantiam inveniendi unum hominem, et custodiendi forestam de Shotover et Sto-*

wode; K. p. 490. Richard de Prestcote held one hide of land in Blechesdon,—*per serjantiam portandi unam hastam porci.*—By the petty serjeantry of carrying a shield of brawn to the king as often as he hunted in the forest of Cornbury, K. p. 244. Joan de Musegrave held the same lands by the same tenure in 13 Edw. III. K. p. 450. Oliver de Standford in 27 Edw. I. held lands in Netlebed *com.* Oxon.—*Per serjantiam espicurnantiæ in cancellaria domini regis,*—By the office of Espigurnel or sealer of the king's writs in Chancery, K. p. 292. Ela countess of Warwick held the mannor of Hokenorton *com.* Oxon.—*Per serjantiam scindendi coram domino rege die natalis Domini, et habere cultellum domini regis de quo scindit,* K. p. 308. The mannor of Broughton *com.* Oxon. in reign of Edw. II. was held by John Mauduit *in capite,*—*Per serjantiam mutandi unum hostricum domini regis, vel illum hostricum portandi ad curiam domini regis,* K. p. 569. •Aston-Bernard *com.* Buck. held in 20 Edw. III. by John Molins from the king *in capite,*—by the serjeantry of being marshal of the king's faulcons and other hawks, K. p. 569. William de la Pole marquess of Suffolk held the mannors of Neddyng and Kittilberston *com.* Suff. by the serjeantry of carrying a golden sceptre with a dove on the head of it, on the coronation day of the king's heirs and successors. As also another scepter of ivory with a golden dove on the head thereof on the day of the coronation of the queen, and all succeeding queens of England, K. p. 631. Sir John de Molins held the mannor of Ilmere *com.* Buck. by the serjeanty of keeping the king's hawks, K. p. 449. Amory de S. Amand held the mannor of Grendon *com.* Buck. and the advouson of the church of Beckley *com.* Oxon. by the petty serjeanty of furnishing the lord of the honor with one bow of ebony and two arrows yearly, or sixteen pence in mony, K. p. 358.—*Summa reddituum assisorum de manerio Banbury,*—*Item de serjantia* cxl. *gallinæ, et* mccc. *ova,* K. p. 354. By the stat. 12 Car. II. when all tenures were turned into free and common soccage, the honorary services of graud-serjeanty were alone excepted.

SERVI. Servile tenants. Our northern *Servi* had alway a much easier condition than the Roman slaves.—*Servis non in nostrum morem descriptis per familiam ministeriis utuntur. Suam quisque sedem, suos penates regit. Frumenti modum dominus, aut pecoris, aut vestis, colono injungit, et servus hactenus paret.* Tacit. de Mor. German. Which plainly describes the condition of our Saxon and Norman servants, natives, and villanes. No author to my knowledge has fixt the distinction between *Servus* and *Villanus,* though undoubtedly their servitude was different: for they are all along in the Doomsday book divided from one another. So in Burcester there were—*quinque servi, et viginti octo villani*, K. p. 65. I suppose the Servi were those whom our lawyers have since called Pure Villanes, and Villanes in gross, who without any determined tenure of land were at the arbitrary pleasure of the lord appointed to such servile works, and received their maintenance and wages at discretion of their lord. The other were of a superiour degree, and were called *Villani*, because they were *villæ et glebæ adscripti*, held some cottage and lands, for which they were burdened with such stated servile offices, and were conveyed as a pertinence of the mannor to which they belonged. The *Ancilla* or woman servant so disposed at the pleasure of the lord. Sir Simon de Meriton granted to the Knights Templars,—*Augnetem de Meriton quæ fuit filia Willielmi patris Walteri ejusdem villæ, et omnia catalla quæ habet vel habere poterit, et omnes proventus qui de ea exierunt vel exibunt*, K. p. 125.

SERVITIUM *Regale*. Royal service, or the rights and prerogatives that within such a mannor belong to the king if lord of it: which were generally reckoned to be these six: 1. Power of judicature in matters of property. 2. Power of life and death in criminal causes. 3. A right in wayfs and strays. 4. Assessments. 5. Minting of money. 6. Assise of bread, beer, weights and measures. All these entire privileges were annext to some mannors in their grant from the king, and were sometimes conveyed in the charters of donation to religious houses,—*Ecclesia S. Georgii data fuit fratribus Osen. et habet ibidem visum franciplegii et totum regale servitium*, K. p. 60.

SERVIENTES *Vicecomitum*. The bayliffs of sheriffs, who had an *Auxilium* or customary aid paid to them, from which some persons were by special privilege exempted. So King Hen. II. granted to the *Homines et Mercatores honoris de Walingford, ut quieti sint de auxilio vicecomitum et servientum*, K. p. 114.

SERVIENS *de manerio*. A Steward who is employed by the lord to occupy such grounds, and to account for the yearly profits of them.—*Computat Walterus de Gaung serviens de Arnikote coram auditoribus de omnibus receptis*, K. p 287.

SEWER, *Dapifer mensalis*. An officer like our clerk of the kitchen, who ordered the serving up of dishes to the table. Dr. Cowel derived it from the old Fr. *Asseour*, a disposer. William Martel sewer to King Stephen, K. p. 97.

SIDELINGE. A ridge or butt of arable land lying along the side of a stream or river.—*Cujus aqua manat ultra et præter dictas buttes, et ideo vocantur Sydelynges, nec pertinent ad furlong de Long-Stanford nec ad Busthames furlong, sed jacent inter medium,* K. p. 531.—*Deinde transeundum est ad furlung de Thromwell cum le Sidelynge adjacente*, K. p. 532.—*Ab hac furlung procedunt le Sidelynges de quibus patet superius*, ib. From Sax. Siò, Sioe. Thence a Side or party, to Side or adhere to, a Sideman or assistant, to Side about or turn. In the North wast-coats are called Side-coats; from a situation on the Side or along by, in Lincolnshire and most northern parts they use the word Side for Long, as a Side-field, a long field: and for high, as a Side-house, a Side-mountain; and by metaphor for proud, as a Side woman, *i. e.* a haughty proud woman: which in Sussex is Sidy, as a Sidy-fellow, *i. e.* an imperious surly fellow.

SIGNUM. A cross prefixt to the name of a subscribing witness as a sign of attestation and approbation to a charter or other deed, commonly used among the Saxons and first Normans, before the use of seals or military coats of arms. ✠ *Signum Roberti episcopi Lincoln.* ✠ *Signum Nigelli de Oily, &c.* K. p. 78.

SIMONY. Upon proof of Simoniacal presentation, the clerk was ejected, the patron lost his next turn, and the bishop collated; as in the church of Bucknel, *an.* 1524, K. p. 619.

SLADE. Sax. Slæd. A long flat piece of ground. *Pratum vocatum le Slade*, K. p. 465.—*Slade-furlong*, K. p. 537,—*furlong de la Slade*, ibid. *de la Slade versus Gravenhull nichil in denariis hoc anno quia remanet ad staurum domini*, K. p. 572. Hence Sax. Slið, Dan. *Slet*, Eng. Sleet, *i. e.* smooth and plain. To Slide, a Slidge or Sledge, to Sleek cloaths with a Sleek-stone, to Slib or Slip, Slape or smooth in Lincolnshire, Slape-ale, *i. e.* plain ale opposed to worm-wood, scurvy-grass, or other medicinal ale. A Slab or smooth plank. A Slate or flat step of a ladder in the North, where butchers' call the tongue and root of a hog killed and cut out a Slot of pork. In Northumberland the Slot of a door is the bolt: and in the South to Slot a-lock is to thrust it back. Slate or smooth mineral stone. A Slappel or smooth piece in Sussex. A Slap or flat box with the open hand. A Slog or Slough of smooth water and dirt. Slaps or seamen's breeches. Slippers. A Sliff or Sleve. To Slubber or run smoothly over. Old Eng. Slidder, small rain or Sleet. A Slape or smooth descent. To Slitter or cut smooth. A Sliver or smooth piece, &c.

SMIGMA, *Migma*, à Gr. Μἱγνυμι, *Misceo.* Soap, or a confection of soap and other unctuous matter for washing and cleansing of boards, cloaths, &c.—*Et in smigmate empto quadam vice ad lavandam aulam prioris* i. *den.* K. p. 574.

SNODDE. A smooth roll or bottom of silk or thread. From Sax. Snoð, a fillet or hair-lace with which women smooth up their hair, which in the North parts of England is now called a Snude, and in Scotland a Snod. Which Snod as an adjective in the North is a common word for smooth. And Snodly for smoothly and neatly, as Snodly geared, *i. e.* smoothly and finely drest. And wheat ears are said to be Snod when they have no beard or awns. And a tree is Snod when the top is cut smooth off. Hence to Snod along, to go close and smooth; to lie Snod and Snug, to lie close.—*Et in octo-Snoden de Pakthread emptis ibidem pro quodam reti faciendo pro cuniculis capiendis hoc anno sex sol.* K. p 574.

SOLARIUM. An upper room, chamber, or garret, which in some parts of England is still called a Sollar.—*Istud cellarium et illud solarium sita sunt intra domum meam,* K. p. 325.—*Pro duobus cellariis et duobus solariis eisdem ad terminum vitæ traditis et concessis,* K. p. 448. The Sax. Sol signified a rope or haltar to tie cattle in their stall, which in several parts of England is still called a Soul and a Sole, whence to Sowl, to pull and tie up; and by easie metaphor to Sowl one by the ears, *i. e.* to pull one's ears, a common phrase in Lincolnshire, upon which Dr. Skinner is thus ridiculously witty: To Sowl one by the ears, *vox agro Linc. usitatissima,* i. e. *aures summa vi vellere, credo a Sow,* i. e. *aures arripere et vellere, ut suibus canes solent.*

SOCAGE, *Soccagium,* Sax. Soc, Soca, right and jurisdiction. Soccage was a tenure of lands by which a man was enfeoffed freely or in fee simple, without any military service, relief, ward, or marriage, paying only to the lord a stated rent in mony or provisions. So the kings of England often firm'd out their demesn lands, as Brill *com.* Buck. let out in Soccage for the reserve of one hundred capons to the king's table, K. p. 52. Tenants who held in Soccage might by custom be obliged to some services of plough or cart which were called *Soccagia,* and sometimes were expresly renounced by the lord,—*Pro omnibus servitiis, tallagiis, soccagiis, et pro omnibus secularibus exactionibus et terrenis demandis,* K. p. 262. To prove the tenure of Soccage was a sufficient discharge from claim of scutage and military service to the lord of the fee,—*Qualiter extincta sunt feoda domini abbatis quæ ab ipso petita sunt— Residuum quod habet de honore Sancti Walerici tenetur de abbate regalis loci per assignationem comitis per soccagium, et non habentur ibidem nisi tria cotogia,* K. p. 305.

SOKA, Soca, Sax. Socn. A liberty or franchise of holding a court and exercising other jurisdiction over the socmen or soccage tenants within the extent of such an honor or mannor.—*Castrum et manerium de Bolyngbroke cum soka, mara, et marisco cum pertinentiis,* K. p. 418. From Soccage, commonly called the plough tenure, in the North they still call a plough-share a Sock or Ploughsock.

SPURARIUM *Aureum.* A Spur Royal. Lat. *Spourones,* Spurs, Sax.

Spopa, a Spur, Spop, a tread or track, whence the Sporling of a wheel, *i. e.* a wheel track in the North. A Sporre-way or Spurr-way in Sussex, *i. e.* a sheer-way or bridle-way. Spopnan, to spurn or to kick. To walk or run a Spurt. To Spur or to strike. A Sparthe or double axe, as Spencer, " He hath a Sparthe of twenty pound of weight.". But this rather from Lat. *Sparus*, Sax. Spæpa, Eng. Spear. Nor is it absurd to think that our English Sport was originally foot-ball-play, though since extended to any other game. —*Pro hac recognitione Johannes dedit prædicto Hugoni unum spurarium aureum*, K. p. 321.

STALLUM. Some think it a contraction of *Stabulum*. Sax. Stal, a Stall, a seat, a standing, and in old Eng. any sort of chair or stool, as Spencer, " A woman at a door sate on a Stall." From Stall as applied to the standing or apartment of horses in a stable, comes the Lat. *Stalonus*, Eng. Stallion, and old Eng. a Stallere, *i. e.* a groom. A Still or stand to set beer upon in a cellar. A Stage. To Stall in Lincolnshire to feed, or fill, or make fat. A Stalled ox, *i. e.* a fat ox. And perhaps the Stale and Staling of horses. Sax. Stal-peopb, Stalwart, strong, as Duglass renders *fortia corpora* in Virgil,—*stalwart bodyis*. The Stalking or walking of a horse.— In the chancel of every conventual church, the religious had each of them a Stall. As now in cathedral quires,—*Willielmi de Long-spe animam Ela abbatissa de Lacock vidit cœlos penetrantem in stallo suo, et coram cæteris sororibus denuntiavit*, K. p. 244.

STALLAGIUM. Stallage, a customary rent paid in fairs and markets for the liberty of a Stall or standing, by the Stallangers or the creamers, *i. e.* those traders who exposed their goods to sale in the said Stalls. To be exempt from this duty, or to have a free standing, was a privilege granted by King Hen. II. to the tenants and merchants within the honor of Walingford,—*ut quieti sint de thelonio, stallagio, &c.* K. p. 114. Edmund earl of Cornwall to the Bonhommes of Asherugge and their tenants,—*ut in singulis burgis et villatis nostris, et etiam in singulis nundinis et mercatis nostris libere valeant emere et vendere omnes mercandisas absque ullo theloneto seu stallagio nobis vel hæredibus nostris inde præsentando*, K. p. 311 From the Stall of wares and goods comes the Staple of merchants, Staple-commodities, &c.

STAPRON. A course apron.—*Et in stipendio Katerinæ Colins facienti mantalia coquinæ hoc anno xx den. et in datis eidem pro uno stapron iii. den.* K. p. 576.

STATUS *de maneria*. All the tenants and legal men met in the court of their lord to do their customary suit, and enjoy their customary rights.—*Apud curiam de Wrechwike tentam in festo S. Andreæ*, an. 17 Edw. III.—*Omnis status de Wrechwike elegerunt*

Hugonem Kyng ad officium præpositi, et juramentum suscepit, K. p. 456.

STAURUM. Any Store or standing stock of cattle, provision, &c —*Computant de quatuor solidis provenientibus de stauro boveriæ,* K. p. 571.—*de duobus coriis vaccarum stauri de la Breche,* ib.

STERLINGI, *Esterlingi.* Sterling money, old Eng. Starlinges, Lindwood has a childish fancy, that a Starling or bird was imprest upon such old coin. Some pretend it was the purer metal which the Easterlings or eastern merchants brought into these parts. Others would presume it first coined at the castle of Sterling in Scotland. But Mr. Somner seems most happy in the derivation of it from the Sax. Steope, a rule or standard, from Steopan, to guide or govern. So as Sterling mony seems to be that sort of coin, which for metal and value was to be a common standard of all current mony. Which seems the more probable, because such mony at the first coming in of the Normans was called *Sterilensis.* As Orderic. Vital. *sub an.* 1082.—*Porrigam quindecim sterilensium.* From the same Sax. Steopan comes our Eng. to Steer right; the Steer or Stern, and the Star-board of a ship. A Steers-man or pilot. To Stare or fix the eyes. To Start. The Stirrop in a saddle. Sterbrech in our old law, *i. e.* a trespass in stopping or molesting the common road, whence a Stray, and to go astray. Mr. Somner does ingeniously conjecture that the termination of Ster in several faculties and trades is owing to the same original and signifies the mastery or command of such an art, as a Maltster, a Gamester, a Spinster, a Songster, &c.—*decem solidos sterlingorum,* K. p. 129.

STRAKYS. The Strakes or Streaks of a wheel, *i e.* the iron plates that shoe the fellows of a wheel, or be nailed round the circumference of it. *A* Lat. *Striga,* a long furrow, Sax. Steplce, Germ. *Streke,* Eng. Stroak or Streak. Whence a small stalk or young strait branch, is in Kent and other parts called a Strig. A Strickle or smooth strait piece of wood to Strike corn in the measure of it. To Stroak down. To Streek in the North, *i. e.* to pull out, or open, or lay smooth.—*In uno pari rotarum vocat. Schozears empt. ibidem, ut patet per prædictum papirum* vii. *sol.* ii. *den. et in* vi. *Strakys ferreis* iv. *sol* K. p. 573.

STRAND. Sax. Strande. Any shore or bank of a sea or river. An immunity from custom and all imposition paid for goods and vessels of such places was granted by King Hen. II. to the church of Rochester,—*Concedo et confirmo in perpetuum cum socner et seke,* strande and stream. Mon. Ang. tom. 3. p. 4. So the same prince granted to all tenants and traders within the honor of Walingford, that—By water and by land, by wood and by strand, *quieti sint de thelonio, pontagio, &c.* K. p. 114. Hence the street in the west suburbs of London, which lay next the shoar or bank of the Thames is called The Strand. Whence a ship or vessel running on the shoar, and being broke to pieces, is said to Strand and to be Stranded. And G. Duglass mentions the Strandis of the sea.

STRATA. Sax. Stpæte, Eng. Street or high-way. Hence to Strout and Strut along, to make Streit or Strait, to Stretch out, &c.—*Extendit se in latitudine juxta altam stratam versus cœmiterium ecclesiæ parochialis de Berencester*, K. p. 325.

STREPITUS *Judicialis*. The circumstances of noise and croud and other turbulent formalities at a process or trial in a publick court of justice.—*Possint eos et eorum successores per omnem censuram ecclesiasticam ad omnium et singulorum præmissorum observationem absque articuli seu libelli petitione et quocunque strepitu judiciali compellere*, K. p. 344.

SUETTA, *Secta*. Suit or service done to a superiour lord. From the Fr. *Suivre*, to follow.—*Pro omnibus servitiis, curiæ sectis, suettis, releviis, &c.* K. p. 262.

SUFFRAGIA *orationum*. The prayers and holy offices performed by the religious for their founders and benefactors. Bernard de S. Walery gave the site and advouson of the abby of Godstow to King Hen. II.—*Salvis tantummodo mihi et hæredibus meis ejusdem ecclesiæ orationibus et eleemosinæ suffragiis*, K. p. 127. Isabel Gargat gave a croft to the canons of Burcester,—*Dicti vero canonici receperunt me et dominam matrem meam specialiter in orationibus suis et suffragiis domus suæ imperpetuum*, K. p. 149. Sir John de Molins was a special benefactor to the canons of St. Marie Overie in Southwark, for which they made him partaker of all their prayers and suffrages, and covenanted to mention him in all their masses, vigils, &c. K. p. 425.

SULCUS *Aquæ*. A small brook or stream of water, which in Essex is called a Doke.—*In fine inferiore ipsius meræ descendit quidam sulcus fluens inter medium de Stanford-more prædicta usque in Nether-Stanford, et ibi vocatur Bygenhull-broke.* K. p 531. From the word Brook comes possibly the fishing term of Brokling or Brogling for eels. In Sussex and some other parts the clouds are said to Brook up, when they gather and threaten rain. To Brookle or Brukle in the North is to make wet and dirty.

SUMMA, *Saugma, Sauma*, à Gr. Σάγμα. Fr. *Saume, Somme*. Properly any load or burden of a horse. In old charters we frequently find *Sauma vini* and *Summa ligni* for a horse load of wine or wood. Mr. Somner believes that this sort of burden gave name to a Sumpter-horse, Lat. *Equus Saumarius*, Fr. *Somiere*. *Summa frumenti*, Sax. Seam and ɼeam-bynben, was the quantity of eight bushels or a quarter, still called a Seam in Kent and other South parts. The Knights Templars gave to the wife of Sir Wido de Meriton,—*duas summas bladi*, K. p. 120.—One Seam of nuts was equivalent to two shillings in 23 Hen. II. K. p. 132. Maud de Chesney gave to the canons of Burcester,—*quinque summas frumenti ad hostias faciendas*, K. p. 158. Hence a sum of mony. The termination of Sum and Some implying a plenty and fullness, as Troublesome, &c. The Summer in building, or chief beam to support the roof. A term in falconry, a hawk is full Summed, when the plumes are full grown, &c.

SUMMONITOR. A Summoner or Apparitor, who was to cite in a delinquent to appear at a certain time and place to answer a charge exhibited against him. Two persons were joined in this office, who in citations from a superiour court were to be peers or equals of the party cited. At least the barons were to be summoned by none under the degree of knights, hence *Summonitores ordinarii, legales, boni.*—*Summone ibidem per bonos summonitores eundem Thomam quod sit coram nobis in crastino S. Johannis Baptistæ responsurus ad hoc quod ei proponetur*, K. p. 177.—*Summonitus ad respondendum*, Legally summoned or cited to answer an action or complaint,—*Johannes filius Nigelli sen. summonitus fuit ad respondendum domino regi de placito quo warranto clamat habere visum franciplegii*, K. p. 313. *Summonitores Scaccarii*, Those officers who assisted in collecting the king's revenues by citing the defaulters into the court of Exchequer,—*De scutagio quod per summonitores Scaccarii exigis*, K. p. 200. Hence in the diocese of Canterbury the apparitors in each deanery are called the Sumners.

SWANEMOTUM. From Sax. Span, a Swain, as Country-swain, Boat-swain, and Gemote, a court or convention. The Swanemote was a court held twice a year by the forest officers, fifteen days before Midsummer, and three weeks before Michaelmas, for enquiry of the trespasses committed within the bounds of the forest. An inquisition *de statu forestæ de Bernwode*, 38 Edw. III.—*Dicunt quod forestarii ut in jure domini regis dictæ forestæ habere debent una vice per annum ad Swanemota sua cum tenta fuerint repasta sua in aliquibus maneriis*, K. p. 449. What Mr. Somner writes Span Sir Henry Spelman makes to be Spang, a labourer, whom Chaucer calls a Swinker, from Spincin, to labour and take pains, whence in Kent a hard labourer is said to Swink it away. From thence Spingan, to thresh, in the North to Swingle, with a flail there called a Swingel, whence to Swinge off, or take a Swinging blow.

SWATHA. Sax. Spað, a Swath or in Kent a Sweath, in some parts a Swarth, *i. e.* a strait row of cut grass or corn, as it lies in the Swath at first mowing of it. A Swathe of meadow was a longe ridge of ground, like a Selion in arable land. William Burward sold his part of five Swaths in a meadow called Bikemore, K. p. 380. *Duæ Swathes dicti prati jacent ut sequitur,* K. p. 399. *Duæ Swathes apud Mathammes,* K. p. 401. Hence in the North a Swath banks is a Swarth of new cut grass or hay: where a green Swarth in a bottom among arable land is called a Swang. Hence Sax. Sƿæðıl, a Swath, or Swaddle, or Swadling-cloaths. To Swaddle or bind up. A Swad or bundle of hay or straw. The Swads or Swods of pease, Sax. Speapð, The Swearth, Swarth, or Sword of bacon. Green-swerd or the turf of grass ground. A Swatch or Switch, a small stick or rod, a Swache in the North is a fally of wood, especially fixt to cloth sent to the dyer. To Swaddle and Swatchel, *i. e.* to beat or strike with a wand or rod that shall bend round the body, or thing so-stricken. As prov. in Kent, " Ile swaddle your sides," *i. e.* with a whip or wand I will strike, and make it bend and meet round your body. By metaphor, Swad in the North is slender, *i. e.* close bound, as a Swad-fellow, a meer Swad. And by a like figure Swath, smooth and calm, as Swathweather.

SWORN-Brothers. *Fratres Jurati.* Persons who by mutual oath covenanted to share each the other's fortune.—*Statutum est quod ibi debent populi omnes et gentes universæ singulis annis, semel in anno scilicet, convenire, scilicet in capite kalendarum Maii, et se fide sacramento non fracto ibi in unum et simul confœderare, et consolidare, sicut conjurati fratres.* Leg. Edw. Confess. cap. 35.—In any notable expedition to invade and conquer an enemies country, it was the custom for the more eminent souldiers of fortune to engage themselves by reciprocal oaths to share the rewards of their service. So in the expedition of Duke William, Eudo and Pinco were sworn brothers, and copartners in the estate which the conquerour allotted to them. So were Robert de Oily and Roger de Ivery, by vertue of which contract, the said Robert gave one of his two honors in this county to his sworn brother Roger; from whom it was first called the mannor of Ivery, as afterwards the honor of St. Walery, K. p. 56. *Robertus de Oleio et Rogerus de Iverio fratres jurati, et per fidem et sacramentum confœderati venerunt ad conquestum Angliæ,* K. p. 57. No doubt this practise gave occasion to our prov. of " Sworn-Brother, and Brethren in iniquity," because of their dividing plunder and spoil.

SYNODI. The ancient episcopal synods (which were held once a year about Easter) were composed of the bishop as president, the dean cathedral as representative of that collegiate body, the archdeacons as at first only deputies or proctors of that inferiour order of deacons, and the urban and rural deans who represented all the parochial priests within their division, K. p. 648.

SYNODALIA. *Synodals* or *Synodies*, a pecuniary rent, commonly two shillings, paid to the bishop at the time of his annual synod by every parochial priest. This burden was sometimes justly laid upon the appropriators: so at Merton appropriated to the abby of Eguesham,—*Solutionem decimæ cujuscunque currentis, ac synodalium, et aliorum censuum ipsam ecclesiam pro tempore concernentium,—Religiosos et eorum succesores supportare volumus,* K. p. 483.

SYNODALES *Testes.* The urban and rural deans were at first so called from informing and attesting the disorders of clergy and people in the episcopal synod. But when they sunk in their authority, the synodical witnesses were a sort of impanelled jury, a priest and two or three lay men for every parish. And at last two for every diocese were annually chosen, till by degrees this office was devolved on the church-wardens, K. p. 649. *Juramentum Synodale* was the solemn oath taken by the said *Testes,* as is now by church-wardens to make their just presentments.

T.

T. R. E. *Tempore Regis Edwardi.* It occurs frequently in the Doomsday Survey, where the valuation of manners is recounted, what it was in the late reign, and what in the present. So—*Manerium de Burcester T. R E. valuit quindecim libras, modo sexdecim,* K. p. 65.

TALLIA, *Talia.* From Sax. Talian or Tællan, to account or estimate: or from the Fr. *Tailler*, to cut. A Tally or piece of wood cut with indentures or notches in two corresponding parts, of which one kept by the creditor, the other by the debtor. As now used by our brewers, &c. and was formerly the common way of keeping all accounts.—*Ut patet per talliam contra Willielmum Spinan collectorem redditus ejusdem anni,* K. p. 570.—*Receptis de redditu in Curtlington per talliam contra Willielmum Newman collectorem redditus ibidem,* K. p. 571. Hence to Tell mony, old Eng. a Talled sum. The Tale of mony. The Tallier (Talliator) of the Exchequer, whom we now call the Teller.

TALLIARI *de certo tallagio.* To be assest or taxt at such a rate or proportion, imposed by the king on his barons and knights, or by them on their inferiour tenants.—33 Hen. III. *Rex illas* xvi. *libras ad quas homines qui fuerint Godefridi de Craucumb in Pydinton—nuper talliati fuerint, assignavit ponendas per visum Hu-*

gonis Gargate,—Et mandatum est vice com. Oxon. quod homines de prædicto manerio pro prædicto tollagio de cætero non distringat, K. p. 241. The inferiour tenants sometimes made a composition with their lord for this Tallage. As the tenants of Hugh de Plessets in Hedingdon,—*Quotiens dominus rex suos dominicos talliare contigerit, dabunt prædicto Hugoni et hæredibus suis quinque marcas, et dictus Hugo concessit pro se et hæredibus suis, quod iidem homines quieti sint de tallagio prœ eisdem,* K. p. 321. This Tallage of the custumary tenants was sometimes fixt and certain, and sometimes at the arbitrary pleasure of the lord.—*Extenta manerii de Ambrosden* 28 Edw. I.—*Sunt ibidem* ix. *cotterii, et reddunt per annum* ix. *sol. et debent talliari per annum de certo tallagio ad sex libras,* K. p. 682. In Burcester King's-end—*Quilibet custumarius dominæ debet talliari ad festum S. Michaelis pro voluntate dominæ priorissæ,* K. p. 401.—*In illo manerio de Pedinton quælibet virgata terræ dabit ad tallagium domini circa natale Domini* ii*s.* K. p. 495.—*Tenent quinque acras terræ et duas acras prati de dominico pro dimidia marca per annum salvo tallagio domini ad festum natalis Domini,* K. p. 495. The lords in Ireland impose an arbitrary tax on their tenants which they call a Cutting, the literal meaning of the French *Taillage.*

TAXA. The Task or labour of a workman. *Trituratur ad taxam,* a Tasker or thresher in the barn, who works by the great, or by the measure, not by the day.—*Et in solutis Johanni Leseby trituranti ad taxam* xlv. *quarteria frumenti ut patet per talliam hoc anno, capiendo pro quolibet quarterio* iii. *den. ob.* K. p. 576.

TAXATIO *Norwicensis.* The valuation of ecclesiastical benefices made through every diocese in England, on occasion of the pope's granting to the king the tenth of all spirituals for three years. Which taxation was made by Walter bishop of Norwich delegated by the pope to this office in 38 Hen. III. and obtained till the 19th of Edw. I. when a new taxation advancing the value, was made by the bishops of Lincoln and Winchester at command of the king and permission of the pope, K. p. 249, 315.

TEMPORALIA. The lands, houses, tithes, and other fixt endowments of a bishoprick or abby, distinct from the spiritualities, which arose more immediately from the function and office, as synodals, pentecostals, &c. These temporalities held by barony, were seised into the king's hands by the eschaetor at the death of every such prelate: and after the election and confirmation of a successor, there was a writ *de restitutione temporalium,* K. p. 330.

TEMPORALIA *Ecclesiæ Parochialis.* The manse, glebe, and tithe, as distinct from the voluntary oblations, and other contingent perquisites. Upon a judgment in the Exchequer against Ichel de

Kerewent rector of Bucknell, *an.* 26 Edw. I. his temporals were seised, and put into custody for two years, K. p. 330.

TENEMENTUM. Tenure or holding.—*Unam virgatam terræ in Meriton,—habendam et tenendam—de tenemento Dominorum Templariorum,* K. p. 129. *Tenementa* were lands or houses or any yearly profits Tenanted or held by tenants.

TENTHS. First fruits and tenths of all ecclesiastical benefices were paid to the see of Rome, and by Pope Innocent IV. the Tenths were first given to King Hen. III. *an.* 1253, for three years, which occasioned the Norwich taxation, *an.* 1254, which proved a great oppression to the clergy, and soon made more grievous. For when the pope had again granted the tenths to the king for three years, for a compensation of what they fell short of the due value, the king in the 53d year of his reign, *an.* 1269, made the clergy pay within those three the tenths of four years, K. p. 312.—*An.* 1288, 16 Edw. I. Pope Nicholas IV. granted the tenths to the king for six years, toward his expedition to the Holy Land, and that they might be then collected to the full value, a new taxation by the king's precept was begun *an.* 1288, and finished *an.* 1291, 19, 20 Edw. I. by the bishops of Lincoln and Winchester, K. p. 315.

TERRA. In the form of inquisitions entred in the Doomsday Register, this word *Terra* put simply, must signifie arable land, as distinct from wood, meadow, and common pasture. So in Berncester,—*Ibi sunt* 15 *hidæ et dimidia—Terra* 22 *carucatarum. De hac terra tres hidæ in dominio.*—So in Bucknel,—*Ibi sunt* 7 *hidæ. Terra* 10 *carucaturam, &c.* K. p. 65. I confess I do not build this on the authority of any author; but there seems to be no sense without this distinction, that the hides were a computation of the whole mannor in gross; which was afterwards particularly described under the distinct heads of *Terra* or arable land, *Pratum* or meadow, *Silva* or wood land.

TERRA *Normannorum.* Such land in England as had been lately held by some noble Norman, who by adhering to the French king had forfeited his estate in this kingdom, which by this means becoming an escheat to the crown was called *Terra Normannorum,* and restored or otherways disposed at the king's pleasure.— 8 Hen. III. *Rex vicecom. Oxon. salutem. Scias quod commisimus Thomæ Basset manerium de Kirtlington quæ est terra Normannorum,* K. p. 197.

TESSELLATA *pavimenta.* The pavements in the tents of the Roman generals made of curious small square marbles, bricks, or tiles, and called *Tessellæ,* from the form of dies, K. p. 12. Such a Tessellated pavement of porphyry marble was laid by King

Edw. I. round the sepulcher of his father at Westminster, K. p. 13.

THANE. Sax. Ðeȝen, a military servant, from Ðenıan, to serve, Ðenınȝ, any duty, charge, or office. Cýnınȝeȝ-Ðeȝen, the king's Theine or Thane was a Saxon lord or nobleman. And after the Conquest the word was sometimes used to denote all persons of superiour degree, K. p. 54.

THASSARE, *Tassare*. To lay up hay or corn into a Tass, Toss, stack or mow, Lat. *Tassa, Tassus, Taesius*, Sax. Taʃ, Fr. *Tas.—Homines de Hedingdon qui carectas non habuerint venient cum furcis suis ad dictum feonum levandum et thassandum*, K. p. 320.—*Qui carectas non habuerint adjuvabunt ad thassandum bladum*, ib.—*Pro victualibus emptis pro factoribus tassiorum prioris* xii, K. p. 550. Hence a Tassel or Tossel, to Tass or Toss, Hay-toss; a mow of corn in a barn is called in Kent the Toss. And by metaphor the yard of a man is called his Tass. Gawen Duglass calls a woodstack or wood-pile, a Tass of green stick. In old Eng. Taas was any sort of heap. As Chaucer, " To ransake in the taas of bodies dead." And Lidgate Troil. l. 4, c. 30.

" An hundred knyghts slain and dead alas
That after were found in the taas."

TITHE. Two parts of the tithe of a mannor or parish were often given to a religious house: of which the reason was this.—Tithe of England in the time of Augustin the monk was divided commonly into four parts: and in the reign of King Alfred reduced to three parts, of which a first part to the repair of churches, a second to the relief of the poor, and a third only to the maintenance of the parish priest. Hence the lords of mannors at their first building of churches did often allot no more than that third part of tithes for an exhibition to the parish priest, and kept the other two parts in their own hands for the uses of the church and poor: till by degrees they either gave in the two other parts to the parochial priest, or else with the bishop's consent assigned them to some religious house, K. p 79. This was the meaning of giving two garbs or theavs or sheaves to the religious, while the third garb remained due to the parish priest, K. p. 81. So Brien Fitz-Count gave a third part of the tithe of his demesne in Hillingdon to the monastery of Evesham, K. p. 100. So Robert de Oily to the secular canons of St. George in the castle of Oxford.—*Duas partes decimæ de omni re quæ decimari solet de omnibus dominicis de Mokenorton, Swerefordia, &c.* K. p. 104. In the parish of Compton-Basset com. Wilts, the Persona or rector had—*tertiam partem decimarum garbarum*: and the prior and convent of Burcester had

144 GLOSSARY.

—*duas partes decimarum garbarum*, K. p. 205. By the laws of King Edgar made about 670 if a Thane or lord should have within his own fee a church with a burial place, *i. e.* a parish church, he must give the third part of his tithe to it. But if it had no privilege of burial, *i. e.* if it were only a chappel of ease depending on a mother church, then the lord was to maintain the priest out of his nine parts, K. p. 594. Two parts of the tithe of the demesne of Heyford-Warine was given to the chappel of St. Georges, and thence transferred to the abby of Oseney, K. p. 513. In the mannor of Chesterton, the abby of Glocester had two parts of the tithe of the demesne land, which they firmed out to the abbat and convent of Oseney, who as appropriators had the third part, K. p. 223. This division of tithe was the occasion of disputes and quarrels, and therefore one part was often bought off, and united to the other : or at least one share rented out to those who had the other, that the whole tithe might be collected together. So the monks of Egnesham compounded with the canons of Burcester to receive a yearly pension of twelve shillings in lieu of their two parts of tithe in Stratton, K. p. 144. Two parts of the tithe of Burcester belonged first to St. George's and then to Oseney abby, till in 28 Edw. I. the abbat and canons of Oseney resigned their right of two parts to the prior and canons of Burcester, who had before as appropriators a third part, for a rent or pension of sixty shillings yearly, K. p. 343. The arbitrary disposition of tithes by lay men was a conceit of Mr. Selden, confuted, K. p. 105. Parochial tithes were sometimes given to the religious for admitting the donor's son into their house and order, K. p. 81. Tithes could not be lawfully detained or enjoyed by a lay man,—*Salvis ecclesiæ nostræ de Missenden decimis ad capellam de Musewell spectantibus, et siqua sunt alia ad dictam capellam spectantia, quæ laico retinere non licet*, K. p. 226. Tithes personal were alway paid in country villages, as well as in populous towns and cities : and in appropriations, because hard to collect, they were generally allotted to the vicar.—So the prior and canons of St. Frideswide to the vicar of Oakle,—*Omnes decimas personales in dictis provenientes de quæstu eorum qui de mercatura vivunt*, K. p. 455. So the prior and convent of Burcester to the vicar of that church,—*Vicarius et successores decimas personales percipient et habebunt, prædialibus eorundem locorum nobis et successoribus nostris omnino reservatis*, K. p. 669.

TITHING-Men. In the Saxon times, for the better conservation of peace, and the more easie administration of justice, every hundred was divided into ten districts or Tithings, each Tithing made up of ten friborgs, each friborg of ten families, and within every such Tithing—*Statuerunt justitiarios super quosque decem friborgos, quos decanos possumus appellare, Anglice vero* Tienheroð, *i. e. caput de decem.* Which Tithing-men or civil deans were to examine and determine all lesser causes between villages and neighbours, but to refer all greater matters to the superiour courts, which had a jurisdiction over the whole hundred, K. p. 633.

TODDE. Perhaps from Sax. Toðælan, to divide or parcel out. A Tod of wool is a parcel containing twenty-eight pounds or two stone, by stat. 12 Car. I. cap. 32. But in these parts the woolmen buy in twenty-nine pounds to the Todd, though they sell out but twenty-eight.—*Computant de decem libris* xviii. *sol.* vi. *den. receptis de* xxiii. *todde lanæ puræ venditæ cuidam mercatori Oxon. hoc anno, per le todde* ix. *sol.* vi. *den.* K. p. 572.

TOFTA, *Toftum.* A Toft, the ground which has been the site of a late messuage, or the place where any mansion or building lately stood.—*Ratum habemus et stabile donum quod fecit de uno tofto et crofto,* K. p. 307.

TOLL. Lat. *Tolnetum, Thelonium,* à Gr. Τελώνιον. In the Saxon charters Thol was the liberty of buying and selling, or keeping a market in such a mannor. In later times it signified the customary dues or rent paid to the lord of a mannor for his profits of the fair or market, called the Toling-pence. Mon. Ang. tom. 2. p. 286. Alexander bishop of Lincoln gave to the abby of Tame—*centum solidos de thelonio Bannebiriæ, i. e.* two hundred shillings yearly rent out of his Toll at Banbury, K. p. 94. King Hen. II. granted a privilege to the tenants and traders within the honor of Walingford—*ut quieti sint de thelonio,* K. p. 114. Edmund earl of Cornwal granted to the Rector and Bonhommes of Asherugge and their tenants—*ut in omnibus burgis et villatis nostris, et etiam in singulis nundinis et mercatis nostris libere valeant emere et vendere omnes mercandisas absque ullo theloneto seu stallagio,* K. p. 311. Hence the Toll-booth or Toll-sey, or place where such custom was paid. This Toll at publick fairs and markets was paid at the sound of a bell, as we have now a market-bell, which possibly might give name to the Tolling of a bell, and to the proverb of being Tolled in, or drawn into a bargain. In Derbyshire they say Thole a while, *i. e.* Stay a while.

TORCEYS, *Torchia,* Fr. *Torche,* Eng. a Torch, à Lat. *Torquis,* Fr. *Tort,* a wreath; or *Torris,* a fire-brand.—*In octo libris ceræ emptis Oxon. eodem die ad faciendum* ii. *torceys versus natale Domini ad aulam prioris* iii. *sol.* K. p. 574.

TORNEAMENTA. Torneaments, military exercises of armed horse-men to improve their strength and activity in war. From the Fr. *Tourner,* to turn about. They were invented in France by

Geffry de Pruilli, who was killed at Anjou *an*. 1066. Justs and Torneaments are commonly joined in representing the celebration of these manly sports; but there was this difference between them, Torneaments implied the mutual engagement of several sides and parties: but Justs were the single combats of any two horse-men, one against the other. The first Torneaments authorised in England were in 5 Rich. I. when one of the three solemn places appointed by the king was Bayard's-green between Mixbury and Brackley, K. p. 153. Piers de Gaveston in 2 Edw. II. proclaimed Torneaments to be kept nigh his castle at Walingford, wherein he highly affronted the English nobility, K. p. 357. Solemn Justs performed at Whitney *com*. Oxon. between Humphrey Bohun earl of Hereford on the one part, and Aymer Valence earl of Pembrook on the other, K. p. 386. King Edw. III. to express his joy for the birth of a seventh son at Woodstock, appointed publick Justs and Torneaments in that town, to which the nobility resorted in great numbers, K. p. 478.

TOTHLANDA. A certain measure of land, in the dimension whereof I can find no direction, and can make no safe conjecture, —*cum una virgata terræ, et cum una tothlanda, et octo acris, quæ fuerunt datæ in dedicatione (Ecclesiæ de Heyford ad pontem) Wulfwini episcopi Dorcestriæ,* K. p. 514.

TOUGH. The beam of a plough, or that part by which it is drawn along. From Sax. Teon, to draw. Hence Tough that can be drawn out in length. To Tow or draw along a boat. Tow in spinning, or ductile flax or hemp.—*Pro uno vomere et una cultura et dimidia toughe cum uno plowsho emptis* xxiii *d*. K. p. 549.

TRACTUS -uum. Traces by which horses draw a cart or waggon. *Par tractuum,* a pair of traces,—*Pro uno cartsadel, uno colero, cum uno pari tractuum emptis* xivd. K. p. 549. Hence prov. He is out of his traces, *i. e.* He is out of his way of business. A Trace or Track, or way drawn or markt out, by which a follower may Trace and Track the foregoer. The Lat. *Traho* was by the Saxons turned into Dnagan, whence to Drag, to Draw, to Drain; to Drate in the North, to Draw out one's words in speaking. Dree in the North long and tedious, as a Dree way. A Dray or cart. A Dray-horse. A Drudge. Old Eng. to Dretche, *i. e.* to protract or spin out the time. A Dretching or delay.

TRANSLATARE, *pro transferre*. To remove or transfer.—*Tunc translatavit se dicta domina usque ad Swaneton, et ibi obiit,* K. p. 282.

TREMUTA, *Treumia, Tremellum*. The Hooper or Hopper in a mill; into which the corn is put to fall from thence to the grinding stones. Perhaps from the similitude to the *Tramela* or *Tramellum,* or net, which we still retain in the word Trammel, a net to catch larks. And possibly the Lat. *Tremellum* and *Tramallum* might be both of Saxon original, from Tpa or Tpe, [so K.] two, and Mæl, a cross, alluding to the travers form of the holes in a net.—*Do libere molere in molendino meo, ita quod immediate post bladum existens in treumia, quod vulgariter dicitur ingranatum, eorum bladum moletur.* Du Fresne, *in voce* Treumia. Baldwin Wac to the priory of Deping,—*Sciendum tamen est quod prædicti monachi facient sectam molendini mei tam de blado suo quam hominum suorum. Ita quod ipsi habeant primam molituram post bladum quod invenerint in tremello.* Mon. Ang. vol. 1. p. 470. a. So Wido de Meriton in his charter to the Knights Templars,—*Concesserunt mihi fratres unam libertatem ad suum molendinum scilicet molendi segetem pro multura reddenda pro segete quæ est in tremuta,* K. p. 120. Our Hopper seems from the Sax. Dop, a circle or Hoop, or Doppan, to Hop, dance, or turn about, to Hobble, &c. as is implied by Chaucer, "The hopper waggeth to and fro." Hence a Hoppet in Lincolnshire is a little hand-basket. A Hop or Hoop in Yorkshire is a measure containing a peck, or a quarter of a strike. A young child danced in the arms is by metaphor called a little Hoppet. Any one whose lameness lies in the hip is called Hopper-arsed.

TRINODA *necessitas.* A threefold necessary tax or imposition toward the repairing of bridges, the maintaining of castles or garrisons, and an expedition against invading enemies. In the grant and conveyance of lands, they were many times excepted from all other secular service,—*Excepta trinoda necessitate*—*Exceptis his tribus, expeditione, pontis et arcis constructione,* K. p. 46.

TUELLA, *Toacula, Toalia, Tobalia,* Fr. *Touaille.* A Towel, or linnen cloth to wipe the hands. Menagius derives it from the Lat. *Torale, quod toro vel mensæ adstruebatur.* But it is as wise to conjecture that our Towel might be from the Sax. Top, *i. e.* Tow or coarse hemp, as well as a Napkin from the Sax. Dnoppe, the nap or lint of cloth.—*Inter ornamenta ecclesiæ—Zona cum duabus tuallis benedictis,* K. p. 598.

TURNUS *Vicecomitis.* The Sheriff's Turn or court kept twice every year within a month after Easter, and a month after Michaelmass, as the court leet of the county, at which all free tenants were obliged to do their suit and service, except those who compounded at a certain yearly sum, for the privilege of sending only one person to attend the sheriff, to represent and excuse the lord and tenants of that mannor.—*Bardulfus de Castreton debet viii. sol. de turno vicecomitis, et cum vicecomes tenet turnos suos in prædicto hundredo, idem Bardulfus mittet ibi unum de suis ad petendam*

148   GLOSSARY.

libertatem suam, et habebit, nec ipse nec homines sui venient ibi, K. p. 318.

TURRIBULUM, *Thuribulum*. The pot of frankincense used in the old offices of religion.—*Inter ecclesiæ ornamenta—Turribulum cum navi*, K. p. 598.

V.

VADIUM. A pledge or surety. *Ponere per vadium*, to take security or bail for the appearance of a delinquent in some courts of justice.—*Edwardus rex vicecom. Oxon. salutem. Præcipimus tibi sicut alias tibi præcepimus, quod ponas per vadium et salvos plegios Johannem de Burey*, K. p. 334.

VALECTUS, *Valettus, Vasletus, Vassaletus*. A young Vassal, at first in an honourable sense for the son of a nobleman, afterward for an *Armiger* or military attendant, and at last for an inferiour servant. Whence a Varlet or vile fellow, a *Valet de chambre*: and hence possibly a servant's Vales or mony given to those Valets,—*Et in blodeo panno empto pro armigeris et valectis prioris*, K. p. 576.—*Et in stipendio Johannis Baldwin valecti cameræ prioris hoc anno* xiii. *sol.* iv. *den.* ib.—*Et in datis cuidam valetto forestæ portanti carnes ferinas priori in crastino ejusdem festi* xii. *den.* K. p. 578.

VANDALEN. A German word to wander, Sax. Ƿanðpıan. Hence the people who came out of Scythia and settled on the coasts of the Baltic sea toward Germany, were called by the Romans *Vandali*, and by the Saxons *Wandalens* and *Wendelens*, who being employed as auxiliary souldiers in this island, gave name to Wendleburg near Alchester, K. p. 14.

VANYS. Lat. *Vannus*, Sax. Fana, A Vane or Fane, a versatile ornament on the top of a house or tower to shew the turning and setting of the wind.[u]—*Cum duobus ventilogiis videlicet Vanys de tyn emptis de fabro de Cherlton ponendis super utrumque finem prædicti dormitorii*, v. *sol.* ii. *den.* K. p. 575. Hence a Fanne with which they ventilate or winnow corn. The Fann of a lady to cool her face.

VASSALLUS. A diminutive from *Vassus*, a military servant; the title was afterwards given to servile tenants, who when they made any grant or assignation of land held by them, the grant was to be confirmed by their lord, K. p. 127. Sir Richard d'Amory computing for the lands of the Knights Templars, escheated to the king 2 Edw. II. accounted fourty shillings and ten-pence for the rent of Vassals and cottagers, K. p. 857.

VASTUM. A waste or common lying open to the cattle of all tenants who have a right of commonage, which right was sometimes determined by a trial at law.—*Thomas de Fekenham debet regi quinque marcas et unum palefridum, sic quod inquisitio fiat utrum membrum illud de manerio de Bruhull, quod idem Thomas tenet, debeat participare de vasto manerii de Bruhull ratione communæ ejusdem manerii, in qua communa nihil habet, ut dicunt,* K. p. 171. *Vastum forestæ vel bosci,* when part of a forest or wood had the trees and underwood destroyed, and lay in a manner waste and barren.—*Sciatis quod de vastis nostris in foresta nostra de Bernwode in com. Buck. dedimus, &c.* K. p. 351.—*Si boscus domini (de Pidenton) abeat in vastum, tum acquietabunt dominum pro dictis Housbote et Haybote,* K. p. 497. To waste or destroy the vert of the forest was a trespass against the assise or laws of the forests.— *Dicunt quod priorissa de Littlemore devastavit boscum suum de Shottore contra assisam forestæ,* K. p. 498.

VENATIO. Sometimes used for the exercise of hunting, and sometimes for Venison. If any without license hunted within the liberties of the king's forest, a severe penalty was imposed at the next swanemote: which fines or amercements were not allowed to the forester, but commonly reserved to the king. So when William Fitz-Nigel enjoyed several privileges as forester of Bernwode, it was—*Exceptis indictamentis de viridi et venatione, quæ domino regi omnino reservabantur,* K. p. 73.

VENTILARE. To fann or winnow corn. *Ventilatrices,* the women who were employed in this work.—*Et in ventilatricibus conductis in grosso ad ventilanda omnimoda grana triturata infra prioratum hoc anno,* K. p. 576. Sax. Pind, Eng. Wind, thence a Windore. In Kent the swaths of grass when turned and a little dried are cast into Windrows, to be farther exposed to the wind and sun. In some south parts the borders of a field dug up and laid in rows, in order to have the drie mould carried on upon the land to improve it, are called by this same name of Wind-rows.

VESTURA, *Vestitura.* A Vest, vesture, advesture. An allowance of some set portion of the products of the earth, as corn, grass, wood, &c. as part of a salary to some officer or servant, for their livery or vest. So foresters had a certain allowance of timber and under-wood yearly out of the forest for this use,—*Annuatim percipiendum tantum de roboribus et brueriis quantum pro vestura indiguerit,* K. p. 620.—*Liberare faciatis eidem tanta robora et brueria quanta indigent usque ad xls. pro vestura sic restricta,* K. p. 621.

DE VI LAICA amovenda. When the bishop of a diocese has certified into the court of Chancery, that the rector or vicar of any church within his jurisdiction is kept out of his benefice by any lay force or power, then may a writ be granted to the sheriff to remove all such violent force and resistance, which writ is therefore entitled *De vi laica amovenda.*—*Edwardus rex vicecom. Oxon. salutem.*—*Præcipimus tibi quod omnem vim laicam quæ se tenet in ecclesia de Bukenhull, quo minus idem episcopus officium suum spirituale ibidem exercere possit, sine dilatione amoveres ab eadem,* K. p. 335.

VICARIA. At first no more than any curacy or donative, till by ordination and fixt endowment it was made presentative, and called perpetual. Five marks were at first the common allotment to a perpetual vicar,—*Vicaria in capella de Hedingdon—consistit in omnibus obventionibus altaris cum minutis decimis totius parochiæ, exceptis decimis agnorum, et decimis casei, de curia domini provenientibus.—Et valet vicaria quinque marcas et amplius, tota autem ecclesia* xx. *marcas,* K. p. 511. An advance was afterward made of ten marks, and sometimes to ten pounds. So in the ordination of Merton vicarage, *an.* 1357, 81 Edw. III.—*Reservata congrua portione pro vicario perpetuo—quam portionem in decem marcis summæ pecuniæ sterlingorum fore et consistere secundum taxationem decimarum,* K. p. 483. The vicarage of Churchill *com.* Oxon. ordained *an.* 14 Edw. III consisted—*in decem libris argenti solvendis vicario ad duos anni terminos per priorem et canonicos de S. Frideswida, et de manso competente et honesto : et in quinque acris terræ arabilis in uno campo, et quinque in altero,* K. p. 506. Endowment of the vicarage of Chesterton, K. p. 543, of Burcester, K. p. 559. The same church had sometimes a rectory and vicarage separate and distinctly endowed. So at Chesterton *com.* Oxon.—*Willielmus archidiaconus London. ratione terræ et hæredis Roberti de Chesterton in manu sua existentium præsentat ad ecclesiam de Chesterton, salva vicaria Ranulphi de Besaciis quam habet in eadem,* K. p. 193. When a vicar was too poorly endowed he complained to the diocesan, who had power to augment his portion out of the appropriated tithe. So the vicar of Ellsfeld nigh Oxford, applying himself to Oliver bishop of Lincoln, got an augmentation of three seams or quarters of corn from the prior and canons of St. Frideswide, who were the sordid appropriators, K. p. 515. Some imperious appropriators, to prove themselves lords over the servile vicar, expresly covenanted for a heriet to be paid them at the death of every vicar,—*Vicarius de Cestreton post ejus decessum dabit heriettam rectori et conventui de Asherugge,* K. p. 543. and sometimes against all equity and conscience laid the repair of the chancel on the poor vicar, *ib.* Yet the case of vicars was generally better in the days of popery, because their own diet, and suitable accommodation for their vicar and clerk, and the keeping of a horse, were commonly allowed them by the convent, and taken *in specie* at their court or mansion-house in the parish, whenever the religious resided there for their health, their business, or their pleasure. So at Burcester, K. p. 559. It was very happy for the interest of the church and clergy, that at the first endowment of vicarages, the portion was assigned in improvable land and tithes, not in a stated sum of mony, K. p. 605. In the new valuation of church benefices, 26 Hen. VIII. vicarages were computed as if the greater tithes were included. So as the first fruits and tenths fell as heavy on the vicar as if he had been really rector of the same church, K. p. 632.

VILLA *Regia*. A title given to those countrey villages where the kings of England had a royal seat or palace, and held the mannor in their own demesne. So Brill com. Buck. was called *Villa Regia*, K. p. 58. So Hedingdon com. Oxon. &c.

VILLATA. A small village opposed to *Burgus* a larger town.— *In omnibus burgis et villatis nostris*, K. p. 311.

VILLANUS. A Villain, or rather a Villane. Some pretend it from the Fr. *Vilain*, Lat. *Vilis*, base and vile. But rather from *Villa* a countrey farm, (as *Rustici*, *Coloni*, &c.) where these men of low and servile condition had some small portion of cottages and lands allotted to them, for which they were depending on the lord, and bound to certain works and other corporal service. They were of two sorts, 1. Villanes in gross, who as to their persons, their issue, and their stock, were a sort of absolute slaves, the sole property of their lord, moveable and alienable at pleasure. 2. Villanes regardant or appendant to a mannor, who were ascribed as members of such a fee, and as a pertinence of it, descended to the heir, or past along to every new lord. For their service they held some small portion of house and land in Villenage. In Doomsday Inquisition these Villanes were recounted as an emolument and appendage of every mannor; so in Burcester twenty-eight Villanes; in Bucknel six Villanes, &c. K. p. 65. Their persons were conveyed along with their lands so held in Villenage. Wido de Areines gave to the abby of Oseney his land in Mixbury,—*Sex virgatas terræ de villenagio, cum villanis et eorum sectis et servitiis*, K. p. 212 William de Longspe confirmed to the priory of Burcester land in Wrechwike,—*Cum villanis et eorum sequelis et catallis*, K. p. 216. So Robert de Amory to the abby of Oseney two hides in Chesterton. So Hamo de Gattone conveyed his lands in Wreckwike,—*Cum omnibus villanis et eorum tenementis et sequelis*, K. p. 272.—*Villanos cum villanagiis omnibus catallis et tota sequela ipsorum*, K. p. 288.—*Una cum villanis, coterellis, eorum catallis, servitiis, sectis, et sequelis*, K. p. 310. In the charter of Gilbert Basset and Egeline his wife to their priory at Burcester,—*Terram nostram de Votesdun et de Westcote cum omnibus pertinentiis suis, scilicet dominium nostrum cum vilnagio,* K. p. 151. The Villanes over and above their operations or custumary labours, paid an annual rent in mony. So in the extent of the mannor of Ambrosden, taken in 28 Edw. I.—*Sunt ibidem triginta et septem villani, quorum quisque tenet unam virgatam terræ, et reddunt per an.* ix *l.* v *s.* K. p. 628. This tenure is now extinct, yet the footsteps of it still remain in those custumary services which are now reserved from some tenants to the lord, as particularly from the tenants of Mr. John Coker lord of the mannor of Burcester King's-End.

VICINETUM, *Visne, Visnage.* Neighbourhood. All persons to be returned on a jury as legal men, were to be *de eodem vicineto,* formerly of the same hundred, as now only of the same county.— *Electi sunt duodecim homines legales de vicineto,* K. p. 134.—*Per sacramentum proborum et legalium hominum de vicineto de Chesterton,* K. p. 367.

VIRGATA *terræ.* A Yard-land. Sax. Gÿrd-land, Gÿrd, a rod or Yard, Gÿrdan, to Girt, in the North to Gyrd. Hence a Yard, a close, a backside, in the North a Garth. A Garden, Fr. *Jardin.* A Garland. A Garret. A Garter. A Girdle. A Horse-girt, &c. A Gird-land or Yard-land was originally no more than a certain extent or compass of ground surrounded with such bounds and limits. And therefore the quantity was uncertain according to the difference of place and custom. They reckoned in some parts fourty, in other thirty, twenty, and at Wimbleton in Surry but fifteen acres. Spelman. Gloss. Five virgates of land made the fourth part of a knight's fee in Otendone *com.* Oxon. 3 King Steph. K. p. 93. Two Virgates or Yard-lands in Chesterton 24 Hen. III. contained fourscore and ten acres, K. p. 224.

VIRIDE, Vert or green. Whatever grows in a forest, and bears boughs and leaves for the covering and shelter of the deer. Either Over-vert, *Haut-bois,* High-wood, Timber-trees; or Nether-vert, *Sou-bois,* Under-wood. All which *Viridarius* the Veredor was to supervise and maintain, and to bring indictments at the Swanemote against those who wasted or trespassed on the Vert. The amercements for such offences were generally reserved to the king. So William Fitz-Nigel held the forestarship of Bernwode.—*Exceptis indictamentis de viridi et venatione, quæ domino regi omnino reservabantur,* K. p. 73. In all inquisitions taken of the state of forests, the Viridar was one of the jury.—*Inquisitio capta—de foresta de Bernwode—domini Walteri Upton, Johannis Graunden viridarii,* &c.—K. p. 209.

Visus *Forestariorum*. View of the forestars. When the liberty of Housbote, Heybote, Fire-wood, or any the like privilege, was granted within the bounds of a forest, it was not to be taken but *ad visum forestariorum*, upon view and approbation of the forestars, K. p. 160. Thomas de S. Walery granted to the nuns of Stodley—*qualibet septimana unam carectam ligni mortui in bosco suo de Horton per visum forestarii sui ejusdem nemoris*, K. p. 170. The profits of this View were firmed or rented from the king.—*Certus visus valet per annum* ii. *sol. et reddit domino regi pro prædicta hida et certo visu* x. *sol.* K. p. 314.

Visus *custodis manerii*. The inspection or care taken by the steward or bayliff of a mannor, for the doing right and justice to the lord.—*Rex illas sexdecim libras et dimidiam marcæ ad quas homines de Pydinton nuper talliati fuerant, assignavit ponendas per visum Hugonis Gargate custodis prædicti manerii in prædicto manerio instaurandum*, K. p. 241.

Visus *Franciplegii*. *Vid.* Franciplegium.

Vivarium. Any place for the nurture and confinement of living creatures, as a park, a warren, a fish-pond, &c.—*Illud tenementum cum vivario, et aliis pertinentiis*, K. p. 224.—*Et in datis prioris servientibus purgantibus vivarium versus molendinum ante idem festum* iv. den. K. p. 578.

W.

Waddemole, now called Woadmel, and in Oxfordshire Woddenell, a course sort of stuff used for the covering of the collars of cart-horses. Mr. Ray in his Collection of East and South Country Words describes it to be a hairy course stuff, made of Island wool, and brought thence by our seamen to Norfolk, Suffolk, &c. Perhaps from the Sax. Ƿeob, grass, hay, weed, and Ɯele, any hollow continent, as if a collar stuft with straw or hay. Or possibly from the Island. *Vadur*, a rope or any Wod of course hemp, and *Mel*, to beat, or *Mall*.—*Et in quinque virgatis de Waddemole emptis pro coleris equinis hoc anno* ii. *sol. i.* den. K. p. 574.

Wake, Vigil, Eve. Feast of the dedication of churches. The original and continued observation historically delivered, K. p. 609.

Wapentachium. A Wapentake. A portion or division of a county in the North, of the same extent as a hundred in other parts. The Laws of Edward Conf. cap. 38, derive it from the Sax. Ƿæpnu, weapons, and Taccape, to confirm, or Tac, a touch, because in their solemn meetings they clattered their arms as a token of agreement. But Jo. Brompton gives this allusion,—*Wapentake Anglice idem est quod arma capere, eo quod in primo ad-*

ventu novi domini solebant tenentibus pro homagio reddere arma sua.
X. Script. col. 957. To which custom Ranulph of Chester refers the word in his Hist. l. 1. cap. 5. This derivation as most agreeable is confirmed by Mr. Somner, who, both in his Glossary and in his Saxon Dictionary, deduces the word from Sax. Ƿæpen, arms or weapons, and Tæcan, or rather Beræcan, to deliver up: from whence, says Mr. Somner, to betake or commit, and Tacke in the North for a firm or any tenement let out for rent.—*Cum molendinis, firmis, wapentachiis, et hundredis affirmatis,* K. p. 354.—*Cum villis et hamlettis, terris, tenementis, hundredis, et wapentagiis,* K. p. 389.

WARANTUM. Right and title to justifie and defend a possession. Spelman and Somner deduce it from the Sax. Ƿeruan, to defend and to beware. But Du Fresne (possibly with less reason) chuses to derive it from the Lat. *Creantare,* to verifie or secure, from whence in his opinion the Fr. *Granter* and *Garantir,* &c. *Placitum de Quo waranto,* an action brought by the king to cite the defendant to prove his right of possession.—*Johannes filius Nigelli sen. summonitus fuit ad respondendum domino regi de placito quo waranto clamat habere visum franciplegii,* K. p. 313. Thence a Warant, or writ to authorize the apprehension of a debtor or delinquent. To Warant any matter, to defend and justifie the truth of it.

WARANTIA. A defence and legal assertion of right and title. *Vocare ad warantiam,* to desire a court of justice to cite or warn in a party to Warant or defend a title, which as superiour lord of the fee he is bound to maintain. So John de Peyto being sued for the mannor of Pidington, which he held under Sir John de Sutton and Isabel his wife,—*Venit in curiam, et per Richardum de Sheldon attornatum suum vocat inde ad warantiam Johannem Sutton de Dudley chevalier, et Isabellam uxorem ejus, ut habeat eos hic in octabis S. Michaelis per auxilium curiæ,* K. p. 477.

WARDA. Sax. Ƿeapð, Guard, Ward, or custody. Before the stat. of 12 Car. II. cap. 24, which dissolved the court of Wards, the heirs of all the king's tenants, who held *in capite* or by military service, during their nonage or minority, were in the Ward or custody of the king, or others by him appointed. The king disposed and committed these Wards as a compensation for debts and services,—*Faciemus eidem Radulpho et hæredibus suis competens escambium in wardis et eschaetis ad valentiam prædicti manerii,* K. p. 203.

WARDE Penny, War-penny, War-scot, Warth. A customary due paid to the sheriff and other officers for maintaining Watch and Ward, payable at the feast of St. Martin. In the beginning of Edw. I. Sir Bardulph de Chesterton held the mannor of Chesterton,—*Et debet, sectam ad hundredum de Chadlinton—et debet quinque denarios de Warde-pennie ad festum S. Martini*, K. p. 318.

WARECTARE. From *Carectum*, a plough. To plough up land in order to let it lye fallow for the better improvement, which ground in Kent we call Summer-land. *Mense Aprili warectandi erit tempus idoneum et amœnum, cum terra fregerit post carrucam*, Fleta l. 2, cap. 33, sect. 4.—*Homines de Hedingdon uno die warectabunt terram domini, prout decet, ad unum diem cum carucis suis*, K. p. 320. Thence *Warectum*, a fallow field, which Sir Edward Coke poorly fancies to be *Warectum, quasi vere novo victum vel subactum.—Campus warectabilis, campus ad warectam, terra warectata, ad warectandum,) tempus warectationis. Wallerus prior Berencestriæ per fratrem Thomam de Meriton fieri fecit quoddam Inhoc in campo warectabili utriusque Ernicote*, K. p. 297. Sir Roger de Amory gave to the nuns of Godestow—*viginti quinque acras in Blechesdon ad seminandum, et totidem ad warectandum*. Mon. Ang. tom. 1. p. 425. *In manerio de Pydinton quælibet acra valet sex denariis tam warectata, quam seminata*, K. p. 495. *In communi pastura, sicut in bosco et in campis ad warectam possunt sustentari* xvi. *vaccæ et unus taurus cum boviculis*, K. p. 495.— *Dominus Lestraunge habet duas separales pasturas in hoc campo, et sunt separales usque ad finem Sancti Jacobi apostoli omni anno, excepto anno quo campus prædictus jacet warectatus*, K. p. 535.— *Communam in campis de Burncester, tam post blada vincta, quam tempore warectationis omni anno*, K. p. 539.

WARRENA. A Warren, from Sax. *Peŋan*, to guard or keep. *Libera Warrena*, free warren was a liberty granted by the king to the lord of a manor, that within such an extent he should keep and preserve, and take to his own use, fish, fowl, and other game, which no other person should hunt or destroy without leave of the lord, K. p. 247.

WAYNSCOTS. Deal boards to wainscote a wall. German *Wandschotten*, from old Teuton. *Wand*, a wall, and *Schotten* to cover or defend.—*Et in sex estregbords videlicet Wayrscots emptis apud Sterisbrugge* ii. *sol*. iii. *den*. K. p. 575.

WEYF, *Wayf, Wavium*. From Sax. *Pæʒ*, a Way, à Lat. *Via*. For the Latin *V* consonant was by the Romans themselves pronounced as our *W*; *Vinum Winum, Vallum Wallum*, &c. which was the reason why the Saxons changed the letter *V* into *W*, as wine, wall, way, &c. To which the Britains prefixt a *G*, as *Vectis*, Wight, *Gwydh*; *Venta*, Went, *Gwent*. So *Viavium, Waif, Gwaif*.—*Recognitum est militibus et liberis hominibus—quod ad nos spectat le Gwaif*, K. p. 196. Waif was felons goods, or things feloniously stolen, left by the thief, and forfeited to the king or to the lord, who enjoys the right by a grant from the crown.—*Emma Cooke domum Johannis Attewelle in Overwynchendon fregit, et* xix. *marcas—felonice furata fuit—quæ seisitæ fuerunt ibidem tanquam weyf in manum prioris, ut de antiqua consuetudine fieri consuevit,* K. p. 506.

WITHBYS. Any low place where willows grow. From Þiðiʒ, a Willow tree, Þroðe, a With or Withe,—*Tres acræ apud le Whitheyes,* K. p. 395. *Dimidia roda jacet ad Witheyes juxta pratum prioris,* K. p. 400.

Y.

YCONOMI *Ecclesiæ. Pro Oiconomi.* Church-wardens.—*Qui ibidem compotum yconomorum dictæ ecclesiæ de Oakle,—Et ipsos onerent sive liberent, et novos yconomos eligant seu deputent,* K. p. 616.

INDEX.

A.
	page
Account of the tenants, rents, and services within the manor of Bicester, 18 Edw. III.	215
Account of the outgoings and incomings of the dairy of La Brech, 8 Hen. IV.	230
Account of the receipts and expenditure of the prior and canons of Bicester Priory, A. D. 1425	234
Adams, John	74
Airson, Thomas	89
Akeman-street, description of	199
Alchester, its etymology	190
———— conjectures respecting its Roman name	191
———— present state	197
———— discoveries on digging among the ruins	195
Aldridge, Richard	87
Aldwinkle, John de	70
Allectus rebels against Carausius, and defeats that monarch at Caversfield	209
———— is slain by Asclepiodotus in battle	210
Altars, the number of, in the church of Bicester Priory	78
———— to whom dedicated	ib.
———— how decorated	79
Annals of the Priory of St. Edburg	57-78
Ardington, tithes of, settled on Bicester Priory	69
Arthur, his battles with the Saxons	204
Asherugge, rector and convent of	68
Aspler, Thomas	87
Audley, James Lord, his benefaction to Bicester Priory	66
Augustine visits Oxfordshire, and raises a dead body to life	206
———— Order, their origin, rules and dress	52
Aulney Abbey	68

B.
Bailiwick of Bicester, when instituted	170
———— with whom remaining	173
Bake-house provided by the lord of Bigenhul for the use of his tenants	31
Banbury, Thomas	75
———— Alice	63
————'Allen, his disputes with Bicester Priory	62
———— founds the Bicester schools at Oxford	63
Basset, Gilbert, obtains the grant of seven knight's fees of the honor of Walingford, which includes Bicester and the neighbouring parishes	151
———— his benefactions to the religious	ib.
———— Gilbert, founds Bicester Priory	55

INDEX.

Basset, Gilbert, grants land for
    the endowment - 58, 59
———— chief events of
    his life - - 151, 152
———— Philip - - 65
———— Philippa - - 64
Battle of Ashendon - - 10
Battle of Basing - - ib.
Battle of Banbury - - 5
Battle of Cirencester - - 6
Battle of Gravenhull - - 10
Bellamy, William - - 70
Bensington Parsonage - - 86
Bicester, situation and etymo-
    logy - - - 1
———— description of the town 16
Bigenhul, village of - 134
———— history of the manor 157
———— present state of - 139
Bird, John - - - 87
———— his epitaph at Wendlebury 89
Blackwall, Samuel - - 89
Blount, Sir Michael - - 87
———— Sir Richard - - 88
Brails, Richard - - 74
Bret, James le - - 60, 61
Brito, Thomas - - 62
Brode, Nicholas - - 69
Brown, William, surrenders Bi-
    cester Priory - - 77
Bruce, Robert - - 75
Burials, none permitted at Strat-
    ton Audley - - 50
Burncester, Walter de - 69
Burrows, Richard, his donation
    for apprenticing poor children 147
Butt's-corner anciently without
    the town - - 16

C.

Campion, William - - 70
Camvill, Richard de, marries the
    widow of T. Verdon - 152
———— his benefactions to the
    Priory of Bicester 58, 60
Carlton, Mary, her benefaction
    to the poor - - 145
———— appoints a sermon
    to be preached on the 2nd
    Sunday in March - 146
Carunam, Robert - - 87
Cattieuchlani - - 188
Caversfield, Richard de - 70
———— Sybil de - - 61

Caversfield, Village of, etymo-
    logy - - - 209
———— battle
    fought - - ib.
Cenwalch - - - 8
Cerdic - - - 5
Chamberlain, Dame Ann - 87
Charity School established - 111
———— scholars taught to
    work in school hours - 112
———— benefaction to 113
Charter of Hen. II. to the inha-
    bitants of the honor of
    Wallingford - - 26
———— for a fair in King's-end 125
Chesney, Maud de - - 75
Chesterton, Ralph de - 64
Church in Bicester, supposed to
    be built by Birinus - 48
———— dedicated to
    St. James - - 49
———— anciently
    stood in Sheep-street - ib.
———— rebuilt - ib.
Clements, Thomas, purchases
    the bailiwick of Bicester 170
———— attempts to retain the
    manorial rights - - 171
Clerk, Robert - - 60
Clifton - - - 86
Coins found at Alchester - 198
Cok, Thomas - - 70
Coker, John, see manor of Nun's
    Place
Coker, Thomas, his donations to
    the poor - - 147
Commonage, description of - 36
———— right of, terminated 39
Constantius opposes Carausius 208
Cooke, S. - - - 90
Cornish, Henry, enters New Inn
    Hall, Oxford - - 120
———— joins the parliament
    party - - ib.
———— is appointed visitor of
    the University - ib.
———— displaced by the king's
    commissioners - ib.
———— settles at Bicester, and
    becomes pastor of a dis-
    senting congregation - ib.
———— his death and character 121
Cottesford, Roger de - - 69
Coventry, John - - 75

INDEX.

Crispin, Milo - - 150
Crockwell, Walter de - - 60
———— Street, account of - 17
———— instances of the extravagant rent of cottages ib.
———— well, where situated ib.
———— Moor - - 61
Culne, Richard - - 66
Curtlington, Robert de - 69

D.

Dadyngton, William - - 75
D'Amory, Sir Richard - 80
Danes enter Oxfordshire - 9
———— defeated at Gravenhill - 10
———— destroy Berincester and the neighbouring villages 12
———— massacred at Oxford - ib.
Deaneries, institution of - 51
Deanery of Bicester, the seal of 52
———————— churches in ib.
Dennant, John - - 122
Derby, Earls of, see Stanley
Derby-hold, its origin - 37, 170
———————— estates converted into freeholds - - 175
Dissenters, their tenets - 118
———— instances of marriages celebrated by their minister - - 121
Dobuni - - - 188
Donations to the parish of Bicester - - 140
Doomsday-book, account of - 21
———————— extract from - 22
———————— explanation of the terms - - ib.
Drayton - - 86

E.

Ethelfleda governs Mercia - 11
———————— her character - ib.
Extracts from the church-wardens' books - - 261
———————— from the king's books 262
Eynesham, the abbat and convent of - - 57
Eyre, Joseph - - 90

F.

Fairs and markets, origin of - 124
———— anciently held in church-yards on a Sunday - - ib.

Fairs and markets, charter for one at Bicester - 125
———— market discontinued, and a new one established in Market-end 127
———————— M. Howlet established three new fairs 129
Farmers, ancient state of - 37
———— alteration in the manners of their daughters 40
Fitz-Count, Brien, wars against King Stephen - 150
———————— takes the cross, and his estates seized by the king - - ib.
Fitz-Michael, Robert - - 61
Forbes, Thomas - - 89
Free-school, account of - 107
Freewald, father of St. Edburg and St. Editha - 57

G.

Gargate, Isabel, her donation to the priory - - 61
———— Muriel - - ib.
Germayn, Robert, the tenure by which he held his lands, cottage, &c. - - 29
Glass-urn found in Alchester - 198
Glynne, William, purchases an estate at Bicester - 173
———————— is created a baronet - - ib.
———————— his benefactions to Bicester church - 104
———————— builds Ambrosden-house - 174
———— Sir William, chosen member for Woodstock - ib.
———————— dies - ib.
———— Sir Stephen, sells the estates of Bicester and Ambrosden - ib.
Grantham, Sir Thomas, his donation to poor widows 146
———————— inscription on his monument 103
Graven-hill, Danes buried there 19
———— the wood given to Bicester Priory - 59
Green, Richard - - 70
Grimsbury, land at, given to Bicester Priory - 65
———— valuation of - 250

INDEX.

Grimsbury, to whom given after the Dissolution - 87
Grote, Peter le - - 70

H.

Hall, William - - 89
Harvest-home, origin of the custom - - 31
——— all the families bound to give their service on the last day of harvest, except their wives and tenants - ib.
——— present mode of keeping the feast - 269
Hearne, Thomas, his opinion respecting Alchester - - 201
Hermitage and chapel of St. John the Baptist - - 115
Hervey, prior of Bicester - 60
Heyford-warrin - 65. 75. 255
Hindlest, Richard - - 75
Hodesham, land in, exchanged for Nyhenaker - - 60
Honour of Wallingford - 21
——— charter granted to the inhabitants - - 26
——— court of, when held, fines levied, discovered to be illegal 34, 35
Hospital, charter for one at Bicester - - 116

I.

Inclosure of King's-end field, substance of the bill obtained for the - - 40
——— names of the proprietors - - ib.
——— width of public roads, &c. - - 41
——— account of the great tythes - - ib.
——— provisoes in the act - - 42
Inclosures of Market-end field, bill obtained - 37-39
——— names of the land owners - - ib.
——— names of those having a right to commonage - - ib.
——— consequence of

inclosures, rise of the rent of land - - 42
Ingeram, Walter - - 62
Inns, scarcity of—Travellers entertained at religious houses 35
Islip, Robert - - 70
Jones, James, establishes a Sunday-school - - 111
Jurdan, Nicholas, obtains a charter for a hospital at Bicester 115

K.

Kennel, John - - 87
Kennett, Sarah, inscription on her monument - - 101
Kennett, White, affecting letter of, detailing the circumstances of her death - - ib.
Kenric - - - 5
King's-end, built on the site of Bigenhull - 20. 135
——— privileges of the inhabitants - - 136
Kirklington, land in - - 58
Kirklington, Walter de - '62

L.

Lacy, Henry, earl of Lincoln, marries Margaret Longspe 156
——— procures charters for fairs - - 157
——— military enterprises ib.
——— death of his son - ib.
——— embassy - - 158
——— joins the barons against Gaveston - - ib.
——— death of his wife - 159
——— marries his daughter to Thomas earl of Lancaster - - ib.
——— dies - - ib.
——— inquisition - - 68
Lacy, Alice, seized by Earl Warren's partisans - 160
——— claimed by Richard as his wife - - 161
——— divorced from the Earl of Lancaster - - ib.
——— marries Eubolo le Strange - - ib.
——— forfeits her estates - ib.
——— death of Eubolo - 162
——— marries again - ib.
——— dies - - ib.

INDEX.

Lamb-ale - 269
Lancaster, Thomas earl of, opposes Gaveston - 160
——— made steward of England - ib.
Law prohibiting men from following any profession except agriculture - 32
Lestrange, Sir Roger - 163
——— Sir John - ib.
——— Sir Richard and lady quarrel with the wife of Sir John Trussel in St. Dunstan's Church - 163
——— perform penance - 164
Letcomb Basset - 85
Longspe, William, marries Idonea de Camvil - 153
——— claims the earldom of Salisbury - ib.
——— his benefactions to Bicester Priory - 63, 64
——— military achievements - 153
——— slain by the Saracens - 154
——— seen by his mother ascending to heaven - ib.
——— miracles at his tomb 155
Longspe, William, son of the above - ib.
——— scheme of his widow to retain her estates after marrying a second husband without the king's license - 156

M.
Magendime, field of - 62
Markland, John - 90
May-Day, amusements of - 267
Meadow-mowing - 269
Meeting-House, description of 122
Missenden Little - 63
Mortar-pits, Derby holders privileged to dig mortar at - 39
Mumping, custom of - 270

N.
Nicholas, Pope, ecclesiastical taxation - 67
Nun's Place, history of the manor - 130
——— granted on lease to John Griffith - 132

Nun's Place sold to Mr. John Coker - 132
——— manor-house rebuilt - ib.
——— the green inclosed, and converted into a pleasure ground - 133

O.
Oilgi, or D'Oilly, Robert, marries Aldith daughter of Wigod 148
——— the greatest man in the county - 149
——— builds Oxford castle, the great bridge, &c. ib.
——— grants the tithe of Bicester and the neighbouring villages to the church of St. George, Oxford - ib.
——— monkish story concerning his illness - ib.
——— death - 150
Osbath, George - 87
Oseney Abbey, description of the dormitory of - 81
Oseney, Abbot, complains of damage in their possessions at Arncote - 66
——— remits the tithe of Bicester parish to that priory - .68
Osmond, John - 70

P.
Paine, Thomas, burnt in effigy 183
Parentyn, Richard - 70
Parish churches, origin of - 44
——— their endowment 45
——— privileged with burying grounds - 46
——— part of the church allotted to the use of the hamlets - ib.
Parish church of Bicester, when built - 91
——— description ib.
——— galleries - 95
——— organ, pulpit, reading-desk, and font - 96
——— monumental inscriptions - 97
——— tower - 107
——— churchyard 108

Patron of the church anciently allowed a seat in the chancel - 46
Patron Saint - 49
Paulyn, John - 70
Payments - 270
Penda - 6
Penrose, Mr., digs among the ruins of Alchester - 195
——— discoveries - 196
Petyrton, Richard - 75
Philip, Ralph - 71
Place-yard, story of a coach and six horses lost in a pond - 83
Plautius, Aulus, leads a Roman army into Britain - 189
——— his wars - ib.
——— plants a garrison at Alchester - 190
Poor of Bicester, an abstract of the returns for the expense and maintenance of, for several years - 43
Population in 1801 and 1811 - 44
Princep, John - 90
Priory of St. Edburg, by whom founded - 55
——— charter of foundation - ib.
——— Patron Saint 57
——— donations, &c. 57, 76
——— description of the buildings at the time of the Dissolution - 81
——— statement of its revenues - 77, 78
——— to whom granted - 85, 173
Priory church, account of - 78-80
——— conjectures respecting its site - ib.
Protestants, account of some confined in Bicester Priory - 271
Pugh, John - 66

Q.

Quakers - 124
Quintin, description of that sport 266

R.

Roads, the ancient and present state of those in the neighbourhood of Bicester 13
——— their repair anciently considered an act of piety ib.

Roads, turnpikes, tolls, &c. - 14
——— Roman - 201
Rosamond Clifford, life of - 213
——— not poisoned - ib.
——— interred at Godstow church - 213
——— extract from an ancient book relative to the opening of her grave by King Henry - 214
——— removal of her body by order of the bishop of Lincoln - 215
Rural Deans - 51
Russel, Mistrys, purchases land at Letcomb Basset, formerly belonging to Bicester Priory 86

S.

Saxons, description of - 3
——— invade Britain - 4
——— settle in Oxfordshire - 6
Serich, Richard - 62
Sheep-street, formerly St. John's-street - 18, 117
Sherborne - 86
Shewring, Thomas - 89
Shobington, Nicholas de - 70
Shore, Thomas - 85
Shrove Tuesday, sports of - 267
Small pox rages at Bicester, and occasions the ruin of the market - 180
Smith, John, his description of a well and coffin found in Place Yard Gardens - 82
Smith, John - 90
Sports and pastimes - 266
Stage-coach - 183
Stanley, George, Lord Lestrange, marries the daughter of Sir John Lestrange - 164
——— given up to Richard III. as an hostage for the fidelity of his father - 165
——— Thomas, Earl of Derby ib.
——— Henry, Earl of Derby, accompanies Wolsey to France - 166
——— suppresses the pilgrimage of grace - ib.
——— persecutes the Wiclifites - 272
——— dies - 166

INDEX.

Stanley, Henry, his son, life of - 167
——— Ferdinand, Earl of Derby, said to be bewitched - ib.
——— detail of his illness and death - 168
——— William, Earl of Derby, involved in a dispute respecting his title to the Isle of Man - 169
——— sells the manor of Bicester - 170
Stapenhull, Thomas de - 70
Staveley, William, his benefactions to Bicester Priory - 75
——— inscription on his monument - 97
Stodham - 86
Stone-pits, Derby-holders privileged to dig stones at - 172
Stratton, village of, its etymology 201
——— anciently an hamlet of Bicester - 50
——— the great tythes given to Egnesham Abbey - 57
——— the chapel conveyed by charter to Bicester Priory - ib.
——— the great tythe conveyed to that monastery for an annual pension - 58
——— tythe of hay given to the same - ib.
——— the inhabitants punished for burying their dead in that village - 71
——— the rectory and advowson of the church granted to the see of Oxford - 86. 245
Stratton, William de - 70
Stukeley, Dr., his observations on Alchester - 191. 194
Suffolk, Duke of, obtains the grant of Bicester Priory - 85
Sunday Schools, account of - 114

T.
Taylor, Thomas - 89
Tenures - 24
Theodore, Archbishop of Canterbury, unites the bishoprick of Dorchester to Mercia - 8
Thornberg, William de - 68

Tithes first granted by the lord of the manor - 45
——— divided into four parts by Augustine - 46
——— anciently collected by itinerant priests - 47
——— Bicester and Stratton given to St. George's church, Oxford - ib.
——— transfer of the grant to Oseney Abbey - ib.
Tooker, John - 71
Tower of Bicester church, tradition respecting - 50
——— bells, &c. - 107
Town Hall - 18
Town-stock, account of - 140
——— orders issued by the court of Chancery relative to the application of the charity - 141
——— present state of the funds, &c. - 143
Tronghton, John, enters St. John's College Oxon - 119
——— is ejected - ib.
——— settles at Bicester ib.
——— his death and character - ib.
Troughton, John, son of the former - 121
Turner, Edward, purchases the priory estates - 174
——— created a baronet ib.
——— dies - ib.
——— Sir Edward, is a candidate for the representation of the county in parliament - 175
——— rebuilds Ambrosden house, and extends the park - ib.
——— dies - 176
——— Sir Gregory, succeeds to his father's estates, and discharges all the workmen employed in the plantations at Ambrosden - ib.
——— pulls down the house, cuts down the timber, and incloses the park - ib.
——— causes of his death 177
——— his will - ib.

INDEX.

V.

Vache, Richard de la, grants lands to Bicester Priory on certain conditions - 66. 69
Valuation of the estates of the Priory of Bicester by the commissioners appointed by Henry VIII. - 250
Vicarage of Bicester ordained - 59
——— its revenues increased by a new instrument granted by the prior and convent - 72
——— Sir M. and Sir R. Blount seize upon some of its revenues - 88
——— are obliged to refund them by a decree of Chancery - ib.
——— the vicarage again injured by the sale of Sir S. Glynne's estates - 90
——— measures taken to obtain redress - ib.
Vicarage-house, description of - ib.
Villains, description of the - 23
——— their services - 29
——— not allowed to sell a stone-horse, or ox, or give their sons any learning, or marry their daughters, without consent of their lord - 30
——— causes of their emancipation - 36
——— instance of manumission granted to two of the king's slaves and their families by Henry VIII. - ib.
——— relics of villainage existing in 1695 - ib.
Visitors appointed to inspect all the monasteries - 76
——— their instructions - ib.
——— report - 77

Volunteer company established 183

W.

Walker, William, his benefactions to the schools - 113. 147
Walsingham, the king at - 68
Wantyng, John - 71
Warde, Roger de - 69
Warkworth, land at, given to Bicester Priory - ib.
Well of St. Edburg, where situated - 83
——— virtue of its waters ib.
——— re-opened by Mr. Coker - 84
——— present name and state - ib.
Wells, Hugh, Bishop of Lincoln, ordains the vicarage of Bicester - 58
——— orders the removal of the body of fair Rosamond 215
Wentworth, Agnes - 87
Whitsun-ales - 268
Wigod de Walingford entertains the Romans after the battle of Hastings - 148
——— marries his daughter to Robert de Oilly - 149
Wilkins, Bennet - 85
Wilkins, John - 87
Worden Pool - 199
Work-house, account of - 19
Wretchwic, how written anciently 200
——— account of, see Priory Estates
Wycomb, Edmund, grants a new instrument of endowment for the vicarage of Bicester - 72
Wykins, Thomas, and T. Clements purchase the bailiwick of Bicester - 170

Y.

Year's-mind, how celebrated - 79

THE END.

www.ingramcontent.com/pod-product-compliance
Lightning Source LLC
Chambersburg PA
CBHW021140240426
43661CB00075B/1592